GAME DESIGN WORKSHOP

GAME DESIGN WORKSHOP:

Designing, Prototyping, and Playtesting Games

Tracy Fullerton

Christopher Swain

Steven Hoffman

CMP**Books**

San Francisco, CA • New York, NY • Lawrence, KS

Published by CMP Books
an imprint of CMP Media LLC

Main office: 600 Harrison Street, San Francisco, CA 94107 USA
Tel: 415-947-6615; fax: 415-947-6015

Editorial office:
4601 West 6th Street, Suite B, Lawrence, KS 66049 USA

www.cmpbooks.com
email: books@cmp.com

Senior Editor:	Dorothy Cox
Managing Editor:	Gail Saari
Cover Layout Design:	Damien Castaneda

Distributed in the U.S. by:
Publishers Group West
1700 Fourth Street
Berkeley, CA 94710
1-800-788-3123

Distributed in Canada by:
Jaguar Book Group
100 Armstrong Avenue
Georgetown, Ontario M6K 3E7 Canada
905-877-4483

For individual orders and for information on special discounts for quantity orders, please contact:
CMP Books Distribution Center, 6600 Silacci Way, Gilroy, CA 95020
Tel: 1-800-500-6875 or 408-848-3854; fax: 408-848-5784
email: cmp@rushorder.com; Web: www.cmpbooks.com

ISBN: 1-57820-222-1

CMP Books

For our families, with gratitude for your faith and support

And for our students, whose creativity and enthusiasm make the game worth playing

Table of Contents

Updates: Want to receive e-mail news updates for Game Design Workshop? To subscribe, you can send a blank e-mail to gamedesign@cmpbooks.com.

Acknowledgments and Credits

The authors wish to thank the many people who have helped us in the creation of this book. They include:

Danielle Jatlow, Waterside Productions

Dorothy Cox, CMP Books

Paul Temme, CMP Books

Jamil Moledina, CMP Books

Frank Lantz, gameLab

Richard Garfield, Wizards of the Coast

Eric Zimmerman, gameLab

David Perry, Shiny Entertainment

American McGee, The Mauritania Import Export Company

Warren Spector, Ion Storm

Peter Molyneaux, Lionhead Studios

Richard Hilleman

Steve Ackrich, Atari

Ray Muzyka, BioWare

Scott Miller, 3D Realms

Lorne Lanning, Oddworld Inhabitants

Sandy Petersen, Ensemble Studios

Rob Pardo, Blizzard Entertainment

Amy Jo Kim

Scott Kim

Jesse Schell, Carnegie Mellon University

Don Daglow, Stormfront Studios

Celia Pearce, UC Irvine

Noah Falstein, The Inspiracy

Bill Roper, Flagship Studios

Bill Fulton, Microsoft Game Studios

Kevin Keeker, Microsoft Game Studios

Brian Hersch, Hersch and Company

Bruce C. Shelley, Ensemble Studios

Brian Tinsman, Wizards of the Coast

James Ernest, Cheapass Games

Graeme Bayless, Electronic Arts

Rob Daviau, Hasbro Games

Alan R. Moon

Nikita Mikros, Black Hammer Game

Trent Oster, BioWare

Marc LeBlanc

Michael Sweet, AudioBrain

Starr Long, NC Soft

Matt Firor, Mythic Entertainment

Josh Holmes, EA Canada

Troy Dunniway, Electronic Arts Los Angeles

Stan Chow, EA Canada

Naomi Kokubo, EA Canada

Chris Taylor, Gas Powered Games

Tom Sloper, Sloperama Productions

Kenn Hoekstra, Raven Software

Rich Liebowitz, Union Entertainment

Jesse Vigil

Jim Vessella

Justin Hall

Sus Lundgren, PLAY Research Group

John Rocco

Ranjit Bhatnagar, gameLab

Bob Greenberg, R/GA Interactive

Neal Robison, Vivendi Universal Games

Matt Kassan, Atari

Vincent Lacava, PopNYC

Rob Roth

Kim Markegard, Casino Studios

Dino Citraro, Casino Studios

Greg Glass

Mike Gresh

Dan Fiden

Tim Lee

Greg Ecker

Neil Dufine

Richard Wyckoff, Pandemic Studios

Peter Duke, Duke Media

Chris Brandkamp, Cyan

Chip Blundell, Eidos

Jay Wilbur, Epic Games

Jordan Mechner

Phil Adams, Interplay

Nick Lefevre, Konami of America

John Garrett, LucasArts

Rhy-Ming Poon, Activision

Dallas Dickinson, Sony Online Entertainment

Steve Weiss, Sony Online Entertainment

Minori Murakami, Namco

Jason Rubin, Naughty Dog

Stephanie Reimann, Nintendo

Leslie Hollingshead, Vivendi Universal Games

Kate Ross, Wizards of the Coast

Steve Jackson, Steve Jackson Games

Gary Gygax

Scott Fisher, USC School of Cinema

Jen Stein, USC School of Cinema

Elizabeth Daley, USC School of Cinema

All of our students at the University of Southern California

IMAGE CREDITS AND COPYRIGHT NOTICES

Cover design by Tracy Fullerton

Dice and chess cover photos by Tracy Fullerton

Image from Hitman courtesy of Eido Interactive. © Eidos Interactive Ltd.

Images from Unreal 2 courtesy of Epic Games, Inc. © Epic Games, Inc.

Image from Jak and Daxter Copyright © 2003 Sony Computer Entertainment America, Inc. "Jak and Daxter" are trademarks of Sony Computer Entertainment America, Inc. Courtesy of Naughty Dog

"Concept Art from Starcraft: Ghost™ provided by Blizzard Entertainment®

Playtesting photos by Tracy Fullerton and Christopher Swain

All diagrams in the book by Tracy Fullerton

Images from You Don't Know Jack™ courtesy of Jellyvision © Jellyvision, Inc.

Photo illustrations by Tracy Fullerton

Scrabble, Monopoly, Milton Bradley's Operation, Lord of the Rings boardgame, Connect Four, and Pit © Hasbro

Image from Chess tournament courtesy of SKBosna

Image from Quake tournament courtesy of Foto

Images from Dark Age of Camelot courtesy of Mythic Entertainment. Copyright © 2003 Mythic Entertainment, Inc. All rights reserved. www.darkageofcamelot.com

PAC-MAN™ © 1980 Namco Ltd,. All Rights Reserved. Courtesy of Namco Holding Corp.

Image from 7th Guest © Virgin Interactive Entertainment

Image from Tomb Raider courtesy of Eido Interactive. © Eidos Interactive Ltd.

Image from Slingo courtesy of Slingo, Inc. © Slingo

SOUL CALIBER II™ © 1982 Namco Ltd. All Rights Reserved. Courtesy of Namco Holding Corp. SOULCALIBUR II ® & © 1995 1998 2002 2003 NAMCO LTD., ALL RIGHTS RESERVED.

Introduction

One of the most difficult tasks people can perform, however much others may despise it, is the invention of good games.
— *C.G. Jung*

Games are an integral part of all known human cultures. Digital games, in all their various formats and genres, are just a new expression of this ancient method of social interaction. Behind the system of every game there lies a designer who has crafted the rules for clarity, balanced the play for fairness, and conducted hours of playtests to find any loopholes in the design. Part engineer, part entertainer, part mathematician, and part social director, the goal of the game designer is to create that elusive combination of challenge, competition, and interaction that players just call "fun."

The cultural impact of digital games has grown to rival television and films as the industry has matured over the past three decades. Game industry revenues have been growing at a double-digit rate for years and have recently eclipsed the domestic box office of the film industry, reaching 9.4 billion dollars in 2001. According to reports in *Time Magazine* and *The LA Times*, 90% of U.S. households with children have rented or owned a video or computer game, and young people in the United States spend an average of 20 minutes per day playing video games. This makes digital games the second most popular form of entertainment after television.

As sales of games have increased, interest in game design as a career path has also escalated. Similar to the explosion of interest in screenwriting and directing that accompanied the growth of the film and television industries, creative thinkers today are turning to games as a new form of expression. Degree programs in game design are currently being developed in major universities all over the world in response to student demand. The International Game Developer's Association, in recognition of the overwhelming interest in learning to create games, has established an education committee to help educators create a curriculum that reflects the real-world process of professional game designers. On their website, the IGDA lists over 82 game design programs in North America alone. Furthermore, *Game Developer* magazine puts out an annual career guide bonus issue in order to connect the study of game development to the practice of it.

In addition to our experience designing games for companies such as Sony, Sega, and Microsoft, the authors of this book have spent seven years teaching the art of game design to students from a variety of different backgrounds and experience levels. In this time, we've found that there are patterns in the way that beginning designers grasp the structural elements of games, common traps that they fall into, and certain types of exercises that can help them learn to make better games. This book encapsulates the experience we've gained by working with our students to design, prototype, and playtest hundreds of original game concepts.

Our students have gone on to jobs in all areas of the game industry, including game design, producing, programming, visual design, marketing, and quality assurance. The method we present here has proven to be successful over and over again. Whatever your background, your technical skills, your reasons for wanting to design games, our goal with this book is to enable you to design games that engage and delight your players.

Our approach is exercise-driven and extremely nontechnical. This may surprise you, but we don't recommend implementing your designs digitally right away. The complexities of software development often hamper a designer's ability to see the structural elements of their system clearly. The exercises contained in this book require no programming expertise or visual art skills, and so release you from the intricacies of digital game production, while allowing you to learn what works and what doesn't work in your game system. Additionally, these exercises will teach you the most important skill in the game design: the process of prototyping, playtesting, and revising your system based on player feedback.

There are three basic steps to our approach:

Step 1

Start with an understanding of how games work. Learn about rules, procedures, objectives, etc. What is a game? What makes a game compelling to play? Part I of this book covers these game design fundamentals.

Step 2

Learn to conceptualize, prototype, and playtest your original games. Create rough physical or digital prototypes of your designs which allow you to separate the essential system elements from the complexities of full production. Put your playable prototype in the hands of players and conduct playtests that generate useful, actionable feedback. Use that feedback to revise and perfect your game's design. Part II starting on page 139 covers these important design skills.

Step 3

Understand the industry and the place of the game designer in it. The first two steps give you the foundation of knowledge to be a literate and capable game designer. From there you can pursue the specialized skills used in the game industry. For instance, you may pursue producing, programming, art, or marketing. You may become a lead game designer or perhaps one day run a whole company. Part III starting on page 317 of this book covers the place of the game designer on a design team, and in the industry.

The book is full of exercises intended to get you working on game design problems and creating your own designs. When you reach the end, you will have prototyped and playtested many games, and you will have at least one original playable project of your own. We emphasize the importance of doing these exercises because the only way to really become a game designer is to make games, not just play them or read about them. If you think of this book as a tool to lead you through the process of design, and not just a text to read, you will find the experience much more valuable.

So if you're ready to get started, it's your turn now. Best of luck!

Part I

Game Design Basics

Since there have been games, there have been game designers. Their names may have been lost to history, but at some point the first clay dice were thrown, and the first smooth stones were placed in the pits of a newly carved mancala board. These early inventors may not have thought of themselves as game designers—perhaps they were just amusing themselves and their friends by coming up with competitions using the everyday objects around them—but many of their games have been played for thousands of years. And although this history stretches back as far as the beginnings of human culture, when we think of games today, we tend to speak of the digital games that have so recently captured our imaginations.

These digital games have the capacity to take us to amazing new worlds with fantastic characters and fully realized interactive environments. Games are designed by teams of professional game developers, working long hours at specialized tasks. The technological and business aspects of these digital games are mind-boggling. And yet, the appeal of digital games for players has its roots in the same basic impulses and desires as the games that have come before them. We play games to learn new skills, to feel a sense of achievement, to socialize, to determine pecking order, and sometimes just to pass the time. Ask

yourself, why do you play games? Understanding your own answer, and the answers of other players, is the first step to becoming a game designer.

We bring up this long history of games as a prelude to a book primarily about designing digital games because we feel that it's important for today's designers to "reclaim" that history as inspiration and for examples of what makes great gameplay. It's important to remember that what has made games such a long-lasting form of human entertainment is not intrinsic to any technology or medium, but to the experience of the players.

The focus of this book will be on understanding and designing for that experience, no matter what platform you are working with. In the first chapter of this section, we'll look at the special role played by the game designer throughout the process: the designer's relationship to the team, the skills and vision a designer must possess, and the method by which a designer brings players into the process. Then, we will look at the essential structure of games—the formal, dramatic, and dynamic elements that a designer must work with to create that all-important player experience. These are the fundamental building blocks of game design and provide an understanding of what it takes to create great games.

Chapter 1
The Role of the Game Designer

The game designer envisions how a game will work during play. She creates the objectives, rules, and procedures, thinks up the dramatic premise and gives it life, and is responsible for planning everything necessary to create a compelling player experience. In the same way that an architect drafts a blueprint for a building or a screenwriter produces the script for a movie, the game designer plans the structural elements of a system that, when set in motion by the players, creates the interactive experience.

As the impact of digital games has increased, there has been an explosion of interest in game design as a career. Now, instead of looking to Hollywood and dreaming of writing the next block-buster, many creative people are turning to games as a new form of expression.

But what does it take to be a game designer? What kinds of talents and skills do you need? And what is the best method of designing for a game? In this chapter, we'll look at the answers to these questions and outline a method of iterative design that designers can use to judge the success of gameplay throughout the design and development process. This iterative method, which relies on inviting feedback from players early on, is the key to designing games that delight and engage the audience, because the game mechanics are developed from the ground up with the player experience at the center of the process.

An Advocate for the Player

The role of the game designer is, first and foremost, to be an advocate for the player. The game designer must look at the world of games through the player's eyes. This sounds simple, but you'd be surprised how often this concept is ignored. It's far too easy to get caught up in a game's graphics, storyline, or new features and forget that what makes a game great is solid gameplay. That's what excites players. Even if they tell you that they love the spe-cial effects, art direction, or plot, they won't play for long unless the gameplay hooks them.

As a game designer, a large part of your role is to keep your concentration focused on the player experience and not allow yourself to be distracted by the other concerns of production. Let the art director worry about the imagery, the producer stress over the budget, and the technical director futz with the engine. Your main job is to make sure that when the game is delivered, it provides superior gameplay.

When you first sit down to design a game, everything is fresh, and, most likely, you have a vision for what it is that you want to create. At this point in the process, your view of the game and that of the eventual new player are similar. However, as the process unfolds and the game develops, it becomes increasingly difficult to see your creation objectively. After months of testing and tweaking every conceivable aspect, your once clear view can become muddled. At times like this, it's easy to get too close to your own work and lose perspective.

Playtesters

Situations like these are when it becomes critical to have playtesters. Playtesters are people who play your game and provide feedback on the experience so that you can move forward with a fresh perspective. By watching other people play the game, you can learn a great deal.

Observe their experience and try to see the game through their eyes. Pay attention to what objects they are focused on, where they click or move the cursor when they get stuck or frustrated or bored, and write down everything they tell you. They are your guide, and it's your mission to have them lead you inside the game and illuminate any issues lurking below the surface of the design. If you train yourself to do this, you will regain your objectivity and be able to see both the beauty and the flaws in what you've created.

Many game designers don't involve playtesters in their process, or, if they do bring in playtesters, it's at the end of production when it's really too late to change the essential elements of the design. Perhaps they are on a tight schedule and feel they don't have time for feedback. Or, perhaps they are

1.1 Playtest group

afraid that feedback will force them to change things they love about their design. Maybe they think that getting a playtest group together will cost too much money. Or they may be under the impression that testing is something only done by marketing people.

What these designers don't realize is that by divorcing their process from this essential feedback opportunity, they probably cost themselves more time, money, and creative heartache than not. This is because games are not a form of one-way communication. Being a superior game designer isn't about controlling every aspect of the game design or dictating exactly how the game should function. It's about building a potential experience, setting all the pieces in place so that everything's ready to unfold once the players begin to participate.

In some ways, designing a game is like being the host of a party. As the host, it's your job to get everything ready—food, drinks, decorations, music, to set the mood—and then you open the doors to your guests and see what happens. The results are not always predictable, or what you envisioned. A game, like a party, is an interactive experience that is only fully realized once your guests partake of the punch. What type of party will your game be like? Will your players sit like wallflowers in your living room? Will they stumble around trying to find the coatroom closet? Or will they jabber and chatter away, hoping the night will never end?

Inviting players "over to play" and listening to what they say as they experience your game is the best way to understand how your game is working. Gauging reactions, interpreting silent moments, studying feedback, and matching those with specific game elements are the keys to becoming a professional designer. Once you learn to listen to your players, you can help your game to grow.

In Chapter 8 on page 196, when we examine the playtesting process in detail, you'll learn methods and procedures that will help you hold professional-quality playtests, and make the most of these tests by asking good questions and listening openly to criticism. For now though, it's just impor-

tant to know that playtesting is the heart of the design process explored in this book, and that the feedback you receive during these sessions can help you transform your game into a truly enjoyable experience for your players.

Like any living system, games transform throughout their development cycle. No rule is set in stone. No technique is absolute. No scheme is the right one. If you understand how fluid the structures are, you can help mold them into shape through repeated testing and careful observation. As a game designer, it's up to you to evolve your game into more than you originally envisioned. That's the art of game design. It's not locking things in place; it's giving birth and parenting. No one, no matter how smart they are, can conceive and produce a sophisticated game from a blank sheet of paper and have it perfected without going through this process. And learning how to work creatively within this process is what this book is all about.

1.2   More playtest groups

Exercise 1.1: Become a Tester

Take on the role of a tester. Go play a game and observe yourself as you play. Write down what you're doing and feeling. Try to create one page of detailed notes on your behaviors and actions. Then repeat this experience while watching a friend play the same game. Compare the two sets of notes and analyze what you've learned from the process.

Throughout this book, we've included exercises that challenge you to practice the skills that are essential to game design. We've tried to break them down so that you can master them one by one, but by the end of the book, you will have learned a tremendous amount about games, players, and process. And, you will have designed, prototyped, and playtested at least one original idea of your own. We recommend creating a folder or notebook of your completed exercises so that you can refer to them as you work your way through the book.

PASSIONS AND SKILLS

What does it take to become a game designer? There is no one simple answer, no one path to success. There are some basic traits and skills we can mention, however. First, a great game designer is someone who loves games. A passion for games is the one thread all great designers have in common. If you don't love what you're doing, you'll never be able to put in the long hours necessary to craft truly innovative games.

To someone on the outside, making games may seem like a trivial task—something that's akin to playing around. But it's not. As any experienced designer can tell you, testing their own game for the ten-thousandth time can become work, not play. As the designer, you have to remain dedicated to that ongoing process. You can't just go through the motions. You have to keep that passion alive in yourself, and in the rest of the team, to make sure that the great gameplay you envisioned in those first, carefree days of design is still there in the exhausting, pressure-filled final days before you lock production. In order to do that, you'll need to develop some other important skills in addition to your love of games.

Communication

The most important skill that you, as a game designer, can develop is the ability to communicate clearly and effectively with all the other people who will be working on your game. You'll have to "sell" your game many times over before it ever hits the store shelves: to your teammates, management, investors, and perhaps even your friends and family. To accomplish this, you'll need good language skills, a crystal clear vision, and a well-conceived presentation. This is the only way to rally everyone involved to your cause and secure the support that you'll need to move forward.

But good communication doesn't just mean writing and speaking—it also means becoming a good listener and a *great* compromiser. Listening to your playtesters and to the other people on your team affords fresh ideas and new directions. Listening also involves your teammates in the creative process, giving them a sense of authorship in the final design that will reinvest them in their own responsibilities on the project. If you don't agree with an idea, you haven't lost anything, and the idea you don't use might spark one that you do.

1.3 Communicating with team members

What happens when you hear something that you don't want to hear? Perhaps one of the hardest things to do in life is compromise. In fact, many game designers think that compromise is a bad word. But compromise is sometimes necessary, and if done well, it can be an important source of creative collaboration.

For instance, your vision of the game might include a technical feature that is simply impossible with the time and resources you have available. What if your programmers come up with an alternate implementation for the feature, but it doesn't capture the essence of the original design? How can you adapt your idea to the practical necessities in such a way as to keep the gameplay intact? You'll have to compromise. As the designer,

it's your job to find a way to do it elegantly and successfully, so that the game doesn't suffer.

Teamwork

Game production can be one of the most intense, collaborative processes you'll ever experience. The interesting and challenging thing about game development teams is the sheer breadth of types of people who work on them. From the hardcore computer scientists, who may be designing the AI or graphic displays, to the talented illustrators and animators who bring the characters to life, to the money-minded executives and business managers who deliver the game to its players, the range of personalities is incredible.

1.4   Team meeting

As the designer, you will interact with almost all of them, and you will find that they all speak different languages and have different points of view. "Computer-ese" doesn't often communicate well to artists or the producer, while the subtle shadings of a character sketch may not be instantly obvious to a programmer. A big part of your job, and one of the reasons for your documents and specifications, is to serve as a sort of "universal translator," making sure that all of these different groups are, in fact, working on the same game.

Throughout this book, we often refer to the "game designer" as a single team member, but in many cases the task of game design is a team effort. Whether there is a team of designers on a single game, or a collaborative environment where the visual designers, programmers, or producer all have input to the design, the game designer rarely works alone.

Process

Being a game designer often requires working under great pressure. You'll have to make critical changes to your game without causing new issues in the process. All too often, a game becomes unbalanced while trying to correct an issue because the designer gets too close to the work,

and in the hopes of solving one problem, introduces a host of new problems. But unable to see this mistake, the designer keeps making changes, while the problems grow worse, until the game becomes such a mess that it loses whatever magic it once had.

Games are fragile systems, and each element is inextricably linked to the others, so a change in one variable can send disruptive ripples throughout. This is particularly catastrophic in the final phases of development, where you run out of time, mistakes are left unfixed, and portions of the game are amputated in hopes of saving what's left. It's gruesome, but it may help you understand why some games with so much potential seem "D.O.A."

The one thing that can rescue a game from this terrible fate is instilling good process in your team from the beginning. Production is a messy business, when ideas can get convoluted and objectives can disappear in the chaos of daily crises. But good process, involving the iterative system of playtesting and controlled changes which we'll discuss throughout this book, can help you stay focused on your goals, prioritize what's truly important, and avoid the pitfalls of an unstructured approach.

Exercise 1.2: D.O.A.

Take one game that you've played that was D.O.A. By D.O.A., we mean "dead on arrival" (i.e., a game that's no fun to play). Write down what you don't like about it. What did the designers miss out on? How could the game be improved?

Inspiration

A game designer often looks at the world differently from most people. This is in part because of

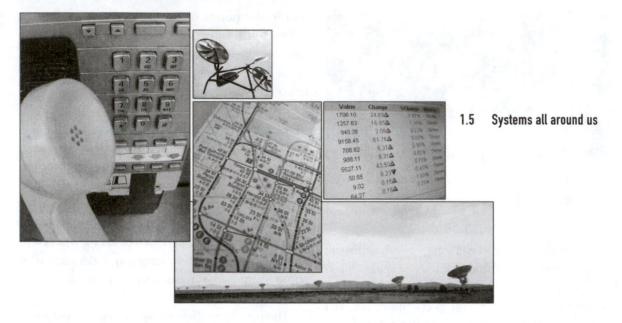

1.5   Systems all around us

the profession and in part because the art of game design requires someone who is able to see and analyze the underlying relationships and rules of complex systems, and to find inspiration for play in common interactions.

When a game designer looks at the world, he often sees things in terms of challenges, structures, and play. Games are everywhere: from how we manage our money to how we form relationships. Everyone has goals in life and must overcome obstacles to achieve those goals. And of course, there are rules. If you want to win in the financial markets, you have to understand the rules of trading stocks and bonds, profit forecasts, IPOs, etc. When you play the markets, the act of investing becomes very similar to a game. The same holds true for winning someone's heart. In courtship, there are social rules that you must follow, and it's in understanding these rules and how you fit into society that helps you to succeed.

If you want to be a game designer, try looking at the world as one giant game made up of millions of smaller games that work independently in

their own structures. Try to analyze how things in your life function. What are the underlying rules? How do the mechanics operate? Are there opportunities for challenge or playfulness? Write down your observations and analyze the relationships. You'll find there is potential for play all around you that can form the inspiration for a game. You can use these observations and inspirations as foundations for building new types of gameplay.

Why not look at other games for inspiration? Well, of course, you can. But if you want to come up with truly original ideas, then don't fall back on existing games for all your ideas. Instead, look at the world around you. Some of the things that have inspired other game designers, and may inspire you, are obvious: personal relationships, buying and selling, competition in the workplace, etc. We could go on and on. But there are subtler areas of the world that may inspire you as well.

For instance, nature offers a wide variety of game-like systems. Take ant colonies: they're organized around a sophisticated set of rules, and there's competition both within the colonies and between competing insect groups. The same holds true for any ecosystem, whether it's lions in sub-Saharan Africa or turtles in your neighborhood pond.

Examine these systems; break them down in terms of objects, behaviors, relationships, etc. Try to understand exactly how each element of the system interacts. This may be the foundation for an interesting game. You can do the same when looking at how people interact, whether in politics, music, or marriage. There is a game in each relationship. By practicing the art of extracting and defining the games in all aspects of your life, you will not only hone your skills as a designer, but you'll open up new vistas in what you imagine a game can be.

Exercise 1.3: Your Life as a Game

List five areas of your life that could be games. Then briefly describe a possible underlying game structure for each.

Creativity

Creativity is hard to quantify, but you'll definitely need to access your creativity in order to design great games. Everyone is creative in different ways. Some people come up with lots of ideas without even trying. Others focus on one idea and explore all of its possible facets. Some sit quietly in their rooms thinking to themselves, while others like to bounce ideas around with a group and find the interaction stimulating. Some seek out stimulation or new experiences to spark their imagination. Great game designers tend to be people who can tap into their dreams and fantasies and bring those to life as interactive experiences.

One of the greatest game designers in the industry, Nintendo's Shigeru Miyamoto, said that he often looks to his childhood and to hobbies that he enjoys for inspiration. "When I was a child, I went hiking and found a lake," he says. "It was quite a surprise for me to stumble upon it. When I traveled around the country without a map, trying to find my way, stumbling on amazing things as I went, I realized how it felt to go on an adventure like this."[1] Many of Miyamoto's games draw from this sense of exploration and wonder that he remembers from childhood.

Think about your own life experiences. Do you have memories that might spark the idea for a game? One reason that childhood can be such a powerful inspiration for game designers is that when we are children, we are particularly engrossed in playing games. If you watch how kids interact in a playground, it's usually through game playing. They make games and learn social order and group dynamics from their play. Games permeate all aspects of kids' lives and are a vital part of their developmental process. So if you go back to your childhood and look at things that you enjoyed, you'll find the raw material for games right there.

Exercise 1.4: Your Childhood

List ten social games you played as a child. For example, hide and seek, four square, tag, etc. Briefly describe what was compelling about each of those games.

Creativity might also mean putting two things together that don't seem to be related—like Shakespeare and the Brady Bunch. What can you make of such a strange combination? Well, the

---

1. David Sheff, *Game Over: How Nintendo Conquered the World* (New York: Vintage Books, 1994), p. 51.

1.6   You Don't Know Jack

designers of *You Don't Know Jack* used silly combinations of high- and low–brow knowledge like this to create a trivia game that challenged players to be equally proficient in both. The result was a hit game with such creative spark that it crossed the usual boundaries of gaming, appealing to players old and young, male and female.

Our past experiences, our relationships, and our identity all come into play when trying to reach our creativity. Game designers must find a way to tap into their creative souls and bring forth the best parts in their games. However you do it, whether you work alone or in a team, whether you stand on your head or bounce off the walls, whether you look to other games for inspiration, or to life experiences, the bottom line is that there's no single right way to go about it. Everyone has a different style for coming up with ideas and being creative. What matters is not the spark of an idea but what you do with that idea once it emerges, and this is where process comes into play.

THE DESIGN PROCESS

Having a good solid process for developing an idea from the initial concept into a playable and satisfying game experience is another key to thinking like a game designer. The approach we will show you in this book focuses on involving the player in your design process from conception through completion. By that we mean continually testing the gameplay with target players through every phase of development. The sooner you can bring the player into the equation, the better. Immediately after brainstorming, we encourage designers to construct a playable version of their game. By this we mean starting with a physical prototype of the game mechanics.

A physical prototype can use paper and pen, index cards, or even acting out. It is meant to be played by the designer and her friends. The goal is to play and perfect this simplistic model before a single programmer, producer, or graphic artists is ever brought onto the project. This way, the game designer receives instant feedback on what players think of the game and comes to understand the core game structures.

This may sound like common sense, but in the industry today, much of the design of the core gaming system comes later in the production cycle, which can result in huge amounts of frustration. People in the industry are realizing that this lack of testing means that many games don't reach their full potential, and the process of developing games needs to change if that problem is to be solved.

There's a reason for this. Because most games are not thoroughly prototyped or tested early on in the process, many of the flaws come out later—in some cases, too late to fix. For a developer, this can become a nightmare. Veteran game developer and former Xbox evangelist Seamus Blackley gave an eloquent speech on this topic at the 2003 D.I.C.E. Summit. "The problem right now is that we're designing for publishers and not the audience." In Blackley's view, playtests "should be used early enough so that the developers can make use of them. Testing can help you to delight the customer and should empower design. And yet today, testing is a scary process that developers are scared of."[2]

Our solution to this problem is never to begin the production, or even the software prototype, without a deep understanding of the game's foundation. This is critical because once the production process commences, it becomes increasingly difficult to alter the design. As you will see, the production process often runs counter to the design process, and therefore, the further along the design is before the production begins, the greater the likelihood of costly mistakes. How can you avoid this paradox? The best way is to take an iterative approach to the design and development process.

Iterative design

By "iterative" we simply means that you design, test, and evaluate the results over and over again throughout the development of your game, each time improving upon the gameplay or features, until the experience meets your criteria. Here is a detailed flow of the iterative process that you should go through when designing a game:

- Idea or system is conceived.
- Idea or system is formalized (i.e., written down or prototyped).
- Idea or system is tested (i.e., playtested or exhibited for feedback).
- Results are evaluated, categorized, and prioritized.

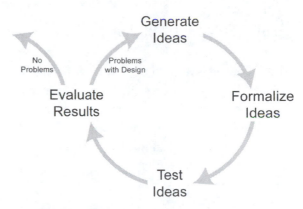

1.7   Iterative process diagram

- If results are negative and idea or system appears to be fundamentally flawed, go back to the first step.
- If results point to improvements, modify and test again.
- If results are positive and idea or system appears successful, the iterative process has been completed.

As you will see, we will apply this process during almost every aspect of game design, from the initial conception through to the final quality assurance testing.

Step 1: Brainstorming

- Come up with as many game concepts as you can.
- Narrow down the list to the top three.
- Write up a short, one-page outline describing each of these ideas.

Step 2: Physical prototype

- Create a playable prototype using pen and paper or other craft materials.

---

2. Seamus Blackley, D.I.C.E. Conference 2003.

DESIGNERS YOU SHOULD KNOW

The following is a list of designers who have had monumental impact on digital games. The list was hard to finalize because so many great individuals have contributed to the craft in so many important ways. The goal was not to be comprehensive but rather to give a taste of some designers who've created seminal works and who it would be good for you, as an aspiring designer yourself, to be familiar with. We're pleased that many designers on the list contributed interviews and sidebars to this book.

Shigeru Miyamoto

Miyamoto was hired out of industrial design school by Nintendo in 1977. He was the first staff artist at the company. Early in his career he was assigned to a submarine game called *Radarscope*. This game was like most of the games of the day—simple twitch-game play mechanic, no story, and no characters. He wondered why digital games couldn't be more like the epic stories and fairy tales that he knew and loved from childhood. He wanted to make adventure stories and he wanted to add emotion to games. Instead of focusing on *Radarscope*, he made up his own beauty and the beast–like story where an ape steals his keeper's girlfriend and runs away. The result was *Donkey Kong*, and the character that you played was Mario (originally named Jumpman). Mario is perhaps the most enduring character in games and one of the most recognized characters in the world. Each time a new console is introduced by Nintendo—starting with the original NES machine—Miyamoto designs a Mario game as its flagship title. He is famous for the wild creativity and imagination in his games. Aside from all the Mario and Luigi games, Miyamoto's list of credits is long. It includes the *Zelda*, *Starfox*, and *Pikmin* games.

Will Wright

Early in his career, in 1987, Wright created a game called *Raid on Bungling Bay*. It was a helicopter game where you attacked islands. He had so much fun programming the little cities on the islands that he decided that making cities was the premise for a fun game. This was the inspiration for *SimCity*. When he first developed *SimCity*, publishers were not interested because they didn't believe anyone would buy it. But Wright persisted on his own, and the game became an instant hit. *SimCity* was a break out in terms of design in that it was based on creating rather than destroying. Also it didn't have set goals. These things added some new facets to games. Wright was always interested in simulated reality and has done more than anyone in bringing simulation to the masses. *SimCity* spawned a whole series of titles including *SimEarth*, *SimAnt*, *SimCopter*, and many others. His game, *The Sims*, is his most ambitious creation yet. And it is currently the best selling game of all time. See "A Conversation with Will Wright by Celia Pearce" on page 133.

Sid Meier

Legend has it that Sid Meier bet his buddy, Bill Stealey, that he could program a better flying combat game than the one they playing were playing, in two weeks. Stealey took him up on the offer, and together they founded the company Micro Prose. It took more than two weeks, but the company released the title *Solo Flight* in 1984. Considered by many to be the father of PC gaming, Meier went on to create groundbreaking title after groundbreaking title. His *Civilization* series has had fundamental influence on the genre of PC strategy games since. His game *Sid Meier's Pirates!* was an innovative mix of genres—action, adventure, and roleplaying—that also blended real time and turn-based gaming. His gameplay ideas have been adopted in countless PC games. Meier's other titles include the *Colonization* series, *Sid Meier's Gettysburg!*, *Alpha Centauri*, *Silent Serv.*

Warren Spector

Warren Spector started his career working for boardgame maker Steve Jackson Games in Austin, Texas. He went from there to the paper-based roleplaying game company TSR where he developed boardgames and wrote RPG supplements and several novels. In 1989 he was ready to add digital games to his portfolio and moved to the developer, ORIGIN Systems. There he worked on the *Ultima* series with Richard Garriott. Spector had an intense interest in integrating characters and stories into games. He pioneered "freeform" gameplay with a series of innovative titles including *Underworld*, *System Shock*, and *Thief*. His title *Deus Ex* took the concepts of flexible play and drama in games to new heights and is considered one of the finest PC games of all time. See his "Designer Perspective" interview on page 39.

Richard Garfield

In 1990 Richard Garfield was an unknown mathematician and part-time game designer. He had been trying unsuccessfully to sell a boardgame prototype called *RoboRally* to publishers for seven years. When yet another publisher rejected his concept he was not surprised. However, this time the publisher, a man named Peter Adkison doing business as "Wizards of the Coast," asked for a portable card game that was playable in under an hour. Garfield took the challenge and developed a dueling game system where each card in the system could affect the rules in different ways. It was a breakthrough in game design because the system was infinitely expandable. The game was *Magic: The Gathering*, and it single-handedly spawned the industry of collectible card games. *Magic* has been released in digital format in multiple titles. When Hasbro bought Wizards in 1995 for $325 million, Garfield owned a significant portion of the company. See his article "The Development of *Magic: The Gathering*" on page 182.

Peter Molyneux

The story goes that it all started with an anthill. Peter Molyneux as a child toyed with one—tearing it down in parts and watching the ants fight to rebuild, dropping food into the world and watching the ants appropriate it, etc. He was fascinated by the power he had over the tiny, unpredictable creatures. Molyneux went on to become a programmer and game designer and eventually the pioneer of digital "god games." In his breakout title *Populous* you act as a deity lording over tiny settlers. The game was revolutionary in that it was a strategy game that took place in real time, as opposed to in turns, and you had indirect control over your units. The units had minds of their own. This game and other Molyneux hits had profound influence on the real-time strategy (RTS) games to come. Other titles he has created include *Syndicate, Theme Park, Dungeon Keeper,* and *Black & White.* See Molyneux's "Designer Perspective" interview on page 18.

Gary Gygax

In the early 1970s Gary Gygax was an insurance underwriter in Lake Geneva, Wisconsin. He loved all kinds of games, including tabletop wargames. In these games players controlled large armies of miniatures, acting like generals. Gygax and his friends had fun acting out the personas of different pieces on the battlefield such as commanders, heroes, etc. He followed his inclination of what was fun and created a system for battling small parties of miniatures in a game he called *Chainmail.* From there players wanted even more control of and more character information about the individual units. They wanted to play the role of single characters. Gygax, in conjunction with game designer Dave Arneson, developed an elaborate system for role-playing characters that was eventually named *Dungeons & Dragons.* The *D&D* game system is the direct ancestor of every paper-based and digital role-playing game since. The system is directly evident in all of today's RPGs including *Diablo, Baldur's Gate,* and *EverQuest.*

Richard Garriott

Richard Garriott—a.k.a. "Lord British"—programmed his first game right out of high school in 1979. It was an RPG called *Akalabeth.* He sold it on his own through a local computer store in Austin, Texas. The packaging for this first version was a Ziploc bag. *Akalabeth* later got picked up by a publisher and sold well. Garriott used what he'd learned to create *Ultima,* and thus one of the most famous game series of all time began. The *Ultima* titles evolved over the years—each successive one pushing the envelope in terms of both technology and gameplay—eventually bringing the world of the game online. *Ultima Online,* released in 1997, was a pioneering title in massively multiplayer online worlds. Garriott continues to push the boundaries of online gaming with work on the much-anticipated title *Tabula Rasa.*

- Playtest the physical prototype using the iterative process described starting on page 11.
- Once the physical prototype is perfected, write up a three- to six-page gameplay treatment, describing how the game functions.

Step 3: Presentation (optional)

- A presentation is often made in order to secure funds to hire the prototyping team. Even if you do not require funding, going through the exercise of creating a full presentation is a good way to think through your game and introduce it to the team members and the upper management for feedback.
- Your presentation should include demo artwork and a solid gameplay treatment.
- If you do not secure funding, you can either return to Step 1 and start over again on a new concept or gain feedback from your funding sources and work on modifying the game to fit their needs. Because you have not yet invested in extensive artwork or programming, your costs so far should be pretty reasonable, and you should have a great deal of flexibility to make any changes.

Step 4: Software prototype

- Once you have your prototyping team in place, you can begin creating a rough computer program which models the core gameplay.
- If possible, try to do this entirely without graphics, or use temp graphics that cost very little to make. This will save time and money and make the process go faster.
- Playtest the software prototype using the iterative process described earlier.
- Once the software prototype is perfected, move on to the documentation step.

Step 5: Design document

- While you have been prototyping and working on your gameplay, you have probably been compiling notes and ideas for the "real" game. Use the knowledge you've gained during this prototyping state to write the first draft of a document that outlines every aspect of the game and how it functions.

Step 6: Production

- Work with all of the team members to make sure each aspect of the design is achievable and correctly described in the document.
- Once a draft of the design document is completed, move on to production.
- Production is the time to staff up and begin the creation of the real artwork and programming.
- Don't lose sight of the iterative process during production—test your artwork, gameplay, characters, etc., as you move along. As you continue to perform iterative cycles throughout the production phase, the problems you find and the changes you make should get smaller and smaller. This is because you solved your major issues during the prototyping phases.
- Unfortunately, this is the time when most game designers actually wind up designing their games, and this can lead to numerous problems of time, money, and frustration.

Step 7: QA

- By the time the project is ready for Quality Assurance testing, you should be very sure that your gameplay is solid. There may still be some issues, so continue playtesting, with an eye to usability. Now is the time to make sure your game is accessible to your entire target audience.

Designer Perspective: Sandy Petersen

Title

Designer, Ensemble Studios

Project list (five to eight top projects)

- *Call of Cthulhu* (paper game)
- *Lightspeed*
- *DOOM*
- *Quake*
- *Rise of Rome*
- *Age of Empires: The Age of Kings*
- *The Conquerors*

How did you get into the game industry?

I backed into it by accident. Took up a job typesetting for a game company to fund my college years and ended up turning an avocation into a vocation.

What are your five favorite games and why?

- *Contract Bridge:* Best card game ever, bar none. It features many different ways to excel, which means not all good players are good in the same way, so games become clashes of different styles.
- *Cosmic Encounter:* The first game to instigate the concept of different players having different abilities. This has become a mainstay of computer games (such as *Civilization*), but *Cosmic Encounter*'s simple autobalancing system still rules supreme as the finest use of this concept.

As you can see, iterative design comes into play throughout the production process, which means you'll be doing lots of prototyping and playtesting at every stage of your game's development. You can't be the advocate for the player if you don't know what the player is thinking, and playtesting is the best mechanism by which you can elicit feedback and gain insight into your game. We cannot emphasize this fact enough, and we encourage any designer to rigorously build into any production schedule the means to continually isolate and playtest all aspects of their game as thoroughly as possible.

- *World in Flames 5th Edition:* Something deep within my soul forces me to replay all of World War II every year or two by using this huge retro-style wargame. There's no excuse for it, really.
- *Civilization* (the boardgame): Brings the economy to the forefront in a way that few games have done successfully. Every decision you make in *Civilization* affects your economy for better or worse, and the card-trading is a blast.
- *Runequest:* My favorite role-playing game.

An astute reader will notice that none of my five favorites are computer games. I myself didn't realize this until after I'd written them down, but it's probably not a coincidence.

What games have inspired you the most as a designer and why?

- *Wolfenstein 3-D:* At its time, it was amazing for the use of 3D. It still has great strengths in that each separate group of rooms or hallways presents a different tactical puzzle.
- *Command HQ:* First really good use of multiplayer in a game.
- *M.U.L.E.:* Best ever economic-based computer game, and maybe the only one ever that was any fun.
- *Zelda:* The whole series is one of my favorite role-playing games. I look forward to the next installment eagerly.

What are you most proud of in your career?

Being voted into the Gamers Hall of Fame in 1990—an award given to only a single person a year, and voted on by game fans, rather than game companies.

What words of advice would you give to an aspiring designer today?

Be familiar with all types of games, not just computer games.

Prototypes and playtesting in the industry

In the game industry today, many designers take a shortcut, skipping the creation of a physical prototype altogether and jumping straight from dreaming up a concept to writing the design document. Seldom is time taken up front to develop original gameplay and test it with players. The problem with this method is that the design document is completed and the software coding has commenced before anyone has a true sense for the game mechanics. How can someone design a game without understanding the core game structure? Surprisingly, it happens all the time. In fact, it's the norm in the industry today, and this is the reason so many games wind up looking and feeling like carbon copies of one another.

DESIGNER PERSPECTIVE: PETER MOLYNEUX

Title

Managing Director, Lionhead Studios

Project list (five to eight top projects)

- 1989: *Populous*: Game Design/Lead Programmer
- 1990: *Powermonger*: Game Design/Lead Programmer
- 1991: *Populous 2*: Game Design/ Lead programmer
- 1993: *Syndicate*: Producer/Game Design
- 1994: *Theme Park*: Producer/ Lead Programmer, Game Design*
- 1994: *Magic Carpet*: Producer/ Game Design
- 1997: *Dungeon Keeper*: Producer/ Game Design/Programming

How did you get into the game industry?

Hmm. This is quite a long story. I set up a company with my then partner Les Edgar programming databases on the PC. We called our company Taurus because we were both Taureans. One day we had a call inviting us to meet with [computer company] Commodore—they gave us the red carpet treatment and were very keen for us to work on the Amiga, asking us how long it would take for us to get "the program" on the Amiga—even giving us several free machines. It was only at the end of the meeting it dawned on me that they had the wrong Taurus—they thought we were a company called Torus. But we kept quiet, took the free machines, and it soon became very apparent that the Amiga was going to be a games machine—we were offered a conversion of *Druid 2* from the ST to Amiga and [our company] Bullfrog was born.

It's difficult to design an original game if you skip the physical prototyping process. What happens is that you are forced to reference existing games in the design document. This means your game is doomed from the outset to be derivative. Breaking away from your design document becomes even more difficult as the production heats up. Once your team is in place, with programmers coding and artists cranking out graphics, the idea of going back and changing the core gameplay becomes unthinkable. The gears are in motion, and everyone is working off the design document. It becomes the set path that you must follow, and any changes to it are met with stiff resistance.

What are your five favorite games and why?

- *Zelda: Ocarina of Time:* Just because it's one of the most complete games ever.
- *Advance Wars:* It's taken me over—I spent my whole holiday playing on the beach and nearly caused a car crash playing it while driving.
- *Command & Conquer: Red Alert:* Because it really brought the RTS genre together and was absolutely one of the most playable games of its time—I love the RTS genre.
- *Half-Life:* Because it proved that the first-person shooter could be more then just a test of reflexes and could be as entertaining as a film with a great story and plot.

What games have inspired you the most as a designer and why?

My inspiration from games started from the earliest games, in particular *Wizardry* on the Apple IIe which, in terms of game design, for me was the equivalent of the invention of the wheel. The ability to explore dungeons, create your own characters and take part in heroic quests had never been seen in a game before. I'd also have to mention *Dungeon Master*, not because it was a great role-playing game, but because it had such an intuitive interface. It certainly was responsible for my belief that interfaces are paramount. I'd also admit to being influenced by the high production values in games such as *Half-Life*.

What are you most proud of in your career?

Building up a team of people whom I have now worked with for over a decade.

What words of advice would you give to an aspiring designer today?

Designing a game is not thinking up a storyline but about what the player does and sees while playing your idea. If you can crack that, then that game's design stands a much higher chance of being a hit.

By using the iterative design approach outlined previously, you have the opportunity to lay out the structure and design of the game before anyone else is involved. This gives you, the designer, full control to manipulate the gameplay and test it without the production process constricting your creativity. If you think about it, it's much easier to make a change to a pen and paper model than to ask several programmers, who have spent a week or more coding the gameplay, to alter something. Sure, they may accommodate the first few times, but designing solid gameplay is an iterative process, which requires continual tweaking. How many times can you ask the programmers to recode the engine before they become disgruntled? After all, from their perspective, you should have perfected the gameplay after the tenth try—but as any experienced game designer knows, ten tries is only the beginning.

The same holds true for the artwork. If you make changes in the gameplay, it affects everything from the user interface design down to the graphics and database objects. Every member of the team has to alter what they're doing every time a change is implemented, and people tend not to like to throw out something they've worked hard to create. So as a designer, you're in an awkward position when you start restructuring the core game mechanics while the wheels are in motion.

There's also a lag time between iterations, and time is money. Programmers and artists aren't cheap, and the further down the path you go and the larger your team grows, the more it costs to make each change. That is why doing the prototyping yourself or within a small group is critical. You will be able to try out dozens of different permutations of your game in the same time it takes you to try out one variation with a larger team.

DESIGNING FOR PLAYERS

The primary advantage of the iterative design process we recommend, besides saving time and money, is that it puts the player at the center of the game design process. This seems logical, but all too often the player comes last, and the production process winds up dictating changes in the game.

Changes and ideas can be tested easily and quickly when you're working with a pen and paper prototype. You simply take out a fresh sheet of paper and rewrite the rules, then test the game again, each time gaining more feedback from the players. The opposite tends to occur when you have a large production team in place. Even if you manage to bring in outside players and get valid feedback, there is no time to change gear on the software and media production based on that feedback. The result is that the game designer is overridden or good ideas are deemed too costly to implement. On the other hand, if you playtest early, using physical prototypes and rough software prototypes, you can get your feedback and make your changes, often without costing the production a dime.

Experimentation

An iterative approach can also foster new ideas because it gives you time to research wild new ideas and craft them to make sure they will be accepted by players. Real breakthroughs seldom come from the first spark of an idea—they tend to come from long-term development and experimentation. By interacting with players throughout the design process, experimental ideas have time to develop and mature.

What will your experiments produce? Perhaps nothing. Perhaps you'll discover 100 ideas that are not fun at all. But you'll never know until you try. And the method we propose can open up your process to experimentation without costing time and money in production.

A golden moment in the design process is the time before production when you are free to experiment with the forms and structures of gameplay to your heart's content, and this is when you just might discover an entirely new form of gameplay.

CONCLUSION

Our goal in this book is to make you a game designer. We want to give you the skills and tools you'll need to take your ideas and craft them into games that aren't mere extensions of the games already on the market. We want to enable you to push the envelope on game design, and the key to doing this is process. The approach you will learn here is about internalizing a method of iterative design and playtesting that will make you more creative and productive, while helping you to avoid many of the pitfalls that plague game designers.

The following chapters in this first section will lay out a vocabulary of design and help you to think critically about the games you play and the games you want to design. Understanding how games work and why players play them is the next step to becoming a game designer.

Chapter 2
The Structure of Games

Exercise 2.1: Think of a Game

1. Think of a game, any game. Now write down a description of the game. Be detailed. Describe it as if to someone who has never played a game like it before.

2. Now, think of another game—a completely different type of game. The more different this game is from the first one, the better. Describe it.

3. Compare your descriptions. Which elements were different and which were similar? Dig deep and really think about the underlying mechanics of each game.

There is no wrong answer to this exercise. The goal is simply to get you to begin thinking about the nature of games and to realize that games, no matter how dissimilar they may seem, do share some common elements. Those common elements are why we recognize certain experiences as games, and not others, and throughout this book they will form the basis for our study of games and game design.

GO FISH VERSUS *QUAKE*

Do all games share the same exact structure? Of course not. A card game has a very different format than a boardgame; a 3D action game is not at all the same as a trivia game. There is something, however, that they must share, because we clearly recognize them all as "games." Take Go Fish and *Quake*. They must have some similarities because if we asked you if each was a game, you'd say, "Yes!" In other words, if these games don't share the same structure, then what *do* they share that makes them games and not two different forms of entertainment?

Before venturing to say what the similarities between them might be, it would help to look more closely at each of the two example games.

Go Fish

This is a game for three to six players using a standard 52-card deck. The dealer deals five cards to each player. The rest of the cards are placed face down in a draw pile. The player to dealer's left starts.

A turn consists of asking a player for a specific rank. For example, if it's your turn, you might say, "Chris, please give me your Jacks." You must already hold at least one card of the requested rank, so you must hold at least one Jack to say this. If Chris has cards of the named rank (Jacks in this case), he has to give you all his cards of this rank. You then get another turn and may again ask any player for any rank that you hold.

If Chris does not have any cards of the named rank, he says, "Go fish!" You must then draw the top card from the draw pile. If the drawn card is the rank you asked for, you show it and get another turn. If the drawn card is not the rank you asked for, you keep it, but the turn now passes to the player who said, "Go fish!"

As soon as a player collects a book of four cards of the same rank, this must be shown and discarded face down. The game continues until either someone has no cards left in their hand or the draw pile runs out. The winner is the player who then has the most books.

Quake

In single-player *Quake*, the player controls a character within a 3D environment. Your character can walk, run, jump, swim, shoot, and pick up stuff, but you have a limited amount of armor, health, and ammo.

In the game there are eight types of weapons: axe, shotgun, double-barreled shotgun, nailgun, perforator, grenade launcher, rocket launcher, and a thunderbolt. Each weapon uses a specific type of ammo: shells are for both types of shotguns, nails are for nailguns and perforators, grenades are for grenade launchers and rocket launchers, and cells are for the thunderbolt. There are also power-ups within the game that will boost your power, protect you, heal you, or render you invisible, invulnerable, or able to breathe underwater.

Your enemies include rottweilers, grunts, enforcers, death knights, rotfish, zombies, scrags, ogres, spawn, fiends, vores, shamblers, and possibly other players. Hazards you might find in the environment are explosions, water, slime, lava, traps, and teleporters.

The goal of *Quake* is to stay alive while you move through the levels. Also, according to the backstory, your overall objective is to find the enemy, codenamed Quake, who is using "slipgates" (transporter devices) to insert death squads inside your bases to kill, steal, and kidnap. You

2.1 Quake and Go Fish

have the authority to requisition anything that you need to achieve your objective.

There are four episodes in the game. The first level of each episode ends in a slipgate—these signify that you've entered another dimension. When you complete an entire dimension (five to eight levels), you encounter another slipgate, which returns you to the start.

Comparison

At first glance, the descriptions of these two experiences could not be more dissimilar: one is a turn-based card game; the other is a real-time 3D action shooter. One requires a piece of commercial software and a personal computer capable of running it; the other can be played with a common deck of cards. One is a copyrighted product; the other is a public domain set of rules, which can be transferred verbally from person to person, generation to generation. And yet we call them both games, and agree, even if we cannot at first verbalize it, that they are similar experiences at some deep level.

If we look closely, though, and try not to ignore ideas that seem self-obvious, there are enough similarities between the experience of *Quake* and the experience of Go Fish for us to begin to understand what underlying requirements we are looking for when we judge whether or not something is a game.

Players

The most obvious similarity in these two descriptions is that both start out by mentioning that the experiences are for players. This sounds like a simple distinction, but what other forms of entertainment are designed to demand active participation by their consumers? Sports are one example, but

2.2   Players

of course, many sports are games. Musicians participate in creating the experience of music, but the primary consumers are the audience, not the players. Similarly, dramatic actors participate in the experience of a play, but again, the experience is primarily created for the audience.

What the term "players" implies in each experience described is the notion of voluntary participants who both partake in and consume the entertainment. Players are active, they make decisions, they are invested, they are potential winners—they are a very distinct subset of people. Throughout this book, we will focus on players and the design of their experience within the game as the primary challenge for the game designer.

Exercise 2.2: Players

Describe the difference between how players interact in Go Fish versus *Quake*.

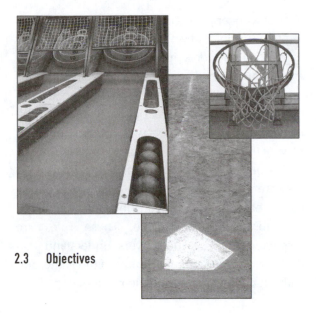

2.3   Objectives

Objectives

The next clear distinction is that both descriptions lay out specific goals for the players. In Go Fish, the goal is to be the player who makes the most books. In *Quake,* it's to stay alive and complete the level of the complex you are in.

This is very different from other experiences in which we may participate in general. When you watch a film or read a book there is no clear-cut objective presented for you to accomplish during the experience—of course, there is one for the characters, but we're talking about the players here. In life, we set our *own* objectives and work as hard as we feel necessary to achieve them. We don't need to accomplish all of our objectives to have a successful life. In games, however, the objective is a key element without which the experience loses much of its structure, and our need to work towards the objective is a measure of our involvement in the game.

Exercise 2.3: Objectives

List out five games, and in one sentence per game, describe the objective in each game.

Procedures

Both descriptions also give detailed instructions on what players can do to achieve the game objectives. For example, in Go Fish, some of these instructions include: "the dealer deals five cards to each player," or "a turn consists of asking a specific player for a specific rank." In *Quake,* the description states that "your character can walk, run, jump, swim, shoot, and pick up stuff." The directions also provide a set of controls for doing so. These controls are the method by which the player accesses the basic procedures of the game. If we played Go Fish on a computer, we'd have to create controls for dealing or asking a player for a card of a certain rank.

Procedures, the actions or methods of play allowed by the rules, are an important distinction of the experiences we call games. They guide player behavior, creating interactions which would

2.4   Procedures

probably never take place outside the authority of the game.

For instance, if you wanted to create a set of four cards of like rank, you wouldn't necessarily ask one player at a time for these cards. You might use a more efficient means, like asking all of the players at once, or simply looking through the draw deck for the cards you needed. Because games, by their nature, have procedures that must be followed, you don't take these more efficient actions. Instead, you follow the procedures, and in doing so, you confirm that these required actions are indeed an important distinction that sets games apart from other behaviors and experiences.

Rules

Both descriptions spend a great deal of time explaining exactly what objects the game consists of and what the players can and cannot do. They also clarify what happens in various situations that might arise. In Go Fish, "the cards are placed face down in a draw pile," or "if Chris has cards of the named rank, he must give me *all* his cards of this rank." And from *Quake*, "there are eight types of weapons," and "shells are for both types of shotguns, nails are for nailguns and perforators, etc."

Some of these rule statements define game objects and concepts. Objects, like the deck of cards, draw pile, and weapons, are the building blocks of each of these systems, upon which the rest of the design depends. Other rules limit player behavior and proscribe reactive events. For instance, if nails are for nailguns, you can't use nails in the thunderbolt. If you have a Jack when you're asked for one, you have to give it up; you can't keep it, or you're breaking the rules of the game. Who will stop you from breaking the rules? Your own sense of fair play? The other players? The underlying code of a digital game?

The concepts of both rules and procedures imply authority, and yet there is no person or body named in either description with whom to associate that authority. The authority of the rules stems from an implicit agreement by the players to submit themselves to the experience. If you don't follow the rules, in a very real way, you are no longer playing the game.

So, our next distinctive quality of games is that they are experiences that have rules which define game objects, proscribe principles, and limit behavior within the game. These rules are respected because the players understand that they are a key structural element of the game, and without them, the game would not function.

Resources

As we've discussed each of these games, we've mentioned certain objects that seem to hold a

2.5   **Rules**

rather high value for the players in reaching their objectives. In Go Fish, the cards of each rank; and in *Quake*, the weapons, their ammunition, as well as the power-ups mentioned in the rule set. These objects, made valuable because they can help the players achieve their goal, but made scarce in the system by the designer, are what we call resources.

Finding and managing resources is a key part of many games—whether those resources are cards, weapons, time, units, turns, or terrain. In the two examples we see here, one depends on direct exchange of resources (Go Fish), while the other offers resources fixed in place by the game designer (*Quake*).

Resources are, by definition, items made valuable by their scarcity and utility. In the real world, and in game worlds, resources can be used to further our aims; they can be combined to make new products or items; and they can be bought and sold in various types of markets.

Conflict

As noted previously, both experiences we described lay out specific objectives for their players. And, as we've also noted, they lay out procedures and rules that guide and limit player

behavior. The problem for the players is that the procedures and rules of games tend to deter them from accomplishing goals directly. For example, as mentioned earlier, you cannot simply ask everyone at the table to give you the other three Jacks all at once when you're playing Go Fish. You have to ask each player one at a time, risking that you may not get a card and lose your turn, while revealing to the table that you have a card of the rank you asked for.

Similarly, in *Quake*, if you could just leave the level of the complex you're on, that would solve the objective, but it's not that easy. To find the exit, you're forced to make it through a maze-like obstacle course of enemies and hazards. In both cases, the relationship between the objectives of the players and the rules limiting behavior creates another distinctive element of games: conflict, which the players work to resolve in their own favor.

Exercise 2.5: Conflict

Compare and contrast the conflict in football to the conflict in poker. Describe how each game creates conflict for the players.

Boundaries

Another similarity between these two experiences, one which is not referred to directly in either description but rather implied, is that the rules and goals that are driving the players apply only within the game and not in "real life." In the case of *Quake*, the architecture of the 3D space forms a physical boundary. Players are precluded from moving their characters out of these boundaries by the underlying code.

In the case of Go Fish, the boundaries are more conceptual than physical. Players are not precisely

2.6   Resources

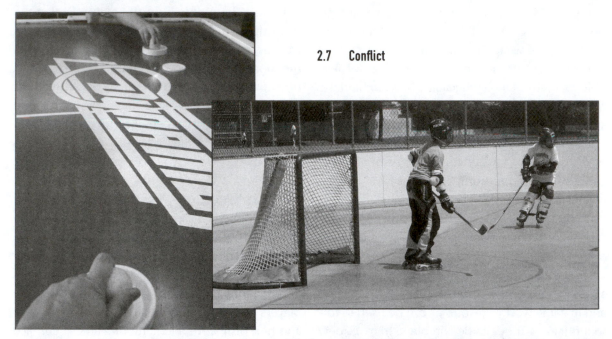

2.7 Conflict

bounded in a physical sense by any of the rules, except that they need to be able to speak to one another and trade cards back and forth. They are, however, conceptually bounded by the social agreement that they are playing the game and that they will not leave the game with some of the cards, or add extra cards to the deck.

The concept that these experiences are somehow set apart from other experiences by boundaries is yet another distinction we can make about the structure of games.

Outcome

One last similarity between both of these experiences is that they are both driving towards measurable and unequal outcomes. For example, in Go Fish, the player who achieves the objective of making the most books by the end of the game wins. In *Quake*, a player can either win (stay alive) or lose (be killed).

The outcome differs from the objective in that all players may achieve the objective, but other fac-

2.8 Boundaries

tors within the system may determine which of these actually win the game. For example, in Go Fish, a number of players may accomplish the objective of creating books, but only one player will create the most books—unless there's a tie, and that type of special case is usually addressed in the rules of a game.

DESIGNER PERSPECTIVES: AMERICAN McGEE

Title	Project list (five to eight top projects)	
Creative Director, The Mauritania Import Export Company	• *DOOM and DOOM II* • *Quake and QUAKE II*	• *Alice* • *Oz*

How did you get into the game industry?

Was working as an auto mechanic and living in Mesquite, Texas. It just so happened that one of my neighbors was John Carmack, owner of id Software. He and I became friends, and after several months of hanging out and beta testing at id, John offered me a job doing tech support. While answering phones I trained myself on the in-house design tools and quickly found myself creating content for *DOOM II*. The rest, as they say, is history.

What are your five favorite games and why?

The Legend of Zelda: The Ocarina of Time, Grand Theft Auto III, Battlefield 1942, Medal of Honor, etc. Games that deliver a sense of an endless world, living environments, and open-endedness always get my stamp of approval. I'm looking forward to the day when emergent gameplay takes us away from the idea of "videogames" and into alternate realities where we decide what the gameplay is.

What games have inspired you the most as a designer and why?

Every game I play inspires me in some way. It could be an elegant solution to a third person auto-camera, or the worst driving physics ever created—even the mistakes have something to teach us.

What are you most proud of in your career?

Just being a part of the industry makes me proud. If you had asked me fifteen years ago where I'd be today I think that "game designer" would have seemed just as unlikely as brain surgeon. All the other events that have transpired since my entry into the industry are gravy.

What words of advice would you give to an aspiring designer today?

Think entertainment, not games. The creative people within our industry need to start thinking about the big picture, not just the boxed game product. When you design, design with toys, books, films, soundtracks, clothing lines, and any other franchise extensions you can think of in mind. In addition to that, design these things for your audience, not for yourself or your team. Games are not about designer versus player any more, they're about your ideas versus the marketplace.

2.9   Outcome

We said in the introduction to this section that people play games to gain a sense of achievement. Outcome is often the measure of that achievement. Providing this sense of unequal outcome is a key element of the experiences we call games.

Formal Elements

The games you described in Exercise 2.1 may also have had other elements we haven't mentioned here: perhaps special equipment, digital environments, complex resources structures, or character definitions. And of course Go Fish and *Quake* each have their own unique elements that we haven't touched upon, such as the turn structure in Go Fish or the real-time element of *Quake*. But what we're interested in right now are elements that all games share—elements that make up the essence of games.

A number of scholars from different fields have examined this same question from other perspectives. Some of the most influential have been those looking at games in terms of studying conflict, economics, behavioral psychology, sociology, and anthropology.

But our perspective is not strictly academic, and our purpose here is not to be definitive. Rather, it is to provide a useful context for us to discuss the process of designing games. The distinctive elements that we discussed starting on page 24 are important concepts for the game designer to understand because they provide structure (and form). Without these elements, a game would lose its "gameness" and become some other activity.

Because they play an essential structural function, we call these the "formal elements" of games. We will look at each of these formal elements in more detail in Chapter 3 and discuss how you can use them in various combinations to achieve exactly the type of gaming experience that you want to create for your players.

ENGAGING THE PLAYER

If the formal elements mentioned provide structure to the experience of games, then what gives these elements meaning for the players? What makes one game capture the imagination of players and another fall flat? Certainly, some players are engaged by pure abstract challenges, but for most players, there needs to be something else that draws them in and allows them to connect

2.10   Chess tournament and Quake tournament

emotionally with the experience. Games are, after all, a form of entertainment, and good entertainment engages us and moves us both intellectually and emotionally.

This sense of engagement comes from different things for different players, and not all games require elaborate means to create it. Next we've listed some elements which allow a player to make an emotional connection with a game.

Challenge

We said that experiences created conflict that the players had to work to resolve in their own favor. This conflict challenges the players, creating tension as they work to resolve problems and varying levels of achievement or frustration. Increasing the challenge as the game goes on can cause a rising sense of tension, or if the challenge is too great, can cause frustration. Alternately, if the challenge level remains flat or goes down, players may feel that they've mastered the game and move on. Balancing these emotional responses to the amount of challenge in a game is a key consideration for the keeping the player engaged with the game.

Exercise 2.6: Challenge

Name three games that you find particularly challenging and describe why.

Play

In addition to providing structured environments for challenge and achievement, games can also provide opportunities for players to use imagination, fantasy, inspiration, social skills, or other more playful types of interaction to achieve objectives within the game space. The play might be serious, like the pomp and circumstance surrounding a Grand Master match in chess, or it might be charged and aggressive, like the marathon play environment of a *Quake* tournament. It might also be an outlet for fantasy, like the rich online worlds of *EverQuest* and *Dark Age of Camelot*. Designing for the type of play that will appeal to your players is another key consideration for keeping players engaged with the game.

DESIGNER PERSPECTIVE: SCOTT MILLER

Title

CEO, Apogee Software (a.k.a. 3D Realms)

Project list (five to eight top projects)

- *Duke Nukem*
- *Max Payne*
- *Wolfenstein 3-D*
- *Raptor*
- *Rise of the Triad*
- *Shadow Warrior*
- over 30 more

How did you get into the game industry?

First as a journalist in 1982, then in 1987 starting my own company, Apogee Software. Apogee is known as the pioneer of shareware gaming—we invented the method of releasing one episode as shareware and selling additional episodes of the game directly ourselves. This allowed us to self-publish our first 20 games without the need of a retail publisher or outside funding. We made millions using this method before finally signing with traditional publishers in the mid-1990s. Id Software and Epic Games mimicked our shareware method and also rose to great success. It's no coincidence that all three companies are among the strongest, most successful, entirely independent development studios in North America. By first self-publishing our games we were able to build strong financial independence. This method allowed all three companies to make original intellectual property (IP) without the publisher getting long-term ownership and control of these IP. In fact, a developer's only chance of long-term success is to create and own an original IP. Without doing this, a studio is constantly under-the-thumb of finicky and often untrustworthy publishers. An IP gives a studio the clout needed to get the best publishing deals. Plus, as 3D Realms and Remedy have shown with the sell of the *Max Payne* IP, for over $45 million, an IP is where the real value of a studio resides. Additionally, 3D Realms has been offered $80 million for our *Duke Nukem* IP by a major publisher. Never doubt that making original IP that your studio owns is the best path to long-term success.

What are your five favorite games and why?

As a long time gamer, my list includes some classic oldies...

- *M.U.L.E.:* A breakthrough, addictive multiplayer game that is begging for a modern remake.
- *Diablo:* The core gameplay is a model of simplicity, the execution borders on perfection, and the game continuously rewards the player through a brilliant system of ever-improving gear.
- *Tetris:* Perhaps the most perfect computer game ever. Simple to learn, near-impossible to master, and equally appealing to either gender.
- *DOOM:* A technical tour de force, and the first game to truly frighten players.
- *Space Invaders:* The game that officially kicked off the arcade's golden years. The most adrenaline squirting game I've ever played.
- *Super Mario Bros.:* I can't leave this game off my list because it was the first game that introduced the idea of a world for the player to explore, an idea that still continues to be seen in many modern games, including the *GTA* series.

What games have inspired you the most as a designer and why?

My self-education mostly comes from the arcade's golden years of the late 1970s and early 1980s, as this was the time that I instinctively learned rules like being fair to the player, simple interface, and dozens more. These early games could not rely on pretty graphics, they had to rely on solid gameplay mechanics, and so even nowadays I think in terms of gameplay first and foremost.

What are you most proud of in your career?

Working on a variety of very successful games, and co-creating two of the most recognizable game heroes in the game industry, *Duke Nukem* and *Max Payne*.

What words of advice would you give to an aspiring designer today?

Learn from other games and designers, but do not copy them. You absolutely must invent something unique and compelling (one without the other is not enough) to be a success. For example, at the time we were working on the concept for *Max Payne*, *Tomb Raider* was just out and a huge hit. We could have easily fallen into the trap of making a male version of Lara Croft, but that would have been recreating another Indiana Jones. So, instead, we looked at what *Tomb Raider* did well, and purposely picked other things for *Max Payne* to do well. It was critical for Max to be seen as a unique character, not a copycat. If you follow in other people's footsteps, you'll never be a leader.

Premise

Another way that games can create engagement is with an overarching premise, which gives context to the formal elements. For example, the premise in *Monopoly* is that the players are each landlords, buying, selling and developing valuable pieces of real estate in an effort to become the richest player in the game. This premise was quite appealing to down-and-out players during the Great Depression when the game was invented. It remains a favorite to this day, and one reason for that continued appeal is its premise—players enjoy the fantasy of being powerful, land-grabbing landlords with plenty of money to wheel and deal.

Many digital games have even richer premises. Our earlier example of *Quake*, for instance, places the game play in an immersive environment, filled with violent, militaristic imagery. The base-level effect of the premise is to make it easier for players to contextualize their choices, but it's also a powerful tool for involving players emotionally in the interaction of the formal elements.

Exercise 2.7: Premise

What are the premises for the games *Risk*, *Clue*, *Pit*, and *Um Jammer Lammy*? If you don't know these games, pick games that you are more familiar with.

Character

Recently, within the last 25 years, games have begun to address another potential tool for engagement, and that is the notion of character. In traditional storytelling, characters are the agents through which dramatic stories are told, and they can function this way in games as well, providing a way for us to empathize with the situation and live vicariously through their efforts. But characters in games can also be vessels for our own participation, entry points for us to experience situations and conflicts through the guise of a mask we create and direct. Character is a rich area for dramatic engagement in games, and many games, especially digital games, have explored this area of potential.

Story

Lastly, some games engage players emotionally by using the power of story within or surrounding their formal elements. Story differs from premise in its narrative qualities. A premise need not go

2.11   Monopoly

anywhere from where it begins, while stories unfold with the game. How story can be integrated into gameplay is an ongoing and fairly contentious debate. How much story is too much? How little is too little? Should gameplay change the story? Should story dictate the gameplay? There is no one answer to this question, but it's clear from the interest of both players and designers that story integrated with play can create powerful emotional results.

2.12   The Evolution of Mario

Exercise 2.8: Story

Have any stories within a game ever gripped you, moved you emotionally, or sparked your imagination? If so, why? If not, why not?

Dramatic Elements

The games you picked in Exercise 2.1 on page 22 almost certainly have one or more of the elements described previously as a part of their design. We call these the "dramatic elements" of games because they engage the players by creating a dramatic context for the formal elements. In Chapter 4 on page 96 we'll look at each of these more closely and discuss how you can use the dramatic elements to create rich experiences for your players.

THE SUM OF THE PARTS

One thing that may not be immediately apparent from your game descriptions or from our examples of Go Fish and *Quake*, is the depth to which each of the elements we've discussed relies on the others. This is because games are systems, and systems, by definition, are groups of interrelated elements that work together to form a complex whole. An important idea to consider when thinking about games as systems is the old saying that the whole is greater than the sum of the parts.

What we mean by this is that a system, because of the interrelationship of its elements, takes on new dimensions when it is set in motion. As an example, think of a system you are familiar with, such as the engine in your car. You can examine and understand the physical make-up of each element in the engine. You can understand their functions and even predict how they will respond in interaction with other elements. But unless you set the system in motion, you cannot observe certain important qualities of the engine as a whole—namely, its primary function of producing motive power. Once the system is started, however, these qualities emerge as a consequence of the interaction of all the elements.

Game systems are much the same. All of the elements we've laid out previously form a potential that remains nascent until the game is played. Once in play, what emerges is a something that cannot be predicted from examining each of the elements separately. The game designer needs to be able to look at a game system not only as separate elements but also as a whole in play.

2.13 Final Fantasy VIII

DEFINING GAMES

Now that we've thought about some of the various aspects of games, it seems natural to try to pull it all together and answer the question we posed at the beginning of this chapter: what is a game? What makes Go Fish, or *Quake*, or any of the games that you can play a game and not some other type of experience?

We've said that games are given structure by their formal elements, that they also have dramatic elements that make them emotionally engaging experiences. We've also said that games are dynamic systems and that their elements work together to produce a complex whole. But we can go even farther in our definition by pulling out

some of the most important elements from the earlier discussion.

When we talked about boundaries, we mentioned the physical and the conceptual, because this is what most games deal with in their rules. What we didn't mention is the emotional boundary between all of the rest of life and a game.

When you play a game, you set the rules of life aside and take up the rules of the game instead. Conversely, when you finish playing a game, you set aside the incidents and outcome of that game and return to the trappings of the outside world. Within the game, you may have slaughtered your best friend, or she may have slaughtered you. But that was within the game. Outside the game, these actions have no real consequences. What we are describing is the fact that game systems are separate from the rest of the world, they are closed.

We already have said that games are formal systems; that they are defined as games, and not some other type of interaction, by their formal elements. Also, we know that it's key to our definition of games to show that these elements are interrelated, so we should include the concept that a game is a system. So the first statement we can make confidently about games is that they are closed, formal systems.

We've talked at length about the fact that games are for players, that the entire purpose of games is to engage players. Without players, games have no reason to exist. How do games engage players? By involving them in a conflict that is structured by their formal and dramatic elements. Games challenge players to accomplish their objectives while following rules and procedures which make it difficult to do so. So the second statement we add to our definition of games is that they engage players in structured conflicts.

Lastly, games resolve their conflicts in unequal outcomes. A fundamental part of gameplay is that it promises to end and that it promises to produce a winner or winners. Games are not experiences designed to prove we are all equal. In fairness to the great breadth of game genres, some games are not exacting in their sense of closure or in the measure of their outcome. However, even if you are playing a game like *EverQuest* that goes on and on ad infinitum, or a game like *The Sims*, which has no specified objective, these games find ways to provide both resolution and measurable achievement to their players.

Drawing these concepts together, we can come to this working conclusion about the nature of games. A game is:

- A closed, formal system, that
- Engages players in structured conflict, and
- Resolves in an unequal outcome.

Exercise 2.9: Applying What You've Learned

For this exercise, you will need a piece of paper, two pens, and two players. First, take a moment to play this simple game:[1]

1. Draw three dots randomly on the paper. Choose a player to go first.

2. The first player draws a line from one dot to another dot.

3. Then that player draws a new dot anywhere on that line.

4. The second player also draws a line and a dot:

- The new line must go from one dot to another, but no dot can have more than three lines coming out of it.

- Also, the new line cannot cross any other line.

- The new dot must be placed on the new line.

- A line can go from a dot back to the same dot as long as it doesn't break the "no more than three lines" rule.

5. The players take turns until one player cannot make a move. The last player to move is the winner.

Identify the formal elements of this game:

- *Players:* How many? Any requirements? Special knowledge, roles, etc.?

- *Objective:* What is the objective of the game?

- *Procedures:* What are the required actions for play?

---

1. John Conway and Mike Patterson, *Sprouts*, 1967.

- *Rules:* Any limits on player actions? Rules regarding behavior? What are they?
- *Conflict:* What causes conflict in this game?
- *Boundaries:* What are the boundaries of the game? Are they physical? Conceptual?
- *Outcome:* What are the potential outcomes of the game?

Does the game have dramatic elements? Identify them:

- *Challenge:* What creates challenge in the game?
- *Play:* Is there a sense of play within the rules of the game?
- *Premise/Character/Story:* Are these present?

What types of dramatic elements do you think might add to the game experience?

CONCLUSION

You'll notice that though we've arrived at a working definition, we've come to no grand conclusion on the absolute nature of games. That's because we prefer to leave the question open to further investigation. The areas of structure we've mapped out are important to the process of design, and as such need to be clear. The areas left in shadow are just as interesting, and we encourage you to think about aspects of games that interest and inspire you.

Our goal in this exercise is to provide a starting point. It's not meant to constrict you as a designer. Having said that, terminology is key. The lack of a single vocabulary is one of the largest problems facing the game industry today. The terms we have suggested here are just that—suggestions. We use them consistently throughout this book so that we can have a common language with you with which to discuss the design process, and to help you evaluate and critique your designs.

Once you've gained experience with this process, then it's up to you as a designer to move beyond any limitations you find with it. Consider everything you read here a starting point from which you can jump off—a launch pad for your expedition into the world of designing games that will hopefully push the envelope and transport players to places they didn't imagine possible.

DESIGNER PERSPECTIVE: WARREN SPECTOR

Title

Studio Director, Ion Storm (also Project Director on *Deus Ex* PC and PS2 as well as several other games)

Project list (five to eight top projects)

- 2000 *Deus Ex:* PC, PS2, Ion Storm, Project Director
- 1994 *System Shock:* PC, Origin/LookingGlass Technologies, Producer
- 1994 *Wings of Glory:* PC, Origin, Producer
- 1993 *Ultima VII, Part 2, Serpent Isle:* PC, Origin, Producer
- 1991 *Underworld: The Stygian Abyss:* PC, Origin/LookingGlass Technologies, Producer
- 1991 *Martian Dreams:* PC, Origin, Producer
- many more

How did you get into the game industry?

I started out, like most folks, as a gamer, back in the days.

Back in 1983, I made my hobby my profession, starting out as an editor at Steve Jackson Games, a small boardgame company in Austin, Texas. There, I worked on *TOON: The Cartoon Roleplaying Game*, *GURPS*, several *Car Wars*, *Ogre*, and *Illuminati* games and learned a ton about game design from people like Steve Jackson, Allen Varney, Scott Haring, and others.

In 1987, I was lured away by TSR, makers of *Dungeons & Dragons* and other fine RPGs and boardgames. There, I worked as an editor, developer and designer. I ended up managing the games division for a while and managed to write some adventures for *AD&D, Marvel Super Heroes* and other TSR RPGs. I also got to collaborate with Zeb Cook on *The Bullwinkle and Rocky* party role-playing games, with Doug Niles on *Top Secret/S.I.* and with Jeff Grubb on the *Buck Rogers Battle for the 25th Century* boardgame. In addition, I wrote a solo adventure book (*One Thing After Another*, featuring the Thing, of Marvel comics fame) and a novel, *The Hollow Earth Affair*, set in the *Top Secret/S.I.* universe.

1989 saw me homesick for Austin, Texas and feeling like paper gaming was a business/art form that had pretty much plateaued. I was playing a lot of early computer and videogames at the time and when the opportunity to work for Origin came up, I jumped at it. I started out there as an Associate Producer, working with Richard Garriott and Chris Roberts before moving up to full producer. I spent seven years with Origin, shipping about a dozen titles and moving up from AP to Producer to Executive Producer.

In 1996 I left Origin to set up an Austin development studio for LookingGlass Technologies and to Executive Produce their role-playing line in Boston. I'd had the honor of working with Doug Church, Paul

Neurath and other LG folks on the *Underworld* games and *System Shock,* and the opportunity to work with them again and get more hands on with the games than I could as an EP at Origin was too good an opportunity to pass up.

A year and a half later, LG lacked the funds to keep the Austin office going, so we shut it down and I left to do a start-up. Instead, I ended up starting an Austin development office for Dallas-based Ion Storm and, even though the Dallas office went away, we're still going strong down here in Austin.

What are your five favorite games and why?

- *The Legend of Zelda: A Link to the Past (SNES): Link to the Past* is simply the most fun I've ever had sitting in front of a game. It's the perfect balance of excitement, challenge, control, narrative, audio, and graphics. Everything in one simple, elegant package. I got done with this game and felt like I'd done something epic, something heroic. And that's a feeling games don't offer often enough.

- *Tetris:* How long ago did *Tetris* first appear? And how many people still play it? Doesn't that tell you everything you need to know? If I were stranded on a desert island (with infinite electricity, of course) and I could have only one game with me, it would be *Tetris*. You can play it forever and not get bored.

- *M.U.L.E.:* I loved this game back in the Atari 800 days. Playing solo it was a ton of fun but it was the first multiplayer game I ever played and it's still one of the best. The gameplay was as simple as *Monopoly* so adults and kids could enjoy it; the graphics were simple and iconic which makes the game timeless; even the music was fun and so memorable the theme song is still stuck in my mind. Just a great, great game.

- *Diablo:* Highly replayable and fun enough that you *want* to play over and over again. A lot of folks (folks with no joy in their souls, no sense of wonder) often say *Diablo* is "just" a watered down *NetHack* with pretty graphics and nice sound. So what's wrong with that? The sounds in *Diablo* are Pavlovian in their power—I salivate when I hear the sound of *Diablo* cash hitting the ground. And that ring sound? Man, give the guy who made that sound a bonus. And talk about a time-passer! I played *Diablo* for fourteen straight hours the first time I booted it up and didn't even notice that any time had passed. I still play it today. It's like a minicourse in behavioral psychology and fun, to boot!

- *Half-Life:* Game—story—game—story. I love games that walk the fine line between gameplay and narrative and very few games have done that as well as *Half-Life*. At some level, it's "just" an incredibly well-executed shooter, but the extra story hooks built in make every shot mean something and every step seems significant. I lost a lot of sleep to *Half-Life*. Love it.

What games have inspired you the most as a designer and why?

There have probably been dozens of games that have influenced me but here are a few of the biggies:

- *Ultima IV:* Richard Garriott's masterpiece. It proved to me (and a lot of other people) that giving players power to make choices enhanced the gameplay experience. And attaching consequences to those choices made the experience even *more* powerful. This was the game that showed me that games could be about more than killing things or solving goofy puzzles. It was also the first game I ever played that made me feel like I was engaged in a dialogue with the game's creator. And that's something I've striven to achieve ever since.

- *Super Mario 64:* I was stunned at how much gameplay Miyamoto and all managed to squeeze into this game. And it's all done through a control/interface scheme that's so simple it shames me. Mario can do about ten things, I think, and yet you never feel constrained—you feel empowered and liberated, encouraged to explore, plan, experiment, fail and try again, without feeling frustrated. You have to be inspired by the combination of simplicity and depth.

- *Star Raiders:* This was the first game that made me believe games were more than just a fad or passing fancy, for me and for, well, humanity at large. "Oh, man," I thought, "we can send people places they'll never be able to go in real life." That's not just kid-stuff. That's change-the-world-stuff. There's an old saying about not judging someone until you've walked a mile in their shoes, you know? Well, games are like an experiential shoe store for all mankind. We can allow you to walk in the shoes of anyone we can imagine. How powerful is that?

- *Ico: Ico* impressed me because it proved to me how powerfully we can affect players on an emotional level. And I'm not just talking about excitement or fear, the stuff we usually traffic in. *Ico*, through some stellar animation, graphics, sound and story elements, explores questions of friendship, loyalty, dread, tension, and exhilaration. The power of a virtual touch—of the player holding the hand of a character he's charged to protect, even though she seems weak and moves with almost maddening slowness. The power of that touch blew me away. I have to find a way to get at some of that power in my own work.

- *Suikoden:* This little PlayStation role-playing game showed me new ways of dealing with conversation. I had never before experienced Suikoden's brand of simple, straightforward, no player choice options unless they're really significant, binary choices—little things like "Do you fight your father or not? Y/N" or "Do you leave your best friend to almost certain death so you can escape and complete your critically important quest? Y/N" will blow you away! In addition, the game featured two other critical systems—a castle-building mechanic and a related player-controlled ally system. The castle-building bit showed me the power of allowing players to leave a personal mark on the world—the narcissistic aspect of game-playing. The ally system, which affected what information you got before embarking on quests, as well as the forces/abilities available to you in mass battles, revealed some of the power of allowing each player to author his or her own unique experience. A terrific game that has a lot to teach even the most experienced RPG designers in the business.

What are you most proud of in your career?

I guess I'm pretty proud of the fact that "freeform" gameplay, player-authored experiences and the like are finally becoming not just common but almost expected these days. From the "middle" *Ultimas* (*44–6*), to *Underworld*, to *System Shock*, to *Thief*, to *Deus Ex*, there's been this small cadre of us arguing, through our work, in favor of less linear, designer-centric games and, thanks to the efforts of folks at Origin, LookingGlass, Ion Storm, Rockstar/DMA and so on, people are finally beginning to take notice. And it isn't just the hardcore gamers—the mass market is waking up, too. That's pretty cool.

I'm hugely proud of having had the privilege of working alongside some amazingly talented people. It's standard practice in all media to give one person credit for the creation of a game but that's nonsense. Game development is the most intensely collaborative endeavor I can imagine. It's been an honor to work with Richard Garriott, Paul Neurath, Doug Church, Harvey Smith and so many others who will now be offended that I didn't single them out here! I know I've learned a lot from all of them and hope I've taught a little bit, in return.

What words of advice would you give to an aspiring designer today?

Learn to program. You don't have to be an ace, but you should know the basics. In addition to a solid technical foundation, get as broad-based an education as you can. As a designer, you never know what you're going to need to know—behavioral psychology will help you immensely, as will architecture, economics, history. Get some art/graphics experience, if you can, so you can speak intelligently with artists even if you lack the skills to become one yourself. Do whatever it takes to become an effective communicator, in written and verbal modes. And most importantly, make games. Get yourself on a mods team and build some maps, some missions, anything you can. Oh, and make sure you really, really, really want to make games for a living. It's gruelingly hard work, with long hours and wrecked relationships to prove it. There are a lot of people who want the same job you want. Don't go into it unless you're absolutely certain it's the career for you. There's no room here for dilettantes!

Deus Ex

Chapter 3
Working with Formal Elements

Exercise 3.1: Gin Rummy

Let's take the classic card game gin rummy. There are two basic procedures to a turn in gin rummy: drawing and discarding. Take away the discard procedure and try to play the game. What happens?

Now take away both the discard procedure and the draw procedure, and then play the game. What's missing from the game?

Put the drawing and discarding procedures back, but take out the rule that says that an opponent can "lay off" unmatched cards to extend the knocker's sets. Is the game still playable with this change?

Now put back the original rules, but take away the objective and play the game again. What happens this time?

What does this exercise tell us about the formal elements of games?

Formal elements, as we've said, are those elements that form the structure of a game. Without them, games cease to be games. As you saw in the opening exercise of this chapter, a game without players, without an objective, without rules or procedures is not a game at all. Players, objective, procedures, rules, resources, conflict, boundaries, and outcome: these are the essence of games and a strong understanding of their potential interrelationships is the foundation of game design.

Once you grasp these basic principles, you can use the knowledge to create innovative combinations and new types of gameplay for your own games.

PLAYERS

It's obvious that games are experiences designed for players, and that without players, games have no reason to exist. It's not as obvious how to structure the involvement of those players in your game. This is one of the key decisions you need to make as a designer. For instance, how many play-ers does the game require? How many total play-ers can the game support? Do various players have different roles? Will they compete, cooperate, or both? The way you answer these questions will change the overall design of your game.

3.1 Costumed players at an *EverQuest* convention

Number of players

A game designed for one player is essentially different from a game designed for two, four, or 10,000 players. And a game designed for a specific number of players has different considerations than a game designed for a variable number of players.

Solitaire and tic-tac-toe are games that require an exact number of players. Solitaire, obviously, supports only one player. Tic-tac-toe requires two players—no more, no less—the system will not function without the exact number of players. Many single-player digital games support only one player. This is because, like solitaire, their structure supports one player competing against the game system.

On the other hand, there are games are designed to be played with a range of players. *Parcheesi* is a game designed for two to four players, while *Monopoly* is designed for two to eight players. Massively multiplayer games like *EverQuest* are designed to function for a variable number of players, ranging into the tens of thousands; however, a single player can be alone in the world of *EverQuest* and many of the formal elements of the system will still function.

Exercise 3.2: Three-Player Tic-tac-toe
Create a version of tic-tac-toe that works for three players. You may need to change the size of the board or other elements of the game to do this.

Roles of players

Most games have uniform roles for all players. In chess and *Monopoly*, there is only one role for all players. But some games have more than one role for players to choose between. In *Mastermind*, one player chooses to be the code-maker, while the other chooses to be the code-breaker. The system requires both roles to be filled or it will not work. Also, many team games, like football, have different player roles that make up the full team.

A major trend in digital games is online role-playing games, which, as the name implies, have a variety of roles for players to choose between. Players can take on the role of healers or fighters or magic-wielders. If you are going to design a game with different roles, the balance of those roles will be a critical consideration in your game design.

Player interaction patterns

Another choice to consider when designing your game is the structure of interaction between a player, the game system and any other players. The following breakdown of interaction patterns is adapted from the work of E. M. Avedon in his article "The Structural Elements of Games."[1] You'll see that many digital games fall into the pattern "single player versus game," and, more recently, "multilateral competition." There's a lot of potential in the other patterns that is rarely taken advantage of, and we offer these ideas to you in the hopes that

1. E.M. Avedon, "The Structural Elements of Games," *The Study of Games* (New York: Robert E. Krieger Publishing, Inc., 1979), pp. 424-425.

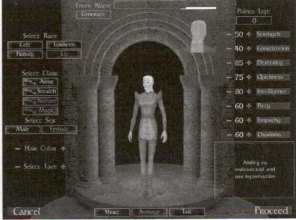

3.2   Create character screen: Dark Age of Camelot

they may inspire you to look at new combinations and possibilities of player interactions to use in your designs.

1. Single player versus game

This is a game structure in which a single player competes against a game system. Examples include solitaire, *Pac-Man,* and other single-player digital games. This is the most common pattern for digital gaming. You'll find this pattern in arcade games, console games, and PC games. Since there are no other human players in this pattern, games that use it tend to include puzzles or other play structures to create conflict. It's perhaps because of the success of this pattern that we now refer to digital games that do have more than one player as "multiplayer" games—when, in fact, games have been multiplayer by definition for thousands of years.

2. Multiple individual players versus game

This is a game structure in which multiple players compete against a game system in the company of each other. Action is not directed toward each other and no interaction between participants is required or necessary. Examples include bingo, roulette, and *Slingo.* This is a rarely used pattern in

digital gaming, although AOL has had a lot of success with their online *Slingo* game. Essentially, this pattern is a single-player game played in the company of other players, who are also playing the same game. This pattern works well for noncompetitive players who enjoy the activity and the social arena (a large percentage of *Slingo* players are women). This pattern also works well for gambling games.

3. Player versus player

This is a game structure in which two players directly compete. Examples include checkers, chess, and tennis. This is a classic structure for strategy games and works well for competitive players. The one-on-one nature of the competition makes it a personal contest. Two-player fighting games such as *Soul Calibur II, Mortal Kombat,* and others have employed this structure successfully. Again, the intense competition marks this pattern for focused, head-to-head play.

4. Unilateral competition

This is a game structure in which two or more players compete against one player. Examples include tag, dodge ball, and the *Scotland Yard* boardgame. A highly undervalued structure, this pattern works

Single Player vs. Game

Multiple Indvidual Players vs. Game

Player vs. Player

Unilateral Competition

Multilateral Competition

Cooperative Play

Team Competition

3.3   Player interaction patterns

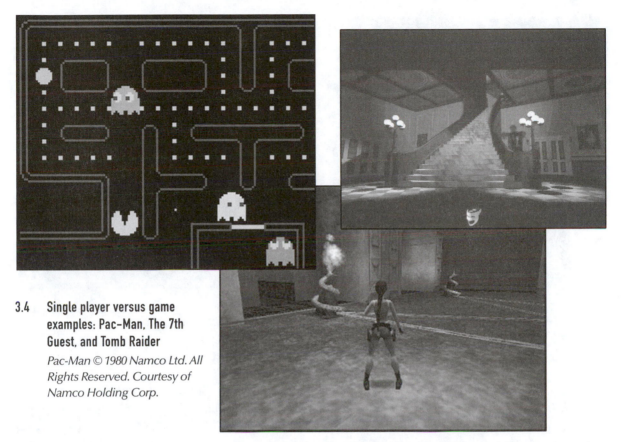

3.4 Single player versus game examples: Pac-Man, The 7th Guest, and Tomb Raider

Pac-Man © 1980 Namco Ltd. All Rights Reserved. Courtesy of Namco Holding Corp.

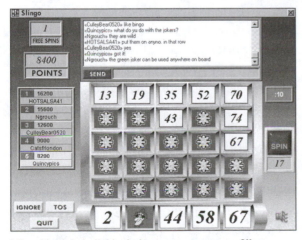

3.5 Multiple individual players versus game: Slingo

as well with "free for all" games like tag, as it does with intensely strategic games like *Scotland Yard.* As does tag, *Scotland Yard* pits one player, "Mr. X," against all the other players. However, unlike tag, *Scotland Yard* has the larger group (the detectives) trying to catch the singled out player (the criminal). This game balances between the two forces because the criminal has full information about the state of the game, while the detectives have to work together to deduce the state from clues left by the criminal. It's a very interesting model for combining cooperative and competitive gameplay that is wide open for digital game development.

5. Multilateral competition

This is a game structure in which three or more players directly compete. Examples include poker,

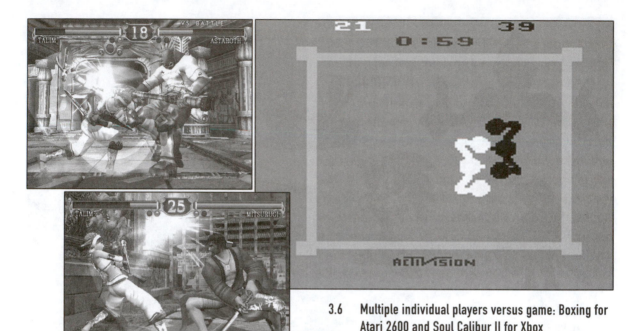

3.6   Multiple individual players versus game: Boxing for Atari 2600 and Soul Calibur II for Xbox

Soul Calibur II © 2003 Namco Ltd. All Rights Reserved. Courtesy of Namco Holding Corp.

Monopoly, multiplayer games likes *Quake*, *War-Craft III*, *Age of Mythology*, etc. This is the pattern that most players are thinking of when they refer to "multiplayer" gaming. Nowadays, the trend is to think of multiplayer in terms of "massive" numbers of players, but as the thousands of years of nondigital "multiplayer" game history supports, there's still plenty of room for innovative thinking in terms of smaller, directly competitive groups. Boardgames with this pattern of player interaction have been "tuned" for generations for groups of between three to six players; clearly there's a social force at work that makes this an ideal group size for direct competition. Want to do something fresh in digital gaming? Try tuning your multiplayer game to encourage the same high level of social interaction that occurs with a three to six person boardgame.

6. Cooperative play

This is a game structure in which two or more players cooperate against the game system. Examples include *Harvest Time*, a *Lord of the Rings* boardgame, and cooperative quests in *EverQuest*. This pattern has received a lot of attention in terms of

3.7   Unilateral competition: Scotland Yard

3.8   Multilateral competition: Super Bomberman and Mario Party

children's boardgames, like *Harvest Time*, but not much in games for adults. Reiner Knizia, the prolific German game designer, tackled this pattern in his *Lord of the Rings* boardgame, in which a group of players cooperate to save Middle-earth. Also, some role-playing games have often featured cooperative quests within a competitive game structure. We'd like to see more designers experiment with this approach.

7. Team competition

This is a game structure in which two or more groups compete. Examples include soccer, basketball, charades, *Battlefield 1942*, and *Tribes*. Team sports have proved the power of this pattern of player interaction over and over, not only for the players but for a whole other group of participants—the fans. As if responding to the need for this particular multiplayer pattern, teams (called clans or guilds) sprang up almost immediately upon the introduction of multiplayer and massively multiplayer digital games. An interesting new cooperative game is Sony's *PlanetSide*, which is a massively multiplayer first person shooter where players work in large teams. Think about

3.9   Cooperative play: Lord of the Rings boardgame

Designer Perspective: Lorne Lanning

Title: President/Creative Director/Co-Founder, Oddworld Inhabitants

Project list (five to eight top projects)

- *Oddworld: Abe's Oddysee* (PlayStation, PC)
- *Oddworld: Abe's Exoddus* (PlayStation, PC)
- *Oddworld: Munch's Oddysee* (Xbox)

How did you get into the game industry?

I convinced my partner, Sherry McKenna, that we needed to get into the game biz and start a development company in order to birth new intellectual properties. In 1994 we raised $3.5 million from venture capitalists and as a result, Oddworld Inhabitants was born.

What are your five favorite games and why?

- *Asteroids:* This is still one of my favorite games to date. The simple combination of analog physics and infinite escalating challenge allow you to always improve your skills and always break a previous high score. Twenty-four years later and I'm still hooked on it.
- *Halo* (Xbox): Though it did little to hook me in single-player mode, it completely hooked me as a cooperative playing game. It blew my friends and me away as we kept going all night for many nights. The cooperative aspect and excellent engineering and design effort brought tired console shooters to a whole new level of chemistry and quality.
- *Driver* (PS): I would argue has the best physics ever in a racing game. I logged over 200 hours into *Driver.* Previous to this I was addicted to *Gran Turismo*, with the belief that *GT* had the best driving physics to date. After *Driver,* I just couldn't bear with the slow acceleration of *Gran Turismo* any longer. *Driver's* burnout button added another dimension to driving simulation and put it much closer to the real deal. When a game can actually train you to handle actual cars more effectively under extremely aggressive driving conditions, then it's really something special. Then consider the open city maps, simulated traffic, and "no rules" mini-games that were part of the package, it really made it an outstanding "stand on its own" game for me. The first fan mail I ever sent to a game developer.
- *StarCraft* (PC): Being a big *WarCraft II* fan, *StarCraft* was all I was hoping for and a bit more. The entertainment value packed into Blizzard's characters has never failed to make me laugh (in a good way). The sheer quantity and scale of activity and battles that could unfold over a multiplayer session would sometimes get just completely overwhelming, which I love. Certain single

player missions I can remember playing dozens of times because of the circumstantial setup with which you prepared for a massive incoming invasion. Seeing hundreds of your troops, that you grew yourself, enter into a massive conflict (in real time), with excellent voices, music, and sound effects is something I don't think I'll ever get tired of.

- *Civilization II* (PC): Because it just never stops challenging your mind or your play strategies. You never play the same game twice, you never play with the same strategy twice, but you always learn more the longer you play. Truly a brilliant game with a sim/economic system that, I believe, will have a larger impact on future game design than any other games in its day.

What games have inspired you the most as a designer and why?

- *Flashback/Out of This World/Prince of Persia:* I felt that all of these platform games brought a new degree of drama and life to game design. Realistic animations combined with interesting story, continued cut scenes, and story conditional oriented puzzle mechanics, inspired a lot of inspiration towards the first *Oddworld* games on the PlayStation. These games were gleaming light posts—indicating that one day films and games would have more in common than previously imagined.

- *Terminator 2* (arcade): I saw this arcade game at a theme park convention before it was released to the public (it was also before I was in the game design business). When I saw this game it became quite evident as to how the future of content would be in amortized digital databases across various delivery mediums. This was the first game that successfully used actual film production assets in the game. It was a signpost for me that read, "This way lies the future of universe oriented digital multimedia properties."

- *WarCraft II:* Really brought home the joy that could be experienced when managing a large group of agents that you've birthed and nurtured over time. This also revealed a huge psychological component to me that emerged via absolute control over their fate. Certainly, other games had touched upon this, but *WarCraft II* enabled a smooth simple control/management interface that allowed the positive emotional reaction to the experience to unfold without frustrating tedium. It also installed a sweet simple blend of sim and strategy that was previously lacking in real time war games.

- *Super Mario 64:* Though the content is very challenging to stay interested in (admittedly, it's for kids), the analog controls mixed with analog animations brought the interactive 3D character to new levels of life and fluidity. It always amazes me how people will tolerate stiff and digital controls sometimes even preferring them. For me, I can't play games that suggest they are dealing with living life forms yet have stiff or digital feeling controls which result in robotic looking/feeling characters. It's always a huge turn off that keeps me from enjoying what might be a good game. On this front, *Mario* set the stage for what constitutes great 3D analog character controls.

- *The Sims:* A record holder when it comes to innovation as well as an amazing example of a developer's ability to nurture and support a mod community that will, in return, nurture and support the shelf life of a product. This is a product that is beyond the norm of traditional genres. This is a game that, if focus tested with the usual suspects in the community, could likely have faced being cut while still in development. However, this series stands tall when it comes to proving that games are not always what we (in the biz) think they should be, while also proving that there is a tremendous market of potential players that are just plain uninterested in what the rest of the industry has to offer them. In many ways, this series is a great white hope for the future of innovation in game design. Not necessarily in terms of the game design structure and chemistry, but more importantly in how different this game is from the rest of the herd.

- *Tamagotchi:* Much like *The Sims*, I know there is an entire breed of games that have yet to be created that will take the concept of "nurturing virtual life forms" to entirely new levels. When games' sociological effects can force a major corporation, like Japan Airlines, to change a policy in response to screaming children that are delaying takeoff (because they were told they needed to turn off all their electrical devices) then you're witnessing something much deeper than people just being addicted to challenging games. We're now watching humans experience new levels of emotional attachment and co-dependency on virtual life forms.

What are you most proud of in your career?

I've been able to pursue a goal, which has created a place (Oddworld) where incredibly talented people can come together, make a good living, and continue to refine and explore their creative capabilities.

My smartest moment was in convincing Sherry McKenna to be my partner. It is critical that the artistic personality realizes his or her inherent disadvantage in fully comprehending the general business practices of the modern world. Without the guidance and prowess of Sherry McKenna, Oddworld would have been out of business before releasing its first game.

What words of advice would you give to an aspiring designer today?

Beyond having an extremely strong work ethic, beyond looking at and studying all the games that you can learn from, beyond being educated and brilliant in programming, design, computer animation, writing, whichever is your skill set—you need to look at and study the life outside of games that is all around you. The best ideas will not come from other games. The best ideas will come from areas that have nothing to do with games. They will come from other areas, art forms, and sciences like sociology, agriculture, philosophy, zoology, or psychology. The more you find inspirational sources that come from areas beyond the spectrum of your intended medium, the more your unique your creations will feel to others.

3.10   Team competition: PlanetSide

your own experiences with team play—what makes team play fun? What makes it different from individual competition? Is there an idea for a team game that comes from your answers to those questions?

Exercise 3.3: Interaction Patterns

For each of the interaction patterns, create a list of your favorite games in each pattern. If you can't think of any games in a particular pattern, research games in that area and play several.

OBJECTIVES

It's obvious that you wouldn't have much of a game if you didn't give your players something to strive for. Objectives do just that. They define what players are trying to accomplish within the rules of the game. In the best-case scenario, these objectives seem challenging—but achievable—to the players.

In addition to providing challenge, the objective of a game can set its tone. A game in which the objective is to capture or kill the opponent's forces will have a very different tone from a game in which the objective is to spell more or longer words.

Some games are constructed so that different players have different objectives, while other games allow the player to choose one of several possible objectives. Additionally, there may be partial objectives in a game that help the players to accomplish the main objective. In either case, the objective should be considered carefully because it affects not only the formal system of the game but also the dramatic aspects. If the objective is well-integrated into the premise or story, the game can take on strong dramatic aspects.

Some questions to ask yourself about objectives as you design your own games are:

- What are some objectives of games you've played?
- What impact do these objectives have on the tone of the game?
- Do certain genres of play lend themselves to certain objectives?
- What about multiple objectives?
- Do objectives have to be explicit?
- What about player-determined objectives?

Here are some examples of objectives from games you might have played:

- *Connect Four:* Be the first player to place four units in a contiguous line on the playing grid.
- *Battleship:* Be the first player to sink all five of your opponent's battleships.
- *Mastermind:* Deduce the secret code of four colored pegs in as few steps as possible.
- *Chess:* Checkmate your opponent's king.
- *Clue:* Be the first player to deduce who, where, and how a murder was committed.
- *Super Mario Bros.:* Rescue Princess Toadstool from the evil Bowser by completing all eight

worlds (32 levels) of the game, each of which have their own mini-objectives.

- *Spyro the Dragon:* Rescue your fellow dragons who have been turned to stone, and defeat the evil Gnasty Gnorc by completing all six worlds of the game, each of which have their own mini-objectives.
- *Civilization:* Option 1: conquer all other civilizations on the board, or Option 2: colonize the star Alpha Centauri.
- *The Sims:* Manage the lives of a virtual household; as long as you can keep your household alive, you can set your own goals for the game.

Are there any generalizations we can make about types of objectives that might help us in our design process? A number of game scholars have made attempts to categorize games by their objectives—here are some of the categories they defined.[2]

1. Capture

The objective in a "capture" game is to take or destroy something of the opponent's (terrain, units, or both), while avoiding being captured or killed. Examples of this type of game are strategy boardgames like chess and checkers, as well as action games like *Quake*, *SOCOM II*, and their brethren. Also in this category are real-time strategy games like the *WarCraft* series and *Command & Conquer*. There are, in fact, so many examples of games with this type of objective that it's difficult to make any generalizations. Suffice to say that the concept of capture or killing the opponent's forces is one that is deeply ingrained in games today and has been since antiquity.

---

2. Adapted from the work of: Fritz Redl, Paul Gump, and Brian Sutton-Smith, "The Dimensions of Games," *The Study of Games* (New York: Robert E. Krieger Publishing, Inc., 1979), pp. 417-418 and David Parlett, *The Oxford History of Boardgames* (New York: Oxford University Press, 1999).

3.11 Capture or kill: SOCOM II and Doom

2. Chase

The objective in a "chase" game is to catch an opponent, or elude one, if you are the player being chased. Examples of chase games include tag, *Fox & Geese*, *Assassin*, and *Maximum Chase*. Chase games can be structured as single player versus game, player versus player, or unilateral competition. For example, tag and *Fox & Geese* are unilateral competitions, or one player versus many. *Assassin* is player versus player with each player chasing and being chased simultaneously. And *Maximum Chase*, an Xbox game, is player versus game, with the player in pursuit of computer-controlled enemy cars. Chase games can be determined by speed or physical dexterity, as in tag and *Maximum Chase*, or by stealth and strategy, as in *Assassin*. Also, a game like *Scotland Yard*, discussed on page 45, is a chase game, but one which is determined by logic and deduction. There is clearly a wealth of possibilities for games using this type of objective.

3. Race

The objective in a "race" game is to reach a goal—physical or conceptual—before the other players. Examples could be a footrace, a board-game like *Uncle Wiggly* or *Parcheesi*, or a simulation game like *Virtua Racing*. Race games can be determined by physical dexterity, such as with the footrace and, to some extent, *Virtua Racing*, or chance, such as with *Uncle Wiggly* and *Parcheesi*. They can also be determined by a mix of strategy and chance, such as in backgammon.

4. Alignment

The objective in an "alignment" game is to arrange your game pieces in a certain spatial configuration or create conceptual alignment between categories of pieces. Examples include tic-tac-toe, solitaire, *Connect Four*, *Othello*, *Tetris*, and *Bejeweled*. Alignment games are often somewhat puzzle-like in that they involve "solving" spatial or organizational problems in order to achieve the goal. They can be determined by logic and calculation, as in *Othello* and *Pente*, or by chance opportunity combined with calculation, as in *Tetris* and *Bejeweled*. Conceptual alignment is used in many games that require the players to make "matches" or "sets" of game pieces.

3.12 Chase games: Maximum Chase

Maximum Chase trademark Microsoft Corporation

3.13 Race games: Pole Position and Gran Turismo 4

Pole Position © 1982 Namco Ltd.
All Rights Reserved. Courtesy of Namco Holding Corp.

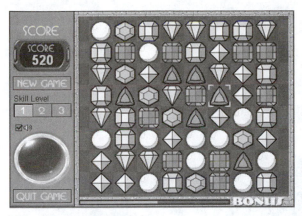

3.14 Alignment: Bejeweled

5. Rescue or escape

The objective in a "rescue" or "escape" game is to get a defined unit or units to safety. Examples are *Super Mario Bros.*, *Prince of Persia 3D*, *Emergency Rescue: Firefighters*, and *Ico*. This objective is often combined with other partial-objectives. For example, in *Super Mario Bros.*, the overall objective, as mentioned previously, is to rescue the Princess. But each of the game levels also has their own objectives that are more puzzle-like (see "Solution" on page 58).

3.15 Rescue or escape: Prince of Persia 3D

3.16 Forbidden act: Milton Bradley's Operation

6. Forbidden Act

The objective in a "forbidden act" game is to get the competition to "break the rules" by laughing, talking, letting go, making the wrong move, or otherwise doing something they shouldn't. Examples include *Twister*, *Operation*, *Ker-Plunk!*, and *Don't Break the Ice*. This is an interesting game type that isn't often found in digital games; perhaps because of its lack of direct competition or the difficulty in monitoring fair play. From the examples it's clear to see that there is often a physical component to games with this objective, sometimes involving stamina or flexibility, and sometimes just plain chance.

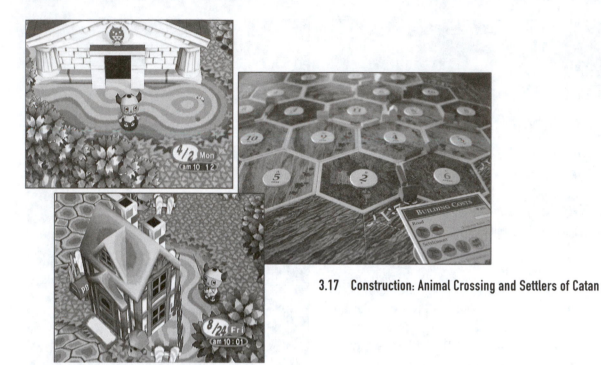

3.17   Construction: Animal Crossing and Settlers of Catan

Not included in the work of the scholars mentioned previously, but interesting nonetheless, are objectives such as the following items.

7. Construction

The object in a "construction" game is to build, maintain, or manage objects; this may be within a directly competitive or indirectly competitive environment. This, in many instances, is a more sophisticated version of the "alignment" category. Examples of this type of game are simulation games like *Animal Crossing*, *Gazillionaire*, *SimCity*, or *The Sims*, or boardgames like *Settlers of Catan*. Games with a construction objective often make use of resource management or trading as a core gameplay element. They are usually determined by strategic choice making, rather than chance or physical dexterity. Also, construction games can often be left open to player interpretation as to what ultimate "success" is within the game; so, for example, players choose what type of city to build

in *SimCity*, or household to encourage in *The Sims*.

8. Exploration

The object in an "exploration" game is to explore game areas. This is almost always combined with a more competitive objective. In the classic game of exploration, *Colossal Cave Adventure*, the objective is not only to explore Colossal Cave but also to find treasure along the way. In games like the *Zelda* series, the objectives of exploration, puzzle-solving, and sometimes combat intertwine to form multifaceted gameplay. Online worlds like *Ultima* and *EverQuest* have also used exploration as one of several objectives in their game structures.

9. Solution

The object in a "solution" game is to solve a problem or puzzle before (or more accurately) than the competition. Examples include graphic adventures like the *Myst* series, text adventures like the classic

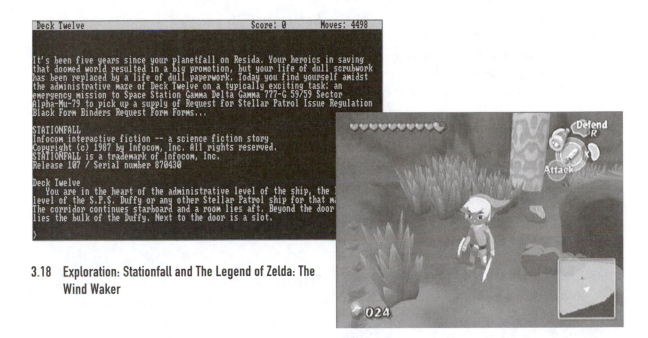

```
Deck Twelve                    Score: 0      Moves: 4498

It's been five years since your planetfall on Resida. Your heroics in saving
that doomed world resulted in a big promotion, but your life of dull scrubwork
has been replaced by a life of dull paperwork. Today you find yourself amidst
the administrative maze of Deck Twelve on a typically exciting task: an
emergency mission to Space Station Gamma Delta Gamma 777-G 59759 Sector
Alpha-Mu-79 to pick up a supply of Request for Stellar Patrol Issue Regulation
Black Form Binders Request Form Forms...

STATIONFALL
Infocom interactive fiction -- a science fiction story
Copyright (c) 1987 by Infocom, Inc. All rights reserved.
STATIONFALL is a trademark of Infocom, Inc.
Release 107 / Serial number 870430

Deck Twelve
     You are in the heart of the administrative level of the ship, the
level of the S.P.S. Duffy or any other Stellar Patrol ship for that ma
The corridor continues starboard and a room lies aft. Beyond the door
lies the bulk of the Duffy. Next to the door is a slot.

>
```

3.18   Exploration: Stationfall and The Legend of Zelda: The Wind Waker

Infocom titles, and many games that fall into other categories but have puzzle qualities. These include some we've mentioned already: the *Mario* and *Zelda* games, *Tetris*, and *The Sims*. Some games of pure strategy fall into this puzzle-like category as well: *Connect Four* and tic-tac-toe.

3.19   Solution: Day of the Tentacle

10. Outwit

The object in a game of "wits" is to gain and use knowledge in a way that defeats the other players. Some games of this type focus on having extra-game knowledge, like in *Trivial Pursuit* or *Jeopardy!* Others focus on gaining or using in-game knowledge: *Survivor* and *Diplomacy*. This second type of game provokes interesting social dynamics, which have yet to be truly explored in digital games.

3.20   Outwit: Diplomacy

Summary

This list is by no means exhaustive, and one of the most interesting things about objectives in games is when they are somewhat mixed. For example, the genre of real-time strategies mixes war with construction, forming a split focus that appeals to gamers who might not be interested in either pure war games or pure construction games. What you can do with a list like this is use it as a tool to look at the types of objectives you like in games, as well as those you don't like, and see how you might use these objectives in your own game ideas.

Exercise 3.4: Objectives

List out ten of your favorite games and name the objective for each. Do you see any similarities in these games? Try to define the type or types of games that appeal to you.

PROCEDURES

Procedures are the methods of play and the actions players can take to achieve the game objectives. One way to think about procedures is: who does what, where, when, and how?

- Who can use the procedure? One player? Some players? All the players?
- What exactly does the player do?
- Where does the procedure occur? Is the availability of the procedure limited by location?
- When does it take place? Is it limited by turn, time, or game state?
- How do players access the procedure? Directly, by physical interaction? Indirectly, through a controller or input device? By verbal command?

There are several types of procedures that most games tend to have:

- *Starting Action:* How to put a game into play.
- *Progression of Action:* Ongoing procedures after the starting action.
- *Special Actions:* Available conditional to other elements or game state.
- *Resolving Actions:* Bring gameplay to a close.

In boardgames, procedures are explained in the rules document. In digital games, they are described in the control section of the manual. Procedures are much easier to distinguish in digital games because they are the things the player does with the controller. Here are some examples of procedures from both a board/tabletop game and a digital game.

Connect Four

1. Choose a player to go first.
2. Each player in his turn drops one of his color checkers down any of the slots in the top of the grid.
3. The play alternates until one of the players gets four checkers of his color in a row. The four in a row can be horizontal, vertical, or diagonal.

Super Mario Bros.[3]

Select Button: Use this button to select the type of game you wish to play.

Start Button: Press this button to start the game. If you press it during play it will pause/unpause the game.

Left Arrow: Walk to the left. Push button B at the same time to run.

Right Arrow: Walk to the right. Push button B at the same time to run.

Down: Crouch (Super Mario only).

A Button

Jump: Mario jumps higher if you hold the button down longer.

Swim: When in water, press this button to bob up.

B Button

Accelerate: Press this button to run. If while holding B, you press A to jump, you can jump higher.

Fireballs: If you pick up a fire flower you can use this button to throw fireballs.

Comparison

Notice that both *Connect Four* and *Super Mario Bros.* specify a starting action. The "progres-

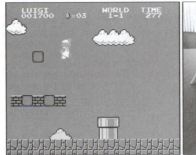

3.21   Super Mario Bros. and Connect Four

sion of action" in *Connect Four* is clearly shown in steps 2 and 3, while in *Super Mario Bros.*, which is a real-time game, the progression is implied by the left and right walk commands, which move the player through the game. *Connect Four* doesn't have any "special actions," but *Super Mario Bros.* has commands that are only applicable in certain situations: i.e., "when in water press this button to bob up," and "if you pick up a fire flower, you can use this button to throw fireballs." *Connect Four* also states the resolving action: when one player gets four checkers in a row. *Super Mario Bros.* does not state the resolving action; this is because the resolution is adjudicated by the system, not the players.

Exercise 3.5: Procedures for Blackjack

List the procedures for blackjack. Be specific. What is the starting action? The progression of action? Any special actions? The resolving action?

System procedures

Digital games can have much more complex game states than nondigital games. They can also have multifaceted system procedures that work behind the scenes, responding to situations and player

---

3. Nintendo, *Super Mario Bros.* Manual, 1986.

Designer Perspective: Marc LeBlanc

Title: Game Developer, Mind Control Software

Project list (five to eight top projects)

- *Thief* series
- *System Shock* series
- *Ultima Underworld II*

How did you get into the game industry?

When I went to school at MIT, I lived on 41st West, a dormitory hall that was home to a number of quirky individuals. Around 1990, several of my 41st West friends (including Dan Schmidt, Jon Maiara, James Fleming, Tim Stellmach, and the ubiquitous Doug Church) joined with Paul Neurath to form Blue Sky Productions. They were working on a game called *Underworld*. The game later became *Ultima Underworld* and the company later became LookingGlass Studios. I joined in 1992, and the rest is history.

What are your five favorite games and why?

- *X-Com: UFO Defense:* Now a classic, this game took two smaller games—strategic resource management and tactical combat—and married them perfectly. *X-Com* is a textbook example of emergent narrative. Through the simplest tricks, it gets the player's imagination to connect the narrative dots between the characters and events of the game. Suit up, son! You're going to Mars!
- *Pikmin:* Real-time strategy games have always had the wrong user-interface for the job. Skilled players have to master complicated finger acrobatics until they become keyboard virtuosos. *Pikmin* does away with all that, creating the first real-time strategy game to truly embrace its "twitchiness." Brilliant!

actions. In a role-playing combat system, character and weapon attributes may be used as part of a system calculation determining whether a particular player action succeeds, and if so, how much damage it causes. If the game were to be played on paper, as many role-playing games are, these system procedures need to be calculated by the players, using dice to generate random numbers. If the game is played digitally, the same system procedures are calculated by the program rather than the players.

Because of this, digital games can involve more sophisticated system procedures and process them more quickly than nondigital games. This does not mean that digital games are "more complex" than nondigital games. When we discuss

- *Star Control II:* Mixed authored storylines with some simple real-time tricks to create a narrative that was both well written and compellingly organic, in a way that has yet to be duplicated. Combine that with twitchy combat that is the worthy heir to *Space War*, and you have a classic.

What games have inspired you the most as a designer and why?

- *Sid Meier's SimGolf:* This game should be mandatory for all game designers. Don't be fooled by the golf theme; this game is a tutorial in level design.
- The boardgames of Reiner Knizia, particularly *Modern Art* and *Tigris & Euphrates*. If you ever find yourself wishing you had faster hardware or more RAM, remember what this guy can do with ten pages of rules and a few slabs of cardboard.
- *Grand Theft Auto III:* While I'm not necessarily a fan of the subject matter, it was heartening to see this kind of open-ended gameplay capture the mainstream console audience.

What are you most proud of in your career?

I'm proud of every time the team I've worked with has had the courage to cut an unnecessary feature. And I'm proud to have had the chance to work with people who have more of that courage than I do.

What words of advice would you give to an aspiring designer today?

1. *Have a critical eye for games.* If you can't say one critical thing about any game, even your *favorite* game, then you're an amateur.
2. *Learn to program.* Designing a game without know how to program is like painting without a brush.
3. *Play lots of games.* Play games in every medium: PC, console, boardgames, party games, and sports. Play the classics. Play *Go*.
4. *Remember that if you're lucky, your game will get played by millions of people.* Design the game for them, not for you.

system structures in Chapter 5 on page 112, we'll look at systems that have simple procedures, which lead to extremely complex results. For example, games like chess or Go are nondigital systems that have intrigued players for thousands of years with their innate complexity, all of which stems from the relationship of very simple game objects and the procedures for manipulating them.

Defining procedures

When you are defining the procedures for your game, it's important to keep in mind the limitations of the environment in which your game will

3.22 SSX Tricky: learn the trick
procedures to score
"Tricky Points"

be played. Will your game be played in a nondigi-tal setting? If so, you will want to make sure they're easy for players to remember. If your game will be played in a digital setting, what type of input/out-put devices will that setting have? Will players have a keyboard and mouse, or will they have a propri-etary controller? Will they sit close to a high-reso-lution screen, or several feet from a low-resolution screen?

Procedures are, by nature, affected by these physical constraints. As a designer, you need to be sensitive to constraints and find creative and ele-gant solutions so that the procedures are intuitive to access and easy to remember.

RULES

We said in the last chapter that rules define game objects and define allowable actions by the play-ers. Some of the questions we might ask ourselves about rules are: how do players learn the rules? How are the rules enforced? What kinds of rules work best in certain situations? Are there patterns to rule sets? What can we learn from those pat-terns?

Like procedures, rules are generally laid out in the rules document of boardgames. In digital games, they may be explained in the manual, or they may be implicit in the program itself. For example, a digital game may not allow certain actions without explicitly stating that fact; the interface may simply not provide controls for such an action, or the program may stop a player from performing that action if it is attempted.

Rules may also close up loopholes in the game system. One classic example of this is the famous rule from *Monopoly:* "Do not pass go, do not collect $200." This rule is applied when a player is sent to jail from any spot on the board. It's important because if it were not stated, a player could make the argument that moving from past "go" all the way to jail entitled him to collect $200, transforming the intended punishment into a reward.

When you are designing rules, as when you are designing procedures, it's important to think of them in relation to your players. Too many rules may make your game unplayable. Too few rules may make your game so simple as to be unchallenging. Poorly communicated rules may confuse or alienate players. Even if the game system (in the case of a digital game) is tracking the proper application of rules, the players need to clearly understand them so that they do not feel cheated by the consequences of certain rules.

Here are some sample rules from several different types of games that we can use as reference for the following discussion:

- *Poker:* A straight is five consecutively ranked cards; a straight flush is five consecutively ranked cards of the same suit.
- *Chess:* A player cannot move her king into check.
- *Go:* A player cannot make a move that recreates a previous situation on the board.
- *WarCraft II:* In order to create knight units, a player must have upgraded to a keep and built a stable.

- *You Don't Know Jack:* If a player answers a question incorrectly, the other players get a chance to answer.
- *Jak & Daxter:* If a player runs out of green mana, they are "knocked out" and return to the last checkpoint of the level.

Even from this short list, there are some ideas that start to emerge concerning the nature of rules.

Rules defining objects and concepts

Games do not inherit objects from the real world; rather, they create their own objects and concepts, usually as a part of their rule set. These may be completely fabricated, or they may be based on real world objects, but even if they are based on familiar objects, they still need to be defined in the rules as to their nature in the game.

Think about the poker rule regarding the concept of a "straight" or a "straight flush." This is a concept unique to the game. There is no "straight" outside of the realm of poker. When you learn the rules of poker, one of the key concepts to learn is the make-up and values of certain hands—a "straight" being one of these hands.

Then again, there is chess. We know that chess has objects in its system called kings, queens, bishops, etc., all of which do have counterparts in the real world. But this is misleading; the king in a chess game is an abstract object with explicit rules defining its nature. A king outside of the game bears no resemblance to this abstract game object. The rules of chess have simply used the notion of a king to give context to the behavior and value of this important piece.

Boardgames and other nondigital games generally define their objects explicitly as a part of their rules sets. Players must read and understand these rules, and then they have to be able to adjudicate the game themselves. Because of this, most nondigital games limit themselves to fairly simple objects, with only one or two possible variables or states for each, usually denoted by some physical aspect of the equipment, board or other interface elements. In a boardgame like chess, the only variables for each piece are color and position, both of which the player can easily track visually.

Digital games, on the other hand, may have objects, such as characters or fighting units that are made up of a fairly complex set of variables, which define their overall state. Players may not be aware of this entire state, since, unlike a board-

game, the program can track the variables behind the scenes. For example, here are the default variables underlying both knights and ogres in *WarCraft II*:

- *Cost:* 800 gold, 100 lumber
- *Hit Points:* 90
- *Damage:* 2–12
- *Armor:* 4
- *Sight:* 5
- *Speed:* 13
- *Range:* 1

While these variables are important to how the play proceeds, and they are in fact available to

	Knight	Ogre	Elven Archer	Troll Axethrower	Mage
Visible Range:	4	4	5	5	9
Hit Points:	90	90	40	40	60
Magic Points:	0	0	0	0	1
Build Time:	90	90	70	70	120
Gold Cost:	800	800	500	500	1200
Lumber Cost:	100	100	50	50	0
Oil Cost:	0	0	0	0	0
Attack Range:	1	1	4	4	2
Armor:	4	4	0	0	0
Basic Damage:	8	8	3	3	0
Piercing Damage:	4	4	6	6	9

3.23   WarCraft II — unit properties

players via the interface, they are not something that players must directly deal with during gameplay. Even the most advanced player probably does not calculate their strategy using these mathematical rules. Rather, they gain an intuitive knowledge of the knight's cost, strength, power, range, etc., versus the other units on the board through their play experience.

When defining your game objects and concepts, an essential thing to keep in mind is how players will learn the nature of these objects. If the objects are complex, will the players have to deal with that complexity directly? If the objects are simple, will players feel they are differentiated enough from each other to make an impact on the gameplay? Do the objects evolve? Are they only available under certain circumstances? How will players learn the nature of each object in the game?

Rules restricting actions

The next general rule concept we can see reflected in our list of sample rules is the idea of rules restricting actions. In chess, the rule that "a player cannot move their king into check" keeps players from losing the game by accident. The example from Go where "a player cannot make a move that recreates a previous state of the board," keeps the players from becoming locked in a never-ending loop of play. Both of these address potential loopholes in the game systems.

Additionally, rules restricting actions may take the form of basic delimitations: "the play takes place on a field of 360' x 160'" (football) or "a team shall be composed of not more than 11 players, one of whom shall be the goalkeeper" (soccer). In both of these cases, we can see that the rules overlap with other formal aspects—namely the number of players and the boundaries of the game.

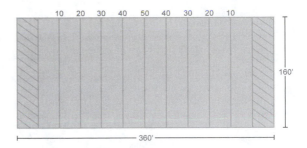

3.24 Dimensions of a football field

This is actually true of all formal aspects, which will be represented in either the procedures or the rules in some way.

Another example of rules that restrict actions is in the type of rules that keep gameplay from becoming imbalanced in one or more players' favor. Think about the effects of the rule from *WarCraft II* where "in order to create knight units, a player must have upgraded to a keep and built a stable." What this means is that one player cannot simply choose to use their resources early in the game to create knights, while other players are still creating lower-level fighting units. All players must progress along a fairly similar path of resource management in order to gain more powerful units.

Exercise 3.6: Rules Restricting Actions

There are many types of rules that restrict action. Here is a list of games: Twister, Pictionary, Scrabble, Operation, *and* Pong. *What rules within these games restrict player actions?*

Rules determining effects

Rules also can trigger effects based on certain circumstances. For example, "if" something happens, there is a rule that "*xyz*" results. In our list of sample rules, the condition from *You Don't Know Jack*

3.25   Jak II — Almost out of mana

falls into this type of rule: "If a player answers a question incorrectly, the other players get a chance to answer." Also, this rule from *Jak & Daxter* is of the same quality: "If a player runs out of green mana, they are 'knocked out' and return to the last beginning of the level."

Rules that trigger effects are useful for a number of reasons. First, they create variation in gameplay. The circumstances that trigger them are not always applicable, so it can create excitement and difference when they come into play. The example from *You Don't Know Jack* shows this quality. In this case, the second player gets a chance to answer the question, already having seen the results of the first player's guess. Because of this, they have an advantage, a higher percentage chance of answering correctly.

Additionally, this type of rule can be used to get the gameplay back on track. The rule from *Jak & Daxter* shows this. Since the game is not "competitive" in the sense that it is a single-player adventure, there is no reason for the player to "die"

when they lose all their mana. However, the designers do want the player to be penalized in some way so that they will take care with their actions and try to keep from losing mana. Their solution is the previous rule: players are penalized, but not badly, for losing all their mana. This gets the game back on track, incentivizing the player to work harder to keep their mana loss in check.

Defining rules

As with procedures, the way in which you define your rules will be affected by your play environment. Rules need to be clear to players, or, in the case of digital games that adjudicate for players, they need to be intuitively grasped so that the game seems fair and responsive to given situations. In general, it's important to keep in mind that the more complex your rules are, the more demands you'll place on the players to comprehend them. The less well that players understand your rules, whether rationally or intuitively, the less likely they will be able to make meaningful choices within the system, and the less sense they will have of being in control of the gameplay.

Exercise 3.7: Rules for Blackjack

In the same way that you wrote down the procedures for blackjack in Exercise 3.5, now write down the rules. It's harder than you think. Did you remember all the rules? Try playing the game as you've written it. You may realize you've forgotten something. What rules did you forget? How did those missing rules affect the play of the game?

RESOURCES

What is a resource exactly? In the real world, resources are assets (i.e., natural resources, eco-nomic resource, human resources) that can be used to accomplish certain goals. In a game, resources play much the same role. Most games use some form of resources in their systems, such as chips in poker, properties in *Monopoly*, and gold in *WarCraft*. Managing resources and determining how and when to control player access to them is a key part of the game designer's job.

How does a designer decide what resources to offer to players? And how does a player control access to those resources in order to maintain challenge in the game? This is a hard question to answer in the abstract. It's easier if we take an example that you're probably familiar with.

Think of a role-playing game like *Diablo*. What are some of the resources you might find in such a system: money, weapons, armor, potions, magic items? Why don't you find things like rubber bands or pieces of pie? While it might be fun to find such random items, the truth is, a piece of pie won't help you achieve the goals of the game. The designers have carefully planned how you can find or earn the very resources that you need to accomplish the goals they've put before you. You may not find or earn as much money as you would like, but if you meet the challenges the game presents, you will gain resources that will allow you to move forward. If you did not gain these resources, the game system would be unbalanced.

By definition, resources must have both utility and scarcity in the game system. If they do not have utility, they are like our piece of pie: a funny and strange thing to find but essentially useless. On the same note, if the resources are overly abundant, they will lose their value in the system.

Exercise 3.8: Utility and Scarcity

What are the resources in the games *Scrabble* and *Doom*? How are they useful to players? How are they made scarce by the game system?

Many designers fall into the trap of copying existing games when it comes to resource management. One way to break your game out of the tried and true rut is to think about resources in a more abstract sense. Look at the basic functions of resource types and try to apply these in new and creative ways. To illustrate what we mean, let's review some abstract examples that you should consider when designing your game.

Lives

The classic scarce resource in action games are lives. Arcade games are built on the management of this primary resource. Examples of this are games like *Space Invaders* or *Super Mario Bros.*, where you have a certain number of lives to accomplish the goals of the game. Lose your lives, and you have to start over. Do well, and you earn more lives to work with. Lives as a resource type are usually implemented as part of a fairly simplistic pattern: more is always better, and there's no downside to earning lives.

Units

A slightly different concept from lives is that of units. In games in which the player is represented in the game by more than one object at a time, you generally have unit resources to manage rather than lives. Units may be all of one kind, as in checkers, or a number of different types, as in chess. Units may keep the same values throughout the game, or they may upgrade or evolve, as in real-time strategy games. Units may be finite (i.e., once they are lost, they are lost for good), or they may be renewable, as in games that allow players to build new units over time. When units are renewable, they often have an associated cost per unit. Determining this cost per unit, and how it balances with the rest of the resource structure

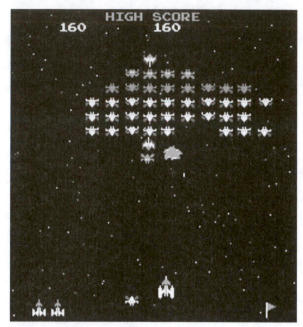

3.26 Galaxian: two lives left

Galaxian © 1979 Namco Ltd., All Rights Reserved. Courtesy of Namco Holding Corp.

3.27 Checkers: simple units

can be tricky. Playtesting is the one good way to determine if your cost per unit is balanced.

Health

Health can be a separate resource type, or, it can be an attribute of an individual life in a game. No matter how it is thought of, when health is used as a resource, it helps to dramatize the loss or near-loss of lives and units. Using a resource like health usually means that there is some way to increase health, even as it is lost as part of gameplay.

How might players raise health levels in a game? Many action games place "medical kits" around their levels—picking one up raises a player's health. Some role-playing games force players to camp in order to heal their characters. Each of these methods has its uses in a particular genre. The action game uses a method that is very fast, while being somewhat unrealistic. The role-playing example is more realistic within the story aspect of the game, but it's slow and potentially frustrating to players.

3.28 Diablo — low health meter on lower left of screen

Currency

One of the most powerful resource types in any game is the use of currency to facilitate trade. As we'll see in Chapter 5 on page 116, currency is one of the key elements of an in-game economy. It is not the only way to create an economy—as many games also use barter systems to accomplish the same goals. Currency in games plays the same role it does in real life: it greases the wheels of trade, making it easier for players to trade for what they need without having to barter using only the goods they have on hand. Currency need not be limited to a standard bank note system, however.

Actions

In some games, actions, such as moves or turns, may be considered resources. An example of this is the game of 20 Questions—your questions have utility and scarcity in this system, and you have to ration them carefully to guess the answer within your limit. Another example is the phase structure of the turns in *Magic: The Gathering*. Each turn is made up of phases; some specific actions can be performed in each phase. Players must plan their turns carefully in order not to waste any potential actions.

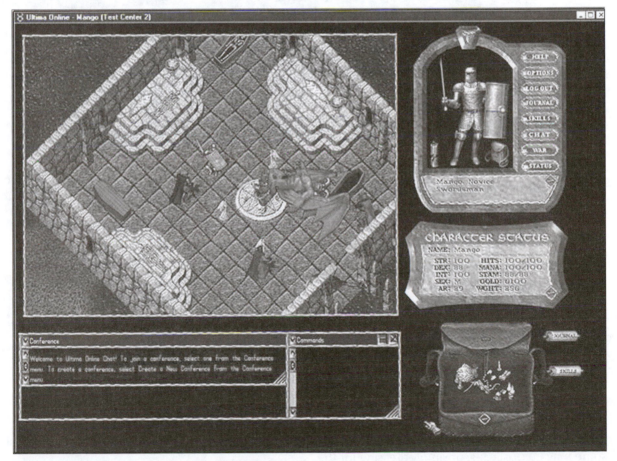

3.29 Ultima Online — player knapsack with sack of gold

3.30   Enter the Matrix — "focus"

Even real-time games can restrict actions that are too powerful, and by doing so, these actions become resources that need to be managed by the players. An example of this can be seen in *Enter the Matrix*, where the "focus" feature allows players to enter bullet time, slowing down the action so they can move more "quickly" relative to their opponents. You have only so much time to "focus," however, before you return to normal time. Managing the use of your focus time is a key part of gameplay.

Objects

Not all objects in a game function as resources; some may be obstacles, or simply dressing for the environment. But if an object has utility and scarcity, as we've defined, it may be considered a resource. We've already mentioned the armor, weapons, and other objects found in role-playing games such as *Diablo*. These objects help players to accomplish game objectives, and they are made scarce by their high price at purchase, or by the opportunity cost of finding them in dungeons guarded by more and greater monsters.

One classic type of object resource is the "power-up." Whether it is magic mushrooms in *Super Mario Bros.* or Blue Eco in *Jak and Daxter*, power-ups, as their name implies, are generally over-powered resources, giving a tremendous boost to the player beyond that of normal resources in the game. However, their power is balanced to their scarcity, in that they are available for a very short time or for only a single instance.

Terrain

Related to objects, but linked solidly to location, some resources are available only by occupying or controlling terrain. Terrain as a resource is an important part of real-time strategy games and map-based war games. In games like *WarCraft II*, the currency of the game (wood, gold, oil) is extracted from special areas of the terrain, so these areas become important primary resources. Other types of games also use terrain as a resource in ways you might not think of. The triple letter squares in *Scrabble* are important resources found on the terrain of the game board, as are the bases on the diamond of a baseball field.

Time

Some games use time as a resource—restricting player actions by time, or phases of the game in periods of time. A good example of time used as a

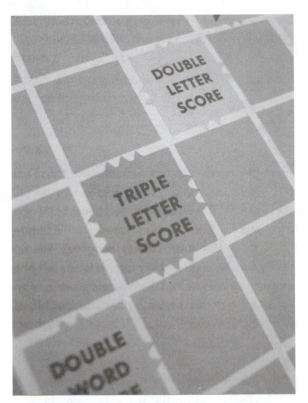

3.32 Scrabble — triple letter score

3.31 **Super Mario Bros. — magic mushroom**

resource can be seen in speed chess, where players have a total amount of time (for example 10 minutes) to use over the course of a game. Players alternate turns as normal, but a game clock keeps track of each player's used time. Another example of time as a resource are the children's games hot potato and musical chairs. In each of these cases, players struggle not to be "it," whether that means holding the hot potato or being the only one without a chair, when the time is up. Time is an inherently dramatic force when used as a resource. We are all familiar with the tension of a countdown deadline, or the anticipation caused by a ticking bomb in an action movie. When used as a resource that players must ration or work against,

3.33   Chess clock

time can add an emotional aspect to a game design.

Exercise 3.9: Resource Types
For each of the resource types (found starting on page 68), create a list of your favorite games that use resources of that type. If you can't think of any games that use a particular type of resource, research games that do and play several of them.

These are just some of the resource types that you should think about using when designing your own games. We challenge you to both create your own original types of resources and take resource models from one genre and adapt them to games where they're seldom, if ever, used. You may be surprised with the results.

CONFLICT

Conflict emerges from the players trying to accomplish the goals of the game within its rules and boundaries. As we've already mentioned, conflict is designed into the game by creating rules and procedures that do not allow players to accomplish their goals directly. Instead, the procedures offer fairly inefficient means toward accomplishing the game objective. While inefficient, these means challenge the player, by forcing them to employ a particular skill or range of skills. The procedures also create a sense of competition or play, which is enjoyable in some way, so that players will submit themselves to this inefficient system in order to gain the ultimate sense of achievement that comes from participating.

Here are some examples of things that cause game conflicts to emerge:

- *Pinball:* Keep the ball from escaping the field of play using only the flippers or other devices provided.

- *Golf:* Get the ball from the tee to the hole, past any obstacles on the course, in as few strokes as possible.

- *Monopoly:* Manage your money and your properties to become the richest player in the game.

- *Quake:* Stay alive while player and nonplayer opponents try to kill you.

- *WarCraft III:* Maintain your forces and resources, while using them to command and control the map objectives.

- *Poker:* Outbid opponents based on your hand or your ability to bluff.

These examples point to three classic sources of conflict in games: opponents, obstacles, and dilemmas. Let's look at each of these more closely to see what they offer in terms of various types of gameplay.

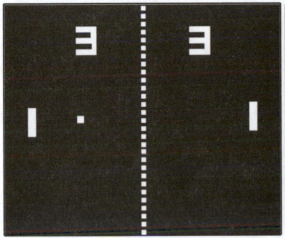

3.34 Pong and Quake III opponents

Obstacles

Obstacles are a common source of conflict in both single and multiplayer games, though they play a more important role in single-player games. Obstacles may take a physical form, such as the sack in a sack race, or the water on a golf course, or the bumpers on a pinball table. Or, obstacles may involve mental skills, such as the puzzles in an adventure game.

Opponents

In multiplayer games, other players are typically the primary source of conflict. In the previous examples, *Quake* uses other players in addition to nonplayer opponents and physical obstacles to create conflict in the game. Also, *Monopoly's* conflict comes from interactions with other players.

Dilemmas

As opposed to physical or mental obstacles and conflict from direct competition with other play-ers, another type of game conflict may come from dilemma-based choices that players have to make. An example of a dilemma in *Monopoly* is the choice of whether to spend money to buy a property or use that money to upgrade a property that is already owned. Another dilemma would be whether to stay in or fold in poker. In both cases, players have to make choices that have good or bad potential consequences. A dilemma can be a powerful source of conflict in both single- and multiplayer games.

Exercise 3.10: Conflict

Explain how conflict is created in the following games: *Tetris*, *Frogger*, *Bomberman*, *Minesweeper*, and solitaire. Does the conflict in these games come from obstacles, opponents, dilemmas, or a combination of these?

DESIGNER PERSPECTIVE: JAMES ERNEST

James Ernest is a prolific designer of board and card games. He publishes many of his creations through his company, Cheapass Games.

Title

President, Cheapass Games

Project list (five to eight top projects)

- Boardgames: *Kill Doctor Lucky*, etc.
- Dice Games: *Button Men, Diceland*
- Friedey's Games: *Give Me the Brain / Lord of the Fries*
- Real-Time Card Games: *Falling, Brawl, Fightball*

How did you get into the game industry?

I was friends with some of the people at Wizards of the Coast in 1993, right before they released *Magic: The Gathering*. I worked with them on support material for that game and designed new games to submit to them for publication. With a backlog of unpublished designs, I started my own game company in 1996.

What are your five favorite games and why?

I like simple games, whether they have deep strategy or not. By time spent playing, my five favorite games would have to be poker (by a wide margin); *Diceland*; blackjack, *Dungeons & Dragons*

BOUNDARIES

Boundaries are what separate the game from everything that is not the game. As discussed in Chapter 2 on page 27, boundaries can be physical—like the edges of an arena, playing field, or game board—or they may be conceptual, such as a social agreement to play. For instance, ten people may be physically sitting in a room where *Truth or Dare* is being played, but two of them may not (although it was fifteen years ago), and my family's unique version of cutthroat pitch. I also play plenty of video games, and sports like bocce and pool.

Poker tops the list because of several factors: I can make money at it, so as a classically trained consumer zombie I'm pretty fascinated by that. The rules are incredibly simple. And it has strong components of both mathematical and psychological strategy, perfected by a society of expert players. I also like games with an element of luck, which is why you'll find me playing poker instead of chess.

What games have inspired you the most as a designer and why?

Magic: The Gathering inspired me both to imitate the things it did right, and to learn from its mistakes. Before *Magic* came out, I'd given very little thought to formal game design (though I'd written a few games, including a chess variant), and being closely associated with it I became acutely aware that games were something you could design for a living. One of the most inspiring things about *Magic* was its original format: to imitate that success I continue to experiment with new formats. I haven't made a hit yet, but at least I deserve a little credit for trying.

What are you most proud of in your career?

In terms of specific game designs, I'm most proud of my most original work: the invention and improvement of my own version of the real-time card game (*Falling*, *Brawl*, and *Fightball*), *Diceland*, and *Button Men*. I'm also proud of the funniest of my games, like the *Doctor Lucky* and *Friedey's* series. On the whole, Cheapass Games is well known and even respected (in some circles), and that's no mean feat.

What words of advice would you give to an aspiring designer today?

Like any creative artist, a game designer will generate a lot of garbage before he creates a masterpiece. Don't be so attached to your work that you refuse to see its flaws. It's easy to fix your game by adding rules, but it's better to take them away. It's easy to copy what you see in the market, but it's better to look for what isn't there. You can try to write a game for a player you don't know, but your best target will always be yourself. That's why the sign in my office says, "Write the game you want to play."

have agreed to play and are therefore outside the boundaries of the system.

Why are boundaries an important aspect of game design? Think about what might happen if there were no boundaries in a familiar game system. Imagine a game like football. What if you tried to play football (either in a physical setting or on a computer) without boundaries? Players could run anywhere they wanted to; they could run as far as they could physically get without being tackled by the other team or blocked by random objects like buildings or cars.

What does this do to the strategy of football? What about the abilities necessary for play? Apply this line of thinking to other games you know. Can you see how they would be intrinsically different if their boundaries were not closed? What if you could add real money to the bank in *Monopoly*? Or if you could add cards to the deck in poker? What if the edges of a chess board were infinitely expanding? It's clear without even playing these that without their boundaries they'd become totally different games.

In addition to the purely practical reason for game boundaries, there's also an emotional one. The boundaries of the game serve as a way to separate everything that goes on in the game from daily life. So, while you may act the part of a cut-throat opponent facing off against your best friend within the boundaries of a game (taking over their civilization or destroying their forces), you can shake hands at the end of the game and walk away without any real damage to your relationship. In fact, you may feel closer to them, having met in this game-world competition.

The play theorist Johan Huizinga calls the abstract space that the boundaries of games create the "magic circle," a temporary world where the rules of the game apply, rather than the rules of the ordinary world.[4]

Are there games that do not have exact boundaries? Some games are very "free form" and do not require strictly defined boundaries to work. An example of this is tag. Tag is usually played with loosely defined boundaries with no detriment to the overall experience. Some modern game designers have also realized that interaction with outside elements might be an interesting design choice for their systems. An example of a more complex game system that has this type of interaction with the environment outside the game system proper is *Magic: The Gathering*.

3.35 Boundaries of a tennis court

In *Magic*, players purchase an initial deck with enough cards to get started, but this is only the surface of the system. To create better decks, players can buy or trade other cards to add to their collection. As time goes on, Wizards of the Coast, the publisher of the game, adds new cards to the system and withdraws old ones. This ever-changing universe of cards within the system creates a game with expansive boundaries, although at any given time, there are actually limits to the universe of cards.

The way that *Magic* treats the boundaries of its system is something of an exception. Most games are "closed" systems. These games clearly define that which is within the game versus that which is

---

4. Johan Huizinga, *Homo Ludens: A Study of the Play Element in Culture* (Boston: The Beacon Press, 1971), p. 10.

outside the game, and purposefully keep the in-game elements from interacting with outside forces. It is up to you as the game designer to determine just where and how these boundaries are defined, and when or if to ever breach them.

Exercise 3.11: Boundaries

What are the boundaries in the game Dungeons & Dragons? Can you think of physical and conceptual boundaries?

OUTCOME

As described previously, the goal of a system is to produce a measurable outcome. In the case of most games, that outcome will be unequal; i.e., there will be a winner or winners. This is not true of all games: many massively multiplayer online worlds do not have the concept of a "winner." Also, simulation games may not have a predetermined win condition either. These games are built to go on indefinitely, and reward players in other fashions than by winning.

For most game systems, however, producing a winner or winners is the end goal. At defined intervals either the players (in the case of a nondigital game) or the system, check to see if a winning state has been achieved. If it has, the system resolves and the game is over.

There are a number of ways to determine outcome, but the structure of the final outcome will always be related to both the player interaction patterns discussed earlier and the objective. For example, in pattern one, single player versus game, the player may either win or lose, or, the player may score a certain amount of points before ultimately losing. Examples of this outcome structure are solitaire, pinball machines, or a number of different arcade games.

In addition to the player interaction patterns described on page 44, the outcome is determined by the nature of the game objective. A game that defines its objective based on points will most certainly

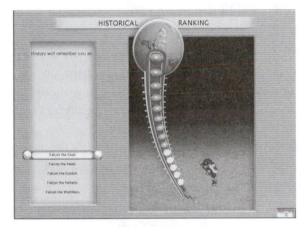

3.36 **Civilization III ranking screen**

tainly use those points in the measure of the outcome. A game that defines its objective as capture, like chess, may not have a scoring system—rather, chess games are won or lost based solely on meeting the primary objective, capturing the king.

Chess is what we call a "zero-sum" game. By this we mean that if we count a win as +1 and a loss as a –1, then the sum for any outcome is "zero." In chess one player wins (+1) and one player loses (–1). No matter which player wins, the sum is always zero.

But many games are not zero-sum games. Ranking systems, statistics, multiple objectives all create outcomes without cutthroat competition. Look at the games you play: what types of outcomes are most satisfying? Does that answer change in different situations, for instance social games versus sporting events? When you determine the outcome for a game that you're designing, be sure to keep these types of considerations in mind.

Exercise 3.12: Outcome

Name two zero-sum games and two nonzero-sum games. What is the main difference in the outcomes of these games? How does this affect gameplay?

CONCLUSION

These formal elements, when set in motion, create what we recognize as a game. As we've seen throughout this chapter, there are many possible combinations of these elements that work to create a wide variety of experiences. By understanding how these elements work together and thinking about new ways of combining these elements, you can invent new types of gameplay for your games.

Exercise 3.13: Revise Rules and Procedures

The rules and procedures of backgammon are fairly simple. Change them so that they are not dependent on chance. How does this affect the gameplay?

Chapter 4
Working with Dramatic Elements

Exercise 4.1: Making Checkers Dramatic

The game of checkers is very abstract: there is no story, no characters, and no compelling reason why you would want to capture all of your opponent's pieces, except for the fact that it's the objective of the game.

For this exercise, devise a set of dramatic elements for checkers that make the game more emotionally engaging. For example, you might create a backstory, give each piece its own name, distinctive look, define special areas on the board, or whatever creative ideas you can think of to connect the players to this simple, abstract system. Now, play your new game with friends or family and note their reaction. How do the dramatic elements improve or detract from the experience?

We've seen how formal elements work together to create the experience we recognize as a game, but now let's turn to those elements we've defined as dramatic—those which engage the

players emotionally with the game experience and invest them in its outcome. Basic dramatic elements, like challenge and play, are found in all games. Other elements, like premise, character, and story, surround the more abstract elements of the formal system, creating a sense of connection for the players and enriching their overall experience.

One way to create more engaging games is to study how these elements work to create engagement and how they've been used in other games—as well as other media. Your exploration of these dramatic elements and traditional tools can help you to think of new ideas and new situations for your own designs.

Exercise 4.2: Dramatic Games

Name five games that you find dramatically interesting. What is it about those games that you find compelling?

CHALLENGE

Most people would agree that one thing that engages them in a game is "challenge." What do they really mean by challenge, though? They don't simply mean that they want to be faced with a task that is hard to accomplish. If that were true, the challenge of games would hold little difference from the challenges of everyday life. When players talk of challenge in games, they're speaking of tasks that are satisfying to complete, that require just the right amount of work to create a sense of accomplishment and enjoyment.

Because of this, challenge is very individualized and is determined by the abilities of the specific player in relationship to the game. A young player, just learning to count, might find a game of *Chutes and Ladders* particularly challenging, while an adult, who mastered that skill long ago, would probably find it boring.

In addition to being individualized, challenge is also dynamic. A player might find one task challenging at the beginning of a game, but after becoming accomplished in the task, they'll no longer find it challenging. So, the game must adapt to remain challenging and hold the interest of the more accomplished player.

Is there a way to look at challenge that's not defined by individual experience? One that can give us some general ideas to keep in mind when designing a game? When you set out to create the basic challenge in your game, you might start by thinking how people really enjoy themselves, and which types of activities make them happy. As it turns out, the answer to this question is directly related to the concept of challenge, and the level of challenge presented by an experience.

The psychologist Mihaly Czikszentmihalyi set out to identify the elements of enjoyment by studying similarities of experience across many different tasks and types of people. What he found was surprising: regardless of age, social class, or gender, the people he talked to described enjoy-

able activities in much the same way. The activities themselves spanned many different disciplines, including performing music, climbing rocks, painting, and playing games, but the words and concepts people used to describe their enjoyment of them were similar. In all these tasks, people mentioned certain conditions that made the activities pleasurable for them:

> *First, the experience (of enjoyment) usually occurs when we confront tasks we have a chance of completing. Second, we must be able to concentrate on what we are doing. Third and fourth, the concentration is usually possible because the task undertaken has clear goals and provides immediate feedback. Fifth, one acts with a deep but effortless involvement that removes from awareness the worries and frustrations of everyday life. Sixth, enjoyable experiences allow people to exercise a sense of control over their actions. Seventh, concern for the self disappears, yet paradoxically the sense of self emerges stronger after the flow experience is over. Finally, the sense of the duration of time is altered; hours pass by in minutes, and minutes can stretch out to seem like hours. The combination of all these elements causes a sense of deep enjoyment that is so rewarding people feel like expending a great deal of energy is worthwhile simply to be able to feel it.[1]*

Based on his findings, Czikszentmihalyi created a theory called "flow," which is illustrated in Figure 4.1. As can be seen in the diagram, there's a dynamic relationship between challenge and ability, frustration and boredom that creates an optimal experience for a person engaged in an activity.

---

1. Mihaly Czikszentmihalyi, *Flow: The Psychology of Optimal Experience* (New York: Harper & Row Publishers, Inc., 1990) p. 49.

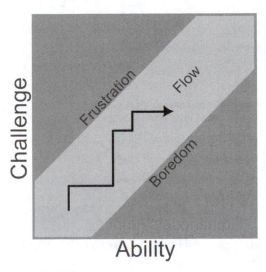

4.1 "Flow" diagram

When a person begins performing an activity, they usually have a low level of ability. If the challenge of the activity is too high, they will become frustrated. As they continue on, their ability rises, however, and if the challenge level stays the same, they will become bored. Figure 4.1 shows a path of rising challenge and ability, balanced carefully between frustration and boredom, which would result in an optimal experience for a user.

If the level of challenge remains appropriate to the level of ability, and if this challenge rises as the ability level rises, the person will stay in the center region and experience a state that Czikszentmihalyi calls "flow." In flow, an activity balances a person between challenge and ability, frustration and boredom, to produce an experience of achievement and happiness. This concept is very interesting for game designers because this balance between challenge and ability is exactly what we are trying to achieve with gameplay. Let's look more closely at the elements that help to achieve flow.

A challenging activity that requires skill

According to Czikszentmihalyi, flow occurs most often within activities that are "goal-directed and bounded by rules ... that could not be done without the proper skills."[2] Skills might be physical, mental, social, etc. For a person who does not have any of the skills a task requires, it is not challenging, but meaningless. For a person who has the skills, but is not completely assured of the outcome, a task is challenging. This is particularly important to game design.

Exercise 4.3: Skills

List the types of skills required by the games you enjoy. What other types of skills do people enjoy that you could incorporate into the games you design?

The merging of action and awareness

"When all of a person's relevant skills are needed to cope with the challenges of a situation, that person's attention is completely absorbed by the activity," Czikszentmihalyi goes on to say. "People become so involved in what they're doing that the activity becomes spontaneous, almost automatic;

4.2 An activity that requires skill: Tony Hawk Pro Skater

2. Ibid.

4.3   Merging action and awareness: Metal Gear Solid 3

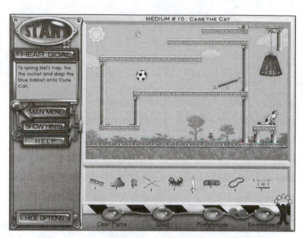

4.4   Clear goals and feedback: Incredible Machine: Even More Contraptions

they stop being aware of themselves as separate from the actions they are performing."[3]

Clear goals and feedback

In everyday life, there are often contradictory demands on us; our goals are not always clearly defined. But in flow experiences, we know what needs to be done, and we get immediate feedback on how well we're achieving our goals. For example, musicians know what notes to play next and can hear when they make mistakes; the same is true whether it's playing tennis or rock climbing. When a game has clearly defined goals, the players know what needs to be done to win, to move to the next level, to achieve the next step in their strategy, etc., and they receive direct feedback as to their actions toward those goals.

Exercise 4.4: Goals and Feedback

Pick three games and list the types of feedback generated in each. Then describe how the feedback relates to the ultimate goal of each game.

Concentration on the task at hand

Another typical element of flow is that we are aware only of what's relevant here and now. If the musician thinks of his health or tax problems when playing, he's likely to hit a wrong note. If the surgeon's mind wanders during an operation, the patient's life is in danger. In game flow, the players are not thinking of what's on TV or how much laundry they have to do; they are focused entirely on the challenges presented in the game. Many game interfaces take over the entire screen of the PC or build impressive audio/visual worlds to focus our attention. Here's a quote from a mountaineer describing a flow experience (but these might as well be the words of an *EverQuest* player): "You're not aware of other problematic life situations. It becomes a world unto its own, significant only to itself. It's a concentration thing. Once you're in the situation, it's incredibly real, and you're very much in charge of it. It becomes your total world."[4]

---

3. Ibid, p. 53.

4.5   Concentration on the task: Asteroids

The paradox of control

People enjoy the sense of exercising control in difficult situations; however, it's not possible to experience a feeling of control unless the outcome is unsure, meaning that the person's not actually in complete control. As Czikszentmihalyi says, "Only when a doubtful outcome is at stake, and one is able to influence that outcome, can a person really know she is in control."[5] This "paradox of control" is a key element of the enjoyment of game systems. How to offer meaningful choice to players, without offering complete control or an assured outcome, is a subject we will return to many times throughout this book.

The loss of self-consciousness

In everyday life, we are always monitoring how we appear to other people and protecting our self-esteem. In flow we are too involved in what we're doing to care about protecting the ego. "There is no room for self-scrutiny. Because enjoyable activities have clear goals, stable rules, and challenges well matched to skills, there is little opportunity for

the self to be threatened."[6] Although the flow experience is so engrossing that we forget our self-consciousness while we're engaged in it, after a flow activity is over, we generally emerge with a stronger self-concept. We know that we have succeeded in meeting a difficult challenge. So, for example, the musician feels at one with the harmony of the cosmos; the athlete moves at one with the team; the game player feels empowered by the efficacy of her strategies. Paradoxically, the self expands through acts of self-forgetfulness.

The transformation of time

"One of the most common descriptions of optimal experience is that time no longer seems to pass the way it ordinarily does," says Czikszentmihalyi. "Often hours seem to pass by in minutes; in general, most people report that time seems to pass much faster. But occasionally the reverse occurs: Ballet dancers describe how a difficult turn that takes less than a second in real time stretches out for what seems like minutes."[7] Digital games are notorious for sucking players in for hours on

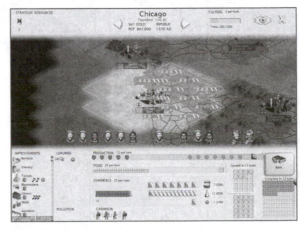

4.6   Paradox of control: Civilization 3

4. Ibid, p. 58-59.

5. Ibid, p. 61.

6. Ibid, p. 63.

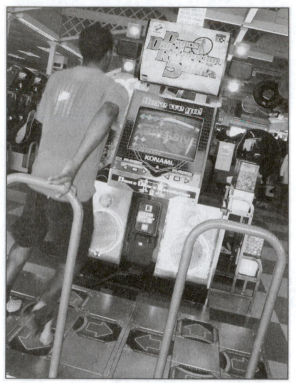

4.7   Loss of self-consciousness: Dance Dance Revolution

end because they involve players in flow experiences that distort the passage of time.

Experience becomes an end in itself

When most of these conditions are present, we begin to enjoy whatever it is that produces such an experience and the activity becomes *autotelic*, which is Greek for something that is an end in itself. Some activities such as art, music, and sports are usually *autotelic*: there is no reason for doing them except to enjoy the experience they provide. Most things in life are *exotelic*. We do them not because we enjoy them but in order to achieve

some goal. Games that achieve flow are both goal-based as well as enjoyable as an end in themselves.

These elements of enjoyment are not a step-by-step guide to creating enjoyable, challenging game experiences; you need to work out for yourself what these ideas mean in the context of your own games. But the focus that Czikszentmihalyi places on goal-oriented, rule-driven activities with clear focus and feedback are clues that might point you in a beneficial direction.

Think about questions like these as you design your game:

- What skills does your target audience have? What skill level are they at? Within that knowledge, how can you best balance your game for your players' abilities?

- How can you give your players clear, focused goals, meaningful choices, and discernible feedback?

- How can you merge what a player is doing physically with what they need to be thinking about in the game?

- How can you eliminate distractions and fear of failure, i.e., how can you create a safe environment, where players lose their sense of self-consciousness and focus only on the tasks at hand?

- How can you make the game activity enjoyable as an end in itself?

Answering these questions is a good first step toward creating an environment where challenge becomes a central attraction, rather than a feature that is too off-putting, or too simplistic to engage their emotions.

7. Ibid, p. 66.

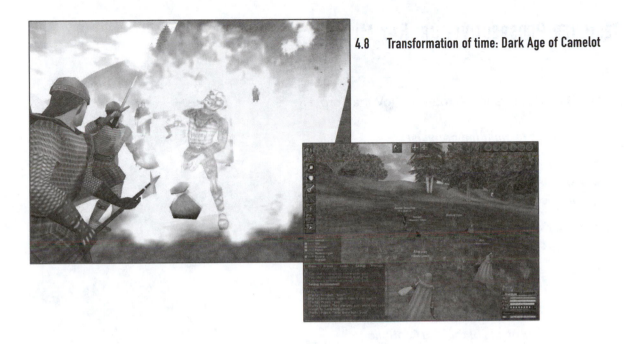

4.8   Transformation of time: Dark Age of Camelot

█   █   █   █   █

PLAY

Another element that engages players emotionally in games is the potential for play. Again, it's important to ask ourselves what we mean by "play" before we begin trying to design it into our games. Of course, we have all played at some point or another, so we all have our own ideas about what the experience is. But does everyone have the same experience as you? Is it possible that play means different things to different people?

The Promise of Play, a recent film investigating the subject, queried a number of people about the nature of play. Here are some of their responses: "Play is boisterous." "It's non directed." "It's spontaneous." "It's not scripted." "Play is loud." "Not work." "It's physical." "It's fun." "An emotional state when you're having a good time." "Play actually is meaningless behavior. You do it for its intrinsic value to you, but play can have utility. That is, you end up developing skills, and those skills can then be used in other arenas." "I think play is one of the ways that we get a feel for the shape of the world." "Play is the central item in children's lives. It's like work is to grown-ups. They play to learn." "Play is child's work. It's all that young children do to learn about the world that they're in."[8]

It's clear from these responses that play has many faces: it helps us learn skills and acquire knowledge, it lets us socialize, it assists us in problem solving, it allows us to relax, and it makes us see things differently. Play is not too serious; it induces laughter and fun, which is good for our health.

---

8. *The Promise of Play*, Institute for Play and InCA Productions, Executive Producers, Dr. Stuart Brown and David Kennard.

Designer Perspective: Dr. Ray Muzyka

Title

Joint CEO and Co-Executive Producer, BioWare Corp.

Project list (five to eight top projects)

- *Baldur's Gate*
- *Baldur's Gate: Tales of the Sword Coast*
- *MDK2*
- *Baldur's Gate II*
- *Baldur's Gate II: Throne of Bhaal*
- *Neverwinter Nights*
- *Neverwinter Nights: Shadows of Undrentide*
- *Neverwinter Nights: Hordes of the Underdark*
- *Star Wars: Knights of the Old Republic*

How did you get into the game industry?

My original background was training and practice as a medical doctor. Dr. Greg Zeschuk and I co-founded BioWare back in 1995 after working on the programming and art for a couple of medical education projects for our university. We met some talented programmers and artists who worked on what became BioWare's first game, *Shattered Steel*. We never looked back and now we have over 160 talented, smart, creative, hard-working employees at BioWare, working on three to six projects at any one time.

On the other hand, play can be somewhat serious: play as a process of experimentation—pushing boundaries and trying new things is an area of common ground for artists and scientists, as well as children. In fact it's one of the few areas where children are seen as experts with something to teach adults. Play is recognized as a way of achieving innovation and creativity because it helps us see things differently or achieve unexpected results. A playful approach can be applied to even the most serious or difficult subjects because playfulness is a state of mind rather than an action.

At the same time, Dr. Bernard Mergen, author of *Play and Playthings*, says, "I think that play enters into it when one doesn't expect a particular

What are your five favorite games and why?

My favorite games cover a lot of platforms and a long time period! Back in the early 1980s I was a big fan of some of the great role-playing franchises, such as *Wizardry* and *Ultima* on the Apple II. Later on, I was a big fan of games like *System Shock* and *Ultima Underworld* on the IBM PC. These too were role-playing games, revolutionary for their time in their interface, graphics, and storylines, and still worth playing. More recently I've enjoyed a number of console RPGs including *Final Fantasy VII*, *Chrono Cross*, and the *Zelda* series. I also enjoy a bunch of other types of games such as real-time strategy (*WarCraft II*, *StarCraft*, *Age of Empires*) and first person action games like *Halo*, *Battlefield: 1942* and *Half-Life*. All of these games share the common traits of being very good at what they set out to do—this is what we try to do in our games at BioWare; we try to make each game better than our last.

What games have inspired you the most as a designer and why?

Probably the same games that I've enjoyed playing over the years—all of them were revolutionary for their time. We play a lot of games and we try to learn from all of them.

What are you most proud of in your career?

We have great employees at BioWare—it's an honor for me to work with all of them.

What words of advice would you give to an aspiring designer today?

Be passionate, but self-critical. Never compromise on quality, but do realize that there is a point of diminishing returns on effort and a point where every game is "as good as you can make it." Most games never reach this point, but if they do, you'll increase the chances of it succeeding by a lot. And for those entrepreneurial types out there, hire smart, talented, creative, and hard-working staff to work with and make sure you treat them extremely well—videogames are not a solo endeavor and the team sizes required to keep the production values high enough for the increasingly sophisticated videogame audiences seem to grow larger every year.

result. Games, competitive games, which have a winner or a loser, are not, in my definition, play."[9]

The one thing that stands out from these meditations on play, is that play is not any one thing—but rather a state of mind, a type of approach to an activity. Dr. Mergen's comment that competitive games are not play touches on an interesting problem. We have said that games are formal systems, that they have strict and explicit rules, and that they are goal-based. Play, on the other hand, is clearly informal, and while it may have rules, it does not depend on those rules for its form, and it's also not driven by goals. So, the comment that games are not play seems

9. Dr. Bernard Mergen, *Play and Playthings* (Westport, CT: Greenwood Publishing Group, 1983)

somewhat accurate. Not *entirely* accurate, however, because we know that while games and play are not the same thing, play does have an important role in our enjoyment of games.

How does play, in all its spontaneity and informality, emerge from within the formal systems of games? In a number of ways, actually. First, some games are simply not so formal or competitive: social games played in not so serious environments lend themselves easily to outright playfulness. Examples might include *Twister* or *You Don't Know Jack*. Second, play can emerge in the "space between" rules, the give and take in the relationships between the game elements, such as the bantering interchange between players at a card table, or the aggressive trash talking on an online game server. Lastly, some games are designed to encourage certain types of play: Role-playing games promote playful fantasy and imagination, adventure games encourage exploration and daring, and sports games produce physicality and sometimes roughhousing. This last idea is worth further discussion, as it offers an active area for the game designer to explore.

Play theorists have identified a number of various types of "players," each with different needs and agendas. Not all of these areas have been thoroughly addressed by today's games, and they offer an interesting area of study for the game designer looking for new areas of play with which to emotionally engage players.

Here are examples of these potential player types:[10]

- *The Competitor:* plays to best other players, regardless of the game.
- *The Explorer:* curious about the world, loves to go adventuring. Explorers seek outside boundaries—physical or mental.

- *The Collector:* acquires items, trophies, or knowledge, the collector likes to create sets, organize history, etc.
- *The Achiever:* plays for varying levels of achievement. Ladders and levels incentivize the achiever.
- *The Joker:* doesn't take the game seriously—plays for the fun of playing. There's a potential for jokers to annoy serious players. On the other hand, jokers can make the game more social than competitive.
- *The Artist:* driven by creativity, creation, design.
- *The Director:* loves to be in charge, direct the play.
- *The Storyteller:* loves to create or live in worlds of fantasy and imagination.
- *The Performer:* loves to put on a show for others.
- *The Craftsman:* wants to build, craft, engineer, or puzzle things out.

Obviously this list includes only a few of the many potential types of players you may want to think about when crafting your gameplay. Combining various types of play into different player roles, as discussed in the previous chapter, is a way of designing games that can engage different types of people.

In addition to types of play, the level of engagement can also be broken down into several categories; not all players need participate at the same level to find the same enjoyment. For example, spectators may find watching sports, games, or other events more satisfying than playing them. We don't tend to think of designing games for spectators, but the truth is, many people use games in this way. How many times have you sat and watched a friend make their way through the

---

10. *The Promise of Play*

level of a console game, waiting for your turn at the controls? Is there a way as a designer to take this "spectator mode" into account when designing the play?

Participant play is the most common way to think about play. As opposed to spectator play, where risk is minimal, participant play is active and involved. It's also the most directly rewarding—for all the reasons we've already talked about.

On last level comes transformational play: this is a deep level of play which actually shapes and alters the player's life. Children experience this level when they learn life lessons through play; in fact, it's one of the reasons they engage in play naturally. Some attempts to create learning through

gameplay attempt to reach this level as well. It's an interesting area to think about if games are to advance as an art form. Certainly other forms of art inspire transformation and deep learning through their experience. Perhaps finding ways to create this level of play can raise the bar for game as an art form as well.

Exercise 4.5: Player Types

For each player type described on page 90, list a game you know that appeals to that variety of player. What type of player do you tend to be?

PREMISE

In addition to challenge and play, games also use several traditional elements of drama to create player engagement with their formal systems. One of the most basic is the concept of premise, which establishes the action of the game within a setting or metaphor. Without a dramatic premise, many games would be too abstract for players to become emotionally invested in their outcome.

Imagine playing a game in which you are a set of data. Your objective is to change your data to increase its values. To do this, you engage other sets of data according to complex interaction algorithms. If your data wins the analysis, you win. This all sounds pretty intangible and rather boring, but it's a description of how a typical combat system might work from a formal perspective. In order to connect players to the game emotionally, the game designer creates a dramatic premise for the interaction that overlays the formal system. In the previous example, let's imagine you play a dwarf named Gregor rather than a set of data. You engage an evil wizard, rather than an opposing set

of data, and you attack him with your broadsword, rather than initiating that complex interaction algorithm. Suddenly, the interaction between these two sets of data takes on a dramatic context over and above its formal aspects.

In traditional drama, premise is established in the exposition of a story. Exposition sets up the time and place, characters and relationships, the prevailing status quo, etc. Other important elements of story that may be addressed in the exposition are the problem, which is the event that upsets the status quo and creates the conflict; and the point of attack, which is the point at which the problem is introduced and the plot begins. While there's not a direct one-to-one relationship, these last two elements of exposition are mirrored in our definition of formal game elements by the concepts of objective and starting action discussed in the previous chapter.

To better understand premise, let's look at some examples from well-known stories from films and books rather than games:

In *Star Wars*, the story is set in a far away galaxy. The protagonist, Luke Skywalker, is a young man who wants to get away from his uncle's remote farm and join the interstellar rebellion, but responsibility and loyalty hold him back. The story begins when his uncle buys two droids carrying secret information that is critical to the rebellion.

In *The Fellowship of the Ring*, the story is set in Middle-earth, a fantasy world of strange races and characters. The protagonist, Frodo Baggins, is a young Hobbit who is happy right where he is—at home. The story begins when Frodo inherits a ring from his uncle, which turns out to be a powerful artifact, the existence of which threatens the safety of all of Middle-earth.

In *Die Hard*, the story is set in a modern office tower in downtown Los Angeles. The protagonist, John McClane, is an off-duty New York City police officer who is in the building trying to make amends with his estranged wife. The story begins when the building's taken over by terrorists and McClane's wife is taken hostage.

These are each examples of how premise is defined in traditional stories. As can be seen, the premise sets the time and place, the main character(s) and objective, as well as the action which propels the story forward.

Now, let's look at examples of premise from games that you may have played. In a game, the premise may be as complex as those previous, involving characters with dramatic motivations, or a game's premise may simply be a metaphor overlaying what would otherwise be an abstract system.

First, here is a very simple game premise: in *Space Invaders*, the game is set on a planet, presumably Earth, which is attacked by aliens. You play an anonymous protagonist responsible for

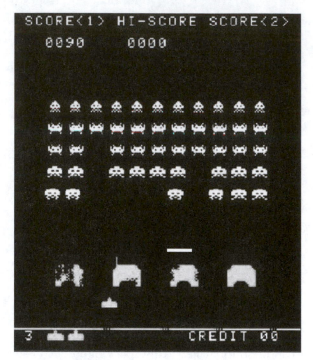

4.9   Space Invaders

defending the planet from the invaders. The story begins when the first shot is fired. Clearly this premise has none of the richness that we see in the earlier stories. It does, however, have a simplicity and effectiveness that made it very powerful as a game premise. No player needed to read the backstory of *Space Invaders* to feel the tension of the steadily approaching aliens.

Now, let's look at some games that have attempted to create somewhat more developed premises. In *Pitfall*, the game is set in the "deep recesses of a forbidden jungle."[11] You play Pitfall Harry, a "world famous jungle explorer and fortune hunter extraordinaire." Your goal is to explore the jungle and find hidden treasures, while surviving various hazards like holes, logs, crocodiles, quicksand, etc. The story begins when you enter the jungle.

---

11. Activision, *Pitfall instruction manual*, 1982.

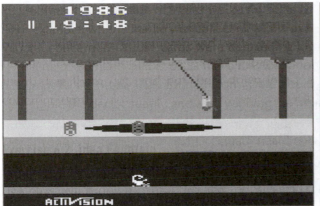 

4.10 Pitfall and Diablo

In *Diablo*, you play a wandering warrior who arrives in the town of Tristram, which has been ravaged by Diablo. The townspeople ask for your help in defeating Diablo and his undead army, ensconced in the dungeon beneath the church. The story begins when you accept the quest.

In *Myst*, the game is set on a strangely deserted island filled with arcane mechanical artifacts and puzzles. You play an anonymous protagonist with no knowledge of Myst Island or its inhabitants. The story begins when you meet Sirrus and Achenar, two brothers trapped in magical books in the island's library. The brothers, who accuse each other of betrayal, each need you to find some missing "pages" of their books to help them escape, but both warn you not to help the other brother.

Exercise 4.6: Premise

Write out the premise for five games that you've played and tell us how this premise enhances the game.

The first task of a premise is to make a game's formal system playable for the user. Rather than

shooting at abstract blocks on a screen, players shoot at aliens in *Space Invaders*. Rather than searching for a generic resource worth 5000 points, players look for diamond rings in *Pitfall*. Beyond simply concretizing abstract system concepts and making the game playable, a well-thought out premise can also create a game that appeals to players emotionally.

For example, the premise of *Myst* not only sends the player on a quest to find the missing pages of one or both of the brothers' magical books, but it also implies that the brothers are not to be trusted and one or both of them may be duping the player. This makes the experience richer for the player, who must determine, by clues found in each age, which, if either, brother to help.

Creating a premise that unifies the formal and dramatic elements is another opportunity for the game designer to heighten the experience of players. As digital games have evolved, more and more designers have begun to make use of more elaborate premises in their designs, which, as we'll see, have evolved to the point where they can be considered fully realized stories.

CHARACTER

Characters are the agents through whose actions a drama is told. By identifying with a character and the outcome of their goals, the audience internalizes the story's events and empathizes with its movement toward resolution.

There are a number of different character types in any story. The main character is called the protagonist. The protagonist's engagement with the problem creates the conflict that drives the story. Another important character is the antagonist, who opposes the main character's attempts to solve the problem. The antagonist may be a person or some other force that works against the main character. Characters may be major or minor: major characters have a significant impact on the story's outcome, while minor characters have a small impact.

In addition to function and impact on the story, characters can be classified by the complexity of their characterization. If a character has several well-defined traits and a realistic personality, it's considered a round character. If a character has few (if any) defined traits and a shallow personality, it's considered a flat character. If a character undergoes a significant change in personality, it's considered a dynamic character. If a character shows little or no change in personality, it's considered a static character. Stock characters are recognizable stereotypes: the lazy guard, the evil stepmother, the jolly doorman, etc. One useful type of character,

4.11 Myst

the foil, shows off elements of another character by comparison and contrast.

All characters are defined within the story by what they say, what they do, what they look like, or what others say about them. These are called methods of characterization. To better understand characters, let's look at some examples of characters in classic stories and in games.

Not to set our expectations too high, but let's first consider one of the most famous protagonists in English drama: Hamlet. He's one of the most complex characters ever constructed. Hamlet is a prince whose father, the king, is killed by his uncle. When the story begins, Hamlet's mother, the queen, has just married the uncle, making him king. Hamlet wants to avenge his father by killing the new king, but wavers between determination and inaction. His fascinating vacillation between the two courses has produced hundreds of years of study.

Without a doubt, Hamlet is an example of a "round" character. In contrast to Hamlet, another character in the same play, Prince Fortinbras, is "flat." Fortinbras has no defining traits and no complexity of character. When presented with a similar decision, Fortinbras simply avenges his father's death and moves on, without any of the soul-searching that plagues Hamlet. Fortinbras provides a foil, however, to Hamlet, which highlights Hamlet's inaction by showing us a character who has no dilemma with decision.

To date, there are no game protagonists with the fullness of character that we find in Hamlet. However, that may be partly because of the structure of the medium itself. Game characters that are controlled by the player do not always have the opportunity to act freely. The player is assuming responsibility for their actions, which limits the degree to which they can demonstrate their own personality and inner thought process. Game

characters also need to strike a balance between being flexible enough so that a wide range of players can identify with them, and being so flexible that they become generic and flat.

Early characters were completely defined by how they looked, with little or no attempt at characterization. Mario, in his first appearance in *Donkey Kong*, was defined by his funny nose and signature cap and overalls. While his motivation, rescuing Pauline, was integrated into both the formal and dramatic aspects of the game, he was ultimately a flat, static character, who did not change or grow over the course of the game. More importantly, Mario would not do anything to accomplish his goal without the player's control.

Some types of game characters are not flat, but both rounded and dynamic, in that they are specific and grow over the course of the game. Many examples of rounded, dynamic characters can be found in role-playing games, where the goal of the game is usually centered in the activity of character creation and improvement.

Sometimes, game characters are not entirely in the control of the player. Characters may have a sense of autonomy and this creates an interesting potential tension between what the player wants and what the character wants. A very early version of this autonomy is the character of Sonic the Hedgehog—Sega's answer to Mario. If the player stopped interacting with Sonic, the little hedgehog let the player know of his dissatisfaction by crossing his arms and tapping his feet impatiently. Impatience was central to Sonic's character: he did everything fast and had no time to spare. Unlike the blazingly fast actions controlled by the player, however, the toe-tapping routine was Sonic's own, and established him as a unique character.

Of course, Sonic's toe-tapping had no impact on gameplay, but the tension between player-controlled action and character-controlled action is an

4.12 **Digital game characters (clockwise from top left): Duke Nukem, Guybrush Threepwood, Munch, Link, Sonic the Hedgehog, Lara Croft, and Mario**
Guybrush Threepwood image courtesy of LucasArts, a division of Lucasfilm Entertainment Company Ltd.

interesting area that has been explored to great effect more recently in games like *The Sims, Oddworld: Munch's Oddysee,* and *Black & White*. If the feature "free will" is turned on in *The Sims*, characters will decide on their own course of action (assuming the player hasn't given them anything specific to do). Players can stop a character from performing an action at anytime, but with this feature on, the game usually unfolds as a complicated dance between what the player desires and what the character "wishes." This sophisticated model produces dramatic results that the player feels both responsible for and yet surprised by.

In general, game characters are evolving to become rounded, dynamic individuals that play an increasingly important part of many games' dramatic structures. A good understanding of how to create interesting and realistic characters using traditional dramatic tools can add to the effectiveness of characters in your games.

Exercise 4.7: Game Characters

Name three game characters that you find compelling. How are these characters brought to life within the game? What allows you to identify with them? Are they rounded or flat, dynamic or static?

STORY

Plays, movies, and television are all media that involve storytelling and linear narratives. When an audience participates in these media, they experience a story that progresses from one point to the

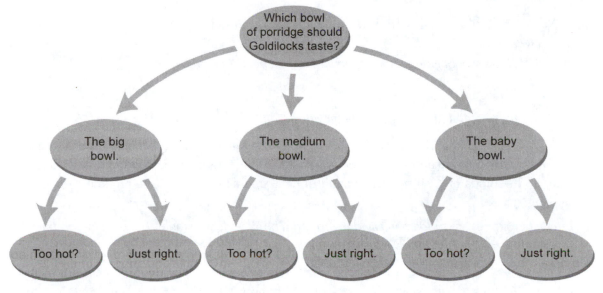

4.13 Branching story structure

next as determined by an author. The audience is not an interactive participant in these media and cannot change the outcome of the story. Game systems are essentially different in this respect: their players are interactive participants who can change the outcome of the game. Because of this, and because game systems are usually nonlinear, it's difficult to integrate traditional storylines into games.

In most games, story is actually limited to backstory: sort of an elaborate version of premise. The backstory gives a setting and context for the game's conflict, and it may create motivation for the characters, but its progression from one point to the next is not affected by gameplay. An example of this is the trend of inserting story chapters into the beginning of each game level, creating a linear progression that follows a traditional narrative arc interspersed with gameplay that does not affect how the story plays out. Games like the *War-Craft* or *StarCraft* series follow this model in their single-player modes. In these games, the story points are laid out at the beginning of a level, and

the player must succeed in order to move on to the next level and the next story point.

There are some game designers who are interested in allowing the game action to change the structure of the story, so that choices the player makes affect the eventual outcome. There are several ways of accomplishing this. The first, and simplest, is to create a "branching" storyline. Player choices feed into several possibilities at each juncture of a structure like this, causing predetermined changes to the story. The diagram in Figure 4.13 shows an example of this type of story structure using a simple fairytale story we are all familiar with.

One of the key problems with branching storylines is their limited scope. Player choices may be severely restricted in such a structure, causing the game to feel simplistic and unchallenging. In addition, some paths may create uninteresting outcomes. Many game designers feel there's better potential for use of story in games if the story emerges from gameplay, rather than from a predetermined structure. For

THE TWO GREAT MYTHS OF INTERACTIVE STORYTELLING

by Jesse Schell, Professor of Entertainment Technology, Carnegie Mellon University

Myth #1: Interactive Storytelling Has Little to Do with Traditional Storytelling

I would have thought that by this day and age, with story-based games taking in billions of dollars each year, this antiquated misconception would be obsolete and long forgotten. Sadly, it seems to spring up, weedlike, in the minds of each new generation of novice game designers. The argument generally goes like this:

> *"Interactive stories are fundamentally different from noninteractive stories, because in non-interactive stories, you are completely passive, just sitting there, as the stories plods on, with or without you."*

At this point, the speaker usually rolls back his or her eyes, lolls his or her tongue, and drools to underline the point.

> *"In interactive stories, on the other hand, you are active and involved, continually making decisions. You are doing things, not just passively observing them. Really, interactive storytelling is a fundamentally new art form, and as a result, interactive designers have little to learn from traditional storytellers."*

The idea that the mechanics of traditional storytelling, which are innate to the human ability to communicate, are somehow nullified by interactivity is absurd. It is a poorly told story that doesn't compel the listener to think and make decisions during the telling. When one is engaged in any kind of storyline, interactive or not, one is continually making decisions: "What will happen next?" "What should the hero do?" "Where did that rabbit go?" "Don't open that door!" The difference only comes in the participant's ability to *take* action. The *desire* to act, and all the thought and emotion that go with that are present in both. A masterful storyteller knows how to create this desire within a listener's mind, and then knows exactly how and when (and when not) to fulfill it. This skill translates well into interactive media, although it is made more difficult because the storyteller must predict, account for, respond to, and smoothly integrate the actions of the participant into the experience.

The way that skilled interactive storytellers manage this complexity, while still using traditional techniques, is through the means of *indirect control*, using subtle means to covertly limit the choices that a participant is likely to make. This way, masterful storytelling can be upheld, while the participant still retains a feeling of freedom. For it is this feeling of freedom, not freedom itself, which must be preserved to tell a compelling interactive story.

Myth #2: Interactive Storytelling Has Little to Do with Traditional Game Design

I am amazed by the vast number of would-be game designers who whine that while they are brimming with great game design ideas, they lack the large team required to implement these ideas, and therefore they are unable to practice their craft.

This is nonsense of the highest order. A game is a game is a game. The design process for a boardgame, a card game, a dice game, a party game, or an athletic game is no different from the process of designing a videogame. Further, a solo designer can fully develop working versions of these nonelectronic games in a relatively short time. Making and analyzing traditional games can often be far more instructive than trying to develop a fully functioning videogame. You can learn much more about game design in a much shorter time, and you won't have to concern yourself with the technical headaches and limitations involved with interactive digital media. If you really want to understand how to create good interactive entertainment, first study the classics, and then try to improve on them. Riddles, crossword puzzles, chess, poker, tag, soccer, and thousands of other beautifully designed interactive entertainment experiences existed long before the world even knew what a computer was.

To sum up: New technologies allow us to mix together stories and games in interesting ways, but there are very few elements that are fundamentally new—most designs are simply new mixtures of well-known elements. If you want to master the new world of interactive storytelling, you would be wise to first understand the games and stories of old.

Author Bio

Jesse Schell is a Professor of Entertainment Technology at Carnegie Mellon, specializing in game design. Formerly, he was Creative Director of the Walt Disney Imagineering VR Studio, where his job was to invent the future of interactive entertainment for the Walt Disney Company. Jesse worked and played there for seven years as designer, programmer, and manager on several projects for Disney theme parks and DisneyQuest (Disney's chain of VR entertainment centers). His most recent work at Disney involves design of family-friendly massively multiplayer worlds, such as Disney's Toontown Online.

example, in *The Sims*, players have used the basic elements provided by the formal system to create innumerable stories involving their game characters. The system provides features that support this emergent storytelling, including tools for taking snapshots of the gameplay, arranging the snapshots in a captioned scrapbook, and uploading the scrapbook to the web to share with other users.

In addition to simulation games, other genres are also addressing the possibility of designing for emergent storytelling. This includes games like *Black & White*, which combine elements of simulation with strategy and role-playing, as well as action games like *Half-Life*, which have "triggered" story sequences depending on player actions, and *Halo*, which uses artificial intelligence techniques in nonplayer characters to create unique and often dramatic responses to player actions.

While it remains to be seen if these attempts to allow emergent storytelling to arise out of formal game structures will have a significant impact on games, it's certain that game designers are still searching for better ways to integrate story into their systems without diminishing gameplay.

Exercise 4.8: Story

Pick a game that you feel successfully melds its storyline with the gameplay. Why does this game succeed? How does the plot unfold as the game progresses?

THE DRAMATIC ARC

We've looked at a number of key elements that can help to create player engagement with the game system. But the most important of these elements is actually one that we've talked about already, and that is conflict.

Conflict is at the heart of any good drama, and, as we've seen in our discussion of formal elements, it's at the heart of game systems. Meaningful conflict is not only designed to keep players from accomplishing their goals too easily, as we pointed out in the discussion of formal elements, but it also draws players into the game emotionally by creating a sense of tension as to the outcome. This dramatic tension is as important to the success of a game as it is to a great film or novel.

In traditional drama, conflict occurs when the protagonist faces a problem or obstacle that keeps her from accomplishing her goal. In the case of a story, the protagonist is usually the main character. In the case of a game, the protagonist may be the player, or a character that represents the player. The conflict that the player encounters may be against another player, a number of other players, obstacles within the game system, or other forces or dilemmas.

Traditional dramatic conflict can be broken down into categories such as character versus character, character versus nature, character versus machine, character versus self, character versus society, or character versus fate. As game designers, we might overlay another group of categories, which are player versus player, player versus game system, player versus multiple players, team versus team, etc. Thinking about game conflict in this way helps us to integrate a game's dramatic premise and its formal system, deepening the players' relationship to both.

Once the conflict is set in motion, it must escalate for the drama to be effective. Escalating conflict creates tension, and in most stories, the

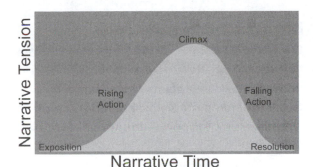

4.14 Classic dramatic arc

tension in a story gets worse before it gets better, resulting in a classic dramatic arc. This arc describes the amount of dramatic tension in the story as it progresses in time. Figure 4.14 shows how tension rises and falls during various stages of a typical story. This arc is the backbone of all dramatic media, including games.

As the figure shows, stories begin with exposition, which introduces the settings, characters, and concepts that will be important to the rest of the action. Conflict is introduced when the protagonist has a goal that's opposed by their environment, an antagonist, or both. The conflict, and the protagonist's attempt to resolve it, causes a series of events that lead to a rising action. This rising action leads to a climax, in which some sort of deciding factor or event is introduced. What happens in the climax determines the outcome of the drama. The climax is followed by a period of falling action, in which the conflict begins to resolve, and the resolution, or dénouement, in which it's finally resolved.

To better understand the classic arc, let's look at in terms of a simple story you are probably familiar with. In the movie *Jaws*, Sheriff Brody is the protagonist. His goal is to keep the people of Amity safe. The antagonist is the shark, who opposes Brody's goal by attacking the people of Amity. This creates a conflict between Brody and

the shark. Brody, who's afraid of the water, attempts to keep the people safe by keeping them out of the water, but this plan fails. The tension rises as the shark attacks more people, even threatening Brody's own children. Finally, Brody must face his fear and go out on the water to hunt down the shark. In the climax of the story, the shark attacks Brody himself. The story resolves when Brody kills the shark and returns the story to the status quo. Simple right? You can look at any story you know and you'll see the dramatic arc reflected in its structure.

Now, let's look at the arc again, this time in terms of a game. In a game, the rising action is linked to both the formal and dramatic systems. This is because games are usually designed to provide more challenge as they progress. Games that also have well-integrated dramatic elements will intertwine those elements with the formal system so that as the challenge rises, the story develops. Here's an example from a classic game: In *Donkey Kong*, Mario is the protagonist. Mario's girlfriend, Pauline, has been kidnapped by the giant ape, Donkey Kong, and taken to the top of a building under construction. Mario's goal is to save Pauline before time runs out. To do so, he must climb the levels of the building, traversing girders, elevators, and conveyer belts, while avoiding flames, barrels, and bouncing rivets thrown at him by Donkey Kong. Each time Mario reaches Pauline, Donkey Kong grabs her and carries her off to the next higher level. Each level builds in difficulty, creating rising tension for the player. Finally, in the climax of the game, Mario must not only avoid Donkey Kong's attacks, but also fight him directly by removing all the rivets on every floor of the level. After the rivets are removed, Donkey Kong falls head first onto a stack of girders and is knocked out, allowing Mario to rescue Pauline and resolve both the formal and dramatic tension.

It's clear from even these simple descriptions that the story in *Jaws* is more developed as to character and story—Brody has a fear which he must overcome in order to solve the problem, and his character changes in motivation as he goes from protecting all the people of Amity, to saving his own family, to defending himself from the shark. While Mario has a goal, and he's certainly vulnerable to attacks from Donkey Kong, he does not have any internal conflict that keeps him from completing his goal, and his goal never wavers. The jeopardy that Pauline is in never increases either, a touch that would have made the formal and dramatic systems of the game better integrated.

What Mario has that Brody does not, however, is that his success or failure is in the hands of the player. It's the player who must learn how to avoid the attacks, moving closer and closer to the goal. And in the climax of the game, it's the player who must figure out how to topple Donkey Kong from his perch and knock him out. So while our response to the climactic moment in *Jaws*, when Brody figures out how to finally kill the shark, is a release of tension built up by our empathy for his character and the character's struggles over the course of the story, our response to the climatic moment in *Donkey Kong* is quite different.

In the case of *Donkey Kong*, we are the ones who have figured out the crucial action needed to resolve the tension, and that tension has built up over a number of levels of play. When we finally resolve that tension, there's a sense of personal accomplishment on top of any sympathetic response that we might have to the resolution of Mario and Pauline's story. This integration of conflict in the formal and dramatic systems can clearly provide a powerful combination for the players in a game experience.

Exercise 4.9: Plotting a Story, Part 1

Choose a game that you've played all the way through. Make certain it's a game with a story involved. For example *Halo, Deus Ex, StarCraft*, and *Star Wars: Knights of the Old Republic*, might be good choices. Now, plot the story against the dramatic arc.

- How is the exposition handled?
- Who's the protagonist?
- What's the main conflict and when is it introduced?
- What does the protagonist do to resolve the conflict?
- What causes the tension in the story to rise?
- What deciding factor brings the story to a climax?
- What happens in the resolution?

Exercise 4.10: Plotting a Story, Part 2

Now, take the same game and plot the gameplay against the dramatic arc.

- What elements of gameplay, if any, support each of these points?
- How is the exposition of gameplay handled?
- Are controls and mechanics clearly explained?
- Are they integrated with the dramatic premise?
- Is the goal clearly stated and integrated with the main conflict of the story?
- How does the gameplay cause the dramatic tension to rise?
- What deciding factor in the gameplay brings the game to a climax?
- What happens in the resolution?
- Do the dramatic elements and gameplay elements help or hinder each other?
- How might they be better integrated to make the game work from an emotional standpoint?

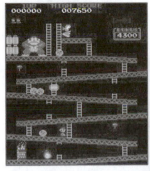

4.15 Donkey Kong

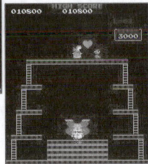

Exercise 4.11: Plotting a Story, Part 3

Take the same game and come up with three changes to the story or gameplay that you believe would make the two better integrated.

CONCLUSION

The elements of drama that we've looked at form the basis of a toolset that the game designer can use to elicit powerful emotional reactions from players. From integral game concepts like challenge and play, to complex integration of characters and narrative, these tools are only as powerful as the inspiration behind their use. Although the media palette of game design has grown to rival film and television, it's clear that the emotional impact of games still has not achieved the depths it is capable of, and which will make it recognized as an important dramatic art from.

What new areas of dramatic possibility do you see? What new ground will your designs break? To answer these questions, you must have a strong grasp of the tools of traditional drama and understanding of good gameplay and the process by which it can be achieved. Before going on to read about system dynamics in games, spend some time with the exercises in this chapter if you haven't already done so, since they're designed to help you practice with some of these traditional tools.

DESIGNER PERSPECTIVE: DON DAGLOW

Title

President, Stormfront Studios

Project list (five to eight top projects)

As Designer or Programmer/Designer:

- *Neverwinter Nights* (first massively multiplayer graphic RPG, published by AOL), 1991–1997
- *Tony La Russa Baseball* (Published by SSI, Maxis and EA on PC, Sega), 1991–1995
- *Earl Weaver Baseball* (Published by EA on PC, Amiga, with Eddie Dombrower), 1987
- *World Series Baseball* (first game to use multiple camera angles, published by Mattel for Intellivision, with Eddie Dombrower), 1983
- *Utopia* (the first sim game, published by Mattel for Intellivision), 1982

As Producer, Executive Producer, etc.:

- *The Lord of the Rings: The Two Towers* (Published by EA for PS2, Xbox, based on the Peter Jackson film from New Line Cinema), 2002
- *NASCAR Racing* (Published by EA Sports for PS, N64, and PC), 1996–1999
- *Racing Destruction Set* (Published by EA for PC, C64), 1985
- *Adventure Construction Set* (Published by EA for PC, Apple II), 1985

As Programmer/Designer on university computers before industry began:

- *Baseball* (the first computer baseball game, PDP-10, 1971–1974)
- *Star Trek* (PDP-10, 1972–1973)
- *Dungeon* (the first computer RPG, first game to display line of sight graphics, PDP-10, 1976–1978)

How did you get into the game industry?

I had been writing games as a hobby on the university mainframe through my college and grad school years, and then while I was a grad school instructor, teacher, and writer.

When Mattel started their in-house Intellivision game design team they advertised on the radio for programmers who wanted to learn how to create videogames. I'd never have thought of looking in the paper for a games job, but I heard the radio ad and called them. When I said "I don't have a computer science degree but I've been programming games for the last nine years" I think they thought I was making up stories, since *Pong* had only been out for about five years at the time.

Fortunately, it all worked out, and I was selected as one of the original five members of the Intellivision game design team at Mattel. As the team grew I ended up being director of Intellivision game development.

What are your five favorite games and why?

I have a hard time separating enjoyment from inspiration, so it's the same list as the one below.

What games have inspired you the most as a designer and why?

Seven Cities of Gold, design by Dan Bunten and Ozark Softscape, published by EA, 1984: Only a handful of resources to manage, and a gigantic map to explore for treasure. Proof that a simple concept with "few moving parts" on a primitive machine with basic graphics can be compelling if the tuning of challenge, suspense and reward is elegant and subtle.

The original *Super Mario Bros.* for Nintendo, design by Shigeru Miyamoto, 1985: The game style has been the subject of endless variations, but this game to me is the foundation on which all the others are built. Just the right balance of eye-hand coordination, environmental and enemy challenges, hidden goodies, and ongoing positive reinforcement made this a game that adults and kids could both play and love.

Sim City, design by Will Wright, published by Maxis, 1989: This game re-defined what a computer "game" could be, and was fun despite breaking many of the commonly accepted design commandments: it had no true opponents (apart from an occasional visit by Godzilla), a score with no clear methodology as to how you earned it, and no clear final goal so you could play for as long as you wanted. Will Wright persevered through repeated rejections before finding a publisher for one of the biggest hits in the history of the industry.

John Madden Football for Sega Genesis, design by Scott Orr and Rich Hilleman, published by EA, 1992: The first console version of *Madden Football* created a monster franchise in the industry, but what made it shine initially was a beautifully tuned head-to-head gameplay mechanic that made playing your buddies an incredibly fun way to pass an afternoon.

Metal Gear Solid 2 for PS2, published by Konami: The cinematic coverage of both stealth and combat advanced the use of cameras in our craft. Where *Final Fantasy* featured episodic tours de force, *Metal Gear Solid* started to blur the line between film and game.

Lord of the Rings: The Two Towers, design by LotR design team, developed by Stormfront Studios, published by EA, 2002 [conflict of interest note: our team created this game]: We started out talking about making the transition from a movie to a game seamless, so you reached a moment of interactivity thinking you were still watching a theatrical film. This is a dream many of us had discussed for years. Unlike many dreams, this time we actually pulled it off. Having now done it once, the result has inspired us about a much wider range of effects we can create in future games.

What are you most proud of in your career?

The fact that I was able to invent the first of several different kinds of games as a designer and programmer in the early years of the industry, and also led big teams that built hit games in the modern high-budget high-stakes era of publishing.

I'm also proud that it appears I've been designing and producing electronic games continuously longer than anyone else (since 1971), which if nothing else proves I'm persistent.

What words of advice would you give to an aspiring designer today?

Enjoy the journey, not just the wrap party.

I see many people enter our industry who are anxious to be the next Shigeru Miyamoto or Will Wright. Most well known designers are the product of the special cases of their era, and rarely are they well known in later phases of industry history. For every Miyamoto and Wright there are many designers who were once trumpeted in the industry press, but who have now faded from the scene and are forgotten.

If I look at the people who have had the most success in the industry over the last ten, fifteen, or twenty years, a simple truth emerges. You have to do what you love, and you have to keep growing as you do it, in all areas of your personal and professional skills.

If you love games and love the process of creating them, it will rub off on everyone around you. If you keep looking for how to do a task better than the last time you did it, you'll grow. Your career will still have ups and downs, but it will advance.

If you embark on a master plan to become a videogame celebrity by age 30, you stop thinking about building great games and start thinking about your personal pride. At that moment the energy that should be going into the craft of game design and execution instead goes into career planning. Which, of course, is the fastest way to sabotage your career.

The person who is unhappy until they achieve their goal spends most of their time unhappy.

The person who enjoys the journey towards the goal—and is resolute about reaching it—is happy most of the time.

Chapter 5
Working with System Dynamics

In the previous two chapters, we looked at games in terms of their formal and dramatic elements. Now, we'll look at how the elements of games fit together to form systems, and how designers can work with system properties to balance the dynamic nature of their games.

A system is defined as a set of interacting elements that form an integrated whole with a common goal or purpose. General system theory, the idea that the interaction among elements of systems can be studied across a wide variety of disci-

plines, was first proposed by the biologist Ludwig von Bertalanffy in the 1940s. Variations of system theory have evolved over time, each focusing on different types of systems. Our goal here is not to look at all the various disciplines of system theory but rather to investigate how we can use an understanding of basic system principles to control the quality of interactions within our game systems, as well as the growth and change of those systems over time.

GAMES AS SYSTEMS

Systems exist throughout the natural and man-made world wherever we see complex behavior emerging from the interaction between discrete elements. Systems can be found in many different forms. They may be mechanical, biological, or social in nature, among other possibilities. A system may be as simple as a stapler, or as complex as a government. In each case, when the system is put in motion, its elements interact to produce the desired goal, for example, stapling papers or governing society.

Games are also systems. At the heart of every game is a set of formal elements that, as we've

seen, when set in motion, creates a dynamic experience in which the players engage. Unlike most systems, however, it's not the goal of a game to create a product, perform a task, or simplify a process. The goal of a game is to entertain its participants. When we talked about formal and dramatic elements, we determined that games do this by creating a structured conflict and providing an entertaining process for players to resolve that conflict. How the interaction of the formal and dramatic elements is structured forms the game's underlying system and determines a great deal about the nature of the game and the experience of the players.

As we mentioned earlier, systems can be simple or complex. Systems may produce precise, predictable results, or they may produce widely varied, unpredictable effects. What type of system is best for your game? Only you can determine this. You may want to create a game in which there is a certain amount of predictability—in which case you might design a system with only one or two possible outcomes. On the other hand, you may want to create a very unpredictable system, in which there are countless possible outcomes, determined by the choices of the players and the interactions of the game elements.

In order to understand why it is that systems act in such different ways, and be able to control the type of system elements that impact the outcome of your own games, we need to first identify the basic elements of systems and look at what factors within these elements determine how a system acts in motion.

The basic elements of systems are objects, properties, behaviors, and relationships. Objects within the system interact with each other according to their properties, behaviors, and relationships, causing changes to the system state. How those changes are manifested depend on the nature of the objects and interactions.

Objects

Objects are the basic building blocks of a system. Systems can be thought of as a group of interrelated pieces called objects, which may be physical, abstract, or both, depending on the nature of the system. Examples of objects in games might be individual game pieces (such as the "king" or "queen" in chess), in-game concepts (such as the "bank" in *Monopoly*), the players themselves, or

representations of the players (such as the avatars in an online environment).

Areas or terrain can also be thought of as objects: the squares on a grid board or the yard lines on a playing field. These objects interact with other game objects in the same way that playing pieces do, and need to be defined with the same amount of consideration.

Objects are defined by their properties and behaviors. They are also defined by their relationships with other objects.

Properties

Properties are qualities or attributes that define physical or conceptual aspects of objects. Generally, these are a set of values that describe an object. For example, the attributes of a bishop include its color (white or black) and its location. The properties of a character in a role-playing game may be much more complex, including variables such as health, strength, dexterity, experience, level, as well as its location in the online environment, and even the artwork or other media associated with that object.

The properties of objects often form a mathematical kernel that can be essential to determining interactions of objects in a game system. The simplest types of game objects have very few properties, and those properties don't change based on gameplay. An example of this type of object would be the checkers in a checker game. Checkers have only three properties: color, location, and type. While the location of checkers changes, their color never does. The type of checker can change from "normal" to "king" if it reaches the other side of the board. These three areas completely define the properties of checkers.

What would be an example of a game object with more complex properties? How about a char-

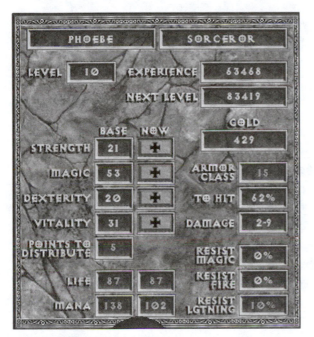

5.1   Diablo: character properties

acter in a role-playing game? Figure 5.1 shows the main properties of a character from *Diablo*.

As you can see, this list defines an object of much greater complexity than our first example. Also, the properties of this object change over the course of the game, and not in a simple binary way, like the checker. Because of its greater complexity, the object in this case will probably have less predictable relationships with other objects in the system than would a simple object like a checker.

Exercise 5.1: Objects and Properties

Choose a boardgame you have at home in which you are able to clearly identify the objects and their properties. Strategy boardgames often have objects with properties that are easy to identify. Make a list of all of the objects and their properties in the game you've chosen.

Behaviors

The next defining characteristics of objects in a system are their behaviors. Behaviors are the potential actions that an object might perform in a given state. The behaviors of the bishop in chess include moving along any of the diagonals radiating from its current position until it is blocked by or captures another piece. The behaviors of the role-playing character described previously might include walking, running, fighting, talking, using items, etc.

As with the sheer number of properties, the more potential behaviors an object has, the less predictable its actions within the system. For example, let's take the checkers example again. A "normal" checker has two potential behaviors: it can move diagonally one space, or jump diagonally to capture another piece. Its behavior is restricted by the following rules: it can only move towards the opponent; if it can jump an opponent's piece it must do so; and if possible, it can make multiple jumps in a turn. A "king" has the same behaviors, but it does not have the rule regarding moving toward the opponent; instead, it can move forwards or backwards on the board. This comprises all the potential behaviors of the checker objects in the game (obviously, a very limited set of behaviors, which result in a fairly predictable game pattern).

Now, let's look at the *Diablo* character again. What are the behaviors of this character? It can move: running or walking. It can attack using weapons in its inventory or skills like magic spells. It can pick up objects, converse with other characters, learn new skills, buy or trade objects, open doors or boxes, etc. Because of the range of behaviors available, the progression of this object through the game is much less predictable than the poor checker.

Does this make the game inherently more "fun," however? We'll discuss this later when we talk about playtesting; the fact is, the greater the complexity of gameplay does not always equate to more fun for the player, or a the better choice for all game designs. For now, it's simply important to note that the addition of more potential behaviors tends to add choice and lessen predictability of outcome in a game.

Exercise 5.2: Behaviors

Take the list of object and properties you created in Exercise 5.1 and add a description of the behaviors for each object. Consider all behaviors in different game states.

Relationships

As we mentioned earlier, systems also have relationships among their objects. This is a key concept in design. If there are no relationships between the objects in question, then you have a collection, not a system. For example, a stack of blank index cards is a collection. If you write numbers on the cards, or mark them in several suits, then you have created relationships among the cards. Removing the "3" card from a sequence of 12 will change the dynamics of a system which uses those cards.

Relationships can be expressed in a number of ways. A game played on a board might express relationships between objects based on location. Alternately, relationships between objects might be defined hierarchically, as in the numerical sequence of cards described previously. How relationships between objects in a system are defined

plays a large part in how the system develops when it's put in motion.

The hierarchy of cards is an example of a fixed relationship: the numerical values fix a logical relationship between each of the cards in the set. An example of a relationship that changes during gameplay is the movement of the checkers on our checkerboard: pieces move toward the other side of the board, jumping and capturing the opponent's pieces along the way. As they do so, their relationship to the board and to the other pieces on it continually changes.

Another example of a relationship is the progression of spaces on a boardgame like *Monopoly*. This is a fixed, linear relationship that constrains gameplay within a range of possibilities. On the other side of the spectrum, objects may have only loose relationships with other objects, interacting with them based on proximity or other variables. An example of this would be *The Sims*, where the relationships of the characters to other objects are based on their current needs and the ability of the objects in the environment to fulfill those needs. These relationships change as the characters' needs change; for instance, the refrigerator is more interesting to a character that's hungry, than a character who has just eaten a huge meal.

Change in relationships may also be introduced based on choices made by the players. The checkers game exhibits such change: players choose where to move their pieces on the board. There are other ways to introduce change into game relationships. Many games use an element of chance to change game relationships. A good example of this is seen in most combat algorithms. Here's an explanation of how the combat algorithm works in *WarCraft II*[1].

Each unit in the game has four properties that

---

1. http://www.battle.net/war2/basic/combat.shtml

determine how effective it is in combat.

- *Hit Points:* these indicate how much damage the unit can take before dying.

- *Armor:* this number reflects not only armor worn by the unit, but its innate resistance to damage.

- *Basic Damage:* this is how much normal damage the unit can inflict every time it attacks. Basic damage is lowered by the target's armor rating.

- *Piercing Damage:* this reflects how effective the unit is at bypassing armor. (Magical attacks, like dragon's breath and lightning, ignore armor.)

When one unit attacks another, the formula used to determine damage is: (Basic Damage – Target's Armor) + Piercing Damage = Maximum damage inflicted. The attacker does a random amount of damage from 50%–100% of this total each attack.

To see how this algorithm tends to introduce chance into the relationship between objects, or units as we've been calling them, let's look at an example from the strategy guide on Battle.net:

An ogre and a footman are engaged in combat. The ogre has a Basic Damage rating of 8, and a Piercing Damage rating of 4. The footman has an Armor value of 2. Every time the ogre attacks the footman, it has the potential to inflict up to (8 – 2) + 4 = 10 points of damage, or it could inflict as little as 50% damage, or 5 points. On average, the ogre will kill the footman in about 8 swings.

The poor footman, on the other hand, with a Basic Damage of 6 and a Piercing Damage of 3, will only inflict 3 or 5 points of damage each time he attacks the ogre, which has an Armor

5.2 **WarCraft II: going up against an ogre**

value of 4 [that's (6 – 4) + 3 = 5]. Even if the footman is extremely lucky and does the maximum amount of damage with every attack, it will take 18 swings to kill that 90 Hit Point ogre. By that time, the ogre will have pounded him into mincemeat and moved on.

This example actually shows two ways of determining relationships: chance and rule sets. As can be seen by the calculation, there's a basic rule set determining the range within which damage can fall. Once that range is set, however, chance determines the final outcome. Some games tend more toward chance in their calculations, while others tend more toward rule-based calculations. Which method is best for your game depends on the experience you want to achieve.

Exercise 5.3: Relationships

Take the list of objects, properties and behaviors you created in Exercised 5.1 and 5.2 and describe the relationships between each object. How are these relationships defined? By position? By power? By value?

SYSTEM DYNAMICS

As we've noted, the elements of systems do not work in isolation from each other. If you can take components away from a system without affecting its functioning and relationships, then you have a collection, not a system. A system, by definition requires that all elements be present in order for it to accomplish its goal.

Also, a system's components must typically be arranged in a specific way for it to carry out its purpose, i.e., to provide the intended challenge to the players. If that arrangement is changed, the results of the interaction will change. Depending on the nature of the relationships in the system, the change in results may be unnoticeable, or it may be catastrophic, but there will be a change to some degree.

Let's say that our example on page 111 of the ogre and the footman from *WarCraft II* was changed; instead of using the properties of basic damage, piercing damage and target's armor to determine the range of potential damage from an attack, let's assume the range for each unit was just a random number between 1 and 20. How would this change the outcome of each individual battle? How would it change the overall outcome of the game? What about the value of resources and upgrades?

If you said that the element of chance in the game would increase in both individual combat encounters and overall outcome, you are right. Also, the value of resources and the upgrades available via those resources would sink dramatically, since upgrades to units and armor would mean nothing in terms of determining outcome. The only strategy open to players in this game would be to build as many units as possible, as sheer numbers would still overwhelm in battle. So

by changing the relationship between units in combat, we have changed the overall nature of the *WarCraft II* system.

Another important feature to understand about the interaction of systems is that systems are greater than the sum of their parts. By this we mean that studying all of the individual qualities of each system element in isolation does not equal studying these elements in relationship to each other. This is important for game designers to realize, as games can only be understood during play when their dynamics become evident.

Exactly how the dynamics of any given game system are affected by the properties, attributes and relationships of its objects is difficult to generalize. A good way to understand how these elements can affect each other is to look at some example systems—ranging from very simple to fairly complex—that exhibit various types of dynamic behavior.

Tic-tac-toe

The objects in tic-tac-toe are the spaces on the board. There are nine of them, and they are defined by their properties, behaviors, and relationships. For example, their properties, are "null," "x" or "o." Their relationships are defined by location. There is one center space, four corners and four sides. When the game begins, the relationship between the spaces is such that there are only three meaningful choices for the first player: center, corner or side.

The second player has between two or five meaningful choices—depending on where the first player put an "x." You can see by the diagram of potential moves, that playing the first "x" in the center reduces the amount of significant next

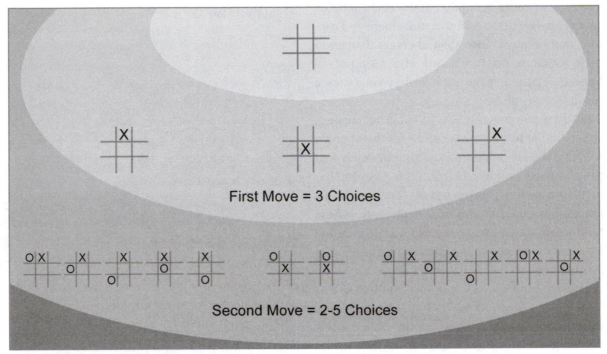

First Move = 3 Choices

Second Move = 2-5 Choices

5.3   Partial tic-tac-toe game tree

moves to 2. Playing the first "x" in a corner or on a side creates up to 5 next moves.

If we continued this diagram of tic-tac-toe out to its conclusion, we would see that the "tree" of possibilities is not very large. In fact, once you learn the best possible moves to make, you can always win or tie at this game because of its ultimate simplicity. What is it about tic-tac-toe that makes its system so easy to learn?

First, we cans see that the game objects themselves are simple: they have only three properties and one behavior. Also, their relationships to each other are fixed: the locations of the spaces on the board do not change. Because of both the objects and their relationships, the system has only a few possible outcomes, and these are all fairly predictable. And as a result of its limited possibilities for play, tic-tac-toe tends to lose the interest of players

once they learn the optimal moves for any given situation.

Chess

An example of a system that has more than one type of object, and more complex behaviors and relationships between objects is chess. First, let's look at the objects in chess: there are six types of units, plus 64 unique spaces on the board.

Each unit has several properties: color, location, and value. For instance, the white queen has a value of nine[2] and a beginning location of D1 (the space at the intersection of the fourth rank of the first file). Alone, these properties do not make the objects in chess more complex than the spaces on the tic-tac-toe board. However, the varied behaviors of and relationships between the objects do

---

2. Some chess texts and programs use different values for the various pieces. This is the standard value given by most texts.

make them more complex. Since each unit has specific behaviors in terms of movement and capture, and because those abilities create changes to their locations on the board, the relationships between each unit are effectively changed as a result of every move.

While it is theoretically possible to create a "tree" similar to the one we drew for the opening moves of tic-tac-toe, it quickly becomes clear that the complexity of potential outcomes beyond the first few moves makes this a useless and physically impossible process. This is not the way players tend to approach the game, and it's not even the way that computer chess applications have been programmed to decide the best move.

Rather, both players and successful programs tend to use pattern recognition to solve problems, calling up solutions from memories of previously played games (or a database in the case of the computer), rather than plotting out an optimal solution for each move. This is because the elements of the game system, once set in motion, create such a large range of possible situations that the tree becomes too complex to be useful.

Why does chess have such a vast number of possible outcomes as opposed to tic-tac-toe? The answer lies in the combination of the simple, but varied, behaviors of the game objects and their changing relationships to each other on the board. Because of the extremely varied possibility set, chess remains challenging and interesting to players long after they have mastered its basic rule set.

One of the most important aspects of a game is the sense of "possibility" that is presented to the players at any given time. As we discussed in the previous chapter when talking about challenge, the goal of the designer is to present a situation that is equal to the abilities of the players, and yet grows in challenge over time with their abilities. It's clear from the two examples that how a system is constructed dramatically changes the dynamics

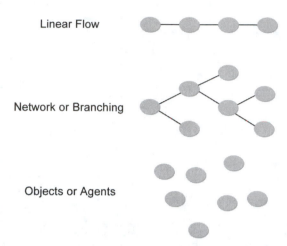

5.4   Various game structures

of that system over time and the range of possibilities that face the player at any given point.

The range and type of possibilities within the system is not a situation where "more is better" in all situations. Many successful games have a somewhat constrained set of possibilities, and yet still offer interesting gameplay. For example, a linear boardgame like *Trivial Pursuit* has very small possibility space in terms of outcome, but the overall challenge of the game is not affected by this. Some console games, like side-scrollers, have a similarly small range of possibilities: you either successfully navigate the challenge or you're stuck. But this range of action works for these types of games. Story-based adventure games often have branching structures with a limited number of outcomes. For players of these games, navigating that defined set of possibilities is part of the challenge.

On the other hand, some new games are attempting to create larger and larger ranges of possibility for their systems. Simulation games (like *The Sims*), real-time strategy games, and massively multiplayer worlds, all use an approach to game systems that focuses on looser, changeable relationships between objects, along with less defined behaviors and goals. This tends to create a larger possibility space for the player and makes for more complex, re-playable game systems—an advantage to capturing a certain type of game player.

There's no one correct way to design a game system, just as there's no one type of game player. But you may find upon analyzing some of your favorite games that they share successful system designs in terms of the properties, behaviors, and relationships of their objects. Studying how the dynamics of these systems work can help focus your own thoughts and explorations.

Exercise 5.4: System Dynamics

Now let's take the game you've been working with in Exercises 5.1, 5.2, and 5.3 and see how we can change the system dynamics by experimenting with the properties, behaviors or relationships of its core objects.

1. For example, if you chose a game like *Monopoly*, change the prices, placement and rent of every property on the board, or change the rules for movement. How you change these things them is up to you, but make significant changes.

2. Now, play the game. What happens? Did your changes affect the balance of the game? Is the game still playable?

3. If the system is still playable, make another change. For instance, take out all the "positive" Chance cards in Monopoly and leave in only "negative or neutral" cards. Play the game again. What happens?

4. Continue doing this exercise until the game is no longer playable.

What was the crucial change you made? Why do you think that change finally "broke" the game?

One important type of system structure often found in games is an economy. We're going to look more closely at this structure because it involves dynamics surrounding the resources in a game, one of the fundamental formal elements of games.

Economies

What is an economy? As we touched on briefly in our discussion of the utility and scarcity of resources in Chapter 3, some games also allow for the exchange of resources—either with the system (i.e., the "bank" in *Monopoly*) or among players. When a game allows exchanges of this kind, the system of trade forms a simple economy. In more complex systems, the rules of real-world economies may apply, but more often, games have severely controlled economies that only vaguely resemble real-world markets. Even so, there are some basic concepts of economic theory that we can use as a barometer for the feasibility of our game economies.

First of all, to have an economy, a game must have items of exchange, such as resources or other barterable items; agents of exchange, such as players or the system bank; and methods of exchange, such as markets or other trading opportunities. Also, an economy may or may not have currency, which helps to facilitate trade. As in the real world, the methods by which prices are set in an economy depend on what type of market controls are in place. Prices of market items in games may be free, fixed or subject to a mixture of controls, depending on the design of the system. Also, the opportunities players have for trade can range from complete freedom to controls on prices, timing, partners, amount, etc. Here are some basic questions a designer should ask before building a game economy:

- Does the size of the economy grow over the course of the game? For example, are resources produced, and if so, is the growth controlled by the system?

- If there's a currency, how is the supply of that currency controlled?

- How are prices set in the economy? Are they controlled by market forces or set by the game system?

- Are there any restrictions on opportunities for trade among participants; for instance by turn, time, cost or other constraints?

To get a sense for how games handle these economic variables, let's look at some examples, ranging from classic boardgames to massively multiplayer online worlds.

Simple bartering

Pit is a simple card game in which players barter for various commodities in order to "corner the market." There are eight suits of commodities, nine cards in each suit. The commodities are worth a varying number of points from 50–100. For example, oranges are worth 50 points, oats are 60 points, corn is 75, wheat is 100, etc. You start with

5.5   Pit

the same number of suits in the deck as there are players—from three to eight. The cards are shuffled and dealt out evenly to all the players. During each round, players trade by calling out the number of cards they want to trade, but not the name of the commodity on the cards offered. Trade continues until one person holds all nine cards of a single commodity—a "corner" on that market.

There are several features to note in this simple barter system. First, the amount of product (i.e., cards) in the system is stable at all times—cards are not created or consumed during play. Additionally, the value of each card never changes relative to the other cards in the deck. The value is fixed by the printed point value set before the game begins. Also, the opportunity to trade is only restricted by number—all trades must be for an equal number of cards. Other than this, trade is open to all players at all times.

In this simple barter system, the in-game economy is so restricted by the rules of the game that there is no opportunity for economic growth, no fluctuation of prices based on supply and demand, no chance for market competition, etc. However, the trading system serves its purpose as an excuse for creating a frenetic, social trading atmosphere without any of the complexities of a real-world economy. To recap the features of this system:

- Amount of product = fixed
- Money supply = n/a
- Prices = fixed
- Trading opportunities = not restricted

Complex bartering

Settlers of Catan is a German boardgame by designer Klaus Teuber in which players compete as pioneers developing a new land. During the course of the game, players build roads and settlements that produce resources such as brick, wood, wool, rock, and wheat. These resources can be traded with other players and used to build more settlements and upgrade settlements to cities, which in turn produce more resources.

As in *Pit*, the bartering of resources is a central part of the gameplay, and the trade in this game is also fairly unrestricted—with the following exceptions:

- You may only trade with a player on their turn.
- Players can only trade resources—not settlements or other game objects.
- A trade must involve at least one resource on each side (i.e., a player can't simply give a resource away). However, trades can be made for unequal amounts of resources.

Other than these constraints, players can wheel and deal as they like for the resources they need. For example, if there is a scarcity of brick in the economy, players can trade two or three of another resource, such as wheat, for one brick.

As you can probably judge already, the economy of *Settlers of Catan* is much more complex than the simple barter system of *Pit*. One of the key differences is the fact that the relative values of the resources fluctuate depending on market conditions, an interesting and unpredictable feature that changes the experience of the game from play to play. If there is a glut of wheat in the game, the value of wheat falls immediately. On the other hand, if there is a scarcity of ore, players will trade aggressively for it. This simple example of the laws of supply and demand adds a fascinating aspect to gameplay that we did not see in the *Pit* example.

Another key difference from the simple bartering in *Pit* is that in *Settlers of Catan* the total amount of product in the economy changes over the course of the game. Each player's turn has a production phase, the results of which are determined by a roll of the dice and the placement of player settlements. Product enters the system during this phase. Product is then traded and "consumed" (used to purchase road, settlements, etc.) during the second phase of the players turn.

In order to control the total amount of product in the system at any time, the system includes a punishment for holding too many resources in your hand. If a player rolls a seven during the production phase of their turn, any player holding more than seven cards has to give half of their hand to the bank. In this way, players are discouraged from hoarding, and encouraged to spend their resources as they earn them.

Another aspect of the economy that is interesting to note is the fact that while the barter system is fairly open, there is a control on price inflation. The bank will always trade 4:1 for any resource; this effectively caps the value of all resources. And, as we also noted, while the trading system itself is quite open, the opportunity to trade is restricted by player turn.

The last difference between these two barter systems is their information structures. In *Settlers of Catan*, players hide their hands, but the production phase is an open process, so by simply paying attention to which players are getting certain resources on each turn, an attentive player can remember some, if not all, of the game state.

- Amount of product = controlled growth
- Money supply = n/a
- Prices = market value w/cap
- Trading opportunities = restricted by turn

Exercise 5.6: Bartering Systems

For this exercise, take the simple barter game of *Pit* and add a new level of complexity to its trading system. One way to do this might be to create the concept of dynamically changing values for each of the commodities.

5.6   Barterable resources from Settlers of Catan

Simple market

The first two examples we've looked at have both been barter systems (i.e., they didn't employ currency). The next type of system we'll look at is the simple market system of *Monopoly*. In *Monopoly*, players buy, sell, rent, and improve real estate in an attempt to become the richest player in the game. The real estate market in the game is finite—there are 28 properties in the market (including railroads and utilities) at all times. Although properties aren't sold until a player lands on their board space, they are still active in the sense that they are available for purchase.

Each player begins the game with $1,500 from the bank, which they can use to purchase properties or pay rent and other fees. The growth of the economy is controlled by the rate at which players can circle the board, passing "go" to collect $200. According to the official rules, the bank never goes broke; if it runs out of money, the player act-

ing as banker can create new notes out of slips of paper.

In terms of trading opportunities, the rules state that buying and trading of properties between players can occur at any time, although "etiquette suggests that such transactions occur only between the turns of other players."[3]

Values of properties in the game are set in two basic ways. First, there is the face value on the title deed; if a player lands on a property, she may purchase it for this amount. If she fails to purchase the property, it goes up to auction and sells to the highest bidder. The auction is not limited by the face value, and the player who passed up purchasing it may bid in the auction. Once a property is purchased, it may be traded between players at any price they agree upon. So, the second and more important value of properties in the game is a true market value set by the competition of the players.

- Amount of product = fixed
- Money supply = controlled growth
- Prices = market value
- Trading opportunities = not restricted

Complex market

For examples of complex market economies, we'll look at two games: *Ultima Online* and *EverQuest*. The two economies have much in common overall, but different emphases in their designs have created unique situations for each system. The key similarity in these and other online worlds is the fact that they have persistent economies that surpass a single game session by any one player. This immediately puts them in a category of complexity far beyond all the other examples we have looked

---

3.   Parker Brothers, *Monopoly* Deluxe Edition rules sheet, 1995.

5.7   Monopoly money and property

complex items than those gained by labor. Items like weapons, armor, and magic items are part of a complex "goods" market.

In both games, goods and labor are traded in two ways: player to player, and player to system. In both games, player to system trade, controlled by the game designers, exists to keep low-level "employment" steady while encouraging the player to player trade in scarce items. For example, shopkeepers will generally buy anything a player wants to sell—even if there is a glut of the object in the market. This keeps newbies steadily "employed." On the other hand, the shopkeepers' offers to buy on higher-level items will not be as competitive as the player to player market, encouraging players to seek out higher prices from one another.

In this way, the games create markets that mimic real-world situations in important ways, and contradict real-world expectations in others. Supply and demand is a factor for players dealing at higher levels of commerce, with scarce or unique items, but it is not a factor for a newbie just trying to get ahead.

The amount of product in the system is controlled by the game designers—although *Ultima* at first tried to create a self-regulating flow in which resources were recycled through the system, available to re-spawn as new creatures and other materials as they were "spent" by the players. This was quickly changed to a system in which the flow of resources into the economy could be directly controlled by the designers. There were several reasons for this, one of which was a tendency for players to "hoard" game objects, restricting the total amount of products circulating in the game.

In both games, a "meta economy" has emerged separate from official gameplay in which characters and game objects are sold between players in real-world markets. Characters have

at so far. The assumption often is that because of the persistence of economy in these games and because they strive to create a sense of an alternate world, that real world economics apply directly to their systems.

In both games, players create characters, or avatars, which begin the game with a small number of resources—a little gold in *Ultima* or platinum in *EverQuest*, some minimal armor and a weapon. Now players must enter the "labor market" to gain more resources. In both games, players begin at the lowest level of the labor market—killing small animals or doing other menial work to earn money. They can sell the results of their labor to system agents (in the form of shopkeepers) or to other players, if they can find interested buyers. In addition to the labor market, players can find, make, buy, or sell more

DESIGNER PERSPECTIVE: ALAN R. MOON

Alan Moon is a prolific designer of board and card games. His games are particularly popular in Europe.

Title: Game Designer

Project list (five to eight top projects)

- *Elfenland:* Spiel des Jahres (German Game of the Year) 1998
- *Das Amulett:* Spiel des Jahres nominee 2001
- *Union Pacific:* Spiel des Jahres nominee 1999
- *Capitol:* Spiel des Jahres selection list 2001
- *San Marco:* Spiel des Jahres selection list 2001
- *Reibach & Co.:* Spiel des Jahres selection list 1996
- dozens of other board and card games

How did you get into the game industry?

I was hired by the Avalon Hill Game Co. in Baltimore to takeover as editor of their house magazine called *The General.* But I never really assumed that job, because when I got to Avalon Hill I started working on developing games. I loved working on games, hated editing. After working as a developer, I also started designing games. Four years later, I left Avalon Hill to go to Parker Brothers in Beverly, Massachusetts as a designer in their video division.

What are your five favorite games and why?

- *Spades:* Best partnership card game ever invented. Endlessly fascinating. Even if you are dealt the worst hand possible, you must still play it well and use it to score as many points a possible.

- *Hunters & Gatherers* (second *Carcassonne* game by Hans im Glueck): On your turn, you draw a tile and play it, and then you can place one of your Meeples or not. That's all you do. But the game is constantly tense and exciting. Every game is different and you always feel like you can win right up until the end.

- *Adel Verpflichtet* (originally F.X. Schmid and Avalon Hill, now ALEA and Rio Grande): Sort of advanced "rock, paper, scissors." Each turn, the five players initially choose one of two locations, dividing themselves into two groups. Then the players in each group compete against each other. The ultimate game about player tendencies and psychology. You have to learn to play against your natural inclinations or you'll become too predictable. Gets better and better the more you play with the same people.

- *Liars Dice / Bluff* (originally Milton Bradley & F.X. Schmid, now Ravensburger and Endless Games): A dice version of the game gamblers play with dollar bills. The dice just provide the mechanic though, as there is little or no luck involved.
- *Crokinole* (Generic): Never thought I'd like an action game or a flicking game. But this one is totally addictive. Most people get better with practice too, which makes the game rewarding as well as fun.

What games have inspired you the most as a designer and why?

When I was a kid, my family played games every Sunday. I can still remember games of hearts, *Risk*, and *Facts in Five*. Hearts and bridge were the foundation for my love of card games, which has grown ever since. My friend Richard Borg described the fascination if cards the best when he said, "Every five or ten minutes you get a new hand, a new chance to get that all-time best hand." *Risk* led to more complex historical simulations, most published by Avalon Hill. European games retain the strategy and decision making of these more complex games, but add the social element of multiplayer, more interactive games, and that is what really keeps me playing and designing games. But if I had to pick one game that inspired me the most, it would be *Acquire* by Sid Sackson. Sadly Sid died last year, but he will always be the dean of game designers. My first big boardgame *Airlines* (Abacus, 1990) was inspired by *Acquire*.

What are you most proud of in your career?

I guess I'm proud of all the friends I've made through games, and the network of contacts I've built up in the toy and game industry. I may never be wealthy, but I'll always be rich in friends. But someday, I hope to be proud of the best game I've ever designed. It just hasn't happened yet.

What words of advice would you give to an aspiring designer today?

Play as many games as you can. It's research. It's the only way you learn. You can't design games in a vacuum, without knowing what has already been done, what's worked, and what hasn't worked. The idea for almost all games comes from other games. Sometimes you play a bad game with one good idea. Sometimes you play a good game and find a new twist to a good idea. Keep playing. Keep designing. Be confident, but remember that there is always more to learn. Like everything, you'll get better with practice. It took me fourteen years to have any real success as a designer. Those fourteen years were tough, but they were worth it.

Playtest your designs as much as possible. Develop a core group of playtesters. You also need to learn when it's time to let something go and work on something else, and when you should keep plugging even though it doesn't seem like the game is ever going to work. Being a game designer is much more than just being creative. You need to be organized, thorough, and flexible. You'll also need to be a good salesman because designing a game is just half the battle. You still have to sell it to someone after that.

been offered on sites such as eBay and Yahoo! Auctions, sometimes selling for hundreds of dollars, depending on the level and inventory offered. While this meta economy was not a planned feature of these role-playing games, there are games that have included the concept of a meta economy in their designs.

- Amount of product = controlled growth
- Money supply = controlled growth
- Prices = market value w/base
- Trading opportunities = not restricted

Meta economy

Magic: The Gathering is somewhat different from the other example games we've looked at, in that the game itself does not include a trading or exchange component. The main system of *Magic* is a dueling game, in which players use custom-designed decks of cards to battle each other. These cards, purchased by individual players, form the central resource in a "meta economy" surrounding the game itself.

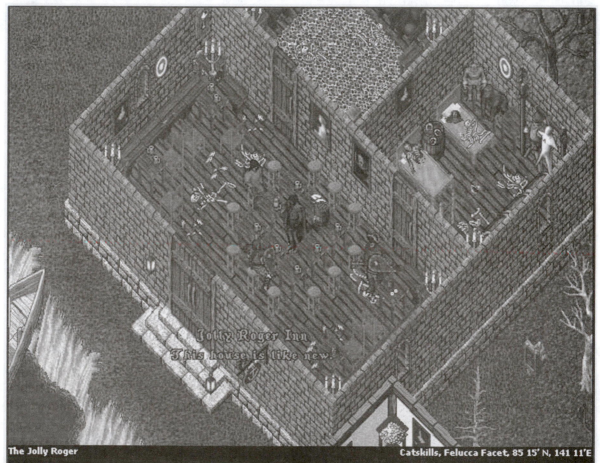

The Jolly Roger   Catskills, Felucca Facet, 85 15' N, 141 11'E

The Jolly Roger Tavern, a dirty but legendary tavern, is the heart of the town of Red Skull Bay and home to fighting contests and some of the best ale in all Britannia. Landlubbers and sailors alike are invited to have a look at this unique bay, and raise a bottle of ale or two with the residents of Red Skull Bay.

5.8   Player-run establishment in Ultima Online

Magic: The Gathering was designed by Richard Garfield and released by Wizards of the Coast, a Seattle-based game company, in 1993. At the time, Garfield was a mathematics professor at Whitman College as well as a part-time game designer. Wizards asked him to design a card game that was quick, fun, and playable in under an hour. But Garfield imagined a game that had the collectible nature of trading cards or marbles, combined with the qualities of *Strat-O-Matic Baseball*—in which players draft and compete their own teams. The result was a collectible card game that has been likened to "gaming crack."

As mentioned, the game Garfield designed is a two-player dueling game with a fantasy theme. Each player has a deck of cards that consists of various spells, monsters, and lands. Land provides mana, which powers spells. These spells summon monsters that you use to attack your opponent. This would seem pretty straightforward, except for the fact that a basic deck of game cards doesn't include all the cards in the system. In fact, it contains a mere fraction of the cards available. Players are encouraged to buy booster sets, and to upgrade their deck as new revisions are released. And, important to our discussion of game economies, players can also buy and trade cards from each other, which they do aggressively. The market for *Magic* cards, and other similar trading game cards, is worldwide, now greatly facilitated by the Internet.

The publisher of the game has control of the overall shape of this economy, in that they gauge how many cards to release—some cards are very rare, some are just uncommon, and others are not valuable at all, because there are simply far too many of them available. But the publisher has no control over where and how these cards are traded, once they have been purchased; and,

other than rarity, they have no control over the prices set for these game objects.

In addition to the collectible nature of *Magic*, and the meta economy formed by the trade of its game objects, there is an in-game aspect to this meta economy. Players choose cards from their collection to build decks, adjusting the amount of land, the type of creatures and spells in order to strike a winning balance.

This process of building and testing decks for effectiveness is similar to the process a game designer would go through when testing the balance of their system, and, of course, the designers of *Magic* do work hard to make sure that any single cards or combinations of cards are not so overpowered as to imbalance the game. But the final decisions regarding resource balance are left in the hands of the player, and are highly affected by the meta economy surrounding the game.

The openness of the *Magic* system, and its success as a business as well as a game, has spawned a whole genre of trading games. As with the current interest in online worlds, it's clear that much of the success of these future games will depend on how their in-game and metagame economies are managed over time.

- Amount of product = controlled growth
- Money supply = n/a
- Prices = market value
- Trading opportunities = not restricted

As you can see, there are a wide variety of economies, ranging from simple bartering to complex markets. The task of the designer is to wed the economic system with the game's overall structure. The economy must tie directly into the player's objective in the game and be balanced against the comparative utility and scarcity of the resources it involves. Every action the player

5.9   Magic: The Gathering cards

performs in relation to the economic system should either advance or hinder their progress in the game.

Economies have the potential to transform rudimentary games into complex systems, and if you're creative, you can use them as a way to get players to interact with one another. There's nothing better for community building than an underlying economy, which makes socializing into a game.

Developing new types of in-game economies is one of the areas in which modern game design has just begun to explore the potential. Even with the success of *EverQuest*, we're just beginning to understand the power of these systems. The fusing of economic models and social interaction is one of the most promising areas for future game

experimentation, and in the next decade, we will see new types of Internet-based games emerge that challenge our conception of what a game can be.

Emergent systems

We've talked about how game systems can display very complex behaviors when set in motion. But this doesn't mean that their underlying systems must be complex in design. In fact, in many cases, simple rules, when set in motion, can beget complex results. Nature is full of examples of this phenomenon, which is called "emergence."

An individual ant is a simple creature—capable of very little by itself and living its life according to a simple set of rules. However, when many ants interact together in a colony, each following these simple rules, a spontaneous intelligence emerges. Collectively the drone ants become capable of sophisticated engineering, defense, food storage, etc. Similarly, some researchers believe that human consciousness may be a product of emergence. In this case millions of simple "agents" in the mind interact to create rational thought. The topic of emergence has spawned dozens of books exploring links between previously unconnected natural phenomena.

One experiment in emergence, which is interesting for game designers, is called the Game of Life. (No, it's not related to Milton Bradley's boardgame *The Game of Life*.) This experiment was conducted in the 1960s by a mathematician at Cambridge University named John Conway. He was fascinated with the idea that rudimentary elements working together according to simple rules could produce fantastic results. He wanted to create an example of this phenomenon so simple that it could be observed in a two-dimensional space like a checkerboard.

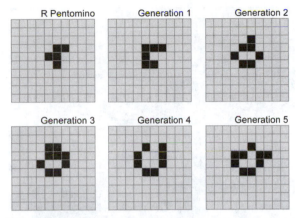

5.10   R Pentomino over several generations

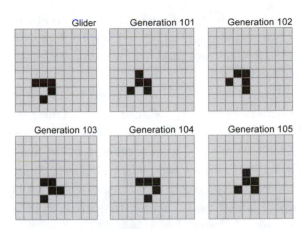

5.11   Glider "walk" cycle

Building on the work of mathematicians before him, Conway toyed with rules that would make squares on the board turn "on" or "off" based on their adjacency to the other squares around them. Acting very much like a game creator, he designed, tested, and revised different sets of rules for these cells for several years with several associates in his department at Cambridge.

Finally he arrived at this set of rules:

- *Birth:* if an unpopulated cell is surrounded by exactly three populated cells, it becomes populated in the next generation.

- *Death by Loneliness:* if a populated cell is surrounded by fewer than two other populated cells it becomes unpopulated in the next generation.

- *Death by Overpopulation:* if a populated cell is surrounded by at least four other populated cells it becomes unpopulated in the next generation.

Conway and his associates set Go pieces on a checkerboard board to mark populated cells and administered the rules by hand. They found that different starting conditions evolved in vastly dif-

ferent ways. Some simple starting conditions could blossom into beautiful patterns that would fill the board and some elaborate starting conditions could fizzle into nothing. An interesting discovery was made with a configuration called R Pentomino. Figure 5.10 shows the starting position for the R Pentomino, followed by several generations.

One of Conway's associates, Richard Guy, kept experimenting with this configuration. He administered the rules for a hundred generations or so and watched a mishmash of shapes appear. Then, suddenly a set of cells emerged from the group and appeared to "walk" on it's own across the board. Guy pointed out to the group, "Look, my bit's walking!"[4] Guy worked on the configuration until it "walked" across the room and out the door. He had discovered what the group would call a "glider." A glider is a configuration that cycles through a set of shapes and moves along the board as it goes. Figure 5.11 shows what several generations of Guy's glider look like.

Conway's system was dubbed the Game of Life, as it showed that from simple beginnings life-form-like patterns could develop. There are a

4.   William Poundstone, *Prisoner's Dilemma* (New York: Doubleday, 1992)

number of emulators online that you can download and experiment with. You'll see that some use different rules and allow you to create your own starting conditions.

Emergent systems are interesting to game designers because games can employ emergent techniques to make more believable and unpredictable scenarios. Games as different as *The Sims*, *Grand Theft Auto 3*, *Halo*, *Black & White*, *Pikmin*, *Munch's Oddysee*, and *Metal Gear Solid 2* have all experimented with emergent properties in their designs.

One recent example is the character AI in *Halo*. Nonplayer characters have three simple impulses that drive them: (1) perception of the world around them (aural, visual, and tactile), (2) state of the world (memories of enemy sightings and weapon locations) and (3) emotion (growing scared when under attack, etc.).[5] These three sets of rules interact—each consulting the other—as a decision-making system in a character. The result is semirealistic behavior within the game. The non-characters do not follow a script written by a designer but rather make their own decisions based on the situation they're in. For instance, if all of their friends have been killed and they're facing overwhelming firepower from the enemy, they tend to run away; otherwise, they stay and fight.

Different games utilize different methods for creating emergent behavior. *The Sims* embeds

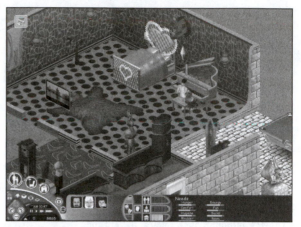

5.12   The Sims

simple rules in both the characters and in items in the environment. Will Wright, creator of *The Sims*, built the household items in the game to have values. When a character gets near an item—such as a bed, refrigerator, or pinball machine—the rules in the character interact with the rules in the items. So if a character's rules say he's sleepy, then an item that provides comfort, such as a bed, may attract his attention.

All of the previous examples share the same basic concept that simple rules beget complex behavior when interacting within a system. This concept is an exciting and fast moving aspect of games today, and it's wide open to experimentation and innovation.

INTERACTING WITH SYSTEMS

Games are designed for player interaction, and the structures of their systems are integrally related to the nature of that interaction. Some of the things that need to be considered when designing for interaction are:

- How much information do players have about the state of the system?
- What aspects of the system do players control?
- How is that control structured?

5.   Steven Johnson, "Wild Things," *Wired* issue 10.03.

- What type of feedback does the system give the players?
- How does this affect the gameplay?

Information structure

In order for players to make choices about how to proceed in a game, they need information about the state of the game objects and their current relationships to each other. The less information players have, the less informed their choices will be. This affects the sense of control they have over their progress. It can also add to the amount of chance in the system and allow space for misinformation or deception as a part of the gameplay.

To understand the importance of information in a game system, think about what types of information you're given in some of the games that you like to play. Do you know the effect of every move you make? What about the other players? Is there information that you only have access to some of the time?

How information is structured in a game has a large influence on how players come to their decisions. In classic strategy games like chess and Go, the players have complete information about the game state. This is an example of an open information structure. An open structure emphasizes player knowledge and gives full disclosure on the game state. It will generally allow for more calculation-based strategy in the system. If this is the type of play you want to encourage in your system, you need to make sure that important information is available to your users.

On the other hand, if you want to create play situations built around guessing, bluffing, or deceiving, you may want to consider hiding information from players. In a hidden information structure, players do not receive certain data about their opponent's game state. A good example of this is the 5-card stud variation of poker—in which all cards are dealt facing down. In this game, the only information players have about their opponents' hands is how many cards they are dealt and the way in which they bet. This hidden information structure allows for a different type of strategy to develop—one based on social cues and deception rather than calculation. And it tends to appeal to an entirely different type of player.

Exercise 5.7: Hidden Information

Many strategy games have open information structures that allow the players access to perfect information about the game state. Examples are chess, checkers, Go, mancala, etc. Take a game with an open information structure and change the system so that there's an element of hidden information. You may need to add new concepts to the game to accomplish this.

Test your new design. How does adding hidden information change the nature of the strategy? Why do you think this is so?

Many games use a mixture of open and hidden information, so that players are given some data about the state of their opponent's game, but not all. An example of such a mixed information structure might be the "7-card stud" variation of poker, where several cards are dealt down and several up over the course of the betting cycle, giving players only partial information about their opponents' hands. Another example of a mixed information structure is blackjack, for the same reasons.

The amount of information that players receive about their opponents' states often changes during the course of the game. This may because they have learned information by interacting with their opponents, or it may be because the concept of a dynamic information structure is built into the game. For example, real-time strategy games, like the *WarCraft* series, use the concept of "fog of war" to provide dynamically changing information to players about their opponents' status. In this game, players can see the state of their opponents' territory if they move a unit into that territory. Once they move the unit out of the territory, the information freezes until another unit ventures back to the territory.

A dynamically changing information structure provides an ever-shifting balance between strategy based on knowledge, and strategy based on cunning and deceit. For the most part, this type of advanced information structure has only been possible since the advent of digital games and the computer's ability to orchestrate the complex interactions between players.

Exercise 5.8: Information Structures

What type of information structures are present in *Unreal Tournament*, *Age of Empires*, *Jak II*, *Madden 2004*, *Lemmings*, *Scrabble*, *Mastermind*, and *Clue*? Do they have open, hidden, mixed or dynamic information structures? If you don't know one of the games, pick a game that we haven't mentioned and substitute it.

Control

The basic controls of a game system are directly related to its physical design. Boardgames or card games offer control by direct manipulations of their equipment. Computer games may use a keyboard, mouse, joystick, or alternate types of control devices. Platform games usually provide a proprietary controller. Arcade games often use game-specific controls. Each of these types of controls is best suited to certain types of input. Because of this, games that require specific input

types have been more successful in some game platforms than others. For example, games that require text entry have not been as popular on consoles as they have been on PCs.

The range of control types for games is extreme, everything from pencil and paper to flight simulations with mock cockpits. The arcade simulation games of Yu Suzuki, for example, offer realistic controls shaped like full-scale motorcycles and racing cars. Some games have as their goal to make control of game systems as realistic and responsive as possible. Others provide a more abstract, less-realistic control system.

One type of control system is not inherently better than another. What matters is whether or not the control system is well suited for the game experience, and it's the job of the designer to determine this. We encourage you to think about the games you like to play. What type of controls do you enjoy? Do you prefer to have direct control over the game elements, such as you might have when moving your character through a 3-D shooter? Or indirect control, as in a game like *SimCity*? Do you prefer real-time control, like in *WarCraft*, or turn-based control, as in *Warlords II*? These decisions will have a huge impact on what type of game you design and how you go about structuring it.

Direct control of movement is a clear-cut way for players to influence the state of the game. Players may also have direct control over other types of input, like selection of items, directly presented choices, etc. Some games do not offer direct control, however. For instance, in a simulation game like *Rollercoaster Tycoon*, players do not have direct control over the guests at their theme park. Instead, players can change ride variables, trying to make certain rides more attractive by lowering price, increasing throughput, or improving the ride design. This "indirect control" offers ways for players to influence the state of the game that is one step removed from the desired changes and provides an interesting type of challenge within certain game systems.

When the designer chooses what type of control to offer to players, he is deciding a very important part of the game. This decision forms the top-level experience that players will have with the system. Control often involves a repetitive process or action performed throughout a game. If this basic action is hard to perform, unintuitive, or just not enjoyable, the player may stop playing the game altogether.

In addition to deciding the level of control, the designer also needs to consider restricting control of some elements completely. As we discussed when we talked about designing conflict, games are made challenging by the fact that the players cannot simply take the simplest route to a solution. This is true in terms of designing controls as well. Some games allow a high degree of freedom in terms of player control. For example, a 3D shooter allows for spontaneous, real-time movement throughout the environment. Other games restrain player control tightly, using this structure to provide part of the challenge. An example of

this would be a turn-based strategy game, like Go or chess.

How do you decide what controls to allow players and what not to allow? This is a central part of the design process. You can see the impact different levels of input have on games if you look at a familiar game and imagine how it would work if you took away some of the player input.

For example, let's look at a real-time strategy game like *WarCraft II*. In this game, the player selects certain units to mine gold, others to chop trees, etc. How many units are doing these tasks at any given time is a function of availability, but is basically under the player's control. What if this opportunity for control was taken away? Imagine how the system would work if the designer determined that system would always assign 50% of the available units to mine gold and 50% to chop trees. How would taking this input away from the player affect the system? Would it create too much balance between various players' resources? Would it take away some tedious parts of gameplay? Or would it take away critical resource management? These are questions a designer faces when thinking about how much and what type of control to give players into the system.

5.13 Indirect control: Rollercoaster Tycoon

Exercise 5.9: Control

For the same games mentioned in Exercise 5.7, describe the methods of control they use: direct/indirect, real-time/turn-based. Are there any cases in which these distinctions are mixed?

Feedback

Another aspect of interaction with the system is feedback. When we use the word "feedback" in general conversation, we often are just referring to the information we get back during an

Score **+** Free Turn   Score **−** Pass Turn

5.14 **Positive and negative feedback loops**

interaction—not what we do with it. But in system terms, feedback implies a direct relationship between the output of an interaction and a change to another system element. Feedback can be "positive" or "negative," and it may promote divergence or balance in the system.

Figure 5.14 shows example feedback loops for two different types of game scoring systems. In the first example, if a player scores a point, they get a free turn. This reinforces the positive effects of the scored point, creating an advantage for that player. A negative feedback loop, on the other hand, like that on the right, works against the effect of the point. In this example, every time a player scores a point, they must pass the turn to the other player. This has the effect of balancing the system between the two players, rather than allowing one player to get a larger advantage over the other.

"Positive" and "negative" are somewhat loaded terms, and some systems theories use the terms "reinforcing" and "balancing" instead. Generally, reinforcing relationships are ones in which a change to one element directly causes a change to another element in the same direction. This may force the system toward one or the other extreme. By contrast, in balancing relationships, a change to

one element causes a change to another in the opposite direction, forcing the system toward equilibrium.

For example, in the game *Jeopardy!* when a player answers a question correctly, they retain control of the board. This presumably gives the leading player an advantage in answering the next question, reinforcing their lead in the game and moving the system toward resolution in their favor. This is a reinforcing relationship, or loop. An example of the same type of relationship, but in the opposite extreme, would be if a *Jeopardy!* player who answered incorrectly was forced to sit out the next question. This is not a rule in the game, but if it were, it would reinforce the repercussions of answering a question wrong.

Reinforcing loops cause output that either steadily grows or declines. Many games use reinforcing loops to create satisfying risk/reward scenarios for players which drive the game toward an unequal outcome based on player choices. In order to keep the game from resolving too quickly however, balancing relationships are also used.

Balancing relationships, on the other hand, try to counteract the effects of change. In a balancing relationship, a change to one element results to a

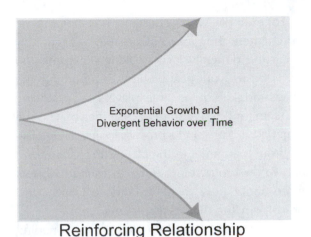

Reinforcing Relationship
or Positive Feedback

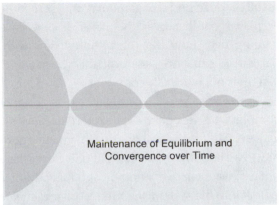

Balancing Relationship
or Negative Feedback

5.15 Reinforcing and balancing relationships over time

change in another element in the opposite direction. The classic example of a balancing relationship is in football. When one team scores, the ball is turned over to the other team. This gives a boost to the nonscoring team, attempting to balance the effects of the points won. If the advantage was given to the scoring team instead, it would be an example of a reinforcing relationship.

Some balancing relationships are not as easy to distinguish. For example, the boardgame *Settlers of Catan* has a procedure that attempts to create balance in the number of resources each player may hold at any one time. In this game, every time a seven is rolled with two six-side dice, any players holding more than seven cards in their hand must give up half of them. This has the effect of keeping prosperous players from becoming too powerful and resolving the game too quickly.

In order to improve gameplay, a good designer must be able to evaluate how quickly or slowly the game is progressing, understand if there are patterns to growth or contraction in the system caused by reinforcing loops, and know when and how to apply a balancing factor.

TUNING GAME SYSTEMS

As mentioned earlier, the only way to fully understand a system is to study it as a whole, and that means putting it in motion. Because of this, once a game designer has defined the elements of their system, they need to playtest and tune their system. They do this first by playing the game themselves, possibly with other designers, and then by playing with other players, who are not part of the design process. There are several key things that a designer is looking for when balancing a game system.

First, she needs to test to make sure that the system is internally complete. This means that the rules address any loopholes that could possibly arise during play. A system that's not internally complete creates situations that either block players from resolving the conflict or allow players to circumvent the intended conflict. This can result in "dead ends" of gameplay and, sometimes, in player conflict over the rules. If players are arguing over how the rules should deal with a particular situation, it's probably because the system is not internally complete.

Once the system is judged to be internally complete, the designer will next test for fairness. A game is fair if it gives all players an equal opportunity to achieve the game goals. If one player has an unfair advantage over another, and that advantage is built into the system, the others will feel cheated and lose interest in the system.

Once a system is internally complete and fair for all players, the designer must test to make sure the game is fun and challenging to play. This is an elusive goal that means different things to every individual game player. When testing for fun and challenge, it's important to test the game with its intended audience of players. Generally, this is not the designer or the designer's friends.

For example, when a designer is testing a game for children, they may not be able to accurately judge the difficulty level, making the game too hard for its young audience. Determining the needs and skills of the target players and balancing a system for them requires a clear idea of who the target players are, and a process for involving players from that target in the playtesting. Chapters 7 and 8, on prototyping and playtesting, will talk more about how to identify those players and bring them into the design process.

Testing for fun and challenge is an ongoing process that will continue throughout the production of a game. When the designer finds problems with the system, he makes changes to address the problems and playtests again. This is a very important part of a game designer's job, which we'll address in detail in Chapters 9 and 10.

CONCLUSION

We've looked at the basic elements of game system and seen how the nature of the objects, properties, behaviors and relationships create different dynamics of interaction, change, and growth. We've looked at how player interaction with these elements can be affected by the structures of information, control, and feedback.

One of the challenges in designing and tuning game systems is to isolate what objects or relationships are causing problems in gameplay and to make changes that fix the issue without creating new problems. When the elements are all working together, what emerges is great gameplay. It is the job of the game designer to create that perfect blend of elements that when set in motion, produce the varieties of gameplay that bring players back time and again.

A Conversation with Will Wright

by Celia Pearce

Will Wright is co-founder of game developer Maxis, Inc. He's famous for thinking outside the box with his game creations and is the mind behind SimCity, The Sims, *and many other hit titles. When Will started work on* The Sims *publishers tried dissuade him from the project on the grounds that no one would play such a game.* The Sims *is the current best-selling title of all time. This is an excerpt of a conversation between Will and game designer/researcher, Celia Pearce. The full discussion appears in the online journal "Game Studies" at http://www.gamestudies.org/0102/pearce/. It is reprinted here with permission.*

On Why He Designs Games

Celia Pearce: *I wanted to start out by talking about why you design games. What is it about the format of an interactive experience that is so compelling to you? And what do you want to create in that space?*

Will Wright: Well, one thing I've always really enjoyed is making things. Out of whatever. It started with modeling as a kid, building models. When computers came along, I started learning programming and realizing the computer was this great tool for making things, making models, dynamic models, and behaviors, not just static models. I think when I started doing games I really wanted to carry that to the next step, to the player, so that you give the player a tool so that they can create things. And then you give them some context for that creation. You know, what is it, what kind of kind of world does it live in, what's its purpose? What are you trying to do with this thing that you're creating? To really put the player in the design role. And the actual world is reactive to their design. So they design something that the little world inside the computer reacts to. And then they have to revisit the design and redesign it, or tear it down and build another one, whatever it is. So I guess what really draws me to interactive entertainment and the thing that I try to keep focused on is enabling the creativity of the player. Giving them a pretty large solution space to solve the problem within the game. So the game represents this problem landscape. Most games have small solution landscapes, so there's one possible solution and one way to solve it. Other games, the games that tend to be more creative, have a much larger solution space, so you can potentially solve this problem in a way that nobody else has. If you're building a solution, how large that solution space is gives the player a much stronger feeling of empathy. If they know that what they've done is unique to them, they tend to care for it a lot more. I think that's the direction I tend to come from.

On the influences of SimCity

CP: When you were first working on *SimCity*, what was going on in the game world at that time? Were you responding to games that were out there, were you wanting something different? Were there things that influenced you at all in the game world or were you just totally in a different mindset?

WW: There were things that influenced me—not many though. There was a very old game called *Pinball Construction Set* by Bill Budge, which was great. He was kind of playing around with the first pre-Mac Lisa interface, which was icon-based. He actually put this in the game, even though it was an Apple II game. He kind of emulated what would later become the Mac interface. But it was very easy to use, and you would create pinball sets with it, which you could then play with. I thought that was very cool.

Also early modeling things, like the very first flight simulator by Bruce Artwick which had this little micro-world in the computer with its own rules, kind of near reality to some degree, but at a very low resolution. But yet it was this little self-consistent world that you could go fly around in and interact with, in sort of limited ways.

So those are some of the influences. But then mostly, stuff I read. I started getting interested in the idea of simulation. I started reading the early work of people like Jay Forrester, starting with that, going forward. When I did *SimCity*, the games at the time really were much more about arcade style action, graphics, very intense kinds of experiences. There were very few games that were laid back, more complex.

CP: They were more twitch-type games at that time?

WW: Yeah, the games that were more complex were these detailed war games. I had played those as a kid, these boardgames. With 40-page rule sets.

CP: Like what?

WW: Oh, like *Panzer Blitz* was a big one, *Global War, Sniper.*

CP: Were those ones with the hex-grid boards?

WW: Yeah, they had a 40-page rulebook, and you'd play with your friend. And it ended up being... I mean, I think it would be excellent training for a lawyer. Because you're sitting there, most of the time, arguing over interpretations of these very elaborate rules. And you could actually combine the rules and say, "well, this was in panic mode so he couldn't go that far." "Well, my indirect fire has a three-hex radius of destruction." So you'd sit there and argue over this little minutia of the rules. And that was kind of half the fun of it—both of you trying to find the legal loopholes for why your guy didn't get killed. So I was familiar with that stuff, but I knew at the same time that most people couldn't relate to that at all. But yet the strategy of those games was actually quite interesting. It was interesting to have a game where you'd sit back and you'd think about it, and the model was far more elaborate than you could really run in your head. So you had to approach it kind of in a different way.

On Experimentation as a Play Mechanic

CP: *I wanted to ask you about this idea of experimentation as a play mechanic. That seems like a big aspect of your games, that play and experimentation are working together.*

WW: The types of games we do are simulation based and so there is this really elaborate simulation of some aspect of reality. As a player, a lot of what you're trying to do is reverse engineer the simulation. You're trying to solve problems within the system, you're trying to solve traffic in *SimCity*, or get somebody in *The Sims* to get married or whatever. The more accurately you can model that simulation in your head, the better your strategies are going to be going forward. So what we're trying to do as designers is build up these mental models in the player. The computer is just an incremental step, an intermediate model to the model in the player's head. The player has to be able to bootstrap themselves into understanding that model. You've got this elaborate system with thousands of variables, and you can't just dump it on the user or else they're totally lost. So we usually try to think in terms of, what's a simpler metaphor that somebody can approach this with? What's the simplest mental model that you can walk up to one of these games and start playing it, and at least understand the basics? Now it might be the wrong model, but it still has to bootstrap into your learning process. So for most of our games, there's some overt metaphor that allows you approach the simulation.

CP: *Like?*

WW: Like for *SimCity*, most people see it as kind of a train set. You look at the box and you say "Oh, yeah, it's like a train set come to life." Or *The Sims*, "it's like a doll house come to life." But at the same time, when you start playing the game, and the dynamics become more apparent to you, a lot of time there's an underlying metaphor that's not so apparent. Like in *SimCity*, if you really think about playing the game, it's more like gardening. So you're kind of tilling the soil, and fertilizing it, and then things pop up and they surprise you, and occasionally you have to go in and weed the garden, and then you maybe think about expanding it, and so on. So the actual process of playing *SimCity* is really closer to gardening. In either case, your mental model of the simulation is constantly evolving. And in fact you can look at somebody's city that they designed at any point and see that it's kind of a snapshot of their current understanding of the model. You can tell by what they've done in the game—"Oh, I see they think this freeway is going to help them because they put it over here." So it gives you some insight into their mental model of the game.

CP: *What's the underlying metaphor of The Sims? The less obvious one, the garden-level one?*

WW: That depends on how you play the game. For a lot of people, the mainstream game is more like juggling, or balancing plates. You start realizing that you basically don't have enough time in the day to do everything that you want to do. And you're rushing from this to that to this, and then you're able to make these time decisions. So it feels very much like juggling and if you drop a ball, then all of a sudden, the whole pile comes crashing down. But other people play it differently. So it's kind of hard. With *The Sims* I've thought about that, and it's not as clear to me what *The Sims* is. I think that *SimCity* has a more monolithic play style, once people get into it, than *The Sims* does. In *The Sims* people tend to veer off in a different direction. Some people go off into the storytelling thing. So eventually the metaphor becomes that of a director on a set. You're trying to coerce these actors into doing what you want them to do, but they're busy leading their own lives. And so you get this weird conflict going on between you and *The Sims* where you're trying to tell a story with the game but they want to go off and eat, and watch TV, and do whatever.

CP: *Like real actors.*

WW: Yes, exactly. Kind of like little actors who just won't do what you want them to do.

On His Favorite Game

CP: *Let's shift gears a little here and talk about your favorite games. And not just limiting it to computer games, but any games you like. What's your favorite game?*

WW: My favorite game by far probably is *Go*. The boardgame.

CP: *That's no surprise to me.*

WW: (Laughs.) That game is just so elegant in that it's got two rules really, one of which is almost never used. But yet from those two rules flow this incredible complexity. It's kind of the boardgame version of John Conway's *Game of Life*, the cellular automata game. It's not dissimilar.

On the Emergent Properties of Games

CP: *When you were talking about Go, I was thinking that when you create a mental model of the environment as it is now, you're also creating a model of how you want it to be. So in Go the mental models have to do with imagining where the players want the game to go, right?*

WW: Right.

CP: *And then as the game fills itself out, as the emergent properties come forth…*

WW: …and of course part of that model is modeling what the other player is likely to do. "Oh, I think they're going to play very aggressively, therefore, my model of them says that this would be the optimum strategy."

CP: *So that's interesting, because there's also this aspect of imagination, which you alluded to earlier.*

And that sort of brings me back to a question about SimCity and The Sims. Each of those games has a different level of abstraction from the other. You can really see the different choices that are made in terms of design. But in terms of this modeling idea, you briefly alluded to the use of The Sims from a directorial standpoint as a storytelling tool, and that in a way, there's a little bit of a dynamic that goes on because the game doesn't want to be, the characters don't want to be used that way necessarily.

So I'm just curious how you grapple with that. I mean you're obviously taking that into account. Are you making a way to use the game as a storyboarding tool, or continuing to play around with the tension that the characters are kind of resisting that kind of control?

WW: It's actually very interesting in *The Sims* how the pronouns change all the time. I'm sitting there playing the game and I'm talking about, "Oh, first I'm going to get a job, then I'm going to do this, then I'm going to do that." And then you know when the character starts disobeying me, all of a sudden I shift and say "Oh, why won't he do that?" or "What's he doing now?" And so at some point it's me kind of inhabiting this little person, and I'm thinking, "It's me; I'm going to get a job and I'm going to do x, y, and z." But then when he starts rebelling, it's he. And so then I kind of jump out of him, and now it's me versus him. You know what I'm saying?

CP: *Yes, I do. But one of things that interests me about the game is that you have these semi-autonomous characters. They're not totally autonomous, and they're not totally avatars either. They're somewhere in between. Do think that's disorienting to the player, or do you think it's what makes the game fun?*

WW: I don't think so. I mean it's interesting. I'm just surprised that people can do it that fluidly, they can so fluidly say "Oh, I'm this guy, and then I'm going to do x, y, and z." And then they can pop out and "Now I'm that person. I'm doing this that and the other. What's he doing?" And so now he's a third person to me, even though he was me a moment ago. I think that's something we use a lot in our imaginations when we're modeling things. We'll put ourselves in somebody else's point of view very specifically for a very short period of time. "Well, let's see, if I were that person, I would probably do *x*, *y*, and *z*." And then I kind of jump out of their head and then I'm me, talking to them, relating to them.

At some level I want people to have a deep appreciation for how connected things are at all these different scales, not just through space, but through time. And in doing so I had to build kind of a simple little toy universe and say, here, play with this toy for a while. My expectations when I hand somebody that toy are that they are going to make their own mental model, which isn't exactly what I'm presenting them with. But whatever it is, their mental model of the world around them, and above them and below them, will expand. Hopefully, probably in some unpredictable way, and for me that's fine. And I don't want to stamp the same mental model on every player. I'd rather think of this as a catalyst. You know, it's a catalytic tool for growing your mental model, and I have no idea which direction it's going to grow it, but I think just kind of sparking that change is worthwhile unto itself.

CP: *But you're more interested in setting up the rule space and letting the outcome evolve with the player's experimentation.*

WW: Right, I mean what I really want to do is I want to create just the largest possibility space I can. I don't want to create a specific possibility that everybody's going to experience the same way. I'd much rather have a huge possibility space where every player has as unique an experience as possible.

CP: *One of the things that I think is interesting about what you do as a role model for interactive designers it that you enjoy the unpredictable outcome. When people do things that you didn't plan on, that seems to be something that you embrace.*

WW: To me, that feels like success.

About Celia Pearce

Celia Pearce is a game designer, artist, teacher, and writer. She is the designer of the award-winning virtual reality attraction Virtual Adventures: The Loch Ness Expedition, *and the author of* The Interactive Book: A Guide to the Interactive Revolution *(Macmillan, 1997), as well as numerous essays on game design and interactivity. She currently holds a position as Lecturer in Studio Art at the University of California Irvine's Claire Trevor School of the Arts.*

Part II
Designing a Game

Now that we've looked at the basic elements of games, it's time to walk through the process of designing a game of your own. This may seem overwhelming at first, especially if your goal is to create a game like the ones you see on the shelves of your local game store—filled with complex animations and elaborate programming. So before we even think of discussing these aspects, let's back away from the ultimate goal and take the process of design step by step from the beginning.

First, we'll discuss conceptualization—coming up with ideas for your games. This may be easy for you—you may already have an idea of the game you want to make. But what if you can't get support for your one idea? What will you do then? We'll show you how you can train yourself to become an "idea person," someone for whom ideas come as easily as breathing. That way, you won't be stuck with just one idea when opportunity knocks.

Once you have your idea, you'll need to formalize it—many designers jump right to writing a design document at this point, but we'll show you how to prototype your idea and get playtesters involved very early in the process. The iterative design process that we outlined in Chapter 1 on

page 11 is detailed in Chapters 7 and 8—"Prototyping" and "Playtesting." By prototyping and playtesting early, you can grasp which aspects of your system are working and which are not. It's only once you've seen players interact with your idea that you have enough knowledge to even think about drafting a design document.

What will you test for? Chapters 9 and 10 discuss strategies for making sure that your game is complete, that it is fair, that it offers meaningful choices, and that it is fun and accessible for your players. In Chapter 11 we will discuss how to conceptualize your design in terms of controls and interfaces, and how to articulate those aspects of design as a preliminary step to a full design specification.

Our goal here is to give you an accurate picture of the design process, if you follow along with the exercises in this section, you'll have designed at least one full game of your own. Going through this process yourself will teach you important methods for conceptualizing, building, and examining your work. By the time you're done, you will understand how to design a game, playtest it, and use your knowledge of the formal, dramatic, and dynamic aspects of games to perfect its gameplay.

139

Chapter 6
Conceptualization

It all begins with a spark. When you're driving in your car and you get that flash: "I could design a game about carrier pigeons! It'll be the coolest carrier pigeon game ever!" Perhaps it will be the only carrier pigeon game ever, but to you it's the beginning of a process. And hopefully, the process we're about to show you will help you weed out ideas that just won't fly, while enabling you to refine and properly prepare the concepts that are worth pursuing.

We believe in a systematic approach infused with inspiration—taking the spark of a creative idea and allowing it to mature without killing it, then developing that idea into a workable structure. As you may have already discovered, some ideas are brilliant, but they simply don't make good games, while other ideas seem dull at first,

but underneath lies a compelling game system. What we hope to do is allow you to wed an exceptional concept with solid gameplay in a manner than doesn't appear to be contrived. That in itself is a huge leap forward.

Now, let's begin with the spark.

Exercise 6.1: Your Inspiration List

List the top ten games you've played in each of the following categories: videogames (computer, console, mobile, and arcade), boardgames, social games, and physical games (like basketball and tag). Next to each one, write down why it is you love this game. One sentence per game is enough.

WHERE DO IDEAS COME FROM?

Great ideas come from everywhere and nowhere. They spring up at any time of day or night, while you're driving, bathing, running a marathon, sleeping, or blundering about. They're impossible to predict or corral, and if you're not paying attention, they slip right past you.

One key to coming up with and retaining great ideas is to carry around a notepad and pen or a PDA. Keep it with you at all times so you can jot down your ideas at moment's notice, whether it's that burst of inspiration that strikes you in shower or the slow trickle that seeps into your consciousness in the middle of the night. If you're driving, a voice recording device is preferable. Having one in your car at all times is critical because the most brilliant ideas are ephemeral and will vanish before they're fully formed, unless you leap onto them, drag them out, and put them down in a coherent form.

Exercise 6.2: Idea Fountain

Turn yourself into an idea fountain. For the next five days, write down every idea that pops into your head — no matter how half-baked it seems. See how they evolve. Keep track of the rate at which ideas come on a day-by-day basis.

You may be surprised. Once you train yourself in the art of continual brainstorming, the idea flow will increase at a dramatic rate. It's like exercise. If you use the creative muscle, it becomes stronger. And if you want to design breakthrough games, you have to think of yourself as an Olympic contender.

You should notice that after a month of training the flow of ideas is significantly higher than on day one—that is, if you don't get lazy. Remember, generating truly innovative ideas is hard work and requires dedication, but the payoff is enormous. If you stick with the program of continual brainstorming, you'll quickly discover that you've amassed more ideas than you know what to do with. This is a problem everyone should have. But it's not an easy one to solve.

We've noticed that as ideas come forth at an ever increasing rate, many people become overwhelmed and begin to shut down. They simply can't handle their own output, and they start feeling as if they're drowning in their own creativity. The problem here isn't with the number of ideas; it's that the ideas aren't being organized in a way that gives them value. If you have a thousand scattered ideas and no way of effectively sorting through them and determining which are relevant to your current goals, then what use are they?

A good solution to this problem lies in creating a system for storing, categorizing, and manipulating your idea pool as it grows. It is only through a systematic approach of classifying and archiving your ideas that you will be able to effectively harness your creativity. One way to do this is to learn how to use a database program. There are many simple databases on the market, some as cheap as $30. Buy one and learn to use it. This will become an extension of your brain and allow you to take the massive flow of material and give it structure.

Exercise 6.3: Organizing Your Brain

Write down 25 different categories of ideas. You can have subcategories if you like. For instance "games" could be one category, and subcategories may include puzzle, strategy, role-playing, etc. Remember not to focus too heavily on games. Many of your best ideas will be cross-pollinations of ideas having to do with philosophy, books, performance, relationships, religion, etc. Now take the ideas you wrote down in the previous exercise and organize them by type.

This is what we call an "ideabase." It's a cross-reference database of concepts that you've come up with. Every night (remember you're an Olympic athlete in training), you should transcribe your ideas from paper, PDA, or voice recording into the database. You should make a system for categorizing your ideas according to the types defined in the previous exercise. Naturally, you will perfect this system over time.

Forcing yourself to transcribe your ideas accomplishes two things. First, it cements the idea in your memory for later retrieval, and second, it gives you a chance to discard the lousy ideas. This is the first step in editing. But don't become too stringent. If an idea has any potential at all, then you should keep it. The beauty of this system is that you are building a powerful creative tool that can be drawn upon for the rest of your life. An idea that seems worthless now may have value ten years from now, and the more you put into your ideabase, the more effective it becomes.

Exercise 6.4: Your Ideabase

Begin creating and organizing your ideabase. It should include at least 100 ideas and 30 categories. These can be drawn from the previous two exercises.

If you've structured your ideabase correctly, you should be able to search on key ideas and see what comes up. Imagine three years from now searching under the key word "baboons" to see what emerges. It may surprise you. You may have

written down notes about a character you were thinking of creating, a painting you saw in an art gallery, a dream you had, and odd behavior you noticed. All of this can be used as building blocks for an element in one of your games. In this way, your ideabase can be used to enhance your brainstorming sessions by providing direct links to your creative past.

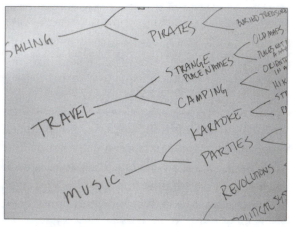

6.1   Example idea tree

BRAINSTORMING TECHNIQUES

What we've given you so far is an informal method of capturing your ideas and organizing them in a coherent and useful form. What comes next is a more formalized system of brainstorming. This is necessary when you are given a specific problem to solve or project to develop and must go deeper than a mere concept.

Structured brainstorming is a powerful skill. And, like any skill, it takes practice to become good. There are brainstorming beginners and brainstorming experts and the difference between their abilities is akin to the difference between an average golfer and Tiger Woods. Expert brainstormers train themselves in how to generate workable ideas and solutions to problems, while

amateurs fling out random ideas and hope something sticks.

Let's take a simple example of structured brainstorming, where you're given the task of coming up with an idea for a game. There are no limitations on the type of game, the budget, resources, or anything else. Where do you begin?

A good place to start is with things you love. The best game ideas tend to come from your heart. We all have things we're passionate about—ideas that make us excited—images lodged in our brain that we won't let go of. Focus on what inspires you: works of art, culture, nature, etc. Think of your fantasies, your hobbies, games you play over and over, childhood dreams, and things in life that spark your imagination. Now begin writing these down on paper. Like any creative work, a game should be an expression of your inner self.

Exercise 6.5: Growing an Idea Tree

Start by planting five trees. Draw five lines on a piece of paper, each representing one sapling. Spread them out so that each line can grow. Now for each line write down one of your passions, whether for sports or adventure or magic or games. You should have five trunks each with the name of something that excites you below it. Then make each of these trunks a branching point, and above each one write down two ideas that stem from it. Now you should have five trunk ideas and ten branching ideas. Repeat the process again, making two more branches sprouting from each of the existing branches. The branching ideas should be in some way related to the ideas below it. Don't edit yourself too much, but try to see the connection between the branches as your idea tree evolves. You can repeat this process as many times as you like and see how the tree takes shape.

What you've created is a systemized structure for your thoughts. Each idea tree embodies a common theme. If you look at them as a group, you'll see patterns of ideas sprouting in all directions. Now as the trees grow, you can apply certain conditions to them. The conditions will yield different growth patterns. The conditions can be as simple as limiting yourself to "dark and scary" ideas. Each of your five trees, under this condition, will yield different fruit. Or your condition can be "medieval adventure." You can have one tree focused on philosophy, another on conflict, and one about history. When you apply the "medieval adventure" condition, it may surprise you how each tree trans-

forms. We call this system idea growth. It's a method for brainstorming and producing ideas that you may not come up with otherwise.

Other techniques

Creating an idea tree is just the beginning. The next sections outline several other methods you can experiment with. There is no single best solution. You may find that some methods work better for you than others. We encourage you to try all the methods and vary your approach. The key to productive brainstorming is finding the right balance of stimulation and structure. If you can do this, you'll improve both the quantity and quality of your output.

List creation

One of the tried and true forms of brainstorming is making lists. List out everything you can dream up on a certain topic. Then create other lists on variations of that topic. You'll be amazed at how many great ideas come out in simple lists. The process of writing them down helps you to freely associate and organize at the same time.

Idea cards

Take a deck of index cards and write a single idea on each one. If you want to be frugal, cut the card up into smaller cards. You can save a few trees this way. Then mix them up in a bowl. Now take out the cards and pair them. For example, "nectar" may appear with "giants." Perhaps, your next game will include "nectar giants," whose bodies are fluid and smell like persimmons. You can concatenate sets of two, three, or four cards. It doesn't matter. And the more wild ideas you throw into the bowl, the richer the combinations become.

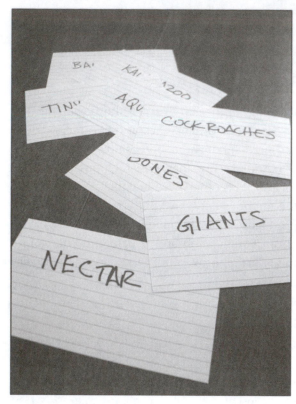

6.2   Idea cards

Shout it out

This is where you shout out whatever comes into your head while a voice recorder is running. After five minutes of auditory abuse, go back and transcribe your mad ramblings. There's often a prized nugget hiding in your verbal blitzkrieg.

Stream of consciousness

Sit down at your computer and start writing like crazy. Don't worry about being coherent. Don't think about punctuation or spelling. Just write as quickly as humanly possible. Whatever comes out is fine. After ten minutes of spewing words on a particular topic, stop and read over what you've done. Sometimes it turns out better than work you've spent days perfecting.

Randomize it

Take a dictionary and open it up to any page, then start with the word you see first. Wherever that leads is fine. The same can be done using a newspaper or magazine. Open it up to any page, then start writing something down in relation to the topic you see. Try to fit what you're writing and seeing into your overall objective of creating a game concept. You can do the same with random web page searches or using the phonebook. Vary the medium but keep the process consistent.

Research

All the previous techniques try to spark your creativity through a certain amount of randomness. On the other side of the spectrum, you might try doing research into a subject that interests you. Always fascinated by ant hills? Find out how ants live and work. Research how they communicate and interact. Is there an idea or concept in this research that you can use in a game?

Exercise 6.6: Research

When you find an idea that you like through brainstorming, do some research to find out more about the topic. Is there already game that resembles the one you have in mind? If so that's fine. How might your game be different?

Extreme measures

As the Greeks proclaimed, moderation in all things is usually a good rule. This isn't true for brainstorming, however. Sometimes extreme measures are needed. This means dragging yourself out of your house, no matter how painful that sounds, and putting yourself into new situations. No, videogames and television are not the extent of the known universe. Force yourself to try something entirely different, like whitewater rafting, bungee jumping, snorkeling, or parachuting. And whenever possible, jot down how you feel and whatever pops into your head.

It's often good to pick activities that in some way relate to the game you're designing. If it's a shooting game, try going to a firing range and unloading a few rounds. If it's a puzzle game, head for the science museum. But don't limit yourself too much. Maybe trying something unrelated will produce the breakthrough you require. We even suggest such simple experiments as locking yourself in a darkened room for 20 minutes and allowing your mind to clear, or turning up the music and dancing wildly. The only rule is to do something you normally do not do.

The best results often come from placing yourself in uncomfortable situations because these make you more aware and introspective. For example, if you've never volunteered your time at a homeless shelter, maybe it's about time. Or if you're the type that seldom goes out at night, perhaps a late night clubbing expedition is in order. Whatever it takes to break your routine and stimulate your brain cells.

The key is to always keep your project in the forefront of your mind. Don't just take a day off. Make that day part of your brainstorming and tie everything that's running through your head into your project. This is harder than it sounds. If you jump out of an airplane for the first time, it's not easy to think of anything but your impending death. But for the sake of designing great games, focus on the experience and see if there are elements you can bring into the game world. The more conscious you are, the more you will retain and be able to use when you return to your home or cubicle. If done right, each experience will enrich the fabric of your life and spark a new wave of inventiveness.

The right environment

The cardinal sin of brainstorming is to self-censor or edit your ideas during the process. This destroys all hope for creativity. Check your critical nature at the door and allow yourself to think freely. The more you open yourself up, the better your ideas will become. There will be plenty of time revise and edit and critique after the brainstorming session is over.

We can't stress this enough. When brainstorming, you must provide a nonjudgmental environment for yourself to think. After all, some of the greatest inventions in history began as mistakes. Let yourself screw up. Encourage sloppy thinking. Strive toward the impractical. Bask in the absurd. Do whatever it takes to push yourself beyond your comfort zone into the realm where anything is possible.

Put it on the wall

Okay, so you're ready to dive into a wild session of brainstorming; now, how do you communicate your ideas effectively to yourself and others in the midst of controlled chaos?

As you may have guessed, sitting at a computer is not always the best solution. The tried and true method is paper. Some people prefer notepads, others like continuous sheets of printer paper that go on and on, while others prefer scraps of paper or sticky notes. Our favorite is writing on a whiteboard, or on large pieces of paper taped to the walls. We feel this helps us express ourselves freely during this phase of the process. For one thing, writing against the wall gets you out of your

Where Do Game Ideas Come From?

by Noah Falstein, The Inspiracy

Game design is my favorite part of game development, and brainstorming is my favorite part of game design. Brainstorming meetings are capricious, at one moment puttering along like an old jalopy on a bumpy road, and at the next zooming like a Ferrari on a racetrack, with the ideas coming so fast there's no time to write them down. Ideas can come from anywhere—books, movies, television, and of course other games are frequent sources, but I've had ideas spawned from personal relationships, from dreams, from scientific principles, from art, from music theory, and from children's toys. Ultimately I think most good ideas come from the subconscious and involve combining dissimilar things in novel ways. When a design client of mine is stuck on a point, I often find it useful as an exercise to pick something apparently totally unrelated to the concept to spark new thought. For example, if a real-time strategy game about rapidly evolving alien creatures needs a new creature type and attack, I might turn for inspiration to frothy romantic comedy films. There's a scene in *When Harry met Sally* where Meg Ryan's character fakes an orgasm in a crowded diner. For the game, that might suggest a siren creature that generates a fake mating cry that causes all enemies of the opposite sex to drop what they're doing and head toward that creature for a few seconds. Ideas are everywhere.

One example of the evolution of one of my favorite ideas was in the original *Secret of Monkey Island* game from LucasArts. Ron Gilbert, the project leader, had worked with me previously on the game *Indiana Jones and the Last Crusade*. For that game we needed a boxing interface so Indy could box with an opponent, and I'd recently been playing *Sid Meier's Pirates!* which had a simple, fun swordfighting interface. By changing swords to fists it worked great for us. The problem is, I neglected to tell Ron where the idea came from, so when Ron was talking to me about *Monkey Island* he casually remarked that he'd realized that the boxing interface would make a great sword-fighting interface for his new game. I confessed to the history of the concept, and for a while we were stumped. Then I suggested that some of the best classic swordplay in movies involved more talking than fighting—thinking of old Errol Flynn movies or the then-recent film *The Princess Bride*. That seemed more appropriate anyway for the comic tone of his game. What if sword-fighting in Monkey Island was about insult and rejoinder, not thrust and parry? And so out of movies, a classic game mechanism was born that proved to be one of the more popular parts of *Monkey Island*.

When I've told this story, some people have asked me if I felt embarrassed adapting an idea from Sid Meier. I might—if Sid hadn't admitted publicly that several of the concepts in his *Pirates!* game were based on what he'd seen in Dani Bunten's *Seven Cities of Gold* game—which Dani said was in turn based heavily on a boardgame. Sometimes I think no idea can ever be truly original.

Author Bio

Noah Falstein has been developing games professionally since 1980. Currently he runs www.theinspiracy.com as a freelance designer and producer. He is also the design columnist for Game Developer *magazine.*

6.3 **Working at the whiteboard**

chair and your blood flowing. It also lends itself to big ideas, sketches, and side notes. When your ideas are on the wall, they can be seen by a group. They can also been seen side-by-side at a glance. This helps spark more ideas and facilitates collaboration.

Writing against the wall is also handy for making mind maps. Mind mapping is a way of expressing ideas visually. You start with a core idea in the center and let related ideas radiate outwards. You can use lines and different colored markers to connect ideas. Mind mapping provides a structure for thinking in a nonlinear manner.

A good practice during brainstorming is to number your ideas. It's helpful to be able to refer back and forth between several ideas quickly using shorthand when you are developing a big concept. The numbers allow you to do this without losing your larger train of thought. Aside from that, it's satisfying to generate lots of ideas in a brainstorming session. The numbers will measure your output, serving a function similar to tracking distance when jogging or reps when lifting weights.

Don't expect too much

Brainstorming is a high-energy activity. A good session will naturally die down after sixty minutes or so. The mind and body need a break after that much focused time. So don't push yourself beyond what's reasonable. Whatever ideas you have after an hour or so can continue to be worked on in the coming days.

TEAM BRAINSTORMING

The idea of brainstorming alone is fine, and it appeals to many maverick game designers and misanthropes, but ultimately, game development is collaborative art, so why not start by including your team in the creative process? The payoff is enormous. Working with others in generating ideas is both stimulating and highly productive. Two or more people bouncing ideas back and forth tend to generate more and better concepts than a single person working alone. The reason is that two or more minds in a dialogue can build upon the core idea being discussed, each acting as a catalyst to inspire the other in ways a single mind can't.

It also helps to verbalize your ideas. Hearing yourself speak can stimulate new thoughts. It's difficult to become excited sitting alone in your room or cubicle. But when you start talking to someone and obtain their instant feedback, a dynamic process results through which concepts transform from vague thoughts into viable solutions. We strongly urge you to seek out partners who mesh with your style of brainstorming and work with them to flesh out the initial plans for your game. You'll find that this type of working relationship becomes more and more valuable as the game design process advances. The type of collaboration which is optional at the start of a project becomes mandatory once you are in full-fledged production and working closely with programmers, artists, producers, and other team members.

Rules of teamstorming

When you are brainstorming with other people, it's important to remember some ground rules—it will help the creativity flow, and it will make sure everyone's equally involved in the process.

1. State a purpose
When you sit down to brainstorm, articulate a purpose for the session. A statement about a problem you are interested in will help you devise a creative solution. Here are some examples:

- "Opponents compete and cooperate at the same time by producing and trading scarce resources."
- "Player creates order from a chaos of shapes."
- "Player has indirect control of volatile agents. Skillful play can convert opponent's agents to the player's team."

2. No idea is bad
Never criticize one of your colleagues' ideas during the brainstorming process. After all, the process itself is about free thinking, and if you begin to criticize or edit their ideas before they're fully developed, it will hamper the flow. Also, certain members of your team, feeling wounded by harsh comments, will limit their contributions, which is the death of creativity.

3. Encourage differing views
This sounds like common sense, but it helps to let everyone know that there is no right answer. It should be emphasized over and over again that there is no right answer in a brainstorm and that everyone in a session is free to approach the subject from a different angle.

4. Vary the structure
Don't rely on just one method for brainstorming. Mix it up. Some structures may work fine for the

group leaders but less well for other members. If you're a leader, make sure to experiment with structures that you aren't comfortable with. Also, ask team members to suggest alternative ways of conducting the brainstorming sessions. You might give them a shot at leading the group. Don't be afraid of losing control—if you are, you've already lost it.

5. Go for lots of ideas

Go for quantity when developing ideas. Try to generate 100 ideas an hour—be free and don't worry if the ideas are outrageous. Don't edit yourself at all during this part of the process. Just let yourself go without regard to feasibility. An idea that initially seems out of place may have value later. Designers often report that ideas that originally seem ridiculous turn into gems later.

Exercise 6.7: Do It

Get a group of friends together for a brainstorm. If you can't get a group together, do the best you can on your own. State a purpose, set up a white board or a sheet of butcher paper, and use the previous techniques to generate 100 ideas related to your purpose in 60 minutes. This may sound like a lot, but if you can keep the energy level up, you can do it!

EDITING & REFINING

What do you do once you've brainstormed? Now you have a zillion ideas but still no game. Okay, now it's time to edit. Change gears and put on your critical hats. Whether you're working alone or as a team, we recommend that you schedule your editing sessions on different days than your brainstorming meetings. Even letting a week go by between the two phases is a good idea. What we don't want to do is blur the line between the two because as soon as you start combining editing and brainstorming, you'll wind up with inferior ideas.

When you begin the editing session, make it clear to everyone involved that the brainstorming is over. This is a time to weed through the morass of ideas and pull out what works. Go through each idea systematically and rank it with a number from one to ten. If it's a group, this can be done like a secret ballot. Tabulate the scores and rank the ideas from best to worst.

The top ten ideas should then be discussed, going over the merits of each idea. Try to keep the discussion positive. Don't bash any ideas. Instead talk about the relative strengths of each idea. If you're working alone, do the same thing in your head. Keeping a positive outlook helps prevent self-censorship when you return to brainstorming.

Narrow down the list from ten ideas to three. Then schedule another brainstorming session on those three ideas. Keep repeating the process until you come up with one idea that everyone feels is superior. Once this has been done, present that idea to other people for feedback, and go through the process yet again, taking their advice and structuring brainstorming sessions around this.

Your ideas should be limited to single paragraph descriptions. Only once an idea has made it through the entire process and received outside feedback should you expand it to about a single-page treatment. The less you write at first, the less attached you'll become to your idea, and the easier it will be to alter your plans if things aren't heading in the right direction.

The goal is to keep the process fluid, so you don't get locked into a single idea too early on or spend too much time perfecting your writing. A better concept may be lurking just around the corner, and until you've gone through several iterations with the first idea, you don't want to lock yourself in.

Exercise 6.8: Describe Your Game

In one or two paragraphs, describe the essence of your game idea. Try to capture what makes it interesting to you, and how the basic gameplay will work.

TURNING IDEAS INTO A GAME

Okay, so you've come up with a single idea that you think would make a good game. But you can't know if it is a gem until you've gone through the entire prototyping and playtesting process. After all, the only way to know if a game works is to play it.

At this point, many game designers try to take a shortcut. They believe that the best way to come up with a game concept is to begin with an existing game. After all, the game mechanics are evident, and it's been proven to work. This is fine to a limited extent. It is important to have an in depth knowledge of games and an understanding of game mechanics, but if you are going to create truly original material, you have to think beyond the games you've played.

We prefer to have you begin by forgetting everything you know about games for one second. Don't think of replicating the latest hit title, or how to combine existing games to create a better one, or features you can layer upon existing game engines. Instead, focus on what you want to say. Work from a vision of the type of game you'd like to play. The structure should be one element of that vision.

Is your game about Africa? Does it have wild animals? If so, as you develop the idea, ask yourself how those animals might interact? What is the role of the player? Does the player have a clearly defined goal? And what are the obstacles in get-

ting to that goal? You see where we're headed. The game mechanics, for the most part, should stem from the core idea. They're an outgrowth of your overall vision.

As you continue to brainstorm, edit, and revise, ask yourself how you'd like your game to look and feel. What is the tone? How should it function? Let your mind wander free and try not to refer to existing games. Write these ideas down in general terms and use the brainstorming techniques to turn them upside down and come up with fresh angles.

There is no right answer. What we don't want to do is lock down the game structure too early in the process. Give yourself time to play around and experiment with a variety of structures to see which fits your vision the best. Refer to the formal and dramatic elements of game design presented in Chapters 2 through 5 of this book. Think about each aspect of your game idea in terms of these elements. If you've forgotten any of them, please go back and review them before proceeding.

Formal elements of game design

- Players
  - ◊ Number of players
  - ◊ Roles of players
  - ◊ Player interaction patterns
- Objectives

- Procedures
- Rules
- Resources
- Conflict
  - ◊ Obstacles
  - ◊ Opponents
  - ◊ Dilemmas
- Boundaries
- Outcome

Dramatic elements of game design

- Challenge
- Play
- Premise
- Character
- Story

One stumbling block many novices run into is allowing themselves to be distracted by the dramatic elements. Story and characters are necessary, but don't let them obscure your view of the gameplay. They should remain secondary until you pin down the mechanics.

What we're trying to do here is to help you to think about the underlying structure without copying existing games. Most games share common elements, and you will probably find a lot of overlap between your ideas and the games you've played, but you should also think about that fact that each of these elements can be used to create new mechanics and types of play. Strive to innovate in your designs, even if only one aspect of your game is an innovation.

Critical thinking skills

One way to hone your design abilities is to develop your critical thinking skills in terms of gameplay. In Chapter 1, we told you to become a

tester, to take notes as you play. This is a great way to begin observing how games work, but designers should also analyze their own observations. After a gaming session, write down what works for you and what could be improved. It's important to describe how you'd improve specific elements of gameplay.

For example, if you're playing a first-person shooter and the control system feels clunky, get out a pen and paper and describe the problem. Why doesn't it work? How might you remedy this problem? Would you modify the GUI, the gameplay, or the graphics? The same holds true for features you enjoy. Write down what you like and make notes as to why each element works. These notes will become priceless later on, and the act of writing them down will help to hone your analytical skills. That way, when you sit down to design your own games, you can learn from other people's mistakes, while building upon the foundation that previous designers have provided.

Simply avoiding mistakes and improving upon existing games seldom yields groundbreaking game design, however. If you want to push the envelope, don't forget to think beyond the game itself to the fundamental gameplay structure. This is where true innovation lies. If you have any brilliant flashes while playing a game, write your ideas down. And even if you don't have any insights, it's good practice to make yourself think of ways of altering the design to yield new results.

The notes you take while playing games will become the basis for your game bible: a list of every game you've ever played, along with detailed analysis of the gameplay mechanisms. Yes, for a true gamer, one who has played thousands of hours of games, this is an enormous amount of work, and we won't ask you to do it all here, but it's something you should start doing today and keep doing for the rest of your life.

As you dissect more and more games, patterns will begin to emerge. This is how you train yourself to think of games in terms of systems that can be deconstructed, manipulated, and transformed. Your goal should be to look at games from a mechanical perspective and take each one apart, much as an auto mechanic works on a car. By taking parts out of numerous game engines, you can learn how they function and eventually construct new, groundbreaking machines.

Focus on the formal elements

Once you have decided on a concept you'd like to develop into a game, you should sit down and lay out the formal elements (or game mechanics). This is easier said than done. For first-time designers, it can be difficult to know where to begin. A good rule of thumb is to go back to your vision of the game and try to derive the mechanics from the subject matter. You may even want to set up separate brainstorming sessions for every element in the design.

As you begin to fill in the elements one by one, you will see a structure emerge. This will become an actual system that you can model and test. At any point, if you get stuck and don't know how to define a particular game element, go back to your game bible and look at other games. See how they function. What devices do they use to solve similar problems? Can you innovate on their approach? Play around with their rules and see what you come up with.

Questions to ask yourself

- What is the conflict in my game?
- What are the rules and procedures?
- What actions do the players take and when?
- Are there turns? How do they work?

- How many players can play?
- How long does a game take to resolve?
- What is the working title?
- Who is the target audience?
- What platform will this game run on? What restrictions or opportunities does that environment have?

The more questions you ask yourself the better. And it's okay if your answers are rough and messy at this point in the process. In the beginning, you can only guess, and you won't know if you're on the right track until you actually play the game and see how it works. But don't let this stop you from conceptualizing the game. You may be working blind at first, but soon the game will materialize before your eyes.

Fleshing out the game structure

- Define each player's goal.
- What does a player need to do to win?
- Write down the single most important type of player action in the game.
- Describe how this functions.
- Write down the procedures and rules in outline format.
- Only focus on the most critical rules.
- Leave all other rules until later.
- Map out how a typical turn works.
- Using a flowchart is the most effective way to visualize this.
- Define how many players can play.
- How do these players interact with one another?

This is the very beginning of a process of prototyping. We won't go into detail here because Chapter 7 will take you through every aspect of

DESIGNER PERSPECTIVE: BILL ROPER

Title: CEO, Flagship Studios

Project list (five to eight top projects)

While at Blizzard Entertainment:

- *Warcraft: Orcs and Humans*
- *Warcraft II: Tides of Darkness*
- *Starcraft*
- *Starcraft: Brood War*
- *Diablo*
- *Diablo II*
- *Diablo II: Lord of Destruction*
- *Warcraft III: Reign of Chaos*

How did you get into the game industry?

I have always been an avid gamer, ever since my mom and dad introduced me to cribbage and black-jack (respectively) to teach me quick addition skills at the age of five. I was doing desktop publishing on the 4:00 P.M.–1:00 A.M. shift for a company called Lasertype when a good friend of mine told me about an opportunity at the small game company where he worked. They needed someone to do the music for a port of one of their games onto the PC because the regular music guy was busy working on their first self-published title. The company was Blizzard and after doing music for the PC version of *Blackthorne*, I was fortunate enough to stay on to do the voice-over work, world design, and manual for *WarCraft: Orcs and Humans*. The day I started in the game industry and turned in my resignation to the desktop publishing company was one of the best in my life.

What are your five favorite games and why?

This list changes slightly every time I think about it, due in great part to the sheer number of games I play. Also, these are from an all-time list, and not necessarily the ones I am playing right now—some of which may be on this list if I wrote it out again in few months.

- *Wizardry:* One of the great early gaming experiences on the Apple II, I can still remember mar-veling at the fact that it looked like you were actually walking down a hallway to fight the mon-sters. The dungeon designs, the puzzles, the interface, the items (Cuisinart the Vorpal Blade) and the story were all fun and exciting. *Wizardry* was definitely a defining title in my high school gaming days on the computer.

- *Carcassonne:* This is a fantastic boardgame out of Germany that centers on the construction of cities and roadways. It changes every time you play it, thanks to the system of people playing a randomly drawn tile on their turn. The game has a lot of social aspects as well since each piece is flipped up and the entire table is supposed to give their advice on how best to play it. I can, and have, played game after game after game of this for hours on end.

- *Diablo II:* Although I worked on this game, it (along with the expansion set) still holds my interest. It is a wonderfully fun romp where just about everything is random, so it simply never gets old. A great community of gamers has grown around the game and hooking up to play over battle.net is so easy, it all makes a terrific package for single- or multiplayer fun, whether I have fifteen minutes or an entire weekend to spend on it.

- *Grand Theft Auto III:* Whether you agree with the edgy premise of the game world, the mechanics and thoughtfulness that went into this game are undeniable. I have played this since it came out, and I am still finding new, fun things to do. The openness of the design and the sheer fun of driving around at breakneck speeds keep this high on my list.

- *Poker:* I honestly think this is perhaps the perfect game. It has simple rules with a limited and easy to understand number of pieces, has innumerable game variations that don't require an expansion set, is played by both core and mass market gamers, is portable, has a scalable risk to reward ratio, and is equal parts skill and luck. Throw in the fact that it is a multiplayer game, and you can hopefully see why it has all the pieces of puzzle for being an amazingly good game.

What games have inspired you the most as a designer and why?

The short answer is every game I have ever played. I think that everything we do in life can act as inspiration for making games, whether reading books, watching movies, listening to music, traveling to different places, playing sports, or just simply living your life. I have always believed that you have to play games to make games, just like a chef eats at a lot of different restaurants to better understand and refine his own craft. I can look to games from *Civilization* to *Monopoly* to *EverQuest* to *Super Mario Bros.* to *StarCraft* to *Bard's Tale* to *Half-Life* to *Madden NFL* and find elements that either really make that game work or could have been done better. The real challenge comes in being able to just sit down and play without completely analyzing every minute element, but I suppose that comes with the territory.

What are you most proud of in your career?

It would be easy to just list the games that I have worked on, but more importantly are the people I had the honor of working with to make those games. I have been privileged to be a part of some simply amazing teams over the past nine years, and the people with whom I am starting a new company are some of the best. Our industry is constantly evolving, and it is rare to have such a good run over such a long period of time. I firmly believe that it was possible because of the dedicated and talented group of developers who had a true passion and respect for what we were doing and who we were doing it for.

And that is the other thing of which I am most proud—having the chance to be so deeply involved in the community of gamers around the world. Staying focused on the players is so vital to making good games. It is easy to become enamored with technology or art or the business side of our industry, but making games that are fun for people who want and escape from the rigors of daily life is really what it's all about.

What words of advice would you give to an aspiring designer today?

To quote a popular ad campaign—"Just Do It." You can't get good at making games unless you make games. Use the level design tools that are a part of many of the best selling titles to work out game ideas. Tear apart boardgames to prototype your ideas. Play around with existing games by changing rules or goals or the strengths and weaknesses of the individual components and see how the balance works. Most importantly, never stop playing.

A Roper Collage:
WarCraft II (right)
Diablo (below)
WarCraft III (lower right)

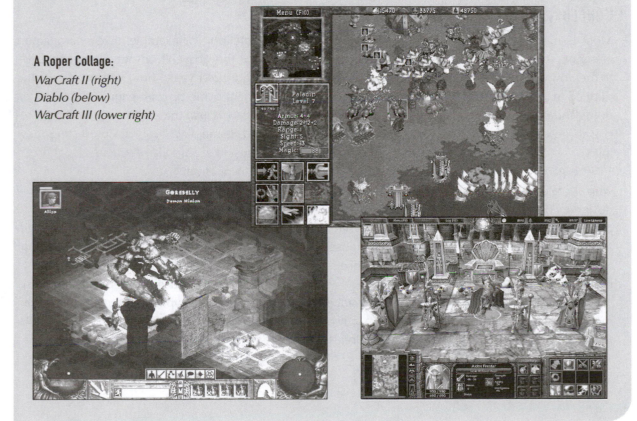

prototyping a game. Suffice to say, that the brainstorming process, as it evolves, naturally segues into prototyping and then playtesting.

For now, the goal is to have an outline of where your game is headed, both in terms of a written treatment and a rough sense of the game mechanics. Whenever you get stuck or feel you can improve upon a particular element, remember to go back and utilize the brainstorming techniques described previously.

Practice, practice, practice

The first time you go through this process will be the hardest. Each time you do it, however, you will become more capable of generating workable ideas. Every accomplished game designer has developed many more concepts than he or she will ever produce. The key is to be persistent and keep practicing.

Exercise 6.9: Write a Treatment

Take the description you wrote in Exercise 6.8 and expand it into a three- to-five-page treatment for your game idea. Ask yourself questions about the formal and dramatic elements as you write. Remember that this is just a draft—when we go on to the prototyping stage we will address these questions again in more details.

CONCLUSION

Most beginning game designers simply borrow elements from successful games and adapt them to their own purposes. This is fine, and many experienced game designers make a career out of doing the same. Our goal, however, is to enable you to go beyond borrowing and begin innovating.

The game designers we admire are the ones who break conventions and go where other designers dared not tread. The advantage of computers is that improvements in technology often allow us to do things that were previously impossible. This gives the designer a unique chance to experiment with novel types of gameplay.

But don't rely solely on technical advancements to open up new avenues of design. Many of the greatest designs come about through tireless experimentation. For example, take boardgames. Technically, they haven't advanced much in the past two hundred years, but every so often, the top designers come up with games that break all the old rules or push the envelope in terms of creativity and gameplay. Look at interesting new boardgames like *Settlers of Catan* and *Carcassonne* for inspiration.

The same is true in the computer world. You'll find that some of the most inventive games were designed on primitive systems. Sometimes limiting yourself to the basics helps you focus your ideas more clearly. With that in mind, it's time to see if those ideas you generated actually work. This is called prototyping and playtesting—the subjects of our next two chapters.

Chapter 7
Prototyping

Prototyping lies at the heart of good game design. The word "prototyping" means to create a working version of the formal system that, while playable, includes only a rough approximation of the artwork, sound, and features. Think of it as a crude model whose purpose is to allow you to wrap your brain around the game mechanics and see how they function.

To many first-time designers, making prototypes seems cumbersome, but if you invest the time, you'll discover that it teaches you about the essence of game design and that there is nothing more valuable for getting a game to work. You don't get bogged down with production-related issues or distracted by the window dressing. All you have are the fundamental mechanics to keep you engaged, and if these mechanics can sustain the interest of playtesters, then you know that you're onto something.

The main advantage of prototyping is that it forces you to define game mechanics in their purest form. If you look at most great games, the core gameplay is not complex. Studies show that human beings can, on average, track and manipulate seven concepts simultaneously. This was first established in 1956 by psychologist George Miller

in his classic paper entitled "The Magical Number Seven, Plus or Minus Two: Some Limits on Our Capacity for Processing Information."[1] In it, Miller showed 7 ±2 as the number of distinct items that humans can hold in short term memory. This strongly influenced the design of the U.S. phone system—e.g., phone numbers are seven digits long. Games utilize this concept successfully as well. For instance, the game *Tetris* includes seven shapes.

If you look carefully at games from *Super Mario Bros.* to *Command & Conquer* to *Halo*, you'll see that underneath the amazing graphics and rich worlds, the gameplay is quite straightforward. These games are engaging largely because they are so easy to understand. In fact, we challenge you to take any addictive game and strip away the graphics, sound effects, and optional features. What you'll find in almost every case is a system that can easily be modeled with a few basic rules. And this is why prototyping makes sense. It helps the game designer to focus on a handful of choices that the player must make and create a viable model for how the game will function given these limitations.

---

1. George Miller, "The Magical Number Seven, Plus or Minus Two: Some Limits on Our Capacity for Processing Information," *Psychological Review*, 1956 vol. 63, pp. 81–97.

How to Prototype

There are two types of prototypes: physical prototypes and software prototypes. The difference is that physical prototypes tend to be created using pen and paper or other real-world materials, while software prototypes are entirely digital and rely on computer code to function.

Physical prototypes

Let's begin with physical prototypes since that's the easiest type of prototype for most game designers to construct on their own. These are typically created using slips of paper, cardboard, and household objects with hand-drawn markings. You are free to use anything you like, from lead figures to plastic army men to pieces borrowed from other games. Whatever you can cobble together is fine.

In early drafts, we recommend that you pay no attention to the quality of the artwork. Stick figure drawings are the norm. The goal is to rough out system components so that you can see how the game operates on a mechanical level. Spending time on the artwork only slows down the process. Also, if you invest too much time crafting the look and feel of the prototype, you may become

attached to your work and be reluctant to make changes. Since the prototyping process is all about iteration and change, this becomes counterproductive.

Think of the prototype as analogous to a blueprint for a building. It might be only an approximation of the final product, but it serves its purpose, and often the limitations of pen and paper enable you to see the underlying forms and structures more clearly.

Battleship prototype

For our prototyping explanation, we're going to use a classic game with a simple system. If you're not familiar with *Battleship*, it's a popular two-player boardgame in which the object is to be the first player to sink your opponent's fleet.

Let's construct a physical prototype of this game. When starting with a prototype, it's best to identify the key elements of a game and then handcraft each element. In this case, take four sheets of paper and draw a 10×10 grid on each. Label the rows on each grid with the letters "A" through "J." Label the columns on each grid "1" through "10." Put the following titles on the four grids: "Player 1 Ocean Grid," "Player 1 Target Grid," "Player 2 Ocean Grid," and "Player 2 Target Grid." The final set will look like Figure 7.2.

Next, find two players and give each an ocean grid, a target grid, and a pen. Players should shield their grids from their opponent's view. Each player distributes the following five ships by drawing on his Ocean Grid. The numbers in parentheses are the ships' sizes on the grid:

- Carrier (1×5 cells)
- Battleship (1×4 cells)
- Destroyer (1×3 cells)

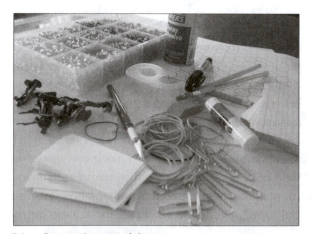

7.1   Prototyping materials

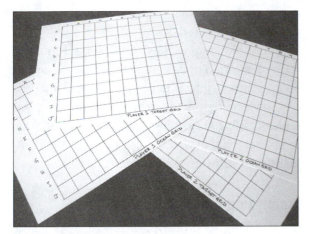

7.2   Battleship grids

- Submarine (1×3 cells)
- Patrol Boat (1×2 cells)

All segments of the ships should be drawn on the playing grid. Ships may not be placed diagonally. Figure 7.3 shows an example of ships placed on the grid.

Now that you have the prototype assembled, it's time to play. On a player's turn, that player calls out grid coordinates—e.g., "B5." If the opponent has a ship on that cell, then he answers, "hit." If not, he answers, "miss." When all segments of a ship have been hit, the opponent says, "You sank my battleship!" Simple enough?

Players track hits and misses on their target grids. If "B5" is a hit, the player marks an "H" on his target grid. Players take turns calling coordinates like this until one player sinks all five of the opposing ships. Figure 7.4 shows an example of what grids will look like during play.

Play this game yourself. Think about it in terms of how it functions as a prototype. Does it accurately represent the game mechanics? Although the artwork is crude and the rules are rough, do they provide enough of an experience for someone to grasp the game and give feedback? If this is the case, then the prototype is a success.

As you can see, making a playable game prototype doesn't require programming skills or art skills. The experience generated by the paper version of *Battleship* is almost identical to the experience generated by the fully produced Milton Bradley version.

The advantage of prototyping is that as you assemble the game, you gain a tactile sense for how the mechanics fit together. Abstract rules suddenly become concrete. You can look at the grid and ask yourself, "What if I made that bigger? How would that affect the gameplay?" And enlarging the grid is simple—just a matter of getting out a

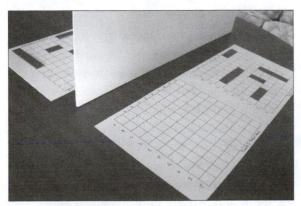

7.3   Battleship grids with ships

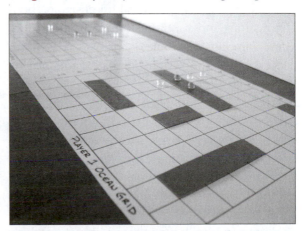

7.4   Battleship grids during play

piece of graph paper and drawing a bigger box. Then you can replay the game and see if the experience is better or worse.

Exercise 7.1: Modifying Your Prototype

Take your *Battleship* prototype and modify three aspects of the game. You can change the grids, the ships, the object of the game, the procedures for playing, etc. Get creative with the changes you make. After each change, play the game with a friend and describe how that particular change affects the gameplay.

As you manipulate elements of the game structure, it will invariably spark more ideas, and it's not uncommon for entirely new systems to materialize during this process. You can then spin some of these systems off into their own games. After you become experienced at prototyping, you'll find that this is probably the most effective way to create gameplay because it takes you right down into the mechanics and permits you to experiment in a way no other process can.

More examples

Physical prototypes are critical for designing both boardgames and sophisticated electronic games. Many famous electronic games are based on paper games. The system for digital role-playing games such as *Diablo II*, *Baldur's Gate*, *EverQuest*, *Asheron's Call*, and *Dark Age of Camelot* are derived from the paper-based system of *Dungeons & Dragons*. Likewise, the system for the famous computer game *Civilization* is based on a *Civilization* boardgame published by Avalon Hill.

The designers and programmers used the paper-based originals to figure out what would work electronically. Remember, there's nothing magical about using a computer. When it comes down to it, it's how people relate to the set of rules

and to each other that matter—not what medium the game is delivered on.

Many videogame designers started out by learning the craft of designing boardgames, and all boardgames begin as paper prototypes. Building and revising paper prototypes instills a deep understanding of gaming principles. And it does so in a setting that isn't bogged down by the complexities of software development.

Prototyping a first-person shooter

It's one thing to prototype a simple boardgame, but is it possible to create a physical prototype of an action-packed videogame? The answer is yes. Doing so is more difficult than prototyping a turn-based game, but it's just as valuable to the design process.

A first-person shooter (FPS) is a popular videogame genre. Examples include *Quake*, *Castle Wolfenstein*, *Battlefield 1942*, *Half-Life*, *Unreal Tournament*, and *Medal of Honor*. The core game mechanics involve units running around shooting other units. That's simple to understand, but how do you model one of these games on paper and what can that teach us? Let's start by defining what we'll need to construct our physical prototype.

Arena map

Take a large sheet of hexagonal graph paper. Hexagons are nice for prototypes because they allow units to move diagonally. You can purchase this graph paper at most boardgame stores or print it out using one of several freeware and shareware programs available online, such as *HexPaper 2*. The grid will serve as the arena for your game.

Cut out a small paper chit and color it red to mark spawning points. A "spawning point" is the cell on the grid where units materialize after they are killed.

7.5 FPS Prototype example

Put lines on the grid to represent walls. Units cannot move or shoot through walls. It's helpful to make walls out of objects that can be repositioned on the grid. Matchsticks are perfect for this. Having moveable walls makes it easier to tweak the system.

You probably already have questions like: "How many hexes should be on the grid?" "How big should each hex be?" "How many spawning points do I need?" and "Do I need lots of walls or only a few?" The answer to all of these questions is: take your best guess. There's no way to know what will work until you play the game. No matter what you decide, you'll probably wind up changing it later on. So pick whatever parameters you deem reasonable and proceed with the process.

Units

Units are "your guys" in this game. You can represent them with coins or plastic army men or other household objects. Whatever you use should fit within one cell on the grid. In addition, a unit should clearly show which direction it is aiming. For example, if you use coins as units, draw an arrow on them to indicate their direction.

This prototype is designed so multiple units can play at the same time. To determine starting cells for the different unit on the grid, roll a die. The player with the lowest number places his unit on the grid first. Go in clockwise order from there and have each player choose a starting cell. An example of what your prototype might look like is presented in Figure 7.5.

Exercise 7.2: Movement and Shooting

If you want a challenge, stop reading now and come up with your own movement and shooting rules. Explain your reasoning behind this set of rules.

Movement and shooting rules

Here is one possible solution for movement and shooting. There are endless other creative possibilities, and we encourage you to experiment with them.

Each player gets the following nine cards:

- "Move 1 space" ×1
- "Move 2 spaces" ×1
- "Move 3 spaces" ×1
- "Move 4 spaces" ×1
- "Turn Any Direction" ×2
- "Shoot" ×3

Play is executed in rounds

1. *Build Stack:* Each player chooses three cards and places them face down on the table in a stack.

2. *Reveal:* Each player turns over his top card.

3. *Resolve Shoot Cards:* Players with a Shoot Card fire in the direction their unit is pointed. They follow an imaginary line across the grid. If this line intersects with a cell containing another unit, the shot hits. If this line comes to a wall or otherwise does not intersect with a unit, it misses. Shots happen simultaneously so that two or more players may hit at the same time.

4. *Resolve Turn Cards:* Players with Turn Cards turn their unit to whatever direction they please. If two or more players have Turn Cards, roll a die to determine who turns first.

5. *Resolve Move Cards:* Players with Move Cards move their units the number of spaces specified on the card. If two or more players have Move Cards, roll a die to determine who moves first. Players cannot occupy the same cell.

6. Repeat steps 2–5 for the second card in the stack.

7. Repeat steps 2–5 for the third card in the stack.

If a unit is shot, then it's removed from the grid, and the player chooses one of the spawning points on the grid and reappears there at the beginning of the next round.

Exercise 7.3: Build it Yourself

Build the physical prototype described just previously and test it out. Describe any problems that you encounter. Also, list out any questions you have while building it.

This process of prototyping an action-based game may seem complex, but if you think about what we've done, it's pretty amazing. In less than five pages, we've completely described how to build a first-person shooter using only pen and paper. When you play with this model, you'll see that it's both flexible and simple to use.

Suggested additions

1. *Add a scoring system,* making players track the number of kills they get. The first player to get ten kills wins the game.

2. *Include a hit percentage.* Say the chance that a shot hits is 100% when two units are standing on adjacent hexes on the grid. This percentage decreases by 10% for each hex of distance added. Calculate hits and misses using a ten-sided die.

3. *Provide hit points.* Have each unit starts with five hit points. One shot suffered removes one hit point.

4. *Drop in first aid.* If a unit stands on a first aid hex on the board for a full round, then his hit points return to their original amount.

5. *Add in ammo.* Units start with 10 rounds each. Every time they shoot, one bullet is removed. If a unit stands on an ammo hex for a full round, he will reload his clip.

6. *Introduce other weapons.* New weapons can be placed on the grid. If a unit stands on the weapon, he can use it in the next round. Enhancements to weapons include more damage per shot, higher accuracy, more bullets, etc.

Exercise 7.4: Features

Add some or all of the features mentioned previously plus a few that you dream up yourself and incorporate them into the physical prototype. Write down how these features affect the gameplay.

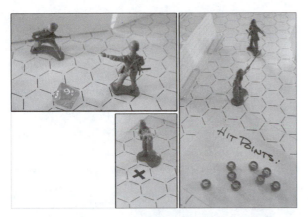

7.6   FPS prototype example with additions—clockwise from top left: hit percentage, hit points, and first aid

New rules and features can continue to be added, altered, and removed. You can use the system to create "capture the flag" games, cooperative play missions, and death matches. You can continue adding, testing, and tweaking until you come up with the right combination. Each time you add a rule or feature, it may spark new ideas and lead you down a path you didn't expect to go. This is the heart of the creative process, and you should encourage yourself to try things that may seem ridiculous or absurd—and just see what happens when you play the game. Completing these exercises will give you insight into how all first-person shooters and 3D adventure games are designed.

Exercise 7.5: Working Backwards

Now let's apply what you've learned to a different type of game.

1. Take two different real-time strategy (RTS) games, such as *WarCraft* and *Age of Empires*, and work backwards. Strip away the external feature set and show what both games have in common. These are the core game mechanics.

2. Translate the core game mechanics for one of the RTS games to paper in a playable format.

Remember, all we care about are the rules that correlate between the two games. These rules represent the core gaming system and will form the basis for your RTS physical prototype.

Perspective on physical prototyping

People not used to physical prototyping may argue that this method doesn't accurately represent the player experience on a computer. They may think a pen and paper prototype might work for a turn-based game, but not for an action-based shooter because gameplay is integrally tied to the 3D environment and the ability of the players to act in real-time. We are not arguing that physical prototyping replaces those things. What we are saying is the overall gaming system can benefit tremendously in its early stages by building a physical prototype.

Physically prototyping allows you to build a structure for the game, think through how the various elements interact, and formulate a systemic approach to how the game will function. The sensory experience created by a digital game—e.g., the feeling of moving through a 3D space—is only one component of an engaging game experience. And although it's a critical component, it can be isolated and left until later in the process. At a minimum, physical prototyping forces you to think through the design elements and define them. You can always change them down the road, but this gives you a framework to build upon, and that in itself can save you from stumbling around blindly when it comes to preparing and launching a production team.

Imagine getting in a room with programmers who know nothing about the project and trying to describe to them the game you have in your head. It's not easy. If you want to create gameplay that people have never seen before, it may be impossible. A physical prototype that they can sit down and play ensures that they will be able to grasp your vision of the game. They also have something solid to work from. A written treatment or design document is good, but when it comes to communicating a complex system, they don't compare to a prototype that someone can actually play.

Software prototypes

Software prototypes are analogous to physical prototypes, except that they are made using programming tools. Like physical prototypes, they include only the elements needed to make the system functional; they are void of polished art and sound; and they serve as the conceptual blueprint for creating the final electronic game.

If you have programming skills, you should prototype using the software tools with which you're most familiar. Again, this is not a book about programming. The de facto standard programming language for today's PC and console games is C++. Electronic Arts, for example, has standardized on C++ and uses it for every new game. Most other game companies do the same. One of the benefits of C++ is that it's an object-oriented language, which means sections of code can be reused. This leads to efficiencies during production and is good for creating large-scale applications where dozens of programmers are working on the same project.

Other popular languages for prototyping are Shockwave (especially for web-based games), Delphi, Blitz Basic, and Visual Basic (because it's so simple to learn), as well as certain types of 3D and 2D graphic engines, like Macromedia Director, which can get you up and running quickly. But if

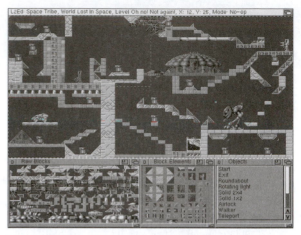

7.7   Lemmings third party level editor (game type: puzzle)

you don't have programming skills, don't be discouraged. Many of the world's greatest game designers are not programmers. You can focus your talents on game design and find programmers to work with you when producing games. See more about working with teams and software development in Part III starting on page 317.

Last but not least, there are software tools that can help you lay out the design in the prototyping phase of a project. These include Visio, for making flowcharts, Excel, for creating spreadsheets, and Access and Filemaker, for structuring the data. It pays to learn some of these tools. They can save you an enormous amount of time when preparing your game concept and presenting it to others.

Level editors

Another useful and fun way to learn about prototyping games with software is to experiment with level editors. Level editors are programs that are used to create custom levels of PC and console games. They are typically "drag and drop" tools, so you don't have to be a programmer to use them. Creating a custom level will expose you to the formal system guts of a game and help you learn how

USING SOFTWARE PROTOTYPES IN GAME DESIGN

by Nikita Mikros, Co-Founder and Lead Game Designer, Black Hammer Game

In a successful game, the rules of the game interact with each other and give rise to interesting but controlled emergent subsystems and compelling play patterns. Having a solid understanding of how one system interacts with another is essential in writing a comprehensive design document, answering questions from the team about the project, resolving unforeseen problems and ultimately creating a compelling balanced game. As games become increasingly complex, it becomes more and more difficult for the game designer to keep a complete image of all the elements or systems of gameplay in his or her mind.

Scientists use simulations and visualizations to gain understanding of complex data. Similarly game designers can employ their own set of tools to gain insight into their own creations. These tools include daily logs, design documents, paper prototypes, and software prototypes. Software prototypes should be one of many tools at the game designer's disposal and although they can be extremely useful, without clear goals they can easily escalate into monsters more complex to build than the problem the designer is trying to solve. The goal in building a software prototype should always be to create a tool to help in your game design efforts, not to show off fancy graphics or elegant software architecture.

When Do You Need Software Prototypes?

Many games lend themselves very easily to paper prototypes, and even if the whole game cannot be modeled this way, isolated parts can often be playtested and designed using this process. However, there are times where one cannot really get a feel for a game without a software prototype. A simple example would be the game of *Tetris*. *Tetris* was inspired by pentominoes, a puzzle/toy based on building shapes out of pieces that are constructed from five basic blocks. In *Tetris*, the pieces are simplified from five to four blocks (tetrominoes) and are dropped at a constant rate, allowing the player to spin and move the pieces trying to construct solid horizontal rows on the bottom of the board. When a horizontal row is created, that row of building blocks is eliminated from the game. The pieces stack up, and eventually the game is lost when the player can no longer fit pieces onto the board. Although they share many similarities, constructing shapes with tetrominoes is very different from playing *Tetris*. How would one model the game of *Tetris* in a physical/paper prototype? Although the game has its origins in a physical puzzle, it is very tightly bound to a type of interaction that can only be modeled on the computer. In this case a physical/paper prototype would be more difficult to construct than a software prototype.

Supremacy: Four Paths To Power

The creation of any software prototyping tools should be carefully considered, due to the costly and time-consuming nature of writing software. The questions that the designer should ask before diving into such a project are as follows:

- Is the tool/prototype really needed?
- What are the requirements of the tool/prototype?
- What is the quickest way to build the tool?
- Will the tool be flexible enough?

In the following section I will address how I attempted to resolve these questions for a particular problem in my current project.

Supremacy: Four Paths To Power is an open-ended strategy war game that is waged on two fronts: the meta game, which is a battle in space, and the ground battles that determine the individual capture of planets. Each type of planet has different natural resources that the player can exploit to build unique military units and ultimately try to defeat his or her enemies. Overzealous players can destroy their own planets due to overproduction.

Is the Tool/Prototype Really Needed?

My first task was to build a paper/physical prototype and test my ideas by getting feedback from the rest of our team who I volunteered to be playtesters. Two separate paper prototypes were created: one simulating battles on the ground, and one simulating the larger battles in space. The ground battle prototype worked fine; the math was straightforward and keeping track of all the stats was relatively simple. Excited by the first prototype, we set out to play the space battle prototype and disaster struck. After much groaning and moaning, we somehow slogged through seven or eight turns in what seemed like as many hours before calling it quits. The accounting of resources that was required was daunting. We were so caught up doing math that we could not see the forest for the trees. When one of the playtesters declared, "This game is hurting my head," I decided it was time to create a software prototype.

What are the Requirements of the Tool/Prototype?

My first impulse was to build a full visual prototype, but upon further consideration I decided to ignore the "programmer within" and opted for a simpler solution. What I decided upon was a nonvisual representation of the game in software and the old paper prototype for visual representation. It was easy for us mere mortals to move pieces, count squares, calculate line of sight, and do all the things that take many person-hours to express in code. Alternatively, it was very easy to program the software to do all the accounting calculations as well as some other tedious tasks like keeping track of turns. The "prototype" looked nothing like a game—it looked like an ugly excel spreadsheet with lots and lots of buttons. It took me about a day and a half to write.

What is the Quickest Way to Build the Tool/Prototype?

My first attempt was to build the tool in a spreadsheet program, but I quickly realized that it was not feasible due to the nature of some of the calculations. I decided to build it using Java and the Metrowerks RAD (Rapid Application Development) toolset. This was a good option because I could quickly and easily lay out my tables, buttons, and other widgets and doodads. I was already familiar with the language and the development environment, so it was a natural choice. For me, writing this type of software is somewhat liberating because the end product is more or less a throwaway. I am far less concerned with software design, architecture, optimization, coding standards, and all the other things that go into building solid software. Remember, the goal is to create a tool to help your game design efforts, not to create elegant airtight software. Ultimately, I believe that you should write your prototypes in whatever language or authoring system you feel comfortable in and which allows you to experiment and change things quickly and easily. If you are not a programmer or are unfamiliar with any type of authoring software then you must rely on your programming team. This can be difficult because ultimately programmers want to write good code and their first impulse is always to build well-engineered reusable code that they can then use in the final product. This is not a bad idea once you have a clear idea of all the elements of your game, but this approach to rapid game design prototyping is like building a tractor to make a sandcastle. It is overkill, and it prematurely locks you into something that you may not be trying to build.

Will the Tool Be Flexible Enough?

Ultimately, you want to be able to change rules and values easily and have the ability to experiment as quickly as you would be able to in a paper prototype. Although this is somewhat of a holy grail, there are things you can do to make your software prototyping tool more flexible. Here are some simple suggestions.

1. Everything is a variable.
2. Try to avoid using any literal constants in your code, in other words a code snippet that looks like this:

```
totalOutput = 15*2
```

should look like this:

```
totalOutput = rateOfProduction*numFactories
```

3. Expose as many variables in the interface as possible.

4. Litter your prototyping tool with editable text fields; any value that has a remote possibility of changing should be editable through these fields. Your tool will be as ugly to look at as your high school yearbook picture, but you'll be happy when you don't need to recompile or go rifling through your code looking for a variable in the middle of a play testing session.

5. Don't even think of reusing this code.

When I was an undergrad studying fine art, I had a drawing professor by the name of Marvin Bileck, and everybody called him Buddy. One day Buddy made us all go buy some sheets of very expensive drawing paper. We all came to class the next week with our beautiful drawing paper, ready to draw. At this point Buddy instructed us to throw the paper on the ground and stomp on it, if we weren't doing a good enough job he came over and joined in on the destruction of our precious paper. At the end of this exercise he declared that we were ready to start drawing. The point of the exercise was clear to me: if you want to be creative don't hold on to anything too tightly, don't make anything so precious that you can't see beyond it. This is the way you should think about your prototyping code. In the end you may wind up reusing parts of the code, but this should not be a goal as you create it. You should be fully prepared to throw it away.

Conclusion

Software prototyping is a tool that can be used to understand and ultimately control the elements of your game. You gain nothing by writing software that prototypes a part of your game that you already thoroughly understand or that you can play test via cheaper methods like paper prototypes. Every game is different, with its own special characteristics and requirements. If we had been working on a first person shooter, or a fighting game, a totally different type of prototype would have been needed. I believe in this particular case the software prototype was successful. It allowed me to visualize emergent behaviors in the game that I would not have been able to see with just a paper prototype. This prototype worked because it addressed the specific problems I was trying to solve and because I could build it quickly and easily.

Author Bio

Nikita Mikros is co-founder and lead game designer for Black Hammer Game. He served as technical director and lead programmer for the award-winning GameBoy Advance title I-Spy Challenger. *Prior to Black Hammer, he joined with John Mikros in 1997 to found Flying Mikros Interactive, a creator of electronic entertainment for the Internet, and of graphics and entertainment software for the Macintosh and PC. Their PC game,* The Egg Files, *was selected as one of ten finalists in the 2002 Independent Games Festival. Other completed titles include* Alien Attack: The Battle over Sector 7G, Monkey Shines 2: Gorilla Warfare, *and* Chick-Tac-Toe. *In addition, Mr. Mikros has taught various programming and game design classes in the MFA Computer Art Department at the School of Visual Arts for the past seven years.*

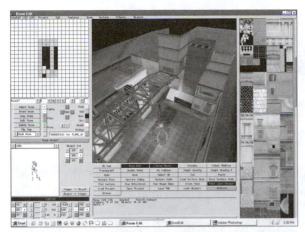

7.8 Tomb Raider: Chronicles level editor (game type: action/adventure)

to prototype your own games. Some level editors come with the games and some are created by third parties. Many can be downloaded from the Internet for free once you've purchased the game.

If you look carefully at the screen shot of the editor for *Unreal 2* in Figure 7.9, you'll notice that they include the same formal elements found in our first-person shooter prototype—a map grid, rooms, units, objects, etc. In fact, spending time

using a level editor is the single best way to get a feel for a specific genre of game, and if you invest the time, you'll find that you aren't alone. Creating "mods," or modifications, is a big part of gaming today. If you go online, you'll discover tens of thousands of mods created by players. Some of the best mod designers are snatched up by large game publishers/developers and can go on to become top designers.

Perhaps the most famous modder is Minh "Gooseman" Le. He took the popular FPS *Half-Life* and modded it to create a version with more team-oriented gameplay. The result was *Counter-Strike*. In this mod, one team plays the role of terrorist and the other plays the role of counter-terrorist. The two sides have different weapons and abilities. They created a variety of maps with creative goals such as hostage rescue, assassination, bomb defusing, and escape. Gooseman and the *Counter-Strike* team released the mod online and it became an instant hit. The game has won dozens of awards for gameplay and has helped sell tens of thousands of copies of *Half-Life*. In fact, many folks

7.9 Unreal 2 level editor (game type: first-person shooter)

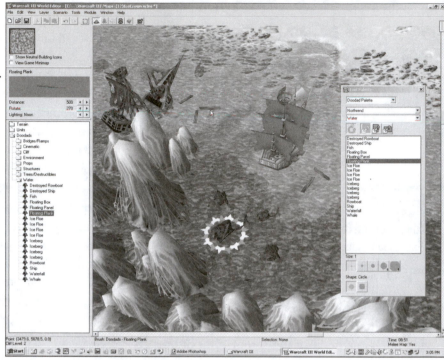

7.10 WarCraft III world editor (game type: real–time strategy)

buy *Half-Life* just so they can play *Counter-Strike*. This is an example of a talented modder becoming a star in the game industry.

    WarCraft III has one of the most sophisticated level editors available. The game developer, Blizzard Entertainment, calls it the "world editor." It allows you to create your own *WarCraft III* maps and manipulate nearly every facet of the game. It's the same editor that the level designers at Blizzard used to make the tutorial on the game CD. If you haven't tried it, you should. Becoming familiar with this level editor is one of the best ways to understand basic RTS game design.

    In Spring 2003, Blizzard conducted a mapmaking contest using the editor. Over one thousand players created their own maps and uploaded them to the Blizzard site. Eleven winners were chosen. Their maps were included on the *WarCraft III: Frozen Throne* CD, and their names appeared in the official game credits.

    The screen in Figure 7.11 shows how you can set the board size for a *WarCraft III* map. Like in most games, a bigger, more complex grid often lengthens the game time, while a smaller, simpler grid makes for a shorter and often more intense experience.

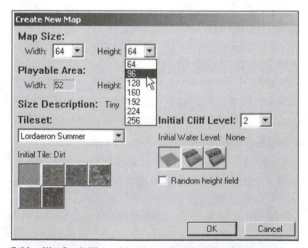

7.11 WarCraft III world editor: choose map size

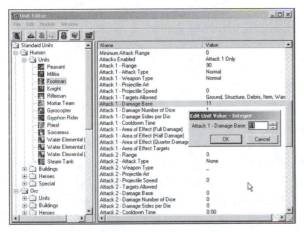

7.12 **WarCraft III world editor: unit properties**

The unit editor in Figure 7.12 allows you to define properties for units in a game session. The default numbers are numbers set by the game designers at Blizzard. As you start to play around with the numbers, you may wonder how the designers came to choose certain values for each unit. The answer is through prototyping and playtesting. More powerful units have higher costs in terms of resources and build time. For instance, the knight unit comes with 800 hit points and a ground attack strength of 25. It is almost two times more powerful than the footman unit which comes with 420 hit points and a ground attack strength of 12.5. The knight has a commensurate cost of 245 gold plus 60 wood compared to the footman's cost of 135 gold and 0 wood. Also the knight has a long build time, 45, compared to the

footman's short build time of 20. So there's always a trade off balanced into the game.

Every unit property in *WarCraft III* had to be meticulously playtested and tweaked based on benefits versus cost until the game system balanced. If any number were out of proportion, experienced players might mass-produce that unit, making all other units irrelevant.

The Aurora Toolset for *Neverwinter Nights* (see sidebar on page 172 and the accompanying figure) was created as a platform to allow gamers to build their own worlds, quests, and storylines. It puts complete control of the world into the user's hands and can be used as a creative toolset for making new kinds of gameplay in a 3D space.

Exercise 7.6: Mapping a Level

Take a game like *WarCraft III*, *Neverwinter Nights*, or another game that ships with a level editor. Study one of the pre-made levels in the game, and sketch out a map of all of its elements, so that you have a clear understanding of how it was designed.

Exercise 7.7: Designing Your Own Level

Use the level-editing tool of the game you chose in the last exercise to design a playable level of your own. You can find a number of example levels online for most games with level editors.

PROTOTYPING YOUR ORIGINAL GAME IDEA

Now that you have some experience creating and modifying prototypes, it's time to take one of your game concepts and create your own original prototype. The first step is to pick one of the ideas that you brainstormed in the previous chapter. If you

skipped Chapter 6, go back and read it now. Once your idea and concept treatment are done, you'll be ready to make your first prototype. But before we dive into the mechanics of constructing the

A Good Mod Kit for First Time Level Designers: The *Neverwinter Nights* Aurora Toolset

by Trent Oster, Producer, BioWare, Inc.

The Neverwinter Nights Aurora Toolset extends a frontier in game development by encouraging and supporting the creation and sharing of user created content on a massive scale. Although the PC mod community has an amazing track record developing original new content from released game titles, much of this development work has historically been limited to "amateur" mod-makers with significant technical skills. When developing *Neverwinter Nights*, BioWare planned from the outset to create an environment that would open the mod community to the average player. Our vision was to enable a Neverwinter mod building community that numbered in the tens or hundreds of thousands.

Although the Neverwinter Aurora Toolset is designed to be accessible to the average person, it still supports all the detail required for professional game story creation. The toolset is based on a simple tile-painting area creation scheme, which allows for fast and easy implementation of environments and quick placement of creatures and items. A powerful and flexible scripting language allows the advanced user extensive control of adventure development while the scripting system supports sharing of custom scripts for the less technical user.

Bioware is a company of determined game players and creators. We often use ourselves as an image of our target market, and as such we create concepts that we believe will appeal to our fans and ourselves. The concept for *Neverwinter Nights* grew from a discussion comparing the relative strengths and weaknesses of massively multiplayer versus single-player games. *Neverwinter Nights* was created to blend the strengths of both formats while at the same time using the Internet itself as a model for distribution and content sharing. By empowering end users to create and host adventures we could create a game that spanned a large cross culture of gamers. In fact, looking at the current *Neverwinter Nights* community, you can easily spot a huge variety of gameplay themes and settings that were not commercially or critically feasible for us to develop. Through the sharing of the toolset, *Neverwinter Nights* has become more than one game; it has become a framework in which users can share varied game experiences.

prototype, make sure you've clearly articulated the core gameplay that will be created.

Visualizing core gameplay

If you try to design the entire game at once, you may become confused and overwhelmed. There are so many elements in a typical game that it's difficult to know where and how to start. What we

recommend is that you isolate the core gameplay mechanism and build out from there.

The core gameplay mechanism can be defined as the one action a player repeats most often while striving to achieve the game's overall goal. Games are repetitive by nature. While the meaning and consequences of what a player does may change over the course of game, the core action tends to

We have been extremely pleased with the results to date—almost 3,000 community-developed modules are providing Neverwinter players a huge variety of adventures, allowing for diverse play styles and storylines that satisfy a range of player preferences. Using the tools, fans have created modules that include everything from the campy "Sex and the Single Sorceress" to a remake of the classic computer game, *Ultima IV.* This large and vibrant mod-making community has extended the lifespan of *Neverwinter Nights* and provided fans a broad range of rich content that could keep the experience fresh for years to come.

Author Bio

Trent Oster is a nine-year veteran of the videogame industry. Through that period he has worked as a development studio owner, an artist, a programmer, and finally a project director. After working on the titles Shattered Steel *and* Baldur's Gate, *he led the development of* Neverwinter Nights *from concept to completion. Trent is currently completing the second expansion pack to* Neverwinter Nights, The Hordes of the Underdark.

**Neverwinter Nights Aurora Toolset
(game type: role-playing game)**

remain the same from beginning to end. For instance, in chess, the core action is moving your pieces on a grid in an attempt to capture your opponent's pieces. That single action defines the entire game. Once you understand that, the overall structure for chess becomes apparent. You can then start to play with other variables and redesign the game. For instance, should certain chess pieces have different attacks or defenses? What should be the size and shape of the grid? What if each piece was assigned health points and damage? How would that change the game?

Suddenly, it becomes clear how to grow the game. By starting from the center and working outwards, you can see the possibilities unfold. This not only works for boardgames like chess but also for videogames. Take the first-person shooter prototype that we created. The core gameplay mechanism was the ability for players to move about simultaneously while attempting to shoot one another with their weapons.

Here are some examples of popular games and their core gameplay mechanisms:

- *WarCraft:* Players build and move units on an overhead map in real time with the intent of engaging opposing units in combat and destroying them.

- *Monopoly:* Players roll two dice and move around a board with the goal of buying up properties and charging rent to anyone who lands on them.

- *Diablo:* In an attempt to amass treasure and become more powerful, a player moves his character about an overhead map, battling any monsters or enemies it comes into contact with.

- *Super Mario Bros.:* A player controls Mario (or Luigi), making him walk, run, and jump, while avoiding traps, overcoming obstacles, and gathering treasure.

- *Atomic Bomberman:* Players move their Bombermen around a maze and drop bombs next to their opponents in an attempt to blow them up.

As you can see, all of the previous descriptions are a single sentence. This is because the core game mechanism should be simple. If you can't write up your gameplay in a single sentence, it means you have a problem. It's extremely difficult to design a game that cannot be articulated concisely. Failure to isolate the core mechanics indicates that the game itself isn't fully thought out or is overly complex.

Exercise 7.8: Understanding Core Gameplay

Define the core gameplay mechanism for five games not described in the previous section.

Now try to answer the following questions about your game. Your treatment from Chapter 6 on page 156 should give you a huge head start with this. If you get stuck on a question, however, just take your best guess. The answers to these questions are going to evolve as you prototype and revise your game, so don't let them slow you down here at the beginning.

Building the physical prototype

Now let's get our hands dirty. Here are four steps that will help you build a physical prototype efficiently.

1. Foundation

Build a representation of your core gameplay. Get some arts and crafts materials such as cardboard, construction paper, glue, pens, and scissors. Draw a board layout or rough map if you want and cut pieces out of the cardboard and paper.

As you do this, questions will come to your mind. How many squares should a player be allowed to move? How will the players interact with one another? How is the conflict resolved? Do not try to answer all these questions as once. In fact, place the questions on the backburner and focus on the core gameplay.

Designing the basic game objects (physical setting, units, resources, etc.) and the key procedures for the game (those repetitive action cycles that keep the game in motion) are the heart of the foundation stage.

Try playing your core mechanic on your own—it may not be much of a game, but you will

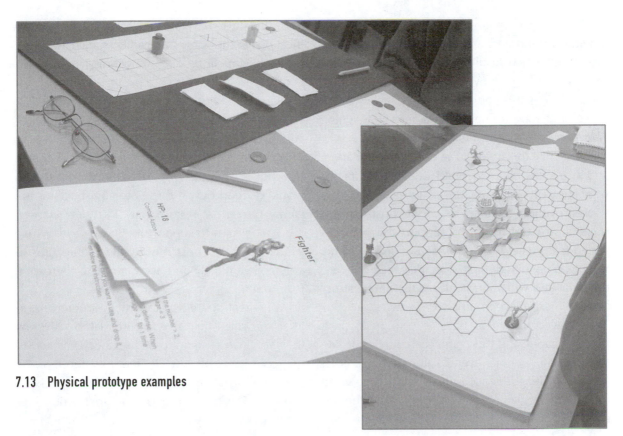

7.13   Physical prototype examples

be able to see if the basic concept is worth pursuing. Once you have your foundation in place, the system takes over and begins to ask you questions you'll want to answer. But watch out. Try to test the game without expanding the rules at this point. If you have to add a rule to make the mechanic playable, then add it, but only do this if it's absolutely necessary. Your goal should be to keep the core gameplay mechanism down to as few rules as possible.

In the FPS prototype, the first element that we fleshed out was simultaneous movement, because this is the core mechanic of the game. The idea that all players should reveal an action card at the same time to simulate real-time movement was conceived. This was a foothold to build upon. From there, the next logical question was: what are options on the action cards? The answer was:

move, turn, or shoot. Other ideas for action cards popped up as well, such as: stand, crouch, go prone, etc. However, we decided to keep the options as simple as possible at first. These lead us to the next stage of our prototype: structure.

2. Structure

Once the foundation is in place and seems to function, it's time to move on to structure. The best technique for doing this is to prioritize what is most essential to the game. In our FPS prototype, some structural elements we added were our three action options—(1) number of spaces a unit could move, (2) procedures for turning, and (3) hit and miss rules for shooting. Our army men were moved and turned on the table, as mock units using the rules.

These experiments solidified some ideas about moving and shooting and caused other ideas to be dismissed, which resulted in a very crude system for simultaneous movement and the basics of shooting. We also considered adding rules about movement and starting points, as well as assigning a turn order to the players.

Think of it this way: you've built the foundation, and now you need to build the framework for your game. It's not a matter of what you think is coolest or most saleable; it's about constructing a skeletal structure that can support the rich and varied feature set that will be your finished game. What you need to do first is decide which rules are essential and which are features that those structural elements have to support.

List every idea you have in your head on a piece of paper, and then rank each one according to what you deem its overall value to the game. If you've ranked them according to their true value in making the game function, the ones at the top should be your essential elements, while the ones at the bottom are your peripheral features.

Now, methodically work down the list. At this point when we were building the FPS prototype, the movement and shooting foundation begged for the structure of a scoring system and unit hit points. As we added these elements, our crude movement and shooting system was re-tested with them in place. The tests illuminated problems that could only be seen with the system in motion. The whole system was revised to address the problems. At this point the system was still messy and ill-defined. Nothing had been written down. There were open questions everywhere. However, the system was basically functional.

When working through this, keep in mind the distinction between what are features and what are rules. Features are attributes that make a game richer, like adding more weapons or new vehicles

or a nifty way to navigate the space. Rules are modifications to the game mechanics that change how the game functions, such as winning conditions, conflict resolution, turn order, etc.

You can add rules without adding features, but you can never add a feature without changing or adding rules. For example, if you added a new type of laser gun to your game, the rules would dictate how this gun could be used, what damage it would do, and how it relates to all aspects of the game. One new feature may introduce ten or more new rules to support it. As you modify your game, you'll be constantly tweaking the rules to enhance gameplay and accommodate a growing feature set.

Your best strategy for adding structure is to focus on rules first and features later. Rules, by their very nature, tend to be inextricably linked to the core gameplay, while features tend to be peripheral. That's a generalization, but if you keep it in mind, it will help you to structure the development of your game.

3. **Formal details**

The next step is to add the necessary rules and procedures to the system to make it into a fully functional game. Focus on what you know about formal elements to decide what your game needs. Is the objective interesting and achievable? Is the player interaction structure the best choice? Are there rules or procedures that you wanted to add, but they weren't part of the core mechanic? The trick is to find an appropriate level of detail to add. Beginning game designers typically add too much. The art of game design often involves paring a bunch of feature ideas down to a small, important set.

At this point in the development of the FPS prototype, we added the hit percentage, health, and scoring. Many other ideas were discussed including: mines, shields, vehicles, mechanisms

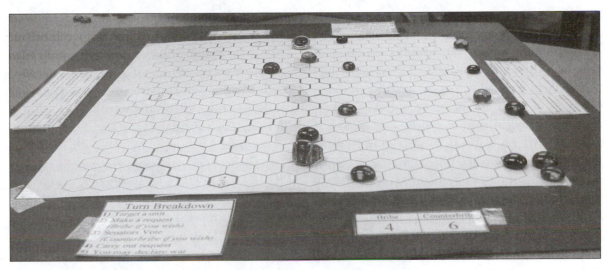

7.14   Physical prototype with procedures outlined

for hiding, and more. However, we scrapped all of them and focused on rules affecting the central gameplay, rather than a set of new features that we believed would create the most interesting game. How did we decide on some elements and not others? It was a creative judgment, backed by input from our playtesters.

One way to add formal details efficiently is to isolate each new rule and test it individually. If you feel the game cannot function without this rule, then leave it in the game and add another rule. But don't overuse this privilege. Not every rule is critical, and the less you add, the cleaner your skeleton. A lot of what you consider to be rules are probably features. Try to draw a clear distinction, and keep your core rule set as clean as possible.

Test each rule, then remove it, and add another rule, and test it. It will be clear that some of the rules are optional and others must be included in the game if you are to continue to expand the gameplay. This is a litmus test. If you can continue to build out the game without a specific rule, no matter how amazing that rule seems, you should

leave it out. You can always add it later, but it shouldn't be included at this early stage.

4.   Refinement

At this point in the process, the prototype is a playable system, although it may still be somewhat rough. By experimenting and tweaking, the play system will become more refined. The play experience created by the game will flow. Instead of questioning the fundamentals of the game (and possibly thinking it will never work), you will switch to questioning the smaller details, and of course, the big question: is your game fun? If not, what will make it fun? This process of refinement may continue for a number of iterations.

During refinement is also the time to add all those great ideas for features that have come up while testing but were not really essential. We went back to those ideas about mines and teleport pads for our FPS at this point. Again, be careful not to get ahead of yourself. It's tempting to slap on five new features, create a bunch of rules to support those features, and then start playing, but this blurs your view of the game. It becomes difficult to tell which features are making the game more fun to play and which are causing problems.

To avoid this, rank the features in terms of necessity. Then introduce and test each one. Test how it affects overall gameplay, and then remove it. This may seem cumbersome, but it will keep your game structure from getting convoluted. If you muck up your game with a bunch of features and rules too early, you'll find yourself losing your grasp on what the game is about. We've seen this happen over and over again, and this is why we caution all designers to postpone the pleasure of creating the ideal game from the outset, and instead recommend that they focus on what's needed step by step.

As you do this, you'll discover that some rules and features that seemed like great ideas actually diminish the playability, while others that appeared dull add a whole new dimension to the game. You can only know this by testing each one

in a controlled environment without the interference of other features. After testing each new twist, write down an analysis. Be sure to use you playtesters and incorporate their feedback into your analysis. They are your eyes and ears. You may love a rule or feature so much that you're blind to its flaws. Trust your testers.

Exercise 7.9: Prototype Your Own Game

Use what you've learned to create a paper prototype of the game idea you described in Exercise 6.9 on page 156. This is a hard task. Break it down into the iterative steps described on pages 174–178 (i.e., Foundation, Structure, Formal Details, Refinement). If you get stuck on a step, just take your best guess and move on. With prototyping you always have room to iterate.

Tools for Visualizing

A tool that can help throughout the design process is a flowchart application. We recommend using popular programs, like Visio, Inspiration, or PDQ to lay out the game as a system. Doing this lets you see the structure take shape before your eyes. If you don't have access to a flowcharting tool, you can use index cards on a corkboard, or even quickly sketched boxes on paper.

There's no right or wrong way to visualize your game. In fact, you may want to make several flow charts, some from the perspective of the players, others where the core game mechanics reside at the center and the rules branch outwards, and others illuminating the turn sequence and gameplay arc, whatever helps you to communicate your game to others and to yourself. When you create these flowcharts, have your team in mind. These

will help your coworkers comprehend the structure of the game. But actually, you will be the one who benefits the most. Forcing yourself to work through the mechanics and express them in a visual format allows you to better internalize the system you've created, which means you can be more creative later on.

As you analyze and refine the structure, make sure to weed out any nonessential rules that slipped into the design. These are luxuries you must do without. When you're done with this process, your core game mechanics should be clearly defined as a body of rules, methods, and procedures that both link to and shape one another.

At this point you can step back and analyze what you've created. Look at the body of rules. Every one should be essential to the game. At the

7.15 **More physical prototype examples**

center, you should have the core game mechanics and around it a clean structure of rules that are required to play a primitive version of what will be the final product.

MAKING THE PHYSICAL PROTOTYPE BETTER

The prototype you've created may or may not be very playable. Parts may be out of balance and rules may conflict. Your game may also feel slow or disjointed. Many designers panic at this point and throw out everything. They feel that their game is hopeless and the only solution is to start from scratch with a new game idea concept.

This may be true, but before you take such drastic measures, it's good to go back to your core game mechanics. Strip away all the additional rules and then reintroduce them one by one in an attempt to isolate the problem. Doing this, you'll come to understand how each rule and feature actually fits into the system. Some features and rules may seem innocuous at first, but as you add and remove them, it will become apparent how they can throw the whole system out of whack.

Think of yourself as a doctor hunting for the source of an ailment. Your game, like the human body, is a complex system, and specific elements may interact with others to produce a result that's unexpected. Your job is to systematically diagnose an ill game and then prescribe treatment. Sometimes this can be a painstaking process, as you rip apart rules and rebuild them over and over again, but it's the only way to truly figure out what part of your game is actually broken.

When you get to the point where you are absolutely certain that your prototype is both playable and fun, then you're ready to start all over again.

Yes, that's right. Just because your game is good doesn't mean it's brilliant. Before you move on to the next stage, you want a great game. And even if it's great, there may be a way to make it better.

Beyond the Physical Prototype

Physical prototyping is only the first in a long set of steps to completing a functional digital game. You (and your team) should use the physical prototype as the systemic blueprint for a software prototype. Because you've spent a lot of time thinking through the core mechanics and most important features of your game by building a physical prototype, articulating those mechanics will be much simpler.

Obviously, taking your physical prototype from a physical to a digital design will change the nature of how players access the game. But the core mechanics of the system are still valid. For example, in the FPS prototype you could lay out the arena, spawning points, ammo, first aid, etc., in the software prototype exactly as you had them in the physical prototype. The programmers would implement a real-time system for movement and shooting, making your card system obsolete, but the basic gameplay would remain intact, and the map you created would provide a good design guide.

The main differences you will find in translating your physical prototype to a digital design are in the controls and interface for the target system. Rather than players moving their army men on the grid, now you have to provide a control map for a keyboard and mouse, a proprietary controller, or for whatever other input device you are designing for. Also, you have to design a visual display of the game environment for a PC screen or television. Chapter 11 goes into more detail on this process.

Design Documents

Since you will probably not be the only person working on your game, it's important to communicate the design to the rest of the team in a document. This design document describes the overall concept, the features, the controls, the interfaces, the flow, etc. While many designers jump right into the design document right after they've come up with a concept, we don't recommend that. Prototyping is really the only way to judge the validity of your concept and gain enough insight to write a useful design document.

We recommend that you build both a physical prototype, and, if possible, a rough software prototype before laying your ideas down in a full design document. While you work on these prototypes, you'll be writing down rules and procedures and blocking out overall concepts for the game. So, when you sit down to write your design document you'll be way ahead in your thinking process. The benefits to your team and your final product will be immeasurable. Chapter 14 on page 370 discusses writing a design document in detail.

Conclusion

Creating an electronic game without a prototype is akin to shooting a movie without a script. A physical prototype will save your team tremendous amounts of time because everyone will have a clear understanding of the game you're making. In addition, a physical prototype will enable you to focus your creative energy on the game mechanics, without becoming distracted by the production and programming process. And most importantly, making a prototype gives you the freedom to experiment—and through experimentation comes innovation.

THE DESIGN EVOLUTION OF MAGIC: THE GATHERING

Magic: The Gathering *is one of the most important and influential games of our time. It was an instant hit when it first appeared at the Gen Con game convention in 1993 and has grown steadily in popularity since. This is a special two-part look at the creation and development of the game as written by the designer, Richard Garfield. Richard wrote the first part "The Creation of* Magic: The Gathering*" nearly 10 years ago when the game was first released. In it he muses about the design challenges of a collectable trading card game, and he recounts the game's fascinating playtest history.*

The second part "Magic Design: A Decade Later" is a retrospective on the original design notes. In it Richard provides insight about how and why the game has evolved the way it has—including thoughts on today's Magic *Pro Tour,* Magic *Online, and the next ten years for the game.*

THE CREATION OF MAGIC: THE GATHERING

by Richard Garfield (written 1993)

The ancestry of Magic

Games evolve. New ones take the most loved features of earlier games and add original characteristics. The creation of *Magic: The Gathering* is a case in point.

Though there are about a dozen games that have directly influenced *Magic* in one way or another, the game's most influential ancestor is a game for which I have no end of respect: *Cosmic Encounter*, originally published by Eon Products and re-released by Mayfair Games. In this game, participants play alien races striving to conquer a piece of the universe. Players can attempt their conquest alone, or forge alliances with other aliens. There are nearly 50 alien races which can be played, each of which has a unique ability: the Amoeba, for example, has the power to Ooze, giving it unlimited token movement; the Sniveler has the power to Whine, allowing it to automatically catch up when behind. The best thing about *Cosmic Encounter* is precisely this limitless variety. I have played hundreds of times and still can be surprised at the interactions different combinations of aliens produce. *Cosmic Encounter* remains enjoyable because it is constantly new.

Cosmic Encounter proved to be an interesting complement to my own design ideas. I had been mulling over a longtime idea of mine: a game which used a deck of cards whose composition changed between rounds. During the course of the game, the players would add cards to and remove cards from the deck, so that when you played a new game it would have an entirely different card mix. I remembered playing marbles in elementary school, where each player had his own collection from which he would trade and compete. I was also curious about *Strat-o-matic Baseball*, in which participants draft, field, and compete their own teams of baseball players, whose abilities are based on real players' previous year statistics. Intrigued by the structure of the game, I was irritated that the subject was one for which I had no patience.

These thoughts were the essence of what eventually became *Magic*. My experiences with *Cosmic Encounter* and other games inspired me to create a card game in 1982 called *Five Magics*. *Five Magics* was an attempt to distill the modularity of *Cosmic Encounter* down to just a card game. The nature of *Cosmic Encounter* seemed entirely appropriate for a magical card game—wild and not entirely predictable, but not completely unknown, like a set of forces you almost, but don't quite, understand. Over the next few years, *Five Magics* went on to inspire entirely new magical card games among my friends.

Ten years later, I was still designing games, and Mike Davis and I had come up with a boardgame called *RoboRally*. Mike was acting as our agent, and among the companies he approached was a brand-new gaming company called Wizards of the Coast. Things seemed to be going well, so that August, Mike, and I made our way to Portland, Oregon to meet over a pizza with Peter Adkison and James Hays of Wizards of the Coast.

Both Peter and James were very receptive to *RoboRally*, but informed me that they weren't really in a position to come out with a boardgame right away. This wasn't what I had come out to hear, of course, but I didn't want the trip to be a total waste. I asked Peter what he would be interested in. Peter replied that he really saw a need for a game that could be played quickly with minimal equipment, a game that would go over well at conventions. Could I do it?

Within a few days, the initial concept for a trading card game was born, based on another card game I had developed in 1985 called *Safecracker*. It hadn't been one of my best games. But then I remembered *Five Magics*.

The first designs

I went back to graduate school at the University of Pennsylvania, and worked on the card game in whatever spare time I had. It wasn't easy; there were three months of false starts on the project, there are so many aspects of card game design that have to be reconsidered when designing trading card games. First of all, you can't have any bad cards—people wouldn't play with them. In fact, you want to prevent too much range in the utility of cards because players will only play with the best—why make cards people won't play with? Besides, homogeneity of card power is the only way to combat the "rich kid syndrome" that threatened the game concept from the start. What was to keep someone from going out and getting ten decks and becoming unbeatable?

It was a major design concern. I had numerous theories on how to prevent purchasing power from unbalancing the game, none of which were entirely valid but all of which had a grain of truth. The most compelling counter to this "buy-out-the-store" strategy was the ante. If we were playing for ante, the argument ran, and your deck was the distilled fruit of ten decks, when I did win, I would win a more valuable card. Also, if the game had enough skill, then the player purchasing their power would surely be easy prey for the players dueling and trading their way to a good deck. And of course there was the sentiment that buying a lot of poker chips doesn't make you a winner. In the end, however, the "rich kid syndrome" became less of a concern. *Magic* is a fun game, and it doesn't really matter how you get your deck. Playtesting showed that a deck that is too powerful defeats itself. On the one hand, people stopped playing against it for ante unless a handicap was invoked; on the other, it inspired them to assemble more effective decks in response.

The first *Magic* release was affectionately named Alpha. It consisted of 120 cards split randomly between two players. The two players would ante a card, fight a duel over the ante, and repeat until they got bored. They often took a long time to get bored; even then, *Magic* was a surprisingly addictive game. About ten o'clock one evening, Barry "Bit" Reich and I started a game in the University of Pennsylvania Astronomy lounge, a windowless, air-conditioned room. We played continuously until about 3:00 a.m.—at least that's what we thought, until we left the building and found that the sun had risen.

I knew then that I had a game structure that could support the concept of individually owned and tailored decks. The game was quick, and while it had bluffing and strategy, it didn't seem to get bogged down with too much calculation. The various combinations that came up were enjoyable and often surprising. At the same time, the variety of card combinations didn't unbalance the game: when a person started to win, it didn't turn into a landslide.

From alpha to gamma

Except for the card mix, little has changed about *Magic* since alpha. In alpha, walls could attack, and losing all your lands of a particular color destroyed the associated spells in play, but otherwise, the rules are much the same now as they were in the early stages of playtesting.

Moving from alpha to the beta version was like releasing a wild animal. The enjoyable game that was alpha now burst the confines of the duel to invade the lives of the participants. Players were free to trade cards between games and hunt down weaker players to challenge them to duels, while gamely facing or cravenly avoiding those who were more powerful. Reputations were forged—reputations built on anything from consistently strong play to a few lucky wins to good bluffing. The players didn't know the card mix, so they learned to stay on their toes during duels. Even the most alert players would occasionally meet with nasty surprises. This constant discovery of unknown realms in an uncharted world gave the game a feeling of infinite size and possibility.

For the gamma version, new cards were added and many of the creature costs were increased. We also doubled the pool of playtesters, adding in a group with *Strat-o-matic Baseball* experience. We were particularly anxious to find out if *Magic* could be adapted for league play. Gamma was also the first version which was fully illustrated. Skaff Elias was my art director: he and others spent days poring over old graphic magazines, comic books, and game books searching for art for the cards. These playtest decks were pretty attractive for crummy black-and-white cardstock photocopies. For the most part, the cards were illustrated with serious pictures, but there were a lot of humorous ones as well. Heal was illustrated by Skaff's foot. Power Sink showed Calvin (of "Calvin and Hobbes") in a toilet; after all, what is a toilet but a power sink? Berserk was John Travolta dancing in *Saturday Night Fever*. Righteousness pictured Captain Kirk, and Blessing showed Spock doing his "live long and prosper" gesture. An old comic book provided a Charles Atlas picture for Holy Strength, and a 98-pound weakling getting sand kicked in his face for Weakness. Instill Energy was Richard Simmons. The infamous Glasses of Urza were some X-ray glasses we found in a catalog. Ruthy Kantorovitz constructed a darling flame-belching baby for Firebreathing. I myself had the honor of being the Goblins. The pictures and additional players greatly added to the game atmosphere. It became clear that while the duels were for two players, the more players playing, the better the game was. In some sense, the individual duels were a part of a single, larger game.

Striking the balance

Each playtest set saw the expulsion of certain cards. One type of card that was common in alpha and beta was rare in gamma, and is now nonexistent: the type that made one of your rival's cards yours. Yes, Control Magic used to permanently steal a creature from your opponent. Similarly, Steal Artifact really took an artifact. Copper Tablet no longer even remotely resembles its original purpose, which was to swap two creatures in play. ("Yes, I'll swap my Merfolk for your Dragon. On second thought, make that my Goblins—they're uglier.") There was a spell, Planeshift, which stole a land, and Ecoshift, which collected all the lands, shuffled them and re-dealt them—really nice for the user of four or five colors of magic. Pixies used to be a real pain—if they hit you, you swapped a random card from your hand with your opponent. These cards added something to the game, often in the form of players trying to destroy their own creatures before their opponents took them for good, or even trying to take their own lives to preserve the last shreds of their decks. However, in the end it was pretty clear that the nastiness this added to the game environment wasn't worth the trouble, and no card should ever be at risk unless players choose to play for ante.

It was around this time that I began to realize that almost any decision made about the game would be opposed, often vehemently, by some players. The huge amount of dissent about what should and should not be part of the card mix has led players to make their own versions for playtesting—a significant task that involves designing, constructing, shuffling, and distributing about 4000 cards. Each of these games had its merits, and the playtesters enjoyed discovering the quirks and secrets of each new environment. The results of these efforts will form the basis of future *Deckmaster* games that use the structure of *The Gathering*, while containing mostly new cards.

To build a better deck

Playtesting a *Deckmaster* game is difficult. Probably the only games harder to playtest are elaborate, multi-player computer games. After developing a basic framework for *Magic* that seemed fairly robust, we had to decide which of the huge selection of cards to include, and with what relative frequencies.

Common cards had to be simple, but not necessarily less powerful, than rare cards—if only rare cards were powerful, players would either have to be rich or lucky to get a decent deck. Sometimes a card was made rare because it was too powerful or imbalancing in large quantities, but more often, rare cards were cards that were intricate or specialized—spells you wouldn't want many of anyway. But these design guidelines only got us so far. The whole game's flavor could change if a handful of seemingly innocent cards were eliminated, or even made less or more common. When it came down to actually deciding what to include and what to do without, I began to feel like a chef obliged to cook a dish for 10,000 people using 300 ingredients.

One thing I knew I wanted to see in the game was players using multicolor decks. It was clear that a player could avoid a lot of problems by stripping down to a single color. For this reason, many spells were included that paralyzed entire colors, like Karma, Elemental Blast, and the Circles of Protection. The original plan was to include cards that thwarted every obvious simple strategy, and, in time, to add new cards which would defeat the most current ploys and keep the strategic environment dynamic. For example, it was obvious that relying on too many big creatures made a player particularly vulnerable to the Meekstone, and a deck laden with Fireballs and requiring lots of mana could be brought down with Manabarbs. Unfortunately, this strategy and counter-strategy design led to players developing narrow decks and refusing to play people who used cards that could defeat them flat out. If players weren't compelled to play a variety of players and could choose their opponent every time, a narrow deck was pretty powerful.

Therefore, another, less heavy-handed way to encourage variety was developed. We made it more difficult to get all the features a player needs in a deck by playing a single color. Gamma, for example, suffered from the fact that blue magic could stand alone. It was easily the most powerful magic, having two extremely insidious common spells (Ancestral Memory and Time Walk), both of which have been made rare. It had awesome counterspell capabilities. It had amazing creatures, two of the best of which are now uncommon.

Blue magic now retains its counterspell capability, but is very creature poor, and lacks a good way to do direct damage. Red magic has little defense, particularly in the air, but has amazing direct damage and destruction capability. Green magic has an abundance of creatures and mana, but not much more. Black is the master of anti-creature magic and has some flexibility, but is poorly suited to stopping non-creature threats. White magic is the magic of protection, and the only magic with common banding, but has little damage-dealing capability.

Sometimes seemingly innocuous cards would combine into something truly frightening. A good part of playtest effort was devoted to routing out the cards that contributed to so-called "degenerate" decks—the narrow, powerful decks that are difficult to beat and often boring to play with or against. Without a doubt, the most striking was Tom Fontaine's "Deck of Sooner-Than-Instant Death," which was renowned for being able to field upwards of eight large creatures on the second or third turn. In the first *Magic* tournament, Dave "Hurricane" Pettey walked to victory with his "Land Destruction

Deck." (Dave also designed a deck of Spectres, Mindtwists, and Disrupting Sceptres that was so grue-some I don't think anyone was ever really willing to play it.) Skaff's deck, "The Great White Death," could outlive just about anything put up against it. Charlie Catin's "Weenie Madness" was fairly effec-tive at swamping the opponent with little creatures. Though this deck was probably not in the high-win bracket of the previous decks, it was recognized that, playing for ante, Charlie could hardly lose. Even winning only one in four of his games—and he could usually do better than that—the card he won could be traded back for the island and the two Merfolk he lost, with something extra thrown in.

In the end I decided that the degenerate decks were actually part of the fun. People would assem-ble them, play with them until they got bored or their regular opponents refused to play against them, and then retire the deck or trade off its components for something new—a *Magic* version of putting the champion out to stud. Most players ended up treating their degenerate decks much like role-play-ers treat their most successful characters: they were relegated to the background, to be occasionally dusted off for a new encounter.

After the pursuit of sheer power died down, another type of deck developed: the Weird Theme deck. These decks were usually made to be as formidable as possible within the constraints of their theme. When Bit grew bored of his "Serpent Deck" (he had a predilection for flopping a rubber snake on the playing surface and going "SsssSssSs" whenever he summoned a Serpent), he developed his "Artifact Deck," which consisted of artifacts only—no land. It was fun to see the "Artifact Deck" go up against someone who used Nevinyrral's Disk. But the king of weird decks was, without a doubt, Charlie Catin. In one league, he put together a deck that I call "The Infinite Recursion Deck." The idea was to set up a situation where his opponent couldn't attack him until Charlie could play Swords to Plow-shares on a creature. Then he would play Timetwister, causing the cards in play to be shuffled with the graveyard, hand, and library to form a fresh library. Swords to Plowshares actually removes a creature from the game, so his rival has one less creature. Repeat. After enough iterations, his rival was bloated with life given by the Swords to Plowshares, having maybe 60 life points, but there were no creatures left in his deck. So Charlie's Elves started in—59 life, 58 life, 57 life—and the curtain closes on this sad game. I still can't think about this deck without moist emotional snorts. The coup de grace is that this league required players to compete their decks ten times. And, since his games often lasted over an hour and a half, he received at least one concession.

Words, words, words

It was not just determining the right card mix that players and designers found challenging. This becomes increasingly clear to me as I participate in the never-ending process of editing the rules and the cards. As my earliest playtesters have pointed out (in their more malicious moods), the original concept for *Magic* was the simplest game in the world because you had all the rules on the cards. That notion is long gone.

To those who didn't have to endure it, our struggle for precision was actually rather amusing. My own rules discussions about card wordings were mostly with Jim Lin, who is the closest thing you will ever encounter to a combination rules lawyer and firehose. A typical rule-problem session would go:

Jim: "Hmm—there seems to be a problem with this card. Here is my seven-page rules addition to solve the problem."

Richard: "I would sooner recall all the cards than use that. Let's try this solution instead."

Jim: "Hmm—we have another problem."

[Repeat until…]

Richard: "This is silly—only incredibly stupid and terminally anal people could possibly misinterpret this card."

Jim: "Yes, maybe we have been thinking about this too long. If you're playing with that kind of person, you should find some new friends."

A specific example of something we actually worried about is whether Consecrate Land would really protect your land from Stone Rain. After all, the first says it prevents land from being destroyed and the second says it destroys the land. Isn't that a contradiction? It still hurts my head getting into a frame of mind where that is confusing. It is perhaps a little like wondering why anyone would give you anything for money, which is, after all, just paper.

But, then again, I could never tell what was going to confuse people. One of the playtesters, Mikhail Chkhenkeli, approached me and said, "I like my deck. I have the most powerful card in the game. When I play it, I win on the next turn." I tried to figure out what this could be; I couldn't think of anything that would win the game with any assurance the turn after casting. I asked him about it and he showed me a card that would make his opponent skip a turn. I was confused until I read exactly what was written: "Opponent loses next turn." It was my first real lesson in how difficult it was going to be to word the cards so that no two people would interpret the same card in a different way.

The Magic marketplace

Another thing I realized in the second year of playtesting really surprised me. *Magic* turned out to be one of the best economic simulations I had ever seen. We had a free-market economy and all of the ingredients for interesting dynamics. People valued different cards in different ways—sometimes because they simply weren't evaluating accurately, but much more often because the cards really have different value to different players. For example, the value of a powerful green spell was lower for a person who specializes in black and red magic than for one who was building a deck that was primarily green. This gives a lot of opportunity for arbitrage. I would frequently find cards that one group of players weren't using but another group were treating like chunks of gold. If I was fast enough, I could altruistically benefit both parties and only have to suffer a little profit in the process.

Sometimes the value of a card would fluctuate based on a new use (or even a suspected new use). For example, when Charlie was collecting all the available spells that produced black mana, we began to get concerned—those cards were demanding higher and higher prices, and people began to fear what he could need all that black mana for. And, prior to Dave's "Land Destruction Deck," land destruction spells like Stone Rain and Ice Storm were not high-demand spells. This of course allowed him to assemble the deck cheaply, and after winning the first *Magic* tournament, sell off the pieces for a mint.

Trade embargoes appeared. At one point a powerful faction of players would not trade with Skaff, or anyone who traded with Skaff. I actually heard conversations such as:

Player 1 to Player 2: "I'll trade you card A for card B."

Skaff, watching: "That's a moronic trade. I'll give you card B and cards C, D, E, and F for card A."

Players 1 and 2 together: "We are not trading with you, Skaff."

Needless to say, Skaff was perhaps a bit too successful in his early duels and trades.

Another interesting economic event would occur when people would snatch up cards they had no intention of using. They would take them to remove them from the card pool, either because the card annoyed them (Chaos Orb, for example) or because it was too deadly against their particular decks.

I think my favorite profit was turned during an encounter with Ethan Lewis and Bit. Ethan had just received a pack of cards and Bit was interested in trading with Ethan. Bit noticed that Ethan had the Jayemdae Tome, began to drool, and made an offer for it. I looked at the offer and thought it was far too low, so I put the same thing on the table.

Bit looked at me and said, "You can't offer that! If you want the Tome you have to bid higher than my bid."

I said, "This isn't an offer for the Tome. This is a gift for Ethan deigning to even discuss trading the Tome with me."

Bit looked at me in disbelief, and then took me aside. He whispered, "Look, I'll give you this wad of cards if you just leave the room for ten minutes." I took his bribe, and he bought the Tome. It was just as well—he had a lot more buying power than I did. In retrospect, it was probably a dangerous ploy to use against Bit—after all, he was the person who was responsible for gluing poor Charlie's deck together once, washing a different deck of Charlie's in soap and water, and putting more cards of Charlie's in the blender and hitting frappé.

Probably the most constant card-evaluation difference I had with anyone was over Lord of the Pit. I received it in just about every playtest release we had, and it was certainly hard to use. I didn't agree with Skaff, though, that the only value of the card was that you might get your opponent to play with it. He maintained that blank cards would be better to play with because blank cards probably wouldn't hurt you. I argued that if you knew what you were doing, you could profit from it.

Skaff asked me to cite a single case where it had saved me. I thought a bit and recalled the most flamboyant victory I had with it. My opponent knew he had me where he wanted me—he had something doing damage to me, and a Clone in hand, so even if I cast something to turn the tide, he would be able to match me. Well, of course, the next cast spell was a Lord of the Pit; he could Clone it or die from it, so he Cloned it. Then each time he attacked, I would heal both of the Lords, or cast Fog and nullify the assault, and refuse to attack. Eventually, he ran out of creatures to keep his Lord of the Pit sated and died a horrible death.

Skaff was highly amused by this story. He said, "So, when asked about a time the Lord of the Pit saved you, you can only think of a case where you were playing somebody stupid enough to clone it!"

Dominia and the role of role-playing

Selecting a card mix that accommodated different evaluations of the cards wasn't enough; we also had to develop an environment in which the cards could reasonably interact. Establishing the right setting for *Magic* proved to be a central design challenge. In fact, many of our design problems stemmed from an attempt to define the physics of a magical world in which duels take place and from building the cards around that, rather than letting the game define the physics. I was worried about the cards' relationship to each other—I wanted them to seem part of a unified setting, but I didn't want to restrict the creativity of the designers or to create all the cards myself. Everyone trying to jointly build a single fantasy world seemed difficult, because it would inevitably lack cohesion. I preferred the idea of a multiverse, a system of worlds that was incredibly large and permitted strange interactions between the universes in it. In this way, we could capture the otherworldly aspects of fantasy that add such flavor to the game while preserving a coherent, playable game structure. Almost any card or concept would fit into a multiverse. Also, it would not be difficult to accommodate an ever-growing and diverse card pool—expansion sets with very different flavors could be used in the same game, for they could be seen as a creative mingling of elements from different universes. So I developed the idea of Dominia, an infinite system of planes through which wizards travel in search of resources to fuel their magic.

In its structured flexibility, this game environment is much like a role-playing world. I don't mean to suggest that this setting makes *Magic* a role-playing game—far from it—but *Magic* is closer to role-playing than any other card or boardgame I know of. I have always been singularly unimpressed by games that presumed to call themselves a cross between the two because role-playing has too many characteristics that can't be captured in a different format. In fact, in its restricted forms—as a tournament game or league game, for example—*Magic* has little in common with role-playing. In those cases, it is a game in the traditional sense, with each player striving to achieve victory according to some finite set of rules. However, the more free-form game—dueling with friends using decks constructed at whim—embodies some interesting elements of role-playing.

Each player's deck is like a character. It has its own personality and quirks. These decks often even get their own names: "The Bruise," "The Reanimator," "Weenie Madness," "Sooner-Than-Instant Death," "Walk Into This Deck," "The Great White Leftovers," "Backyard Barbeque," and "Gilligan's Island," to name a few. In one deck I maintained, each of the creatures had a name—one small advantage to crummy photocopied cardstock is the ease of writing on cards. The deck was called "Snow White and the Seven Dwarves," containing a Wurm named Snow White and seven Mammoths: Doc, Grumpy, Sneezy, Dopey, Happy, Bashful, and Sleepy. After a while I got a few additional Mammoths, which I named Cheesy and Hungry. There was even a Prince Charming: my Veteran Bodyguard.

As in roleplaying, the object of the game in the unstructured mode of play is determined largely by the players. The object of the duel is usually to win, but the means to that end can vary tremendously. Most players find that the duel itself quickly becomes a fairly minor part of the game compared to trading and assembling decks.

Another characteristic of *Magic* which is reminiscent of role-playing is the way players are exploring a world rather than knowing all the details to start. I view *Magic* as a vast game played among all the people who buy decks, rather than just a series of little duels. It is a game for tens of thousands in which the designer acts as a gamemaster. The gamemaster decides what the environment will be, and the players explore that environment. This is why there are no marketed lists of cards when the cards are first sold: discovering the cards and what they do is an integral part of the game.

And like a role-playing game, the players contribute as much to an exciting adventure as the gamemaster. To all the supporters of *Magic*, and especially to my playtesters, I am extraordinarily grateful. Without them, if this product existed at all, it would certainly be inferior. Every one of them left a mark, if not on the game itself, then in the game's lore. Any players today that have even a tenth of the fun I had playing the test versions with them will be amply pleased with *Magic*.

MAGIC DESIGN: A DECADE LATER

By Richard Garfield (written 2003)

Magic and the trading card game industry have undergone a lot of changes since the time I wrote those design notes. In the meantime *Magic* has grown stronger with each successive year—as the game itself is improved, and more people are brought into trading card games from products such as *Pokémon* and *Yu-Gi-Oh!*.

It is difficult for people these days to appreciate how little we knew about the game design space we were entering in the early nineties. My design notes failed to mention what in my mind is the strongest sign of that—after describing the concept of a trading card game to Peter Adkison I concluded with the cautious statement "of course, such a game may not be possible to design." It is hard for me to imagine that state of mind today, in a world where trading card games have reached every corner and are a part of almost every major entertainment property. This is a world where trading card games have left their mark on all areas of game design, from computer games to boardgames; and where trading card games have directly inspired games ranging from trading miniature games to trading tops games. This is a world where Jason Fox, from the comic strip *Foxtrot*, complained that a deck of cards coming with only four aces was some sort of ploy to get people to buy expansion kits.

That could be left as the end of the story; *Magic* was designed—as the design notes of a decade ago portray—and 10 years later it was still going strong. But this leaves out a large part of the story, since *Magic* was anything but a static game since then. The changes and improvements to *Magic* warrant design notes of their own.

First and foremost—a game

One thing that may look arcane in my notes to people who know something about the game market, is my reference to the form of game that *Magic* launched as a "trading card game," rather than a "collectable card game." I still use TCG rather than CCG, which became the industry standard despite my efforts from its earliest days. I prefer "trading" rather than "collectable" because I feel it emphasizes the playing aspect rather than the speculation aspect of the game. The mindset of making collectables runs against that of making games—if you succeed in the collectable department then there is a tendency to keep new players out and to drive old ones away because of escalating prices. One of the major battles that *Magic* fought was to make it perceived principally as a game and secondarily as a collectable. Good games last forever—collectables come and go.

This was not merely theoretical speculation—*Magic*'s immense success as a collectable was severely threatening the entire game. Booster packs intended to be sold at a few bucks were marked up to 20 dollars in some places as soon as they hit the shelves. While many people view this time as the golden age of *Magic* the designers knew that it was the death of the game in the long run. Who is going to get into the game when it was immediately inflated in price so much? How many people would play the game if doing so was wearing holes in some of their most valuable assets? We might be able to keep a speculation bubble going for a while, but the only way *Magic* was going to be a long term success—a classic game—was for it to stand on its game play merits, not on its worthiness as an investment.

During "Fallen Empires," the fifth *Magic* expansion, we finally produced enough cards that the speculative market collapsed. The long-term value of *Magic* could perhaps thrive—but it wouldn't immediately price itself out of the reach of new players before they got a chance to try it. There was an inevitable negative patina that *Magic* got for a while, and "Fallen Empires" still has, but from this point on *Magic* was sinking or swimming on its game merits. Fortunately, *Magic* turned out to be a strong swimmer.

Binding the unbounded

The part of my notes, which I believe, reveals my biggest change in thinking over the last decade is the statement that in the future we would publish other games with mechanics similar to *Magic*. What I was referring to is what became "Ice Age" and "Mirage," two expansions for *Magic*. Why did I think these would be entirely new games, rather than what they ended up being—expansions for the main game?

We all realized from the start that we couldn't just keep adding cards to *Magic* and expect it to stay popular. One reason for that is that each successive set of cards were a smaller and smaller percentage of the entire pool of cards, and so would necessarily have less and less impact on the whole of the game. This was illustrated vividly by players of "Ice Age" talking about how the entire set introduced two relevant cards to the game. One can imagine how the designers felt—working for years to make "Ice Age" a compelling game to have it boil down to a mere two cards. Another, perhaps more important reason, is that new players wouldn't want to enter a game where they were thousands of cards behind, so our audience would inevitably erode.

Initially we saw two solutions to this problem:

1. Make cards ever more powerful. This is a route many trading card game makers followed—and one I greatly dislike. It feels like strong-arming the players to buy more and more rather than really providing them more game value. But it would bring new players in, because they wouldn't need the obsolete old cards.

2. Eventually conclude *Magic: The Gathering*, and start a new game—*Magic: Ice Age*, for example. I advocated this approach, because I believed we could make exciting new game environments indefinitely. When one set was finished, players wouldn't be forced to buy into the new game to keep competitive, they could move on if they wanted a change—and new players could begin on equal footing.

When it actually came time to do "Ice Age," it was absolutely clear that players would not stand for a new version of *Magic*, we had to think of something else. Additionally, we were also worried that fragmenting the player audience was a bad idea; if we made a lot of different games, people would have a harder and harder time finding players.

The solution we found was to promote different formats of game play—many of which involved only more recent sets of cards. Today there are popular formats of play which involve only the most recently published cards, cards published in the last two years, and cards published in the last five years, in addition to many others. While this does fragment the player base—since you may not be able to find players who play your format—it is less draconian than different games since you can apply your cards to many different formats over time. This was a far more flexible approach than the first—as it didn't command players to start fresh—it allowed them to, and allowed new players to join the game without being overwhelmed.

Trading card games are not boardgames

I used to believe that trading card games were far more like boardgames than they are. This is not surprising, since I had no trading card games before *Magic* to draw examples from, and so was forced to use the existing world of games to guide my thinking on TCGs. A lot of my design attitudes grew from this misconception. For example, my second trading card game was designed to be best with four or more people, and took several hours to play. These are not bad parameters for a boardgame, but trading card games really want to be much shorter—because so much of the game is about replaying with a modified, or entirely new deck.

In a similar vein I used what I saw boardgame standards to be when it came to rules clarifications. It was common in boardgames to find a different group played a slightly different way, or had house rules to suit their tastes. With boardgames different interpretations of the rules and ways of play were not a major problem because players tended to play with fairly isolated groups. This led me to be quite anti-authoritarian when it came to the "correct" way to play. It turned out that a universal standard for a trading card game was far more necessary than a boardgame, because the nature of the game form made the interconnectivity of the game audience was far greater.

This meant that we had to take more and more responsibility for defining the rules and standards of play. In some ways this is analogous to being forced to construct the tournament rules for a game. The rules to *Bridge* are not that complex but when you write out the official tournament rules—really try to cross the Ts and dot the Is you have a compendium.

I had also hoped that players could moderate their own deck restrictions. We knew that certain card combinations were fun to discover and surprise someone with, but not fun to play with on an ongoing basis. So we figured players would make house rules to cover those decks and the responsible cards. The highly interconnected nature of *Magic* made it unreasonable to expect that, however, since every playgroup came up with a vast number of restrictions and rules, and they all played with each other. This meant we had to take more responsibility in designing the cards and when necessary, banning cards that were making the game worse.

The Pro Tour

All this precision invested in the design of the rules and cards made *Magic* a surprisingly good game to play seriously. We began to entertain ideas of really supporting a tournament structure with big money behind it—big enough players could, if good enough—make a living off of playing *Magic*. This was a controversial subject at Wizards of the Coast for a while—the worry being that making the game too serious would make it less fun. I subscribed fully to the concept of a Pro Tour—thinking of how the NBA helped make basketball popular and didn't keep the game from being played casually as well.

The Pro Tour had an almost immediate effect. Our players rapidly became much better as the top level ones devoted time to really analyzing the game and as that game tech filtered down through the ranks. Before the Pro Tour I am confident that I was one of the best players in the world, now I am mediocre at best.

Now there are thousands of tournaments each week, and many players have earned a lot of money playing *Magic*, some in the hundreds of thousands of dollars. At the last World Championship there were 56 countries competing. There is a never-ending buzz of *Magic* analysis and play as players attempt to master the ever-changing strategic ground of *Magic*. I believe this is a major part of *Magic's* ongoing popularity, if even a small group of people take a good game very seriously, there can be far reaching effects.

Magic Online

Online *Magic* didn't come into its own until last year. For a long time I have wanted to see an online version of *Magic* that duplicated real life *Magic* as closely as possible. That is, the online game would connect people, run the games and the tournaments, and adjudicate rules—but little else. At first we tried to form partnerships with computer game companies to do this—but our partners always had other ideas about how to do computer *Magic*. Eventually we hired a programming studio to do it our way and now we have *Magic Online*.

One of the striking things about *Magic Online* is that we use the same revenue model as in real life. Despite exhortations to use a subscription model, we chose to sell virtual cards, which you could trade with other players online. This allows players to buy some cards and then play them indefinitely with no further fee—as in real life.

It was important to us that we not make it a better deal playing online than off—we wanted it to be the same. That is because we feel the paper game contributes a lot to *Magic*'s ongoing popularity, and it could be threatened if many of its players go to the online game.

For this reason one of the prime targets for the online game was going to be lapsed players. Many studies had been done on how long people play *Magic* and why they leave the game, and for the most part they didn't leave because they were bored with the game; they left because they had life changes which made it more difficult to play—for example, getting jobs or having kids. These players would potentially rejoin the game if they could play from their own home on their own hours.

Magic Online is still a bit to young to be sure about, but it appears to have acquired a dedicated sizeable audience of players without hurting the paper game. Many of the players are formerly lapsed players, as we had hoped.

The next ten years

Who knows what the next decade will bring? Ten years ago I had no clue at all, it was an exciting time and we were riding a roller coaster. Now I am more confident—I believe that *Magic* is fairly stable, and that there is every reason to believe that it will be around and as strong in another ten years. At this point it is clear that *Magic* is not a fad, and as many new players are coming in each year as are leaving the game.

Certainly *Magic* has stayed fresh for me. I get into the game every few months; joining a league, constructing a deck, or perhaps preparing for and participating in a tournament. Every time I return I find the game fresh and exciting, with enough different from the previous time to keep me on my toes, but enough the same that I can still exploit my modest skills at the game. I look forward to my next ten years of the game.

Chapter 8
Playtesting

Playtesting is the single most important activity a designer engages in, and ironically, it's often the one designers understand the least about. The common misconception is that playtesting is simple—just play the game and gather feedback. This is fine for a weekend gamer, but if you are a professional, playing the game is only the beginning of a process which involves selection, recruiting, preparation, controls, and analysis.

Another reason that designers often fail to playtest properly is that there's confusion over its role within the game development process. Playtesting isn't when the designer and her team play the game and talk about the features. That's called an internal design review. And playtesting is not having the quality assurance team go through and rigorously test each element of the software for flaws. That's bug testing. And it isn't when you have seven marketing execs sitting behind a two-way mirror watching a representative sample group play and discuss the game while a moderator asks them how much they'd pay for this product. That's focus group testing. And it's not when you systematically analyze how users interact with your software by recording their mouse movements, eye movements, navigation patterns, etc. That's usability testing.

So, what is playtesting? Playtesting is something the designer performs throughout the entire design process to gain an insight into how players experience the game. There are numerous ways you can conduct playtesting, some of which are informal and qualitative, and other which tend to be more structured and quantitative. But the one thing all forms of playtesting have in common is the end goal: how to gain useful feedback from players in order to improve your game.

As you develop the game, other groups will perform other types of tests. The marketing people will try to determine who is going to buy the game and how many units can be sold. The engineering team will utilize the QA department to test for hidden bugs and compatibility problems. The interface designers will employ a variety of tests to see if people can operate the game in the most efficient and user-friendly way. But as a designer, your foremost goal is to make sure the game is functioning the way you intended, that it is internally complete, balanced, and fun to play. And this is where playtesting comes in.

PLAYTESTING AND ITERATIVE DESIGN

You'll recall that we said the primary role of the designer is as an advocate for the player. This does not just mean in the early stages of design—the game designer must keep that relationship with the players' needs and perspective throughout the design and production process. Often, as teams work at a project long days and nights for months at a time, they forget the player in their own quest to make the game live up to their vision.

A continual iterative process of playtesting, evaluating and revising is the way to keep the game from straying during that long arduous process of development. Of course, you can't keep changing the game fundamentally or your team will rebel. After all, the goal is to release a product eventually. Figure 8.1 shows how the testing cycle gets tighter and tighter as production moves forward, signifying smaller and smaller issues to solve and changes to make, so that your are merely perfecting the game as the process draws to a close, not changing it fundamentally. This method, of continually testing your assumptions with players, will keep your game on track in the darkest days of production.

You may be thinking: but testing is an expensive process, isn't it? Wouldn't it be better to wait until we have a fully working game—say about the time we have a beta product—and test it then? That way, players will get the best experience. We can't argue against this way of thinking strongly enough. By that time in the process, it is really too late to make any fundamental changes to your game. If the core gameplay isn't fun or interesting,

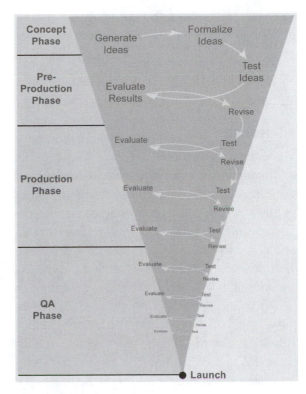

8.1   Model for iterative game design: playtest, evaluate, and revise

you are stuck with it. You might be able to change some top-level features, but that's it.

We advise playtesting and iterating your design from the very moment you begin. And we can show you how to do it without much expense—just your own time and some volunteers. The expense you will save is the cost of changing your game at the very end of production, or releasing a game that doesn't live up to its full potential.

Recruiting Playtesters

Before you can playtest, you must have playtesters. But how do you begin and who should you trust? In the early stages, when you're creating your first prototype, the single best tester you have is yourself.

Self-testing

As you build a working version of your game, you'll naturally try it out repeatedly to understand how it functions. If you're collaborating with other designers on the prototype, you'll self-test both as a group and as individuals. Self-testing is most valuable in the foundation stage of a prototype when you are experimenting with fundamental concepts. It is a large part of the process that enables you to come up with the core mechanics for the system. It is also where you create solutions to glaring problems with the play experience. Your goal at this stage is to make the game work—even if it's only a rough approximation of the final product. You will continue to self-test throughout the life of the project; however, as you progress and your game evolves, you will have to rely on outside testers to gain an accurate understanding of what it is you've created.

Exercise 8.1: Test it Yourself

Take the original game prototype that you developed in Exercise 7.9 and playtest it yourself. Describe in detail what goes through your head as you play the game. Start a playtesting journal in which you record all of the feedback you get from yourself and other testers.

Playtesting with confidants

Once you move past the foundation stage and the prototype is playable, test it with people you know well—such as friends and colleagues outside the design team. These people will bring fresh eyes to the project and will uncover things you haven't considered. You may need to be present to explain the game to them when you begin. This is because the prototype will likely be incomplete in the structure stage. The goal is to get to a version that people can play using only the materials provided and without any intervention from you. You should be able to give some playtesters the prototype materials, and they should have enough information to complete the game. With a physical prototype, this will require that you write a full set of rules. With a software prototype, the user interface will need to be completed and you may need some written rules.

Once your game is playable and you have a clearly defined set of rules, you must wean yourself from your confidants. Testing with friends and family may feel like it works, and it does in the early stages, but it won't suffice once the game matures. The reason is that your friends and family have a personal relationship with you, and this obscures their objectivity. You'll find that most of them are either too harsh or too forgiving. It all depends on how they're used to interacting with you. Even if you believe that your confidants are providing balanced feedback, it's best not to rely too heavily on a small group of individuals. They will never give you the objective, broad criticism that you require to take your design to the next level.

Exercise 8.2: Test with Confidants

Now take your original prototype and give it to some confidants. Have them test it. Write down your observations as they play. Do your best to determine what they think of the game without asking them any direct questions.

Playtesting with people you don't know

It's often hard to show your incomplete game to strangers. It feels comfortable to be around people you know and trust. Our advice is to get over your fear of the unknown. It is only through the process of inviting total strangers into your office or home and allowing them to fiddle around and criticize your creation that you will gain the fresh perspective and insight you require to improve your design. This is because outsiders have nothing to lose or gain by telling you honestly how they feel. They are also untainted by any knowledge of the game or personal ties. If you chose them carefully and provide the right environment, you will see that they can be as articulate and dedicated as your coworkers and confidants. There is no substitute for finding good playtesters. Make them an extension of your team, and the results will become apparent immediately.

Finding the ideal playtesters

So how do you find these perfect playtesters, who have never heard of you or your game? The solution is to tap into your community. You can recruit playtesters from your local high school, college, sports clubs, social organizations, churches and computer-users groups. The possibilities are endless. You can also find a broader demographic of recruits by posting online or putting an ad in a local paper. The more sources you try, the better your candidate pool will become. It's as simple as putting up a notice in a local game store, college dorm, library, or recreation center. You'll find that people want to be part of the process of creating a game, and if your invitation sounds attractive, you shouldn't have trouble lining up testers.

The next step in recruiting is actually screening out and turning down applicants. You can only do this once you get enough applicants. What you should be looking for is a group of testers who are articulate enough to convey their opinions to you. If they can't hold a decent conversation on the phone, they probably won't be of much use. We don't expect you to be an expert in demographics or sampling, but it doesn't hurt to ask a few questions to help sort out which applicants are going to be useful and which are a waste of time. Questions may include: What are your hobbies? Why did you respond to my bulletin? How often to you buy this type of game? If the tester isn't a consumer of the type of game you're making, his feedback will be less useful.

Playtesting with your target audience

The ideal playtester is someone who represents your target audience. You want testers who actually go out and spend their hard-earned money to buy games like yours. These people will give you far more relevant feedback because they will have a gut instinct for what works. They will also be able to compare your game to others and provide you with additional market research. And most importantly, they know what they like and what they dislike, and will be able to tell you this in excessive detail. Once you tap into your audience, you will uncover a wealth of information and gain an insight into your game that no one else can provide.

Exercise 8.3: Recruiting Playtesters

Now, it's time for you to recruit several total strangers to playtest your game prototype. Make sure that they are in your target audience. Set up a time with these playtesters to conduct the test. Exercises 8.4 will help you prepare to get the most from the session.

The more diverse a group you can recruit, the better. By diverse, we mean a broad range of people within your target audience. You want to tap people who play your games, but you don't want to focus on too narrow a section of your total audience. Your pool of testers should represent the entire spectrum of consumers of your product. Posting notices on gaming web sites is a great way to recruit testers in your area.

If you're worried about someone stealing your ideas, have them sign a nondisclosure agreement (NDA). This is a simple agreement where a person promises not to tell anyone about your product until it is released. In game companies, playtesters are typically paid in cash or free games. With independent games and personal projects the testers are typically not paid but gain the satisfaction of contributing their thoughts.

The level of caution you take is up to you, but remember this: don't be paranoid. The fact is that 99.99% of the people out there have no intention of stealing your ideas, and even if they did, the vast majority wouldn't know what to do with your game once they stole it. The benefits of using playtesters far outweigh the perils. In fact, the risk of using testers is negligible when compared to what else can go wrong during a production.

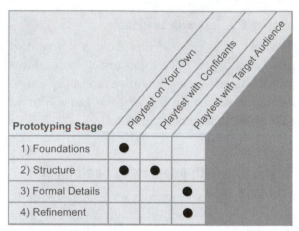

Prototyping Stage	Playtest on Your Own	Playtest with Confidants	Playtest with Target Audience
1) Foundations	●		
2) Structure	●	●	
3) Formal Details			●
4) Refinement			●

8.2   **Types of playtesters appropriate for each stage of prototyping**

Last but not least, you may want to provide snacks and drinks while your testers are playing. Not only is this common courtesy, but it makes your testers feel as if they owe you something, which means that they are more likely to provide you with detailed feedback. It also makes it more likely that your recruits will return at a later date to test again. You'll want to use the same testers periodically throughout the production to gauge how they feel the game is progressing. You may even find that features which you removed or changed don't work as well, and these testers will be able to point that out. But don't become too dependent on a handful of testers. It's still smart to keep fresh recruits streaming in throughout the process. There's nothing like a pair of virgin eyes. Figure 8.2 shows the various stages of prototyping and the types of playtesters you should involve at each stage.

CONDUCTING A PLAYTESTING SESSION

So now that you have all these strangers in your office or living room, what do you do with them? At this point, many game designers panic. They don't know how to present their game or where to begin. First, take a deep breath, and then think of your role. Your job is no longer that of the game designer and auteur, but that of an investigator and guide, who must lead these individuals through the game and uncover what they truly think.

The most common mistake is for the game designer to sit down and begin reading off the rules and describing their vision for the game. Especially if it's a physical prototype, the designer feels compelled to start by jabbering away for thirty minutes, making certain to articulate every facet of the game, even those that aren't there yet, until the testers' eyes glaze over. Remember, people learn by playing, not by listening. Let them start playing. Allow them to make mistakes. See how each person approaches the game. Maybe your rules are confusing. Provide answers if they get stuck, but for the most part, let your testers figure it out. You will tend to learn more the less you speak.

A good way to control your impulses is to create a "script" for yourself to follow. In this script, you take on the character of a researcher, not the game designer. Your script should include at least the following sections, perhaps several others, depending on the type of test you are doing:

- Welcome the playtesters and thank them for participating.
- Remind the playtesters that you are testing the game, not their skills. Any difficulties in playing

the game will help you to improve your design. Give the playtesters the rules (physical prototype), or let them start the application (software prototype).

- Ask the playtesters to begin playing as soon as they are ready.
- Ask them to talk out loud throughout the game about what they are thinking, questions they may have. Warn them that you won't be able to answer their questions; you just want to know what they are. You are just an observer here. You won't be stepping in to help them, not because you don't want to, but because you need to see where problems exist with the game and how they solve those problems.
- When they are finished playing, interview the playtesters or use the following discussion methods to elicit any additional feedback.
- Thank the playtesters for their assistance and feedback. Provide a token gift of thanks if you can afford it.

Exercise 8.4: Writing a Playtest Script

Write a script for the playtest session you set up in Exercise 8.3. Be sure to cover areas of your game that you have questions about. Don't lead or suggest ideas to the playtesters.

The most difficult part about this process will be learning to listen without responding to every point. You, as the designer, invariably feel a strong attachment to whatever it is you've created. This game is your masterpiece. It is something people will judge you by. It's an extension of yourself. And most designers have the overpowering urge to

The Iterative Design Process

by Eric Zimmerman, Co-Founder and CEO, gameLab

The following is adapted from a longer essay entitled "Play as Research" which appears in the book Design Research, edited by Brenda Laurel (MIT Press, 2004). It appears here with permission from the author. Iterative design is a design methodology based on a cyclic process of prototyping, testing, analyzing, and refining a work in progress. In iterative design, interaction with the designed system is the basis of the design process, informing and evolving a project as successive versions, or iterations of a design are implemented. This sidebar outlines the iterative process as it occurred in one game with which I was involved—the online multiplayer game SiSSYFiGHT 2000.

What is the process of iterative design? Test, analyze, refine. And repeat. Because the experience of a player cannot ever be completely predicted, in an iterative process design decisions are based on the experience of the prototype in progress. The prototype is tested, revisions are made, and the project is tested once more. In this way, the project develops through an ongoing dialogue between the designers, the design, and the testing audience.

In the case of games, iterative design means playtesting. Throughout the entire process of design and development, your game is played. You play it. The rest of the development team plays it. Other people in the office play it. People visiting your office play it. You organize groups of testers that match your target audience. You have as many people as possible play the game. In each case, you observe them, ask them questions, then adjust your design and playtest again.

This iterative process of design is radically different than typical retail game development. More often than not, at the start of the design process for a computer or console title, a game designer will think up a finished concept and then write an exhaustive design document that outlines every possible aspect of the game in minute detail. Invariably, the final game never resembles the carefully conceived original. A more iterative design process, on the other hand, will not only streamline development resources, but will also result in a more robust and successful final product.

Case study: SiSSYFiGHT 2000

SiSSYFiGHT 2000 is a multiplayer online game in which players create a schoolgirl avatar and then vie with three to six players for dominance of the playground. Each turn a player selects one of six actions to take, ranging from teasing and tattling to cowering and licking a lolly. The outcome of an action is dependent on other players' decisions, making for highly social gameplay. *SiSSYFiGHT 2000* is also a robust online community. You can play the game at www.sissyfight.com.In the summer of 1999, I was hired by Word.com to help them create their first game. We initially worked to identify the project's play values: the abstract principles that the game design would embody. The list of play values we created included designing for a broad audience of nongamers, a low technology barrier, a game that was easy to learn and play but deep and complex, gameplay that was intrinsically social, and finally, something that was in line with the smart and ironic Word.com sensibility.

These play values were the parameters for a series of brainstorming sessions, interspersed with group play of computer and non-computer games. Eventually, a game concept emerged: little girls in social conflict on a playground. While every game embodies some kind of conflict, we were drawn towards modeling a conflict that we hadn't seen depicted previously in a game. Technology and production limitations meant that the game would be turn-based, although it could involve real-time chat.

Once these basic formal and conceptual questions had begun to be mapped out, the shape of the initial prototype became clear. The very first version of *SiSSYFiGHT* was played with post-it-notes around a conference table. I designed a handful of basic actions each player could take, and acting as the program, I "processed" the actions each turn and reported the results back to the players, keeping score on a piece of paper.

Designing a first prototype requires strategic thinking about how to most quickly implement a playable version that can begin to address the project's chief uncertainties in a meaningful way. Can you create a paper version of your digital game? Can you design a short version of a game that will last much longer in its final form? Can you test the interaction pattern of a massively multiplayer game with just a handful of players?

In the iterative design process, the most detailed thinking you need at any moment is that which will get you to your next prototype. It is, of course, important to understand the big picture as well: the larger conceptual, technical, and design questions that drive the project as a whole. Just be sure not to let your design get ahead of your iterative research. Keep your eye on the prize, but leave room for play in your design, for the potential to change as you learn from your playtesting, accepting the fact that some of your assumptions will undoubtedly be wrong.

The project team continued to develop the paper prototype, seeking the balance between cooperation and competition that would become the heart of the final gameplay. We refined the base ruleset—the actions a player can take each turn and the outcomes that result. These rules were turned into a spec for the first digital prototype: a text-only version on IRC, which we played hotseat-style, taking turns sitting at the same computer. Constructing that early, text-only prototype allowed us to focus on the complexities of the game logic without worrying about implementing interactivity, visual and audio aesthetics, and other aspects of the game.

While we tested gameplay via the text-only iteration, programming for the final version began in Director, and the core game logic we had developed for the IRC prototype was recycled into the Director code with little alteration. Parallel to the game design, the project's visual designers had begun to develop the graphic language of the game and chart out possible screen layouts. These early drafts of the visuals (revised many times over the course of the entire development) were dropped into the

Director version of the game, and the first rough-hewn iteration of *SiSSYFiGHT* as a multiplayer online game took shape, inspired by Henry Darger's outsider art and retro game graphics.

As soon as the web version was playable, the development team played it. And as our ugly duckling grew more refined, the rest of the Word.com staff was roped into testing as well. As the game grew more stable, we descended on our friends' dot-com companies after the workday had ended, sitting them down cold in front of the game and letting them play. All of this testing and feedback helped us refine the game logic, visual aesthetics, and interface.

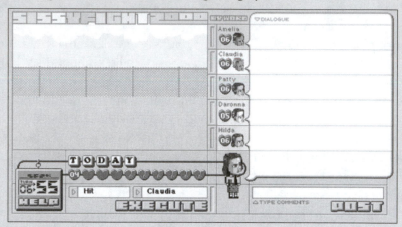

SiSSYFiGHT 2000 interface from software prototype

The biggest challenge turned out to be clearly articulating the relationship between player action and game outcome: because the results of every turn are interdependent on each player's actions, early versions of the game felt frustratingly arbitrary. Only through many design revisions and dialogue with our testers did we manage to structure the results of each turn to unambiguously communicate what had happened that round and why.

When the server infrastructure was completed, we launched the game to an invite-only beta-tester community that slowly grew in the weeks leading up to public release. Certain time slots were scheduled as official testing events, but our beta users could come online anytime and play. We made it very easy for the beta testers to contact us and e-mail in bug reports.

Even with this small sample of a few dozen participants, larger play patterns emerged. For example, as with many multiplayer games, it was highly advantageous to play defensively, leading to standstill matches. In response, we tweaked the game logic to discourage this play style: any player that "cowered" twice in a row was penalized for acting like a chicken. When the game did launch, our loyal beta testers became the core of the game community, easing new players into the game's social space.

In the case of *SiSSYFiGHT 2000*, the testing and prototyping cycle of iterative design was successful because at each stage, we clarified exactly what we wanted to test and how. We used written and online questionnaires. We debriefed after each testing session. And we strategized about how each version of the game would incorporate the visual, audio, game design, and technical elements of the previous versions, while also laying a foundation for the final form of the experience.

To design a game is to construct a set of rules. But the point of game design is not to have players experience rules—it is to have players experience play. Game design is therefore a second-order design problem, in which designers craft play, but only indirectly, through the systems of rules that game designers create. Play arises out of the rules as they are inhabited and enacted by players, creating emergent patterns of behavior, sensation, social exchange, and meaning. This shows the necessity of the iterative design process. The delicate interaction of rule and play is something too subtle and too complex to script out in advance, requiring the improvisational balancing that only testing and prototyping can provide.

SiSSYFiGHT 2000 game interfaces

In iterative design, there is a blending of designer and user, of creator and player. It is a process of design through the reinvention of play. Through iterative design, designers create systems and play with them. They become participants, but do so in order to critique their creations, to bend them, break them, and re-fashion them into something new. And in these procedures of investigation and experimentation, a special form of discovery takes place. The process of iteration, of design through play, is a way of discovering the answers to questions you didn't even know were there. And that makes it a powerful and important method of design. *SiSSYFiGHT 2000* was developed by Marisa Bowe, Ranjit Bhatnagar, Tomas Clarke, Michelle Golden, Lucas Gonze, Lem Jay Ignacio, Jason Mohr, Daron Murphy, Yoshi Sodeka, Wade Tinney, and Eric Zimmerman.

Author Bio

Eric Zimmerman is a game designer and academic exploring the practice and theory of gaming. Eric has been making games in the game industry for ten years, and presently runs gameLab, a company he co-founded with Peter Lee. GameLab creates experimental online single-player and multiplayer games. Before gameLab, Eric collaborated with Word.com on the underground online hit, SiSSYFiGHT 2000 (www.sissyfight.com). Other titles include the PC CD-ROM games Gearheads (Philips Media, 1996) and The Robot Club (Southpeak Interactive, 1998). Eric has taught game design at MIT, NYU, Parsons School of Design, and School of Visual Arts. He is the co-author with Katie Salen of Rules of Play (MIT Press, 2003) and the co-editor with Amy Schoulder of RE:PLAY (Peter Lang Press, 2004). *See also his article on page 312.*

become defensive. They don't want anyone criticizing their baby and will do anything to elicit positive feedback.

Please don't succumb to the devil of playtesting. Ignore your ego. If you're going to gain anything from a playtesting session, you have to transform yourself. Imagine that you are someone else. You are no longer the designer of this game. Instead, you are an analyst hired to uncover the truth. Your job is not to have these people love the game or you, it's to discover what they don't want to tell you or know how to tell you.

Far too many designers fail in this regard. Either they refuse to allow in any negative comments or they stop testing altogether, because it's too painful. If you pressure your testers or try to control them, you'll find that they'll gladly fall in line. You invited them to your office or home, and they don't want to upset you. They want to please you. And they will tell you whatever it is that you want to hear. So if you are determined to hear only good news, then that's what you'll get. It may make you feel like a genius, but it won't make your game any better.

Embrace the criticism you receive from your playtesters. Even if you feel awful inside, remind yourself that you need to hear the problems because you cannot fix the problems if you don't know what they are. And it's better to hear the bad news now than later from a game critic. Don't let this chance slip past.

There are times when the criticism can get a bit heavy. If you are using a group, one tester may be particularly nasty and begin to sway the others. There's a nice way to give feedback and a not so nice way, and some people don't know the difference. They probably haven't been trained in how to give constructive criticism or participate in group discussions, so please be forgiving. Your job

is not to change them or make them better people—it's to learn what you can from them.

Many professional usability facilities isolate testers for this very reason. However, you may not have that luxury. So, it helps to make it clear at the beginning of the session that you are open to feedback and want everyone to be honest, but at the same time there is a certain etiquette you'd like the testers to follow. Everyone should respect each other's opinions. There is no right or wrong answer, and no tester should ever criticize another tester's ideas. Above all, everyone should stick to the game, keeping their comments focused on how the game functions. If you lay down some good rules for the discussion at the outset, you should avoid most problems.

On rare occasions, there will be a tester who acts particularly destructive. This is especially damaging in group settings. If you spot this problem, the best thing to do is politely guide the conversation towards the comments of other testers. If that person continues to behave inappropriately, you should excuse them or ask them to complete a task on their own, like a survey.

Be careful not to abuse your authority. Most people want to be helpful, and it's rare that someone is trying to sabotage the playtesting session. Before you take any action, be sure to look inside yourself for the answer. Are you being too sensitive? Is the criticism truly harmful or is this person unaccustomed to giving feedback? How are the other testers reacting to this person? It's true that one bad seed can skew results, casting a negative spin on everything, but do not jump to conclusions. Your ultimate goal is to take what you are given and learn from it, not silence anyone who says something that you don't like. It's a fine line that many people have trouble seeing, but with time and experience, you should be able to hone your skills.

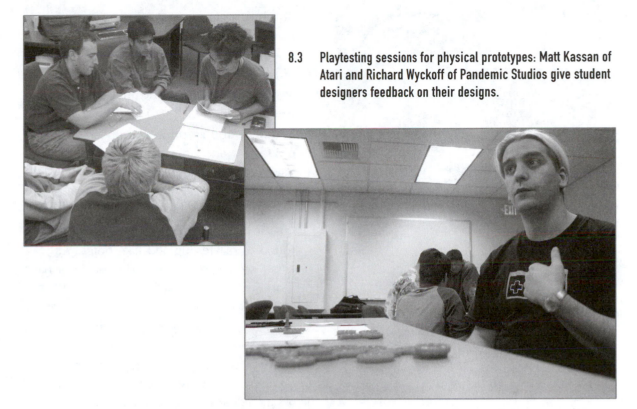

8.3   Playtesting sessions for physical prototypes: Matt Kassan of Atari and Richard Wyckoff of Pandemic Studios give student designers feedback on their designs.

You'll make mistakes, but if you're dedicated, it will serve you well. Becoming a good session leader is something that will help you throughout your career. The same skills can be applied to your production team. In addition to playtesters, you need your team's input and constructive criticism, and the best way to elicit this is to make your entire production a safe environment, where everyone is encouraged to speak their mind while being careful not to personally criticize each other. If you apply the same rules described earlier to all of your group meetings, you will wind up with a far more productive and motivated team that feels invested in the product you are creating together.

Exercise 8.5: Playtesting Your Game

Conduct the playtesting you set up in Exercise 8.3. Use the playtesting script you wrote in Exercise 8.2 to keep the session on track. Take notes in your playtesting journal from Exercise 8.1 recording feedback and problems.

METHODS OF PLAYTESTING

Most professional usability testing takes place individually. It's a generally accepted rule that group dynamics are good for generating ideas, but very bad for evaluating ideas. On the other hand, you may have no choice, depending on the nature of your prototype and environment. So, don't feel

8.4   More playtesting sessions for physical prototypes: Steve Ackrich of Atari and Neal Robison of Vivendi–Universal give student designers feedback on their designs.

like you can't playtest just because you don't have the "perfect" set-up.

Here are a number of different ways you can structure your tests, each with their own positives and negatives, but one or more should work for the environment you have available.

- *One-On-One Testing:* You sit down with individuals and watch over their shoulders as they play the game. You take notes and ask them questions along the way.

- *Group Testing:* You get a group of people and allow them to play your game together. You observe the group and ask questions as they play.

- *Feedback forms:* You give each person who tests your game a standard list of questions to answer after playing, and then compare the results.

- *Interview:* You sit down face-to-face with the playtesters and give them an in-depth, oral interview after the playtesting session. This is not a discussion, it's more of a verbal quiz.

- Open Discussion: You conduct either a one-on-one discussion or a group discussion after a round of playtesting and take notes. You can either promote a freeform discussion or have more structure approach where you guide the conversation and introduce specific questions.

You can combine the previous approaches to fit your game and your space. For instance, you may have players play a game together and have a group discussion afterwards, but then ask each to fill out a feedback form individually. You'll be surprised how differently people respond when there is no group dynamic.

Over time, you'll find out which methods work best for you at each stage of testing. Our goal is to encourage you to test no matter what your limitations are. If none of the structures on our list work for you then think creatively and come up with your own methods. Try some of these different processes if you can. You'll see how each method produces different results, and you'll broaden your testing techniques and experience.

THE PLAY MATRIX

One valuable playtesting tool you can use is the play matrix. We developed the play matrix to help playtesters and students give context to their discussions about game systems.

The horizontal axis of the play matrix is a continuum between skill and chance. The vertical axis is a continuum between mental calculation and physical dexterity. We chose these two continua because they are core aspects of

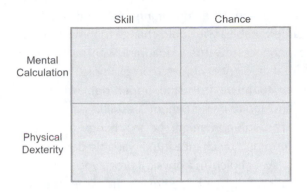

8.5   The play matrix

interactive experiences, and all games can be plotted along them. Think about the game of chess. It's a game of pure strategy, a type of skill. There is absolutely no chance involved. So on the skill versus chance continuum, it would be plotted to the far left. It's also a game of pure mental calculation. There is no physical dexterity required to play the game. So on the mental calculation versus physical dexterity continuum, it's plotted at the very top. When chess is plotted on both these dimensions at the same time, it appears in the top left corner.

Now let's think about the game of blackjack. It involves chance—but the outcome is not determined purely by chance. So it falls somewhere to the right of center on the continuum. No dexterity is required to play, so it plots at the top of the mental calculation versus physical dexterity line.

Exercise 8.6: The Play Matrix

Now it's your turn to use the play matrix. Plot a popular videogame, such as *WarCraft*, *Quake*, or *Atomic Bomberman*, on the play matrix. Compare this to a game like *Twister* or "pin the tail on the donkey." Now try plotting a boardgame like *Monopoly*, *Risk*, or *Clue*. Describe the differences and similarities between the three types of games. What does the play matrix show you?

The play matrix is not an absolute system which produces the same results every time. Different people may have different opinions on where games plot, which is okay. Everyone's opinion has value. It's best to use the play matrix as a tool for stimulating discussion and analyzing gameplay. The goal is to get your playtesters to think about the game and verbalize their feelings.

Figure 8.6 shows the play matrix with several games plotted in each quadrant. Can you see patterns in the types of games that fall in different quadrants? Many popular videogames fall in the lower left (physical + skill). Many popular boardgames and turn-based videogames fall in the upper left (mental + skill), many gambling games fall in the upper right (mental + chance), and many games for very young children fall in the lower right (physical + chance).

Exercise 8.7: Plotting Your Favorite Games

Take five of your favorite games and plot them on the play matrix. Describe what pattern you see. What does this tell you about yourself?

When conducting a playtesting session, it is sometimes helpful to ask your testers to plot your game on the matrix. Then follow by asking them these questions: (1) Is the outcome of the game

	Skill		Chance	
Mental Calculation	Go Civilization Chess		Poker Backgammon	Blackjack Chutes and Ladders
	Warcraft Starcraft Tetris			
Physical Dexterity		Devil Unreal Dice Halo	Operation Kerplunk	Pin the Tail on the Donkey
	Basketball Dance Dance Football Revolution		Whack-a-mole Tag	Twister

8.6   The play matrix including games

determined more by chance or by the skills of the players? (2) Is the outcome determined more by mental skill or physical dexterity? Ask playtesters if they would move the game more towards one quadrant or another, what would they prefer? Different audiences often gravitate towards one quadrant of gameplay, even if they enjoy different genres. For example, players who enjoy strategy games from the upper left corner may also gravitate toward other mental + skill based play, such as trivia or puzzles. Young children often gravitate toward games in the lower right, focusing on physical + chance, but as they get older, they choose games requiring mental + chance.

If players are dissatisfied with your game, they may be able to verbalize it by placing games they do enjoy in other quadrants. Ask yourself what game variables you could change to move the play experience towards a quadrant with games your target audience enjoys. For example, you may want to move from the upper right (mental + chance) to upper left (mental + skill).

The solution might be to change a variable determined by chance into a variable determined by player choice. In a physical prototype this might be accomplished by removing dice from the system and replacing them with cards that a player can choose to play. In an electronic game, this might be accomplished by giving the player a choice of where to start or what weapons to use, instead of randomly generating them.

Taking Notes

As mentioned, it's imperative to keep notes of your playtests. You think you will remember all of the comments later on, but what you will really remember is those comments you expected to hear or wanted to hear. If you don't keep notes, you'll lose all the really important details of the playtesters' reactions. These notes should be filed chronologically in a notebook or folder, or entered into a database. Each time you conduct a test, write down the date of the test, all feedback gathered from your testers, and any of your own observations.

Figure 8.7 is a form you can use to capture observations and playtester comments. It is broken into three parts: (1) in-game observations, which are thoughts that you write down while the testers are playing the game; (2) post-game questions, which are questions designed to help elicit opinions about the key aspects of a game system; and (3) revision ideas, which is a space for you to articulate ideas for making the game better.

You may be asking yourself right now, "What should I be testing for?" Don't worry—that's the subject of the next two chapters. For right now, here are some general questions you might ask of your playtesters. After you've gone through Chapters 9 and 10, you can create your own questions, specifically geared for your own game.

Sometimes it's more effective to interview people and write down their comments than have them fill out forms. This is because filling out forms is a chore. Interviewing playtesters one-on-one is a very good method, but if you can't do that, then group interviews are also fine. Just make sure to encourage everyone to speak their mind, and try to keep the more aggressive members from dominating the discussion.

You'll find that sometimes not all of the questions on the form will be relevant. For example, if you are testing for interface flaws, then data about the overall play experience may be less important to capture. We encourage you to tailor this form to

8.7 Observations and Playtester Comments

IN-GAME OBSERVATIONS

[Your thoughts as you watch the testers play.]

IN-GAME QUESTIONS

[Questions you ask the testers as they play.]

1. What did you feel as your turned ended?
2. Does the navigation seem confusing?
3. Why did you move to that location?
4. Why are you pausing there?

POST-GAME QUESTIONS

[Questions you ask the testers after they've played.]

General questions

1. What was your first impression?
2. How did that impression change as you played?
3. Was there anything you found frustrating?
4. Did the game drag at any point?
5. Were there particular aspects that you found satisfying?
6. What was the most exciting thing about the game?
7. Did the game feel too long, too short or just about right?

Formal elements

1. Describe the objective of the game.
2. Was the objective clear at all times?
3. What types of choices did you make during the game?
4. What was the most important decision you made?
5. What was your strategy for winning?
6. Did you find any loopholes in the system?
7. How would you describe the conflict?
8. In what way did you interact with other players?
9. Do you prefer to play alone or with human opponents?
10. What elements do you think could be improved?

Dramatic elements

1. Was the game's premise exciting?
2. Did the story enhance or detract from the game?
3. As you played, did the story evolve with the game?
4. Is this game appropriate for the target audience?
5. On a piece of paper, graph your emotional involvement over the course of the game.
6. Did you feel a sense of dramatic climax as the game progressed?
7. How would you make the story and game work better as a whole?

Procedures, rules, interface, and controls

1. Were the procedures and rules easy to understand?
2. How did the controls feel? Did they make sense?
3. Could you find the information you needed on the interface?
4. Was there anything about the interface you'd change?
5. Did anything feel clunky or awkward?
6. Are there any controls or interface features you'd like to see added?

End of session

1. Overall, how would you describe this game's appeal?
2. Would you purchase this game?
3. What elements of the game attracted you?
4. What was missing from the game?
5. If you could change just one thing, what would it be?
6. Who do you think is the target audience for this game?
7. If you were to give this game as a gift, who would you give it to?

REVISION IDEAS

[Ideas you have for improving the game.]

GETTING THE MOST OUT OF FOCUS GROUPS

by Kevin Keeker, Designer, Microsoft Game Studios

Kevin Keeker spent the early years of his career working on game projects as a usability engineer. Here he shares some insight into the psychology of focus groups and how to get the most out of them.

Many people believe that focus groups are a good way to evaluate their games. I've learned that focus groups aren't the best way to gauge the quality or popularity of your ideas. Instead, focus groups should be used to generate ideas for your game. A well-run focus group is one where the participants are encouraged to speak freely and disagree with one another if necessary. This environment can generate ideas that will fuel your own creativity and provide a glimpse into the common points of wisdom and key disagreements in your gaming audience. This sidebar describes why focus groups are better for generating ideas than evaluating them. Then it provides a few pointers to help you achieve either objective.

Let's say that you're designing a snowboarding game and you're feeling pretty good about it. You know that you're making the game for teens and young adults. You know that you need a great sense of speed, big air, tons of attitude and crazy tricks. You've been tuning the basic play of the game with usability feedback from your teens and young adults. They're able to pull off the tricks and find some of the fun scenarios that you've positioned around the course. Meanwhile, you've got to refine the attitude part.

Music is a huge part of snowboarding culture. You know that. You know that the kids like the punk rock. After all, you make videogames. You're just a 30-year-old man-child. So, you talk to some labels, pick some tunes and plan a focus group to validate your musical choices.

This is all a lot of fun, until the dozen boarders in your focus group room go into heavy posturing. "What are your favorite bands?" Some start eagerly throwing out names. Others snipe at these suggestions. A third set of participants sinks sullenly back in their seats, while a couple of boarders drift away into the powder.

To reel everyone back in, you remind the group that this is a brainstorm by eagerly accepting all suggestions and going around the room one-by-one. This generates a pretty sizable list of bands with most of the overlap in tastes centering on (expensive) bands with some widespread popularity.

Thankfully, lots of the bands mentioned could be labeled punk if you're just a little generous in your categorization. At least you can be confident that you've validated punk as an enjoyable musical style for most of the snowboarding crowd.

Now you move on to the music you've picked. You play a song. Ask people to give it a thumbs-up or thumbs-down. And please explain their opinion. You notice the participants noticing each other. They look around the room as they make their decision. In the end the bands that are familiar names receive the clearest enthusiasm. At least a few people have heard of them. Most of the songs receive half-hearted enthusiasm. A few of them no one likes. During the wrap-up, you ask for an overall consensus on the musical selection. A few people passionately argue for something other than punk music. The group as a whole agrees that variety is the key.

You're left with a very uneasy consensus. What do you do now? You could go with your gut. But then the focus group has been a waste of time and a truckload of money. You try to sum thumbs and go with the songs that evoked the least ire. But that leaves you at risk of a very bland musical selection.

This scenario points out the fundamental problem in focus groups. They're very good for generating ideas and very poor at validating them.

Group interaction seeds individual creativity by encouraging us to examine differences between our opinions and those of others. The thoughts of others remind us of the way we feel ourselves. The differences between our ideas and others spur us to distinguish our ideas. They also encourage us to try out alternate perspectives and potentially incorporate elements of those perspectives into our own ideas. Creativity is this process of incorporating new elements into our ideas and putting together disparate ideas to create new ideas.

However, a similar process can lead people to avoid stating differences with others. It takes effort to disagree with others and to generate a plausible reason why you differ from others. Furthermore, there's a good chance the other people won't like you if you disagree with them. These are two good reasons to avoid disagreeing by accepting a common consensus. Disagreeing becomes significantly harder if you perceive that you're the only person with an opinion. This perception comes quickly in group settings where one person may state an opinion and others may quickly agree. The onus is then on the dissenters to come forward. But the dissenters may take time to reevaluate their position. These delays in disagreement further support the appearance that there is consensus.

So, what do you do? As a designer who has worked in user-testing, I have a leg up. I know how to ask questions the right way. When you want to generate ideas, you create a group brainstorming session (focus group) and do everything that you can to encourage people to disagree in a safe and constructive fashion.

When you want to evaluate ideas, you survey people individually. Give each person a concrete list of alternatives and ask them to choose or rank those alternatives. To get a clear answer, you need to present people with trade-offs. Do you want this song or that song? Rank these songs in terms of which songs you'd most like to see in the game. Preferably you also present these choices in the context of a clearly defined value system. It's not enough to know that X is better than Y. You need to know that X and maybe Y are good enough to be included in the game. Ask each user to clearly mark the boundary above which songs are good enough to be in the game and below which songs should be dropped. Another way to do this is to ask users to compare the songs to ones that they think would be good, bad, or adequate for the game.

Author Bio

Kevin Keeker trained as a social and personality psychologist at the University of Illinois and at the University of Washington before stumbling into usability engineering. Since 1994 he has worked on a variety of entertainment and media-related products at Microsoft. After managing Microsoft Game Studios' usability group, he shifted focus to apply his user-centered design experience as a game designer on Xbox sports titles.

your specific needs. Many of the questions will be unique to a game, so it's important for you not to rely on our questions but to create your own. Questions designed to get at issues that you have with your particular game will be the most valuable to you.

A good way to begin is to identify key areas of your game you need input on and create questions geared to get feedback on those areas. Write down more questions than you plan to use and then rank them in order of importance. Then group the top questions by type, as we did previously. You can develop your own categories of questions and structure. It really comes down to the type of information you wish to gather and how your playtesting sessions are structured.

One thing to avoid is getting carried away and overwhelming your playtesters. If you ask someone twenty or more questions in a row, they'll become exhausted and may stop answering accurately. Remember, it's not the number of questions you ask but the quality of the responses.

Basic Usability Techniques

Asking questions is a vital part of conducting a playtesting session, but there are other methods for eliciting good responses. Some of these include techniques commonly employed in usability labs. Usability research involves real people using products and giving their feedback before those products are marketed to the public. In the next sections we've listed three techniques that you can apply to game testing.

Don't lead

You'll learn the most from your testers by quietly observing them play. If a playtester asks a question, respond by asking them to describe what they think they should do. If they reach an impasse while playing, then you've identified something important that needs to be fixed.

Ask testers to think out loud

It's easy to see where testers have problems by observing them. However, it's often harder to understand why. Ask your testers to explain to you what's going inside their heads as they play. Their commentary will provide a window into the game and will help you figure out solutions to problems you might not even know existed. Most people aren't used to thinking out loud, so you may have to help them get started.

Quantitative data

In addition to taking notes on what players like and don't like, on what they pick up quickly and have difficulty grasping, use feedback forms to generate data that shows trends. After a playtest session, you can use this quantitative data to prioritize the severity of issues.

Some game companies work with professional usability experts who may employ more sophisticated methods and use special facilities for playtesting. If you have the budget, this can be extremely beneficial. Not only do professional labs tend to produce superior results, but you can learn from the process and apply some of their methodology to your in-house playtesting sessions.

Data Gathering

So far we've mostly discussed how to obtain qualitative feedback, but you may also want to go after quantitative feedback, such as recording the time it takes someone to read the rules, or counting the number of clicks its takes to perform a certain function, or tracking the speed at which a player advances in level. You may also ask testers to rank ease of use of certain features on a scale of one to ten, or to choose between several options to see what features are most important to them.

The type of data you gather depends upon the problems you wish to solve. If the game feels clunky and people are taking too long to get started, then measuring the time they spend on procedure to determine where the trouble spot is, might be a good approach. However, if the problem is that the game doesn't feel dramatic enough, a series of qualitative questions may produce superior results.

Exercise 8.8: Gathering Data

Go back to your original prototype and think of three pieces of quantitative data you can measure that will answer three clearly defined questions you have about the gameplay.

If you're successful at gathering quantitative data, you may suddenly find yourself buried in statistics. It's nice to have stats on every conceivable aspect of your game, but if you don't know how to interpret the numbers, they aren't much use. We recommend that you conduct your data gathering with clearly defined objectives in mind. Before you set out to measure something, write down your assumptions and purpose. What is it you want to prove or disprove? Then structure your test to either affirm or deny the hypothesis. For instance, you may feel that a certain feature in the game is causing a problem, so you design an experiment that measures the time it takes people to reach a specific point in the game with and without that feature. You may also combine this with a qualitative approach, where you ask the testers how they feel about the new feature. The combination of the qualitative and quantitative should give you the answers you are looking for.

You can take your data gathering as far as your imagination and creativity will permit. Some computer game developers even create software tools to record game statistics in special files during playtesting sessions. This is a sophisticated form of keeping version notes. The developers then write special code to help analyze this data and determine the effectiveness of different game elements and features.

For example, the developer might analyze the effectiveness of all units in an RTS prototype using the statistics gathered from actual playtests. If the data shows that one unit is dominating the others, the developer can then tweak that unit's variables accordingly and re-test. They may make the dominating unit more expensive to build or less powerful. Or they may tweak the variables of other units to balance the game.

Although statistical analysis techniques like this are powerful tools, it is not a replacement for the designer's creative judgment on how to tweak game variables. This is because statistics can be misleading. If playtesters are new to the game, they may not be using certain units as efficiently as they could because they haven't learned the subtleties of play yet. Or, at the other end of the spectrum, if the testers are experienced with the game, they may have set opinions about how to use the units and not see some innovative new way of playing. The bottom line with all data analysis is that it's a good tool that should be used in combination with other playtesting methods in order to have the best overall results.

TEST CONTROL SITUATIONS

A tool for improving the efficiency of your playtesting sessions is to utilize controlled game situations. A controlled game situation is when you lay down parameters that force players to test a specific portion of the game mechanics, such as:

- The end of the game
- A random event that rarely takes place
- A special situation within a game
- A particular level of a game
- New features

You can set up to test different aspects of your game independently of one another during different prototyping stages. In the foundation stage, you may test basic functionality without worrying about balancing or fairness. In later stages, you may want to test for loopholes and dead-ends. Or you may focus sessions on the accessibility of the interface or navigation system.

This type of controlled test situation is vital because it allows your testers to repeatedly experience an event under a variety of conditions. For instance, let's say you were designing *Monopoly*, and you wanted to test the "going to jail" feature. Instead of waiting for it to happen by chance, you could force this event to occur and see the results under various conditions. How does going to jail affect a player who owns very little property versus another player who owns a vast amount of property? You may choose to start the game in the middle with the player already in jail, then play for thirty minutes and observe what takes place. Then repeat the experiment with a change in the player's financial position.

Exercise 8.9: Test Control Situations

Create three test control situations for the original prototype that you created. Describe the purpose of each control and how it functions. Then try it out and make note of your observations.

You don't have to have your testers start from the beginning and play the game all the way through. You can start at any point: beginning, middle, or end. You can make one of your players grossly more powerful than the others and see what happens. Testing isn't about being fair to your testers or making sure that they enjoy the game. It's about seeing what happens under every possible condition. Many of these are rare cases and need to be forced so that they materialize at key moments in the game. This way you can see how it affects the gameplay. Does it ruin the experience? Or is it a nice surprise?

Also, when testing, your time is limited, and some games take days to play. If you don't have the time, you'll find yourself relying on test control situations almost every session. One of the most common control situations is starting a game near the end. To do this, you set up the prototype to simulate where players would be in the final conflict. You define the parameters to create the type of ending that you want to test, and then you start the session from this control point and study how the end game plays out. Since it is a controlled situation, you might be able to test the end game four times in one hour.

This is one of the reasons that cheat codes exist for electronic games. They are tools that the game developers use so that the team can test controlled situations. For example, the designers of a real-time strategy game may find it helpful to have a cheat code for turning off the fog of war. This would allow them to better monitor the AI for the computer-controlled units, while a cheat code for infinite resources would allow them to test how the game plays with the maximum number of units. It has become a tradition among game developers to leave the cheat codes in the final releases of game titles. One reason is so that players can have fun experimenting with different game situations that would otherwise be impossible.

PLAYTESTING PRACTICE

We've found it's easier for designers to learn the process of playtesting by using a game that they have no emotional connection with—it's easier to be objective when your design skills aren't on the line. For the next few exercises, we'll take a simple, familiar game and use it to learn the essence of playtesting. As we do this, much of what we discussed earlier will be come apparent, as well as some new concepts.

Connect Four

Many of us grew up playing the game *Connect Four*. It's where two players take turns dropping checkers into a vertical grid. The first player to get four units in a row (horizontally, vertically, or diagonally) wins the game.

1. Create the prototype
First, you need to create a simple prototype for *Connect Four*. To do this with pen and paper, draw a seven squares wide by six squares tall grid on a piece of paper. One player will use a black pen to represent black units on the grid and a second player will use a red pen to represent red units. Make sure to have a stopwatch handy to time your playtest sessions. Next, decide who goes first. Each player, on his turn, chooses a column in which to place a unit. He then draws units at the bottom of the chosen column as if gravity dropped them from the top. Units stack on top of one another when they "land" in the grid.

2. Prepare your questions and script
Write down the questions you plan to ask in advance and prepare a script for the session.

3. Recruit testers
Go out and find two playtesters.

4. Playtesting
Introduce your testers to the game and let them begin playtesting.

5. Testing the grid size
Play according to the previous description a few times. Use your stopwatch and mark how long each game takes to resolve next to the game grid. Next, draw the game grid at 8×6 instead of 7×6. Play this a few times, using the same rules. What happens to the play experience in the 8×6 version? What happens to the time it takes to resolve? Which version is more interesting? Why? Does changing the grid size give you ideas for changing other variables?

6. Testing the objective
Go back to a 7×6 grid, and this time change the objective, so that winning requires connecting five in a row. Play this a few times. What happens?

Does changing the objective give you ideas for changing other variables as well? For example you might find that a 7×6 grid is too small. If so, try the "connect five" version on a 9×7 grid.

7. Testing gravity

Now go back to the original rules (i.e., Connect Four on a 7×6 grid). This time remove gravity from the system. Players can now place a unit in any open cell on the grid. Play the game as usual from there. What happens? Does the game work anymore?

8. Alternate versions

How do these alternate versions compare with the original? Are they better, worse or just different? It's easy to see that changing system variables has a direct effect on the play experience, and the only way to determine this affect is through playtesting.

Final analysis

Compile your questions and write down your thoughts. Take time to go over each answer and analyze your results. What changes would you make to the game as a result of this playtesting session? Do your qualitative and quantitative data point to any conclusions?

The previous exercise exposes you to the basics of playtesting and revision. Playtesting is the process of playing a game with various users, making observations, and gathering data, while revision is the process of taking the critiques and data generated and tweaking the variables in the game to make it a compelling experience. The iterative process of playtesting and revising over and over is fundamental to the creation of good games.

Conclusion

As you can see, playtesting is an involved task, but it's a critical part of game design that cannot be rushed through or sidelined. Your job as designer is to make sure playtesting remains at the heart of the game design and development process. As soon as you let it slip into the background, then you give up your chance to see your game as the players will see it when they open the box for the first time.

Playtesters are your eyes and your ears. They allow you, as the designer, to keep your finger on the pulse of the game, even after you've played it to death. If you listen to your playtesters and analyze what they are saying, you will be able to see the game mechanics for what they are, not what you want them to be or imagine they should be. And that is the key to designing. It's understanding what it is you've created and being able make it even better, not in one flash of brilliance, but step by step over months and even years. If you can master this process, then you have mastered one of the key skills to being a great game designer.

How Feedback from Typical Gamers Can Help Avoid "Disappointing" Outcomes

by Bill Fulton, Games User-Testing Group, Microsoft Game Studios

The Problem

Compared to the giddy expectations of the developers at the kick-off of a project, most games are disappointing, commercially, critically, or both. After all, few people set out to spend that much time and money to produce a game resulting in ambivalent reviews and low sales. Solving this problem is one of the holy grails of game development, as it would remove substantial risk from making games.

The Traditional Analysis of This Problem and the Solution

Why does this disappointment happen? The traditional analysis of the problem is that it is because teams are "too close" to their game to see it objectively, much the way that many parents seem to believe their child is above average. Because of this analysis, a myriad of ways to get feedback from fellow game development professionals (co-workers, publishers, journalists, playtest teams, etc.) has sprung up. While the traditional analysis has some merit and the solution to combat the problem is quite useful, it doesn't seem to explain (or fix) the whole problem.

An Alternative Analysis and Solution

An alternative analysis for why games don't live up to the expectations of the developer is that professional game developers aren't like the people for whom they are designing the game: typical gamers. Game developers are so knowledgeable about games and game development that they have a hard time designing for the typical gamer who knows comparatively little about games. (See figure for an illustration.)

This situation of game developers being very unlike typical gamers suggests that when the game is fun for the developers, it may not (yet) be fun for typical gamers, who may find it too hard, or may not find the fun that is in the game. This is similar to the way that modern art is often unappreciated by anyone without a degree in art history. But to make games for the masses, it is the responsibility of the game developer to show typical gamers how to have fun with the game.

Many publishers and developers have come to see the problem this way, and have engaged marketing research firms to do focus tests on the game to combat this problem. But often the goal of the focus test is to learn how to sell the game, not how to make the game more fun and accessible for more players. Furthermore, focus tests are often done too late in development to make many changes

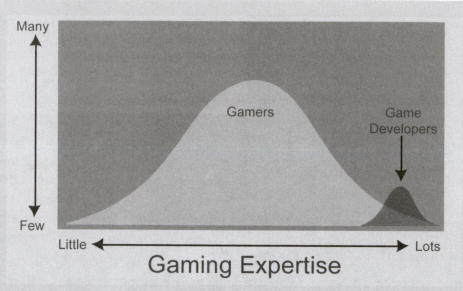

Many

Few

Gamers

Game
Developers

Little ◄─────────────────────────► Lots

Gaming Expertise

Gaming expertise

A comparison of hypothetical distributions of gaming expertise for typical gamers and typical game developers. This figure illustrates how all game developers know more about games than all but the most dedicated gamers. The point of this figure is to show how game developers can't simply make games that are only accessible to people like themselves, if they want to make a game that the majority of gamers can understand and enjoy.

to the game. Because of the constraint of schedule and emphasis on selling as opposed improving the game and time, many game developers are mixed about focus testing.

User-Testing From an HCI Perspective

Getting feedback from consumers for the purpose of improving products is a major goal of the field of usability, a subset of the human-computer interaction (HCI) field. Most major software companies have usability departments staffed with HCI professionals. The games industry has been slow to adopt this practice.

But this is changing—the use of HCI professionals in game development is gaining greater acceptance. One major game publisher has been doing some form of usability work on games since 1998, but other game publishers and developers are beginning to experiment with usability methods as a way to make their games more fun. As more game developers and publishers do usability testing on their games in development, the typical quality of games from those developers and publishers will only get better.

An Example of User-Testing from Age of Empires 2: Age of Kings

Age of Empires 2 (AoE2) is an excellent example of how user-testing from an HCI perspective can improve games. The first AoE game was both a critical and commercial hit. In fact, it sold so well that the only way the sequel (AoE2) could sell any better would be if it expanded beyond the kinds of gamers who played the first AoE.

The developers and publisher decided to "aim for the stars" and make the game accessible to nongamers—that AoE2 would be a game that someone who had never played a computer game would be able to pick up and play. This was a lofty goal, because AoE2 is a complicated game and non-gamers lack the background to learn the game on their own, and because we knew from testing that the first AoE was a difficult game to learn for some experienced gamers.

In order to achieve this level of accessibility, it would be necessary to provide a robust tutorial and do a great deal of user-testing. The details of the testing are better described in a different article, but the following anecdote from the final test of the tutorial gives a bit of flavor:

The final test of the tutorial was done on a Sat., at 10 a.m. At 9 a.m., I noticed an elderly lady (maybe in her 70s or 80s) waiting outside the building. I thought she was lost or looking for someone, but it turned out that she had been scheduled for the test. I was surprised, but she technically fit the kind of people we were looking for (never played a retail computer game, could operate a computer, was older than 40), so I let her in. I apologized for her being given the wrong time for the test, but she told me that she was told 10 a.m. was the time, "but always showed up an hour early for appointments."

I was a little concerned that she might be put off by the nature of the game (build a nation, raise an army, destroy your neighbors), and offered that she could leave if she wanted. But she thought the idea of testing a game was "interesting" because her grandkids played them, and she wanted to be helpful. So we let her go through the test like all the other middle-aged folks. It was a bizarre sight to see dozens of parent and grandparent types playing Age of Empires 2 in the lab.

After they had completed the tutorial, they were instructed to play a random map game against the computer. Towards the end of the test, I went by the elderly lady and saw that she had the semblance of a nation going—she had several villagers collecting all four resources, and had many of the right buildings built (barracks, granary, mining, etc.). When the Mongol hordes came over the hill and invaded her nation, she did several things right—she hid her villagers, and started to build a (woefully inadequate) army. Unfortunately, she was too slow and got overrun; Age of Empires 2 had just crushed grandmother's nation. When I escorted her from the lab, I asked her what she thought—she said she could see how her grandkids would like it, but the game wasn't her "cup of tea."

While the grandmother didn't enjoy the game, after completing the tutorial she was able to understand the basics of the game and responded reasonably to being attacked. This was a dramatic improvement over the original AoE, where sometimes even experienced gamers got stuck and couldn't figure out the game without going to the manual. The reliance on testing AoE2's tutorial with real people and not just paid game-industry professionals, resulted in a game that almost anyone can pick up and play.

In the end, AoE2 sold dramatically more units than did the first version, in large part due to improvements to the game that stemmed from doing user-testing throughout the development of the game.

Author Bio

Bill Fulton has been doing HCI work on games since 1997, and is one of the founders of the Games User-Testing Group at Microsoft Game Studios. The group's mission is to get feedback from typical gamers for the purposes of improving games in development. By Dec. 2002, there were 28 HCI professionals providing feedback from typical gamers to games in development including Age of Empires 2, Halo, Project Gotham Racing, Rise of Nations and Freelancer throughout the development process. To read more about HCI and games, see their web site at http://www.microsoft.com/playtest/publications.htm.

Microsoft playtesting lab (Photo by Kyle Drexel) (above)

Tape of Halo user test. The inset shows a player's hand responses monitored (right)

Chapter 9
Functionality, Completeness, and Balance

Now that you've tried your hand at the playtesting process, you are probably wondering what to do with all the comments your testers are giving you. How can you prioritize all these ideas and comments into a helpful list of changes to your game? Unless you are superhuman and can process hundreds of details at once, you need a way to focus your thinking. You need a way to take your game step by step from a crude mock-up of the core gameplay to a fully functioning model of your entire system. This chapter provides some tangible steps you can take to make sure your game is functional, complete, and balanced.

The process we suggest here is based on years of watching student and professional game designers work through this very problem. What we've found in this experience is that it's important to break the playtesting process down into several discreet phases—each phase focusing on specific aspects of the design, perfecting these aspects, and only then moving on to the next phase.

Of course, as we've discussed, games are dynamic, interrelated systems. A change to one part of the system can completely change the player's perception of another. We realize this, and the process we're about to walk through is a vast simplification of what you will actually experience when you try this yourself. What's important to take away from this process is the need to focus your mind on the distinct goals of each phase, not try to fix everything in your game all at once. We want you to feel in control of this process, and giving you these goal-based phases and a method to move your game through them is a good way to do that.

What Are You Testing For?

When you built your original prototype, we discussed the four basic steps of design: foundations, structure, formal details, and refinement. These four steps allowed you to visualize first the core gameplay or foundation, then carefully add structure to the system, one rule or procedure at a time.

Only then did we go on to the formal details and refinement.

When we talked briefly about these steps in Chapter 7 on page 174, we spoke mostly in terms of prototyping, getting your ideas into physical form—we didn't talk much about playtesting, revision, or your goals at each of these stages. At that point, we just wanted you to get some experience building out a design of a game from scratch. Now that you have a handle on the art of prototyping and playtesting, we can go back to these basic steps and discuss the design goals you should keep in mind as you work your way through each of these phases of development, using the iterative process and playtesting at each step along the way.

Foundation

During this stage, your main concern is that the basic idea for your game is fun. Your prototype may only consist of a main core mechanic with which to engage, and there may not be much else. You may have infinite loopholes, dead ends, etc., but don't worry about all of that right now. At this point, you just need to get a sense that the core of the system you've thought of, so that you can judge whether or not it is the compelling base for a game. As we mentioned in Chapter 8, at this stage, you will probably be playtesting the system on your own. The game is really only valid as an exercise in confirming your intuition that the idea makes a good foundation for a game.

Structure

Once you have a solid foundation, your next goal is to add enough structure to make the prototype functional for playtesters other than yourself—probably your close friends or co-workers, but still, someone other than yourself. We'll dis-

cuss the essence of "functionality" in detail, but intuitively, you already know what it means: your prototype works at a basic, albeit clunky, level. You need to build out the rules and procedures to the extent that the system can be played by people who don't have a full vision of the end experience in mind.

What you want to know when you get to this stage is: was your intuition right? Does the foundation hold up under the rigors of a real playtest with real players? Your focus here is on both functionality and fun. Are the formal elements working together, even in this basic state? Is there a beginning, middle, and an end to the experience? Can the players reach the objective? Are they engaging in the conflict you've designed? Are they enjoying that engagement? Is there a spark to your game? Should you even continue with this idea, or is it time to head back to the drawing board?

Formal details

Let's say the spark is there—you're on to something. Now you've got the problem of having to build out a fully functional version of the game system you envisioned. What should you do first? You know there are problems; they've already come up in the first few playtests, but where to start? The answer to that question is the basis of this chapter. During the formal details stage, your focus should be on making sure the game is (1) functional, (2) internally complete, and (3) balanced.

These three tasks may seem deceptively simple at first, but they require skills that you may never entirely master—you will only get better and better as you learn the craft of game design. Every game is intrinsically different, so the answers you found during one playtesting process are not the right answers next time. Experience will help you judge what decisions to make, what choices will make your game a clean, well-balanced system. But this process is really an art—a game can sink or swim during the formal details stage.

What about fun you say? Why don't we test for fun during this stage? Of course, you are always keeping your eye out to make sure your game stays "fun" as it develops, but remember, we're trying to focus here, to break down the process so that you don't have to worry about everything all at once. Making sure your game is functional, complete, and balanced is huge undertaking.

Refinement

During the refinement state, we're going to assume your game is functional, complete, and balanced. You tested primarily for fun in the first two stages of design—by yourself and with confidants, and if your core gameplay was fun to begin with, completing and balancing the game shouldn't have detracted from that, on the contrary, it probably added to it. But perhaps something of that original spark got lost in the process. Now is the time to focus all your energy on making sure the fun you envisioned from the start is there in spades.

You probably noticed the quotes we use around the word "fun." This is because fun is such a broad term that it is almost impossible to define what it is and how you make sure your game has it. And yet, if you ask a player what they want in a game, nine times out of ten they say it should be "fun." We all know when we're having fun, even if we can't define it—as Supreme Court Justice Potter Stewart said about pornography: "I know it

Prototyping Stage	Functional?	Internally Complete?	Balanced?	Fun?	Accessible?
1) Foundations				●	
2) Structure	●			●	
3) Formal Details	●	●	●		
4) Refinement				●	●

9.1   What are you testing for?

when I see it." Your playtesters know fun when they see it. And so Chapter 10 is all about how you can make your game more "fun" for players, with strategies and ideas for adding that elusive emotional pull to a game system that keeps players coming back for more.

Last, but not least, during the refinement stage, you will be testing for accessibility. Remember, your game has to stand on its own without you there to explain it. You may have the most functional, complete, balanced, fun game in the world, but if it isn't accessible, players won't ever know this. And so this final aspect is as critical as any of the others that come before.

When you feel overwhelmed by the process of playtesting and revision, review Figure 9.1 to remind yourself of the stage of design you are in and where your design focus should be. If you don't try to solve every issue in your game at once, your tasks will suddenly become simpler, and your next steps much clearer. With these steps in mind, let's look at functionality, completeness, and balance in detail.

IS YOUR GAME FUNCTIONAL?

Before you can even think about completeness, you must have a functional game. By functional we

mean the system is established to the point where someone who knows nothing about the game can sit down and play it. It doesn't mean the tester won't run into trouble or that the experience will be thoroughly satisfying, but it does mean that they can interact with the game unaided by you. In a paper prototype this means the players can play the game—following the rules and procedures properly—and not reach an impasse. In software prototypes it means players can use the controls and make the game progress. In both types of prototypes it means that the components of the system interact properly and a resolution can be achieved.

Beyond this, deciding your game is "functional" is really a matter of judgment. If your players can make it through a session without help from the designer, let's call the game "functional" and move on to more demanding questions.

Exercise 9.1: Testing for Functionality

Take the original game prototype you developed in Exercise 7.9 and test it for functionality. Give the game to a group of people who have not played the game before with no verbal instructions—only the challenge to "play the game." See if they can play your game from start to finish without any input or assistance from you. If they can, your game is functional. If not, figure out what was missing, and revise the game to make it functional.

Is Your Game Internally Complete?

As you playtest, you will invariably notice places where your game is functional, but incomplete. For example, early in the first-person shooter prototyping process, we established movement and shooting rules so the system could function, but we had no rules about hit percentages or winning conditions, so it was still incomplete. Some of these missing elements are obvious, but others are much more difficult to discern. Only by testing every possible permutation under all conditions, can you be certain that there are no sections of the game that are left unfinished. Your job as game designer is to identify and resolve these issues.

This sounds simple, but it's not. Most games are quite complex systems which can act in unexpected ways under different conditions. The more you test, the more you'll discover how malleable your game is. Players will do things that you could have never anticipated. There may be gaps in the rules that made sense on paper but when they are actually implemented in the game, they lead to irresolvable situations or gray areas. In board-games, this often leads to arguments between players—each side interpreting the rules in their own way. In software, it leads to a loophole that players can exploit, a dead-end in the player experience, or a complete breakdown of the system. You'll often hear your testers making comments like, "The rules don't say either way," "I'm completely stuck," or "You can't do that!" These types of reactions are red flags that something within the game isn't complete and needs attention.

After identifying an incomplete portion of your game, the first thing to do is go back to the rules. Whether you're working on a digital game or a boardgame, you should have a design document or a rule sheet, which clearly describes how your game is to be played. What you'll discover is that what you thought was a clear set of rules actually has holes in it. You now have to plug the hole (or complete the rules) so that it makes sense. Doing this can often affect other parts of your game, so it's a delicate task and may require several testing sessions and revisions before you get it right.

Exercise 9.2: Testing for Completeness

Take the original game prototype you've been working with since Exercise 7.9 and test it for completeness. This time, look specifically for moments in which players reach an impasse, question the rules, or have to make a judgment call about what happens next. If players argue about the rules or reach a dead-end, your game is not complete. Revise your game to deal with the issues you find and test again.

You'll find that sometimes playtesters uncover problems in a system despite the fact that the rules are unambiguous. For an example, let's go back to the first-person shooter prototype from Chapter 7 on page 160. Is it internally complete?

Here's a potential problem that plagues many first-person shooters, including our prototype: When more than two people play this game, it's possible for players to camp near both of the spawning points on the arena map. When a recently killed opponent appears at either spawning point, the campers can promptly shoot the opponent. Players stuck in the position of being shot are furious at this seemingly unfair tactic.

The problem is that the rules are comprehensive and the players are behaving within the bounds of the rules, but certain players have figured out a way to gain an advantage that the designer didn't expect. Thinking as the designer, how would you alleviate this "spawn camping" problem? For a challenge, stop reading now and think through your own solution. Then compare yours with the following four possible solutions.

Solution # 1

The number of spawning points on a map should be equal to the number of players in the game.

- *Pros:* Players will always have at least one safe point on which to spawn.
- *Cons:* Have to design arena maps specific to the number of players that will play on it. Maps cannot facilitate a fluctuating number of players as most online FPS games allow.

Solution # 2

A force field shield surrounds each spawning point hex. A spawning player can fire and move outward through the force field. However no one can shoot or move back in. The force field incinerates a spawning player if he remains on the spawning point hex for more than one turn.

- *Pros:* Players are safe when they first spawn. And they can fire upon a single camper.
- *Cons:* Multiple campers can still wait nearby making the turn after spawning difficult for players.

Solution # 3

Players can choose to spawn on a randomly generated hex. If the hex is occupied by a wall or another player, then a different hex must be randomly generated.

- *Pros:* Reduces player interest in camping by spawning points.
- *Cons:* Adds an element of luck to the system.

Solution # 4

Don't fix this because it's a feature, not a problem.

- *Pros:* Some players think spawn camping is just part of the game. Leaving the system as is will force players to fight for choice camping spots which will create a game in itself.

- *Cons:* Other players are extremely frustrated by spawn camping.

Discussion

The options listed illustrate that there are many creative ways to tweak this system during the process of making a game internally complete. As we noted, the spawn camping problem is not unique to our first-person shooter prototype. If you do an Internet search on the phrase "spawn camping," you'll see dozens of web sites discussing the pros and cons. You'll also notice that many fans have created numerous work-around mods to alleviate the spawn camping problem. Some of the mod solutions are similar to the options we listed previously. Some are different. One solution makes a player invisible for two to three seconds after spawning. This lets a player run around and shoot without being seen, giving them a fighting chance.

Exercise 9.3: Spawn Camping

Write down three original solutions to the spawn camping problem not mentioned previously. Describe why you feel these solutions are inferior or superior to the ones mentioned.

Loopholes

Finding loopholes is an essential part of testing for completeness. A loophole can be defined as a flaw in the system which users can exploit to gain an unfair or unintended advantage. As long as loopholes exist, your game cannot be considered complete. Your mission as a designer, is to close off all loopholes before the product is shipped.

This is no simple task, especially with videogames. The very nature of a computer program makes it easy for loopholes to go undetected. In most videogames, there are so many possibilities that no designer can test them all, and some gamers actually make a point of ferreting them out. To these gamers, the challenge of finding loopholes is irresistible. They love to tout their discoveries and use them to their full advantage when competing against other players. If you don't believe us, go online and read the fan sites. Gamers make sport out of finding loopholes in games, and they post the flaws on their web sites for everyone to see.

Consider an example from the PC game *Deus Ex*. We should first state that *Deus Ex* is widely regarded as one of the most innovative games to be released in recent times. It's a pioneering piece of work in that the game environment is open and flexible rather than being tightly scripted. One of the weapons available in the game is called a "LAM." LAMs can be attached to walls and used like proximity mines—meaning they explode a few seconds after someone stands in close proximity to them. They are great for blowing up doors and for killing unsuspecting opponents. Apparently, however, they are also good for something the designers never anticipated.

Creative players learned that they could attach multiple LAMs to a wall, and then quickly run up them like a ladder before they detonated. Doing this allowed players to climb into places on game maps in ways that the designers hadn't anticipated. This meant that some levels were less challenging than originally planned. If this can happen to world-class game designers, it can happen to you. Players are much more creative and resourceful than you'd ever imagine.

Another example comes from the Atari game, *Asteroids*. This game was a smash hit in the

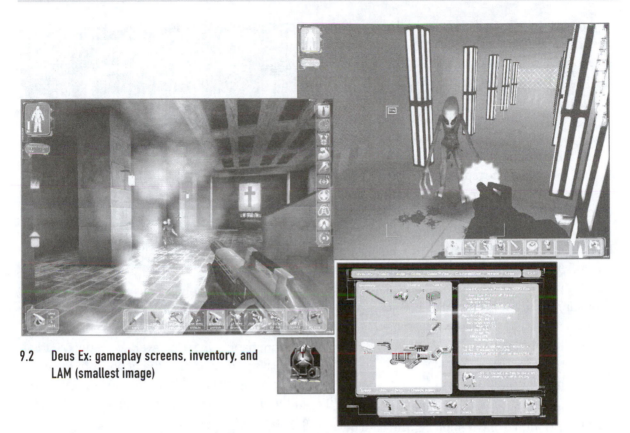

9.2   Deus Ex: gameplay screens, inventory, and
       LAM (smallest image)

arcades when it was released in 1979. In this game you control a spaceship and must blast your way out of a field of floating asteroids, and also gun down flying saucers that come on screen to shoot you.

Engineers at Atari played the game incessantly for six months before it was released and had recorded a company high score of 90,000 points. No one believed that a normal player—someone not familiar with how the game was programmed—could ever achieve a score like that. However shortly after the game's release Atari began receiving reports that players all over the country were scoring three and four times that many points. In fact, the players were "beating the machine" because the *Asteroids* scoreboard maxed out at 99,990 points and, once surpassed, the score started over at 0.

The engineers at Atari were stunned. So they drove out to an arcade to investigate firsthand. Eugene Lipkin, then president of Atari's coin-operated–game division was quoted in *Esquire* magazine in 1981 as saying, "What had happened, was that a player had been smart enough to understand the movement and the programming on the product and had then come up with an idea of how to work around it. It took about three months for that to happen. Then, all of a sudden, we began hearing the same thing from all over. People had figured out that there was a safe place on the screen."

The safe place on the screen occurred because the player's bullets can "wrap around" the screen—meaning when firing off the right side screen they reappear from the left on the same trajectory, whereas the flying saucer bullets cannot wrap around. Players learned that if they destroyed all but one asteroid floating on the screen they could lurk near an edge and pick off the flying saucers as they appeared.

The small flying saucer is normally very formidable and is worth 1,000 points. With the lurking strategy, however, a player could shoot a flying saucer with wraparound bullets and get it from behind, or if the saucer appeared on the same side of the screen as the player, they could quickly blast it before it could get off a shot. It still takes a lot of skill to do it effectively but once mastered, this lurking practice allows players to rack up huge scores. *Asteroids* purists regarded the practice derisively. However this did not keep players from exploiting it to the fullest. Atari had to wait until the next version of the game, *Asteroids Deluxe*, to fully fix the problem.

Loopholes versus "features"

Sometimes it's debatable whether a system issue enables a loophole or whether it is actually a benefit to the game. You'll see heated arguments online, where gamers take both sides of the issue. The first-person shooter spawn camping loophole discussed on page 227 is one example of this. When you identify one of these subjective issues, you must make a creative choice on how to handle it. Sometimes it's possible to make variants on the game to satisfy different types of players.

As an example, let's look at how massively multiplayer online role-playing games (MMORPGs) have dealt with one specific type of "loophole." Ever since MMORPGs were introduced, players have debated the pros and cons of being able to kill other players. MMORPGs are persistent online worlds where players role-play and interact as virtual characters. Most people dislike players who maliciously kill other players. These people are

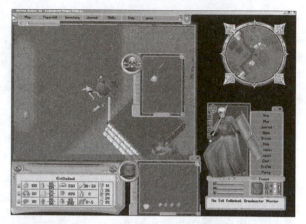

9.3   Ultima Online: EvilIndeed makes a kill

called "player killers." The remaining players would prefer that the game designers, for a given MMORPG, tweak the system to prevent player killing from happening. However, some people think that player killing adds to the richness of the game because evil characters are free to play evil roles, and it creates a more intriguing and challenging environment.

Which side is correct? Does the presence of player killing mean that an MMORPG has a loophole and that the game is not internally complete? The solution that MMORPG designers developed over time—through playtesting with real players—was to provide spaces for both types of players. In essence, many MMORPGs have two variants: one where players cannot hurt one another, and another where they can. Each variant is internally complete in its own way. The following are examples of how several well-known MMORPGs have evolved through play and revision to deal with player killing.

Ultima Online is one of the first MMORPGs. Early in the game's history, new players complained about being bullied and killed for no reason by more powerful players. Newbies had no protection. The problem was spoiling the fun for many players and deterring others from joining. People generally loved the game but hated the player killers—who they called cowards. They filled online message boards with complaints. Articles appeared in magazines about the problem. The designers at *Ultima Online* needed to tweak their game system to alleviate the tension.

In response, *Ultima Online*'s designers created a reputation system for characters in the game. Players who murdered other players were given red name banners and designated as "dishonorable." When law-abiding characters saw a red character, they would likely not trust or cooperate with them. This made it harder and less fun to be a player killer. In addition, and perhaps more dissuasive, was the fact that experienced law-abiding characters would (and do) band together to hunt down red characters. This created a system of vigilante law in the game, which greatly alleviated the tension, but also developed its own set of problems.

Over time, the game designers continued to tweak their system to make it less and less appealing to be a player killer. For example, they placed invincible computer-controlled guards at the entrances to all but one city in the game world. The guards killed red characters on sight. This meant that the cities were safe for law-abiding characters and player killers were relegated to an outlaw's existence, either out in the wilderness or in the one town that accepted them—a dangerous place called Buccaneer's Den. This solution accommodates both law-abiding players and player killers. It also meant that player killers could camp outside of towns, ready to pounce on any hapless players who might wander outside the city limits.

Today, the world of *Ultima* is divided into two separate spheres—one in which player killers run free, and one in which player killing is disabled by the system.

Asheron's Call is another popular MMORPG that had to deal with the same problem but came up with a very different solution. In the first version of *Asheron's Call*, the designers created an allegiance and fellowship system. When a new player came into the world, he had the option of swearing allegiance to another player character. In return, the new player might receive protection or even money and weapons from the experienced player—who was designated as his "leader." From that point onward, a share of the new player's experience points would go to his leader. Likewise, a share of the leader's experience points would go on to that character's follower (if she had one) and so on. This created a mutually beneficial pyramid structure that helped protect players.

In addition, *Asheron's Call* players had the option of joining fellowships. Fellowships were temporary agreements with other players, usually formed to go on a quest or pursue a goal. Experience points generated while the players were a fellowship were distributed across the group. Individuals in the group received a share of the points based on their experience level. For example a third-level character received a bigger share of the points generated by the fellowship than a second-level character, etc. The designers at Turbine Entertainment developed these systems as an elegant way of rewarding players for working together. They made it more fun to cooperate and less fun to be a spoiler.

Even with these systems in place, law-abiding players of *Asheron's Call* still complained about player killers. Turbine responded by tweaking the game so that, by default, players could not be attacked by other players. The story of the game was tweaked to say that the powerful magic of the world of Dereth protected them from one

Designer Perspective: Rob Daviau

Rob Daviau is a prolific designer of board and card games. He works on staff at Hasbro Games.

Title

Senior Game Designer, Hasbro Games

Project list (five to eight top projects)

- *Risk 2210 AD*
- *Axis & Allies Pacific*
- *Trivial Pursuit 20th Anniversary*
- *Star Wars Epic Duels*
- *The Game of Life: A Jedi's Path*
- *Battleship Card Game*
- *Nemesis Factor*

How did you get into the game industry?

Right place, right time. I played games all my life and spent a lot of time fading in and out of role-playing campaigns. After five years as an advertising copywriter I was looking for a change. I applied as a copywriter for Parker Brothers (mostly writing rules and box bottom copy) at the exact time they were looking for a game designer with a writing background. I ended up getting the designer job and the bulk of my work still involves copy-heavy projects. In my interview, I named two of my favorite games from childhood. Turns out the guy interviewing me had designed both those games. It was luck on my part but I advise that as a good tactic when interviewing somewhere. Just don't make it look like you planned it.

another. This made all players completely safe from one another, but it was disappointing to players that wanted the thrill of battling other live players. In response, Turbine created a way for players to voluntarily convert to player killer status. The interested player had to find a special altar in the game world to do it. After conversion, the player could kill and be killed by other player killers. In this approach, all players could inhabit the same game space, but only players designated as player killers could battle one another. This approach continues to be utilized today.

EverQuest, an MMORPG developed by Sony Online Entertainment, uses a similar system to *Asheron's Call*. In *EverQuest*, only players who choose to convert to player killer status can kill or

What are your five favorite games and why?

Tough one. For me, I admire games that create a whole new way to think about games—games that create a new type of game. So my top five (in no order) are: *Dungeons & Dragons*, *Diplomacy*, *Magic: The Gathering*, bridge, and *Monopoly*.

If I had to list my five favorite games (that I have played), I'd go with *Acquire*, *Settlers of Catan*, *Queen's Gambit* (I had very little to do with that game, so I'm not being egotistical), *Scrabble*, and hearts.

If I had to pick the five games I'm most excited to play right now, the list would be: hearts, *RoboRally*, *Game of Thrones* boardgame, *The Riddle of Steel* RPG, and a game we're working on here. That list is for today, in a week a few would probably change. By the time this is published, most will have.

What games have inspired you the most as a designer and why?

Every game—okay most games—have something in them that is clever or new or cool. I keep a mental list of the cool mechanic, the cool piece, the new storage tray, or different artwork in the games I play. I think of it as creating a palette to paint my own pictures. Offhand, in no particular order, the things I find clever right now are: the Spiritual Attributes that force munchkins to be role-players in the *Riddle of Steel* RPG, the bidding mechanism in the German game *Lowenhertz*, the shoot the moon aspect of hearts, the simplicity of *TransAmerica*, the simultaneous planning of *RoboRally*, the interconnectedness of the turns of *Puerto Rico*, the one-hand but two-purpose nature of cribbage, the artwork of *Mystery of the* Abbey—the list could go on and on.

What are you most proud of in your career?

The Avalon Hill line when it first got to Hasbro, which I was part of as a designer and copywriter from 1999 through 2001. I think there are some really good games there.

What words of advice would you give to an aspiring designer today?

It's very easy to hide behind a gimmick—graphics, sound, a license, nice video segments—but game players are smart. They'll figure out if it's all smoke and mirrors with no real game. Think about how well your game would play as a card game. There's nothing sexy about cards, no gimmick to hide bad gameplay. If your game would still seem fun as a card game, then it's a good idea and a good game.

be killed by other players. To further appease player killers, *EverQuest* offers player killer only game servers. On these servers, all players are susceptible to attack from one another. These servers are popular with hardcore fans. This version is the second variant described previously. By responding to player feedback—a form of playtesting—the Sony designers succeeded in closing a disruptive problem and made their game internally complete in regard to the player killer issue.

In most cases, you'll never find all the loopholes before the release date, and this is why some game developers opt for a public beta test. It's a risky proposition because it can dampen sales of the game, but in some cases, especially with massively multiplayer online games, it's a valuable tool.

9.4   EverQuest

Whether you initiate a public beta or not, it is your responsibility to make sure that there are no loopholes which will ruin the player experience.

Whenever a loophole is discovered, your job is to tweak the system and perform another playtest to see if the disruptive technique works. Eventually, you'll find a solution that eradicates the loophole. It's an iterative process, and each loophole can take days or even weeks to solve. By the time a game is released, most designers manage to do a pretty good job at eliminating the obvious flaws, but even with the most sophisticated testing schemes, some loopholes seem to find their way into the final products. This is because the number of people who play a released title is so much larger than the number of dedicated testers any company could manage to recruit, and all it takes is one player to uncover the flaw that everyone else missed. Here are some tips for finding and weeding out loopholes:

- Use control situations, as described in Chapter 8 on page 216, to test aspects of the system in isolation. This will force testers into situations they might otherwise avoid, exposing flaws that otherwise wouldn't be apparent.

- Do a series of playtests where you instruct testers to attempt to disrupt the system. Challenge them to see who can come up with the most creative way to get ahead.

- If possible find testers who enjoy figuring out alternative or subversive solutions. Computer hackers are good at finding loopholes in games. A person doesn't have to be a programmer to have this personality trait.

Exercise 9.4: Loopholes

A loophole is a system flaw that a player can exploit to her advantage; take your original game prototype and test for loopholes. In this exercise, use seasoned playtesters who know your game inside and out. As advised previously, instruct testers to disrupt the system. Challenge them to see who can come up with the most creative way to subvert the rules.

Dead-ends

A dead-end is another type of common flaw that disrupts the gameplay experience. Dead-ends are not loopholes, in that they do not allow a player to exploit a game, but like loopholes, they must be fixed before a game can be considered internally complete.

A dead-end occurs when a player gets stranded in the game and cannot continue towards the game objective no matter what they do. Adventure games, where players have to collect objects in the world and then use these objects later to solve the puzzle, are susceptible to this. If the player cannot solve the puzzle because they are missing a piece, they've reached a dead-end.

Dead-ends can also occur in other types of games. For instance, in a strategy game, a dead end can be a situation where the players cannot resolve the conflict because their forces wind up without resources. In an FPS, a dead-end can be a virtual space that a player stumbles into and cannot get out of. Most titles have ironed out dead-ends before they are released, but now and then, one slips through the playtesting cracks.

Wrapping up completeness

The idea of completeness can be summed up by the following statement: An internally complete game is one in which the players can operate the game without reaching any point at which either the gameplay or the functionality is compromised.

This is both an objective and subjective decision. You can say your game is complete at almost any point, and that will hold true until someone uncovers a flaw. In reality, no game is ever complete. There is always room for improvement, and in most cases, there are unknown or irresolvable issues lurking within the game system.

Schedule and budget constraints often preclude designers from ever fully completing this stage of the process. But your job as designer, and specifically your focus during the formal details stage of design, is to enforce a high enough standard and to lay out rigorous enough tests so that you can be certain beyond a reasonable doubt that there are no critical deficiencies lurking within your game. Only once you have accomplished this can your game can be considered internally complete.

IS YOUR GAME BALANCED?

As with "fun," the concept of balance is often used to describe the process of making a game "better." We offer a specific definition of balance here. Your game may require specific balancing techniques not addressed in this definition. But hopefully this will help you get started, and help you focus your thoughts as you step through this sophisticated process.

"Balancing" a game is the process of making sure the game meets the goals you've set for the player experience: that the system is of the scope and complexity you envisioned and that the elements of that system are working together without undesired results. In multiplayer games, it means that the starting positions and play are fair (i.e., no player has an inherent advantage) and no single strategy dominates all others. In single-player games it means that the skill level is properly adjusted to the target audience. For short, we call these four balancing areas "variables," "dynamics," "starting conditions," and "skill."

Resolving issues of balance is one of the most difficult parts of designing a game. This is because the notion of balance encompasses so many different elements, all of which are dependent on one another. Many of the concepts involved in balancing also involve complex mathematics and statistics, which you may or may not be skilled at computing. Don't let that deter you from the process, however. Balancing is as much about gut instinct as it is about numbers—with enough experience, you'll be able to tweak the variables in your physical prototype, or give detailed feedback to the programmers for your digital game without a degree in calculus.

Balancing variables

The variables of your system are a set of numbers that define the properties of your game objects, whatever those might be. These variables may define how many players the game is designed for, how large the playing area is, how many resources are available, the properties of those resources, etc. In the *Connect Four* example from Chapter 8 on page 217, the properties included two players, a 7×6 game grid, 21 red units, and 21 black units. Indirectly, these variables also determine important aspects of how your game will work when it's set in action.

For example, in *Connect Four*, when you changed the grid size from 7×6 to 8×6, you had to increase the number of units from 21 of each color to 24 of each color—if you didn't, your players may have run out of units before the game was over. This is because we need enough units to fill every cell on the grid: $8 \times 6 = 48$, $48 \div 2 = 24$. Hence, the change in one game variable necessitated a change in another.

Changing the grid size changed some other aspects of *Connect Four*, which you undoubtedly discovered during your playtest as well: (1) the playing time was increased and (2) the game became less exciting. The reason for the first discovery is somewhat obvious—with more area to fill, players had more options to explore, and less contention for the space.

The second discovery is an interesting and perhaps unexpected one. With eight columns, rather than seven, the game is less exciting. Why is this? In the game with seven columns, the center column is flanked by three columns on each side. This means any horizontal or diagonal row of four units must include a unit in the center column. This places great importance on that center column. The battle for control of it draws the players into conflict with each other quickly and makes the overall experience more exciting.

Thus, the original size of the grid is more successful than the 8×6 grid. We can only learn what scope will be most effective for a system through repeated testing with alterations in the game variables.

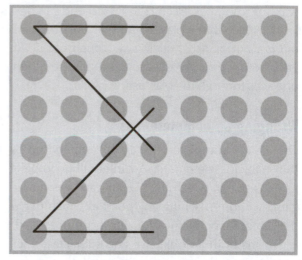

9.5 Connect Four—center column is flanked by three columns on either side

Digital games operate under the same principles. In *Super Mario Bros.*, you start with three lives. If you started with one life, the game would be too hard. If you started with ten lives, the game would be too easy. Changing lives changes how the game plays. Playtesters act differently when they have ten lives versus one, so the experience and balance of the game shifts.

Many variables in videogames are hidden in the computer code. This makes them more difficult for us to analyze, but we can conceptualize them. We've already looked at several examples of game variables: the unit properties in the *WarCraft II* editor (Figure 7.12 on page 171) as well as the map size for the *WarCraft III* editor (Figure 7.11 on page 170). Although it is not as easy to visualize, the number of resources available at any given time in the world of *EverQuest*, as well as the running speed and jumping height of a game character like Mario are also variables that can be adjusted to control the experience of the game.

Can you imagine playing Mario if he moved like a slug? It would be boring. Likewise can you imagine if Mario moved really, really fast? It might be frustrating because he'd be too hard to control. Game designers at Nintendo tweaked the numbers for these variables up and down to arrive at a comfortable speed that would appeal to the majority of players.

The purpose of manipulating variables all comes back to your basic goals for the game—the experience you are trying to create. You can only effectively judge the viability of your system variables if you have a clear picture of that experience.

Exercise 9.5: Game Variables

List out the game variables in your original game prototype. Make a change in one variable and observe how it affects other variables. This is an opportunity to test how your system plays under different conditions. Can you make easy, medium, and hard levels simply by tweaking the variables?

Balancing the dynamics

When we talk about balancing the dynamics, we mean the forces at work when your game is in action. As we discussed in Chapter 5, when systems are set in motion, sometimes there are unexpected results. Sometimes, a combination of rules creates an imbalance. Sometimes it's a combination of objects, or even a "super" object that unbalances play. Other times it may be a combination of actions that provide an optimal strategy for player who know the trick. Whatever it is, these types of imbalances can ruin gameplay. You'll need to identify them and either fix the rules that create the problem, change the values of the objects, or create new rules that mitigate the optimal strategies.

Reinforcing relationships

As we saw in Chapter 5 on page 129, a reinforcing relationship occurs when a change in one part of a system causes a change in the same direction to another part of the system. For instance, if a player earns a point, they would be rewarded with an extra turn, thereby strengthening their advantage. This starts a cycle that rewards the stronger player over and over until the game concludes, probably prematurely, with that player the winner.

This type of problem might be solved by changing the reinforcing relationship you've set up into one that balances the power more fairly—for example, when a player earns a point, the turn is passed to the other player, thereby balancing the effect of the point advantage.

Basically, you want to keep the strong player from accumulating too much power from a single success. Instead, they might receive a small, temporary bonus, but nothing that throws the game out of balance. In many cases, designers make the winner pay a price for taking a strategically important position. This tends to balance out the gains, ratchet up the tension, and provide the loser with a chance to come back.

Other techniques include adding an element of randomness, which can come into play and alter the balance of power. This can take the form of external events, like shifting alliances, natural disasters, and unfortunate circumstances. You may also want to enable the weaker players to group together to battle the dominant one, or have a third party intervene.

The goal is to keep the scales balanced without stagnating the game. After all, this is a competition and someone has to be able to win eventually. Naturally, in the last stages of a game, the scales will tip, and when this happens, let the scales tip dramatically. There's nothing as satisfying as a sweeping victory. This makes the winner feel good and provides for a swift, merciful defeat for the loser. You never want to drag out the ending. Think of your game as a movie. Once you've passed the climax, wrap it up fast.

A game that deals creatively with this type of problem is the strategic multiplayer shooter, *Battlefield 1942*. In assault matches, one team starts with a single spawning point and the other team controls every other spawning point and area of the map. The attacking team must fight to take ground. An example of a map that works like this is "Omaha Beach" which simulates the D-Day invasion. The Allies start on board a ship and must take spawning points on land from the Germans. *Battlefield 1942* incorporates a "tickets" system. Each side begins with a certain number of tickets that are reduced whenever a player is killed in action and subsequently re-spawns. When the number hits zero, the game is over. However, fulfilling certain victory conditions will cause the opposing team's tickets to slowly deplete, until they manage to reverse the situation by reclaiming a required control point. This gives teams a chance to come back from the brink of disaster, or at least, it gives players the resolve to stay in a losing game and manage a minor, rather than a total, defeat based on the percentage of tickets by which they lost.

Exercise 9.6: Reinforcing Relationships

Analyze your original game prototype for reinforcing relationships. Is it common for the player who gets an early lead to win the game? If so, you may have a reinforcing relationship that is creating an imbalance in the system. Identify the issue and change the relationship to balance the play.

Dominant objects

A good rule of thumb is to keep similar game objects within a game proportional in terms of strength. For instance, in a fighting game, no single unit should be significantly more powerful than the others. "Super units," as they're sometimes called, ruin the gameplay by becoming so valuable that none of the other units matter. One of the best ways to keep every element in proportion but still provide a range of choices is to think in terms of strengths and weaknesses. Every unit can be balanced by giving it a special advantage and a corresponding drawback.

Think of the classic "rock, paper, scissors" game. This game works because each element has a clearly defined power and failing. In this game, two players simultaneously choose one of three items: rock, paper, or scissors. Each item wins, loses, or ties depending on what is played by the opponent. Rock beats scissors, scissors beats paper, and paper beats rock. When illustrated in a payoff matrix, it looks like Figure 9.6.

On the matrix, 0 equals a tie, +1 equals a win, and –1 equals a loss. It shows that the three options balance each other out. This concept, sometimes called "rotational symmetry," is often used to balance digital games as well. For example, as Ernest Adams points out in his article "A Symmetry Lesson" on Gamasutra.com, *The Ancient Art of War* by Brøderbund was designed so that knights had an advantage over barbarians, barbarians had an advantage over archers, and archers had an advantage over knights.[1]

Many games use this technique in one form or another. In fighting games, each unit or character has his killer moves and Achilles' heel. In racing

	Rock	Paper	Scissors
Rock	0	+1	–1
Paper	–1	0	+1
Scissors	+1	–1	0

9.6   "Rock, paper, scissors" payoff matrix: rotational symmetry

---

1.   Ernest Adams, "A Symmetry Lesson," *Gamasutra.com*.

games, some cars are good at going up hills but handle poorly on corners. In economic simulations, some products are more durable but cost more, while others have a limited shelf life but higher profit margins. Assigning strengths and weakness is one of the fundamental aspects of game design and should be kept in mind whenever balancing gameplay.

Let's take *WarCraft II*, in which players can play a human or an orc civilization. The two sides are symmetrical in many respects but have minor differences. Both civilizations have the same types of units and buildings, which yield the same types of abilities. For instance, the humans have a "peasant" unit that has the exact same hit points, cost, build time, and abilities as the orc's "peon" unit. The name and the artwork associated with human peasants and orc peons are different, but from a formal perspective, they are identical.

An example of a difference is the orcs' "bloodlust" ability versus the humans' reciprocal "healing" ability. Taken only at face value, bloodlust is more powerful than healing. It enables orcs to deal triple damage in battle. A gang of bloodlusted orcs can easily slay a same-sized gang of humans in direct combat. In order to balance out this discrepancy, the designers at Blizzard gave the humans other abilities and strengths. However, the player must choose an appropriate strategy in order to benefit from them. Healing is not very useful in direct combat with orcs, but it can be effective when utilized as part of a "hit and run" strategy. To do this, the humans must attack the orcs, then retreat quickly, heal their units and attack again. This works particularly well as a strategy for gryphons, because they can fly away.

Humans also have slightly more powerful magic spells than the orcs. However, they also require both skill and strategy to employ. The human mage unit can make other units invisible

9.7   WarCraft II—Bloodlusted orcs attack a human stronghold

so they can sneak into an orc camp for a surprise attack. Or the mage can cast a polymorph spell that will change an orc unit into a harmless sheep. Both of these spells are expensive in terms of mana and require the player to execute complex maneuvers, but the payoff is there. Overall, the orcs are more powerful in direct ground combat, but humans can compete through crafty choices and acquired skills. The point is that there are discrepancies between orc and human units, but overall, the game does a good job of balancing the strengths and the weaknesses, which is no easy task.

Dominant strategies

Sometimes players can discover one or two strategies in a game that effectively dominate all others. This has the effect of narrowing the number of overall choices in the game, because no one will choose the weaker strategies once the dominant ones are known.

For instance, if one way of attacking is far superior, the players will gravitate towards this method. Even a minor imbalance in this regard can have a significant effect upon a game's playability. When balancing a game, make sure there is ample choice in all areas, and that as the game progresses, nothing limits the players' options. When players focus on only a limited set of options in pursuit of a win, games often become dull.

Can you imagine trying to play a game in which your opponent has already calculated the dominant strategy and simply executed it? The game would be frustrating for you and boring for them. If you both knew the dominant strategy, it would be a rote entry of choices on each of your parts, resulting in an experience that you could have predicted from the outset. Tic-tac-toe is a game in which there is a dominant way of playing and thus it isn't an exciting game.

What makes games interesting and challenging is the fact that their systems do not offer a dominant strategy—at least, not at first glance, or even upon repeated play. As a designer, you should always be on the lookout for dominant strategies. When you see one, find a way to get rid of it or obscure it so that players don't simply latch onto that method at the expense of everything else.

One word of caution: a dominant strategy is not the same as a favorite strategy. If hardcore players discover a way of playing your game that they like to employ over and over, but it is not always effective, this is not a dominant strategy. If the game is balanced properly then other players may have ample choice of opposing strategies to counter with.

Exercise 9.7: Dominant Strategy

In your original game, can you identify a dominant strategy that limits player choice? If you can't find one, list out some strategies that do work. What are the opposing strategies that players may utilize?

Balancing positions

In balancing the starting positions for your game, the goal is to make the system fair so that all players have an equal opportunity to win. This does not always mean giving each player the exact same resources and set-up. Although many games are symmetrical in this way, just as many others are not. As we saw in our discussion of player interaction patterns in Chapter 3 on page 44, there are various and interesting ways to design the competition in your game—a symmetrical competition is only one.

Additionally, the challenge of balancing multiplayer games is different from that of single-player games. This is because single-player games often involve a computer "player," or AI that competes against the human player. To understand how this affects balancing, let's look at two basic models for multiplayer games: symmetrical and asymmetrical.

Symmetrical games

If you give each player the exact same starting conditions and access to the same resources and information, then your system will be symmetrical. In chess, black has the same sixteen units as white, opponents start in a mirror-image configuration of each other on the board, and opponents have the same amount of space on the board to maneuver. *Connect Four, Battleship, Othello,* checkers, Go, and backgammon are likewise symmetrical systems.

In turn-based games like the ones just mentioned, there is one asymmetrical aspect that must be dealt with. It is the issue of who moves first. This issue could throw off the fairness of the game if not balanced correctly. In his article on symmetry mentioned previously, game designer Ernest Adams points out that you can reduce the effects of one player going first by establishing a system where the first move provides little strategic advantage.[2] Chess is set up so that only the pawn or the knight can move at the opening. These are two of the weakest pieces in the game. Additionally, four rows separate the opponents at the opening, which means neither side can threaten the other with the first move.

Another option is to balance the system so that a game takes many moves to resolve. This renders the first move of little strategic significance. Chess is a fairly long game; so going first has little effect over the course of a whole game. Contrast chess with a very short game such as tic-tac-toe. In tic-tac-toe, moving first is an enormous advantage. So much so that it enables a rational player to always win or tie.

Adams also points out that you could incorporate chance elements to reduce the effect of one player going first. Symmetrical boardgames like *Monopoly* and backgammon require players to throw dice to move. The dice are chance elements. Since the first player could have a bad roll and the second player could have a good roll, the first mover advantage is mitigated.

Asymmetrical games

If you give opponents different abilities, resources, rules, or objectives, your game will invariably be asymmetrical. An asymmetrical game, however, must still be fair. As a designer, your goal is to tweak the variables so that the system balances out. If played properly, each opponent will have roughly the same chance of winning, regardless of the other factors.

This type of asymmetry is powerful in games because it can be used to model conflicts and competitions from the real world. Historical events, nature, sports, and other aspects of life are full of situations where opponents compete with differing positions, resources, strengths, and weaknesses. Imagine trying to recreate a WWII battle where the players had to begin with the same units on a symmetrical board. It wouldn't make sense. For this reason, the vast majority of digital games tend to be asymmetrical. Let's look at a few games and see how they deal with the issues of asymmetrical abilities and resources.

In the fighting game *Soul Calibur II* there are twelve different characters, each with its own set of ability statistics. A typical character has about a hundred fighting moves and a distinct fighting style. As in many fighters, a move can inflict a variable amount of damage—from none, all the way up to a kill—depending on the countermove played by the opponent. Each time one character attacks another, a damage payoff is determined for one or the other or both of the characters. Mastering the game requires an understanding of how and when to play fighting moves in different situations against different characters. In this example of asymmetry, designers at Namco balanced a system where opponents have the same objective and same basic movement resources but different abilities.

In the RTS game, *Command & Conquer: Generals*, players choose one of three different armies: America, China, or an underground terror organization called the Global Liberation Army. Players adopt a playing style that matches the strength of their chosen army. The Americans utilize high tech weaponry, the Chinese swarm opponents with sheer numbers, and the Global Liberation Army relies on cunning and sneakiness. The key to this game is that the armies have different resources that are balanced, so that, if played skillfully, any

---

2. Ibid.

9.8 Command & Conquer: Generals

one of them has ample choices to beat the other two.

Another game with asymmetrical resources is *NetRunner*. It's a collectible card game designed by *Magic: The Gathering* creator, Richard Garfield. In this game, one player plays a corporation using purple backed cards, and another player plays a runner (kind of like a cyber hacker), using green backed cards. The cards in the two decks are completely different. The corporation uses cards to build and protect data forts, with the ultimate goal to complete corporate agendas. The runner uses his cards to hack corporate security. He tries to steal agendas before the corporation can complete them. The competing sides in this asymmetrical game utilize completely different resources and abilities, but they share the same overall objective: to score seven agenda points.

Exercise 9.8: Symmetrical versus Asymmetrical Games

Is your original game prototype symmetrical or asymmetrical? Describe how and why.

Asymmetrical objectives

Another type of asymmetry involves offering each player different objectives. This can add variety and intrigue to a game. You can offer asymmetrical victory conditions when opponents are otherwise equal, or you can combine asymmetrical objectives with asymmetrical starting positions for a real balancing challenge. In this case, your motive might be to add variety or evoke a real-life situation. Following are several models for offering asymmetrical objectives. Notice that in each case the differing objectives are still balanced against each other to keep the game fair.

Designer Perspective: Graeme Bayless

Title

Supervising Producer, Electronic Arts, Tiburon

Project list (five to eight top projects)

Wow, tough list. I've been doing this for sixteen years, and have been involved in shipping over 60 titles. I could go just by raw sales figures, but that's not necessarily the ones I'm proudest of (though I'm certainly proud of them as well). I guess I'll just mix the two. Here are some titles, in no particular order:

- *NFL Street* (releasing early 2004, one of the most exciting titles I've ever worked on)
- *Madden NFL 2001, 2002,* and *2003* (certainly the most successful titles I've helped lead)
- *MissionForce: CyberStorm* (not a huge success, but a fun game that emphasized some design concepts I wanted to explore)
- *Battles of Napoleon* (still one of the best reviewed war games ever, 1988 release)
- *Kid Chameleon* (old Genesis "jump and bonk" game—when we designed it, it was the most massive game of its type ever, with 100+ levels)

How did you get into the game industry?

Well, I got in a long time ago (1987) when the industry was still trying to find its identity. I had always been a gamer (I've played games as my primary form of recreation since I was eight, and submitted my first paper-game design when I was fourteen) and thus I spent my weekends at the local game store, playing various paper-games or miniatures games. One day, I noticed a posting on the bulletin board of the store I frequented. The posting was an advertisement for a part-time weekend playtester. I figured, "Hey, I can do that," especially since the company was Strategic Simulations Inc., a company that made computer war games which I played heavily. I applied, and got an interview with their manager of testing (who was also their manager of customer service). As the interview went on, she became more and more impressed with my game knowledge, so she asked me if I'd like to interview for their customer support position. I agreed, and came back for another interview. The second interview round included a programmer who was temporarily helping customer support until they could hire someone. This programmer was impressed with my design sensibilities, and suggested I return for a third interview for a "game developer" position (effectively an associate producer). I agreed, and the next thing I knew I was at lunch with the company president (Joel Billings) and vice president (Chuck Kroegel). The interview went well, and I was hired. I spent the next 30 months shipping about 30 SKUs, operating as the testing department, writing manuals, and participating in design on numerous war game and RPG titles.

What are your five favorite games and why?

It's very difficult to pick just five, but I'll take a stab at it.

- *M.U.L.E.:* This was a superb title published by Electronic Arts in 1983. It was simple, yet one of the most elegant game designs ever. The fun factor was undeniable, and it had replay value because the game was randomly generated every time you played. The most memorable part of this game is the trading interface, a truly brilliant game design. Players needed resources of varying types, and would have to bid on them through an interface where players literally scrambled for resources—with the seller able to dance higher and higher on price as folks raced to buy. Brilliant and fun.

- *Advanced Strategic Confrontation:* This was the rough translation from the Japanese name. The game was a Sega Genesis title released around 1990 that became the inspiration for the entire series of *Panzer General* games that kept Strategic Simulations going for years. This game was incredibly original, with a simple war game style that made war games accessible for the rest of us. All units had "10 hit points," and could heal by sitting on friendly cities. Infantry captured cities, and tanks were for killing other units. They had artillery and air units, allowing the full "rock, paper, scissors" strategy matrix. Though it wasn't released in the U.S., it was extremely successful in Japan, and still resides in my collection.

- *Star Control II:* The only sequel on my top list. It took all of the arcade fun of the first game and combined it with a single-player RPG story that was both fun and, at times, hilarious. The replay value was mostly in the arcade mode, but the RPG side was deep enough that it was worth playing more than once to see what you might have missed. The only action RPG of its type, *Star Control II* has never been successfully imitated since. Note that the sequel, *Star Control III*, did not live up to its predecessors and effectively terminated the franchise.

- *EverQuest:* I'd be remiss to leave this off my list, given how much of my life it has sucked out of me. The first true 3D MUD, this game still endures as the top massively multiplayer game of its genre. Filled with bugs, even after four years of constant development, *EverQuest* is still undeniably addictive (more so than alcohol or tobacco some might argue) and plain old fun. It is the perfect operating example of how powerful the concept of "toy factor" is in a game—the base concept being the more toys players have to play with and sort through, the better. Of particular note regarding *EverQuest* is the incredible change the game has undergone, literally evolving to mimic the desires of the player base. *EverQuest* is perhaps the best example of a "living game" we've ever seen.

- *Fallout:* The original post-apocalyptic RPG, this masterwork helped maintain the vitality of the single-player RPG. *Fallout* had a deep storyline, yet didn't overwhelm the player with so many options that they got lost. It was long, but not so long players couldn't finish it in a reasonable timeframe (unlike the sequel). Add in a nice mixture of dark humor, and you have a game that is still top of the heap for single-player RPGs. *Fallout* spawned two sequels, and neither has lived up to the original, unfortunately.

What games have inspired you the most as a designer and why?

That's a difficult one—I'm inspired by literally every game I play. Though not every game is fun, nearly every game has some small spark that one can take away and apply to a good design. However, there have been a few that I could say were truly inspiring.

- *Diablo:* The simplicity of the game combined with the idea of there always being more and better toys to get made this game amazingly addictive. The random nature of the design made replayability limitless, and caused the game's addictive nature to be only more powerful as there was always a bigger, better toy you could get. This game significantly influenced the way I have approached design elements on subsequent titles—even for non-RPGs. Most notably, it made me aware of the value of world/item generation systems in extending the replayability of a game.

- *Doom:* The original modern FPS, *Doom* showed us all that a game needed smooth and fun gameplay far more than it needed elaborate back story or beautiful graphics. *Doom* was actually pretty ugly, graphics-wise, but the gameplay was so fun and the game so cohesive that it set in motion an entire new genre for modern gaming. *Doom* likewise showed me the import of maintaining the illusion. The game is seamless and stays totally within itself, never breaking the illusion with clunky interface, bad audio effects, or buggy gameplay.

- *Eastern Front:* The original hardcore war game for videogame systems (Atari 400/800), this game was Chris Crawford's first major work and still is regarded as a landmark title. With clever and robust AI, *Eastern Front* is what inspired me directly to seek out videogames as a possible career path.

- *Star Fleet Battles:* This is the gargantuan boardgame that expands, and is inspired by, the original *Star Trek* TV series. *Star Fleet Battles* (*SFB*) was the first game I helped work on professionally, and it taught me several important lessons about game design—not the least of which is that players know just as much as designers, and they are a very valuable resource. I spent several years working with the *SFB* design team (for no pay) helping design and write for them. That helped springboard me to my career, and inspired me directly to seek out design as a path.

What are you most proud of in your career?

Honestly, I think I'm proudest of the fact that I've never shipped an unsuccessful title. Every title I've been responsible for has made money and met or exceeded sales expectations. Though I've been blessed to work with some amazingly talented programmers, artists, designers, writers, and marketers—without my contributions these products may well not have been as successful as they were. My strongest suit is as a leader, using my design skills and sensibilities in combination with my ability to help guide others to successfully lead design and programming teams to deliver their absolute best.

What words of advice would you give to an aspiring designer today?

I would urge any prospective designer to become a complete package. It is not adequate to merely learn how to generate good designs; a skilled designer must also know how to communicate those ideas to others both in written and verbal form. A good designer must also be able to communicate concepts through visual tools, allowing the viewer to see what is in the designer's head. Likewise, interpersonal skills are also key, as a designer must sometimes negotiate for resources and/or for the ability to take a product in new directions when that designer isn't also the company CEO.

I will note that the theme of this book—and how it approaches game design—very much mirrors my own beliefs. I strongly support the idea of paper design prior to electronic implementation. Playtest your ideas thoroughly long before a coder codes. Use prototyping whenever possible to avoid inefficiencies that may end up costing you features later when time and money limit the scope of your project.

Ticking clock

Many electronic games allow maps to be set up where a weak defender must fend off a strong attacker. The defender's objective is to hold out for a set amount of time. The attacker's objective is to kill all defenders before time runs out. The second mission in *StarCraft* works this way. In it you must build a small human base and hold out for 30 minutes before being overrun by a horde of attacking Zerg.

The ticking clock is a staple in mission-based games including *Homeworld*, *WarCraft*, and *Command & Conquer*. The model is also used in turn-based military boardgames such as *Panzer General*. Here the ticking clock victory condition is measured in a set number of turns versus a set amount of time. The weaker defender must hold out for 30 turns.

The multiplayer mode in the RTS game *Age of Empires* lets players choose to start the ticking clock as a victory condition on their own. They start it if they choose to build an expensive building called a "wonder of the world." When one player builds a wonder, all opponents see the ticking clock start on their screen. The player must now defend his wonder from being destroyed by all other players. If he can hold out until time runs out, then he wins the game. In this case the ticking clock is a victory condition chosen strategically by a player. It is balanced into the game to enable richer methods of play.

Protection

This is a variant on the ticking clock, and it can be equally dramatic. In this model one side tries to protect something (such as a princess, magic orb, secret document, etc.) and the other side tries to capture it. If the defenders protect or sneak the thing to safety, they win. If the attackers capture the thing, they win. Many games include missions that work like this. One example is the beach invasion map in the WWII-based game, *Return to Castle Wolfenstein*. On this map, the Allies' objective is to storm a beach held by the Axis. Then they must penetrate a seawall, infiltrate the base, and steal several top-secret documents. The Axis objective is to protect these things and keep the Allies from completing their goals.

Combination

It's also possible to combine ticking clock and protection devices. Take, for example, multiplayer assault maps in the FPS game *Unreal Tournament*. These maps have a ticking clock (usually four to seven minutes long), as well as objectives that

9.9   **NetRunner—corporation cards versus runner cards**

need to be protected. The attackers' goal is to reach the headquarters, steal the code, or blow up the bridge. They try to do this as quickly as possible, while the defenders protect the objectives for as long as possible, or until the ticking clock runs out. When the goal has been met, the time to beat is displayed. The two teams then switch roles. They play the same map, but the team who was just attacking is now defending. The new attackers try to beat the time set by their opponents in the previous round. This type of game can be extremely exciting because of its clear objectives and dramatic use of time.

Exercise 9.9: Asymmetrical Objectives

Take the original game prototype you've developed and create a variant with asymmetrical objectives. If your game is a single-player game, add a choice of objectives. Describe what happens to the gameplay when you test the game with these changes.

Individual objectives

In the classic boardgame *Illuminati*, the designers use asymmetrical objectives in a novel way. It's a game of politics, diplomacy, and sabotage in which opponents vie for control of societal groups such as the Mafia, the C.I.A., the "Boy Sprouts," Trekkies, and convenience stores. Each player can play for a shared objective—to control twelve groups—or go for their own individual objective. For instance, the individual objective for the *Illuminati* group is to destroy any eight groups. The individual objective for another is to control five "weird" groups. Players must watch to ensure that no one gets the shared objective while also battling and negotiating to ensure that other players cannot achieve their individual objectives. The differing objectives

9.10   Illuminati Deluxe

create an environment of shaky alliances and mutual distrust. The game is balanced so that, to win, players must cooperate with one another in some instances, and betray one another in others. The winner almost always succeeds by meeting her individual objective as opposed to meeting the shared objective.

The previous models are only a few ways to think about asymmetrical objectives in games. Like many concepts in game design, there are other ways to go about it—some of which can be found in existing games and some of which have yet to be invented.

Complete asymmetry

Scotland Yard is a popular boardgame in which just about everything is asymmetrical. In this exciting boardgame, one player takes on a group of opposing players who work as a team. This player is the fugitive, Mr. X, and the other players are a team of Scotland Yard detectives trying to track him down. To make this contest fair, the designers at Ravensburger balanced the system so that Mr. X has the ability to hide. He also has unlimited subway, bus, and taxi tickets (i.e., resources) from which to choose. Mr. X moves around London invisibly but must surface every four or five turns according to a turn schedule. The detectives use information about where Mr. X was last sighted and work in coordination to try to surround him and cut off potential lines of escape. The detectives have a set number of movement tickets. If one of them runs out of a type of ticket, he can't use that mode of transportation anymore. Mr. X's objective is to evade capture for 24 turns. The detectives' objective is simply to catch Mr. X at any time. Essentially, the following are balanced against one another: Mr. X with unlimited resources and the ability to hide, versus four or more detectives with limited resources and the ability to work in coordination. The game variables are tuned so that over the course of a whole game each side has an equal chance of winning.

In the symmetrical and asymmetrical multiplayer models we've just looked at, the most important balance to work out is between the various players. Because most models of multiplayer interaction employ other players as the basis of the game conflict, the question of balance often comes down to a question of how resources and powers are distributed to each party at the start of the game.

In single-player games, however, conflict is usually provided by the game system—either in the form of obstacles, puzzles, or AI opponents, which we discuss on page 251. As with the multiplayer models, single-player games can also employ symmetrical or asymmetrical forms of play.

Balancing for skill

Balancing for skill involves matching the level of challenge provided by the game system to the skill level of the user. The challenge with this is that every user has a different skill level.

For some games, it's practical to simply offer multiple skill levels. For instance, the original *Civilization* offers five skill levels: chieftain, warlord, prince, king, and emperor. Each of these levels is progressively more challenging to play. The difference between the skill levels in this system is simply a different balance of numbers in the system variables (see Figure 9.11).

When you play *Civilization* at the easy level, chieftain, you start with cash reserves of 50, and when you play at the emperor level, you start with cash reserves of 0. At chieftain, the computer opponents attack at .25 strength, whereas at emperor their strength is multiplied by 1.25. Figure 9.11 on the next page shows a chart of the system variables for each *Civilization* skill level.

Exercise 9.10: Skill Levels

Does your original game have skill levels? If so describe how they work and the method you used to balance them. If not, why not? Can you add skill levels and how would they affect the gameplay?

What if it is not practical to offer multiple skill levels for your game? Perhaps your design is not as dependent on starting variables as the *Civilization* example. In this case, your best bet is to balance the system variables against the median skill level of your target players.

Balancing for the median skill level

Balancing for the median skill level requires extensive playtesting with players from your target audience across the range of ability levels—from novice to hardcore gamers.

A good way to find the proper ability levels is to first set the high water mark of difficulty by testing with hardcore gamers.[3] Next, set the low water

---

3. Tim Ryan, "Beginning Level Design Part 2: Rules to Design by and Parting Advice," Gamasutra.com.

Feature	Chieftan	Warlord	Prince	King	Emperor
Endgame Year	2100 AD	2080 AD	2060 AD	2040 AD	2020 AD
Starting Cash	50	0	0	0	0
Content Citizens Number of Citizens per city born content.	6	5	4	3	2
CP Rows of Food Number of Rows in Computer Player's food storage box.	16	14	12	10	8
CP Resource Cost Multiplier Computer Players have cost to build units and improvements multiplied by this amount.	1.6	1.4	1.2	1.0	.8
CP Lightbulb Increment per Advance Each time an advance is discovered, the cost of the next advances by this amount.	14	13	12	11	10
Human Player Lightbulb Increment per Advance Each time an advance is discovered, the cost of the next advances by this amount.	6	8	10	12	14
Barbarian Unit Attack Strength Multiplier Barbarian's attack strengths are multiplied by this number.	.25	.50	.75	1.00	1.25
Parley Coin Demand Multiplier Peace payment demands are multiplied by this number.	.25	.50	.75	1.00	1.25
Civilization Score Multiplier Used to convert final score to percent for High Score ranking.	.02%	.04%	.06%	.08%	.10%

9.11   Civilization difficulty levels

mark by testing with novices and progressively adjusting the difficulty level downwards.

Once you have these boundaries established, you can balance the system variables to be in the median between these two marks. In games that are structured in progressive levels of play, which is most single-player videogames, you can incrementally increase the difficulty level for the player as you move from level to level in the game. Of course, each level will have to be balanced individually.

Balancing dynamically

In some types of games it's possible to program the system to adjust to the ability level of the players as they play. Take *Tetris*, for example. In this famous game, different-shaped blocks fall down-

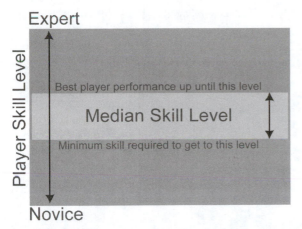

Expert

Player Skill Level

Best player performance up until this level

Median Skill Level

Minimum skill required to get to this level

Novice

9.12 **Balancing for the median skill level**

ward from the top of the screen. The player rotates the blocks and moves them left or right as they fall in order to attempt to fit them together at the bottom. If the player fits pieces together to fill a row completely across, that row disappears and points are scored. When the game starts, the blocks fall slowly, so it's fairly easy for the player to fit them together at the bottom. But as the score increases, so does the speed at which the blocks fall. The system is balanced so that the difficulty increases automatically as the player's ability increases. In this case, difficulty is directly related to the variable of speed.

Single-player racing games such as *Gran Turismo 3*, *Project Gotham Racing*, and *Mario Kart 64* have a self-balancing mechanism. In these games, when a race starts, the computer opponents (i.e., the other cars) accelerate up to their maximum speed. This speed is slightly slower than the maximum speed achievable by a human player if he drives perfectly. The computer opponents remain at max speed as long as the human is close or leading the race—meaning the pack will be tight. When the human crashes his car, the rules for the computer opponents change. They slow down to a reduced speed so that the human can catch up.

Once the human player closes in on the computer opponents, they accelerate back to their maximum speed. The human players may be unaware that this is going on. The ideal is for the human players to feel that they are successful because of their own abilities, but at the same time, keep the game balanced so that novice players aren't shut out from the possibility of winning.

Balancing computer-controlled characters

A problem with designing computer characters is that they must seem to be human and make mistakes. Otherwise a computer-controlled racecar could whiz through a track at maximum speed without crashing; a computer-controlled rifleman could hit an opponent between the eyes with every shot. This would clearly be no fun for a human player. Designers solve this problem by designing a character to act within a range of possibilities. Here's how the flying saucers work in *Asteroids* as explained by the programmer, Ed Logg: "Sluggo [the big saucer] fires at random. Mr. Bill [the little saucer] aims. Mr. Bill knows where you are, and he knows what direction you're mov-

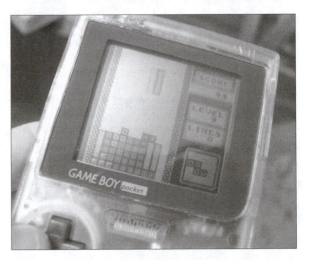

9.13 **Tetris for Game Boy**

9.14 MotoGP and Road Rash
MotoGP © 1998 2000 Namco Ltd., All Rights Reserved. Courtesy of Namco Holding Corp.

ing in. He takes this information and picks a window bounded a few degrees on each side of you, and then shoots randomly inside of that. For this reason, you should never move straight at him. It makes you bigger relative to him. [Also] the higher your score the more accurate Mr. Bill becomes. When your score reaches 35,000, he narrows down his firing window and increases his chances of hitting you."[4]

In this example the saucer aims randomly within a few degrees of the player. This provides a variable that can be tuned to balance the game. If the number of degrees is increased then the sau-

cer is more likely to miss and the game is easier. If the number is decreased then the saucer is less likely to miss and the game is harder. The result is a balanced, challenging, but not impossible, computer opponent.

Programmers have created many clever ways of coding their computer-controlled characters. In fact, there are many books just about programming game AI. What's important for you as a designer is not how the characters are coded but that they can be tuned to provide a balanced and satisfying experience.

TECHNIQUES FOR BALANCING YOUR GAME

As you work through these aspects of balancing your game, you may be tempted to dive right in and change everything at once. The playtesters say they want more of "X" and less of "Y," they want to change procedure "A" and make a new rule "B." Before you know it, you have a real mess on your hands—your balancing process is out of control.

On the following pages are some techniques for keeping a calm head and making changes that truly improve your game.

Obviously, these apply at all stages of revision, but right about now is probably when you need them most. If you master these techniques, you will be able to take a game that works marginally

---

4. Own, "Invasion of the Asteroids."

well and fine tune it without making changes that lose your previous work.

Think modular

Most games aren't comprised of a single system, but a set of interrelated subsystems. A good way to simplify a game is to think in terms of modularity. Breaking your game up into discrete functional units allows you to see how the mechanics of each unit interrelate. If you think of a game like *WarCraft*, it has a combat subsystem, a magic subsystem, and a resource management subsystem. Each of these subsystems is a part of the greater game system. The more interconnected the various pieces, the harder it can be to make alterations because one change can throw off the balance of seemingly unrelated parts of the game.

The key to dealing with this problem is to isolate the subsystems and abstract them from one another. This type of functional independence is a critical part of large-scale game design. It's similar to object-oriented programming, where each object is clearly defined with a set of input and output parameters, so you when make a change somewhere else in the code you can track how it affects every other object. The same holds true for game design. If you keep your subsystems modular, when you tweak one element of your game, you know exactly what impact it will have on the other parts.

Purity of purpose

Along the same lines, try to design your game with a purity of purpose, meaning every component of your game has a single, clearly defined mission. Nothing is fuzzy, nothing exists for no reason, and nothing has more than one function. To accom-

plish this, break your game mechanics down into building blocks using a flow chart and define precisely what the purpose is of each block. This will help you to avoid creating a morass of rules and subsystems, which will grow increasingly convoluted as your game evolves. When this principle is adhered to, tweaking an element only changes one aspect of the gameplay, rather than several aspects, and the job of balancing your game will become methodical, rather than a haphazard guessing game.

Exercise 9.11: Purity of Purpose

Think about your original game prototype. Are there any extraneous elements—elements that have no purpose? Remove the least important element of your game and test the system without it. Does the game still function? Is it complete? Balanced? Remove another element. Continue stripping elements from your game and re-testing until you reach a point where your game no longer functions. Now again answer the question—are there any extraneous elements in your design?

One change at a time

Train yourself to make only one change at a time. Limiting yourself to just a single change often feels cumbersome because after each change, you have to test the entire system again and gauge the affects. However, if you change two or more variables at once, it becomes difficult to tell what affect each of those changes has on the overall system.

Spreadsheets

When balancing a game, nothing is more valuable than a good set of spreadsheets. As you design, you should track of all your data in a spreadsheet program like Excel. This will make the job of balancing your game much smoother.

If possible, your spreadsheets should mirror your game's structure. This will allow you to better communicate with your programmers. We strongly recommend sitting down with your technical team and laying out the spreadsheets together. Each subsystem within your game, whether it is combat, economic, or social, should have its own set of interconnecting tables. Apply the same principles of purity of purpose and modularity to your spreadsheets. Look at the spreadsheets as both your starting point—a great tool for laying out the game design—and your ending point—a tool used in refining and perfecting the gameplay.

Exercise 9.12: Spreadsheets

Take the game variables you listed in Exercise 9.5 and put them into a spreadsheet program like Excel. Make sure that the structure of the spreadsheet parallels that of the game system. Now you can use this tool in balancing your game.

CONCLUSION

Congratulations, by now your original game should be functional, internally complete and balanced. That means you are ready to begin refining your game, the final stage of the design process. But before we move on, one word about how you "know" your game is really balanced. We have filled you up with rules, tools, and methods, but when it comes to balancing a game, much of what you do will depend on your gut.

We mentioned this briefly early on. There is no way to teach you how to use your instincts in a book. Intuition is both a gift and a learned skill. The more you design, the finer your gut instincts will become. You'll know when a game is out of balance without a tester raising an eyebrow, and you'll be able to spot a loophole or dead-end immediately and implement the proper fix. Our goal in this chapter has been to give you a head start, and hopefully, when you combine this with your natural sense for game design, you'll be able to master the process quickly and see your game reach its full potential.

A Conversation with Rob Pardo

Rob Pardo is the Director of Game Design at Blizzard Entertainment in Irvine, CA. Blizzard makes some of the most respected and best-selling games in the industry including the WarCraft, Diablo, and Star-Craft series, among other games. Below Rob shares some details about the game balancing process he's developed with the team at Blizzard and also some of his views on being a professional game designer today.

On His Role at Blizzard

Game Design Workshop: Can you tell us about your role at Blizzard?

Rob Pardo: My title here is "Director of Game Design." I am the lead designer on games with our Team One development team, which is the group that did *WarCraft III*. Now we're working on an all-new secret game. Along with that I also pinch-hit on some of our other projects. For instance right now I'm assisting on *World of WarCraft* and *StarCraft: Ghost*.

GDW: One of the things we're interested in for this conversation is the process that goes into balancing a Blizzard game. Is a lot of what you do involved with game balancing?

RP: Well, I do that, but game design includes lots of things. For example on *World of WarCraft* right now I'm doing a fair amount of balancing and I'm helping out on the different classes for the game. So I'm trying to hone the skills for each class and put in the right balance numbers and work with the designers to make each class stand on its own.

On *WarCraft III*, as lead designer, I had broader responsibilities. It went to unit design; it involved working with Chris Metzen, our storywriter; it went to working with our level designers and determining the gimmicks and play features for each level and how they all fit together. It went to, you know, "how does the mini-map work?" spec'ing out the design documentation and giving it to programmers and artists where appropriate. It's basically all areas of the game that the player sees and interacts with.

Game balance is just one small, but important, part of what we do.

On the Process of Designing WarCraft III

GDW: Can you tell us about the process of designing WarCraft III?

RP: Sure. *WarCraft III* was interesting because it went in a couple of different directions. First of all, it was our first 3D game. So that presented some challenges. Also we wanted to do something different from *StarCraft*. We had just rolled off *StarCraft* and we felt that we'd nailed that form of gameplay—you know: macromanagement, action, RTS—whatever you want to call it. When we rolled onto *War III* we thought about the fantasy elements of the game and we wanted to take a new tack. So we decided to add a lot of RPG elements.

With 3D we decided to bring the camera down quite a bit and try out some things. The problem was with the camera pulled all the way down it became a pseudo-third–person experience. It was disorienting when you went around the map and it was difficult to select units in battle because your camera frustum was pointed in one direction so you didn't have a good view of the battlefield. It was a challenge because we still wanted a fun strategy game. Eventually we pulled the camera into a more traditional isometric view and that's when we really started making progress.

GDW: *That's great. What were the first things that you built for WarCraft III? Did you make a prototype?*

RP: Yes. Since it was our first 3D game it was really important to get the 3D engine up and running. And we had to get the art path ready so the artists could start testing art files with the new engine. Something we did for the first time on *War III* (and now we've been doing on all our projects) is we committed to making a build that ran every day. So, when we finally got the engine running we could immediately put art in it. From that point forward every day the team could come in and boot up the newest version of *WarCraft III* and it would work. Obviously not every day did the new build work—there would be bugs sometimes—but that was a commitment and it really helped us see where we were. On *StarCraft* it wasn't until right before beta that we started getting stable builds on a regular basis. So that was a big step for us. So we spent a lot of time prototyping the look of the world and what we wanted to do with the camera and what elements we wanted to go with.

GDW: *It sounds like figuring out where to put the camera was a part of the prototyping process.*

RP: Yes, for sure. Something we believe in strongly here at Blizzard is iterative design. You know, prototype can mean a lot of different things. We didn't really have a prototype that was made of blocks that we could test gameplay on like are often made at other companies. In this case we did more of a technology and art prototype rather than a gameplay prototype. So once we had the art and the actual 3D engine in there that's when we actually started messing with the camera; messing with the units; trying to figure out exactly what kind of game we wanted to make for *War III*.

On Developing the WarCraft III Races and Units

GDW: Can you tell us about the process for developing the races and units?

RP: We knew we didn't want to do *StarCraft*. We knew we wanted to add role-playing elements to the game and we knew we were going the 3D route. Some people on the team wanted a lot of units. Some people wanted to do a few units. That was a contentious topic in the early days.

One of the first things we came up was the concept of "heroes." In the old days we called them "legends." We actually referred to the game itself as "Legends." We didn't want to refer to it as *WarCraft III* because we felt we might end up making just a sequel to *WarCraft II*. So we referred to the game entirely as "Legends" with the thought that we might release it with that name.

Early on we designed a lot of legend/hero units. We designed many heroes including the Archmage, and Warlord. We built them in prototype form and started playing around with different spell kits and tried to figure out how they should work. We asked: "Should they work like *Diablo* heroes?" We tried to figure out what a hero was; what that meant in a strategy game versus a pure role-playing game. We experimented with stuff like "Well maybe you can only have units when they are following their heroes."

Those concepts formed a lot of the core gameplay early on. But it was a baseless sort of gameplay at that point. Then on the art side we were trying to figure out what we could do with 3D: what was possible, what wasn't. At the same time we were also experimenting with different network models and technological concepts that were going to dictate certain game play elements. So there was inter-linking between gameplay, art, and technology.

GDW: So the idea of hero units was an early concept that you built on. What about the four races in the game? How were they developed?

RP: Early on we had lots of discussions about races. We talked about different cool abilities and play styles they might have and quickly decided that Undead should be a race. It was interesting: in the early days we sketched ideas for nine totally different races. That was never really reasonable though—it was more like nine core concepts from which we could draw the coolest ideas. Nine races went down to six and then that later went down to five. We really thought we were going to release with five for a long time. So in the beginning we had lots of races and units designed on paper.

We started implementing Humans and Orcs first and then the Undead. The fourth race, the Night Elves, was next. They were a compromise between early race concepts we had for Dark Elves and High Elves. We wanted to get elves in the game in a way that hadn't been done before. The fifth race was Demons. We didn't cut them until probably right before alpha. The problem was: we wanted Demons to be the ultimate bad guys in the story line but we also wanted to be able to balance them into multiplayer play. We were having a lot of kit issues with how they should work and how they should interact with the other races. Ultimately we decided to keep them as bad guys in the story but drop them as a full-blown playable race.

GDW: Interesting. You said you had "kit" issues?

RP: Yes. When we look at a race we think: "What's this race about? Is it a sneaky race? Is it a micro-management race? Is it a heavy ground race? Is this race supposed to be really versatile? Is it magic?" When we looked at Demons we said, you know: "Really powerful. Good at Fire Magic. Lots of incredibly tough units." It seemed weird to come up with say a Peon or Footman unit for the Demons. They just didn't lend themselves to that. We decided we'd make Demons less cool by filling out all the roles that races need to fight each other on Battle.net.

On "Concentrating the Coolness"

GDW: Game balancing always seems to involve tuning system variables numbers up and down. Sounds like with WarCraft III you guys thought really big early in the project and then tuned some numbers downward as you went along.

RP: That's right. Early on we brainstorm tons of cool ideas. We have lots of sharp, creative people here so we come up with way more ideas than we could ever put in a game. Then the designer's job over the next year or two years (however long the dev cycle is before the beta) is to hone all those ideas. Some we have to get rid of, some we have to modify, and some become a corner-stone of the gameplay.

One of our mantras—we have lots of mantras around here—is "concentrating the coolness." With *War III*, for example, we could've blown out to 20 or 30 units per race if we wanted to but we wanted each unit to be meaningful. And we wanted to make sure each race had a unique feel. So even though every race has flying units and worker units they still all do things in different ways.

We wanted that idea to carry through to heroes too. Each race should have a little set of heroes that made it unique. When we started detailing out the heroes' spell kits we originally had four heroes per race. But the spell kits were muddled with overlap so we cut down to three heroes. That decision created a big controversy with our fan base because it lead to us cutting the Human's Ranger hero. The Ranger ended up on the cutting room floor and there were petitions and all kinds of stuff like that online. So it was quite a contentious cut.

GDW: *Wow. Talk about a rabid fan base. They were petitioning the loss of a character before they'd even played the game.*

RP: Yeah. Crazy isn't it (laughs)? We like to have a big fan community going even before we go beta. It's great to have fans that are really into it. The downside is you can't just blackbox a game and bring it to market. Lots of people are watching.

The day the Ranger was cut was big. People knew about her because we'd shown her on our web site. When she disappeared one day it caused quite a ruckus. Again it was that kit argument I was talking about. Humans already had a ranged magic hero with the Archmage and they had a cool tank-like hero with the Mountain King and they had the Paladin hero as well. I was a little heartbroken to see the Ranger go too. But I looked at the Night Elves and they had lots of archer units. Even looks-wise the Ranger looked like an Elven archer. We had to differentiate the races so she got cut. It was still really tough.

On the Effect of Balancing Heroes in WarCraft III

GDW: *That's interesting. The heroes have really affected the game play dramatically. One thing I notice in WarCraft III is that I end up playing with smallish parties of units and not the huge armies that I play with in StarCraft.*

RP: That's right. When we started developing *War III* a lot people wanted another game with *Star-Craft*-style gameplay. You know macro-management and that. But we wanted to branch out a bit. We wanted a game with units that were tougher and more meaningful. In *StarCraft* you can just throw lots of units into the battlefield and not care whether they live or die. You can get an army of 50 to 100 units going and it's no big deal.

For *War III* we wanted to get rid of what we call the "fodder" unit. We want you to care about every grunt and every footman. Part of the reasoning for that was the increased focus on heroes. We wanted a hero to be a dominant force in the battlefield because, well, that's what you think of as a hero. So if we know there's going to be 50 units on the battlefield then we'd have to make the hero ridiculously powerful for him to have a meaningful impact. If you have a battlefield with say 10 or 20 units then the hero could be more realistically balanced. For *War III* to work the way we'd envisioned the hero had to be balanced proportionally to the number of units that could be in a battle. Right? If the game was designed for 50 unit battles and then a hero gets into a fight with say only 10 units around then he'd just mop them up. In *War III* it's normal to see people running around with maybe 12 to 15 units. That's like an army in *War III*. 24 units is almost the max.

Trying to enforce that mechanic though was a challenge. It was like "How do we do that?" We had the mechanic in the game, "food", which kind of limited the number of units you have. We also had gold and lumber intakes for resources. But what was happening early on was that with just those mechanics in place players would build up to the cap in the game and just play there. Then if they lost their units they'd have this big gold and lumber surplus that they'd just spend to rebuild their army and max out again. It just didn't play very fun.

GDW: *This sounds like how you came up with the system for "upkeep."*

RP: Right, that's where upkeep came from. Upkeep was a concept that was pretty controversial and we tried a bunch of different ideas beforehand. But that's what we eventually settled on.

The concept of upkeep is: the bigger your army is the more it saps your gold income. If you build up a big army then upkeep siphons off your excess gold income so you can't get these huge gold surpluses. The idea was to encourage you to fight more when you have fewer units.

Originally we tried to encourage small armies just through tweaking unit numbers and costs. But as we watched people play around here—with giant armies—we realized we'd have to go back to the drawing board. We sat down and said "We want a game that plays with fewer units where heroes feel important. How do we make that happen?"

Everyone brainstormed up a bunch of ideas and we talked through each one. We just kept picking at it and testing ideas for a couple of weeks until we had a system that worked. Actually lots of people hated upkeep at first so getting it implemented was controversial. Part of the problem was we originally called it "Tax." I guess it gave people, I don't know, like April 15 flashbacks or something (laughs). They couldn't accept the game dynamic just because of the name. Once we came up with the name "upkeep" though the last people opposing it said "Okay, let's try it."

Upkeep was a game mechanic that got developed to encourage the hero-based game play we had set as a goal. As a game designer figuring stuff like that out is series of big conversations to little ones to mini-battles to see which elements work, which don't, which need to be changed, and which need to be yanked. You know, it's an ongoing process every day.

On Iterative Design and Balancing a Game after it Has Been Released

GDW: *So it sounds like iterative design is a key component for how this gets done.*

RP: Absolutely. We hone system variables over and over as we play and test a game. We're not afraid to pull a unit, pull a major design system, or put in a new one all the way up until beta. In fact with *War III*, we actually introduced a couple of spells post beta. We had designed them ahead of time knowing we might need them. I figured we should go into beta with about 90% of the racial units and spells in the game. I'd learned from previous betas that, no matter how great we think the units play, once pro gamer-types—who're going to play much more than we'll ever play and at a much higher skill level—get a hold of it that we're going to have to change things.

So I went ahead and left some holes in each race so we could fill them with different things if we needed to. And sure enough we did that.

GDW: *Interesting, so you were still balancing things after beta. The game's been out for a year now. Is it still being balanced?*

RP: Yep. We did patches to the *StarCraft* balance for two years after we released it. It definitely evolves. You could probably do a sociology class on the evolution of a game community.

There are two things that I see that happen once a game's been released. First of all imbalances are discovered that just were never discovered before. This is because a million people playing a game is a lot different than a thousand people playing from the beta. Somebody out there will come up with a creative play technique that no one else has thought of. Then once that he starts using it on Battle.net every person he plays sees the imbalance and it spreads across the community like a virus. That forces our hand into doing something.

The other thing that happens is just evolution of gameplay. Sometimes I see things that I want to patch slowly. Like, suddenly one race might be winning a larger proportion of games on Battle.net for a couple of weeks and it seems like a dominant strategy has emerged. And we could certainly go in and "fix" it. But usually what's happening is just an evolution of how people play. You see spikes and valleys. What happens is—let's say the Humans become dominant for a couple of weeks. Well, you've got to give the community a chance to see the new strategy and develop a counter strategy. You see the same thing happen in professional sports sometimes. You know in NFL football the 3–4 defense dominated for a few years. It wasn't an imbalance that they had to go to the rules committee and say, "We need to outlaw the 3–4 defense because it's too bad-ass." The offensive coordinators just had to scheme and develop their playbooks to attack it. I see the same thing sometimes in our game community. It can be really challenging sometimes post-release to decide what to patch and what not to patch. So it's a process.

GDW: *Tell me a about the software tools you use to do this. You can track what players are doing pretty closely via Battle.net?*

RP: Yes. For *War III* we hired a web programmer to make a system that could track all kinds of data. We found someone who had created a really amazing fan site that tracked statistics from our other games and gave him a job. Like we'll say, "We want to see how races play against each other on a map by map basis." And he can make a report of that. We do that pretty often. So they'll be times when my game balance designer wants to make an adjustment to the Orcs or something. And I'll say, "Okay, that sounds reasonable but let's look at the stats too." And we'll look at the stats and we'll go "Hey, actually Orcs aren't really having that problem so let's hold off for a while."

GDW: So you use the data to determine whether the imbalances are perceived or real.

RP: Yeah. We're not slaves to it though. It's just one of many tools we use. You have to have an intuitive sense of it also. Luckily the game balance guy on *War III* is a really good player.

We also we have a group of top-level players that send us feedback directly. Like if we see something like the Undead hammering the Humans in a peculiar way then we might gather replays from top-level players and look at exactly what they're doing.

GDW: Sounds like there's a symbiotic thing going on between the fan community and the development team. For example you hired the web programmer from the fan base.

RP: Yes, our webmaster had one of the top *WarCraft II* web sites back in the day. He got hired as a QA tester and then moved himself up on the web side. Even if you're the best programmer in the world we're not going to hire you unless you're a game enthusiast. If someone's a fan of our games and they have development skills too then that's perfect.

GDW: It must be a dream job for them.

RP: Yeah. They tend to be pretty happy employees (laughs).

On Playtesting at Blizzard

GDW: Okay, this is a good segue way to the next point: I'm curious about your process for playtesting early versions internally.

RP: Sure. Before we go beta we're—as a development team—playing on a fairly regular basis. We don't have structured play sessions like where we say "Friday is playtest day" or something because, like I said, we're all a bunch of gamers. Everyone here loves to play these games. So once the game gets playable everyone on the team is playing it. They'll be lunchtime sessions where all the artists play together. They work in a bullpen so they're really close. And the designers will be playing together and the programmers will be mixing and matching. One way we know when a game is fun is when we have to say to some people "Hey you're playing too much of the game. Start working some more." (laughs).

On Being a Game Designer

GDW: Tell us something you've learned about the craft of being a game designer.

RP: One thing I've learned from starting young to where I am now is: yes you need to have all the game design skills, and you need to know about different development disciplines so you can design smart. A designer needs to wear a lot of different hats. But the other side of it that I don't see talked about much is the skill of working with your team.

The game designer, at least here, is not the primary idea generation guy. He's the primary vision holder for the game. I struggled early on when I used to really fight for my ideas versus other people's ideas. What I learned was "Hey, I'm in a position where I can put in a lot of the game design elements and it's really important for me to be a conduit for everyone else's ideas." When I made that mental shift it was a pretty big day.

Now I look at my job and see that it's really important to listen to everyone else on the team and try to get their ideas in when they are good for the game. Sometimes a team member will have great idea but not know how to package it within the overall framework of the game. So that's where I come in. I might work with them and try to get it into the game in a way that works from a game system perspective. Once you do that then you're job becomes a lot easier. Everyone trusts you more. And it's just this domino process: you're not fighting your ideas versus their ideas; you're not explaining to them why their ideas suck. You're working with them and you're their tool for getting good ideas into the game. Then everything just flows better.

Warcraft III

Chapter 10
Fun and Accessibility

Remember when you first started testing your core idea, when you had just built out the foundations and structure of your game? All we were worried about at that point was making sure the idea was fun, i.e., was it a good idea for a game? Now that we've gone on and created a functional, complete, and balanced game, it's time to go back and really make sure the essence of what you thought was fun is still there. Of course, you've been paying attention to whether or not your game was fun throughout that process, we know that, but now is the time to make fun and accessibility your primary focus.

Before we can test for fun, we have to define what we mean by "fun." Unfortunately, "fun" is one of the most elusive concepts you'll ever try to pin down. As with many aspects of art and entertainment, fun is subjective, contextual, and an entirely up to personal taste. You may think washing dishes is fun (we don't), or you may think shooting bad guys is fun. Your favorite game may be entirely based in strategy, while a friend's requires physical skill and dexterity.

In order to have a useful guideline for our testing process, we can at least determine why we want our games to be fun. Games are voluntary activities; they require player participation—a high level of participation. Unlike movies or television, the "show" does not go on if players cease to play. So if your game has no emotional appeal, players are apt to stop playing, or never pick it up in the first place. So, fun appeals to the emotions. And all of the emotional and dramatic elements that drive a player to pick up your game, to try it out, and to continue to play it, are usually what players cite when asked about what makes a game "fun." So those elements are what we will look for when testing your games during this next stage.

IS YOUR GAME FUN?

How can you tell if your game is fun? By this time, you know the answer: ask the playtesters. But playtesters are not often able to articulate exactly where the fun is lacking, so you'll need some tools to help you identify the "fun factor" yourself.

When we discussed the dramatic elements of games, we talked about the fact these elements are what engage the player with the formal system, what get them and keep them emotionally involved in the game. Challenge, play and story can all provide emotional hooks that captivate players and invest them in the outcome so that they will keep playing.

Challenge

In Chapter 4 on page 81, we talked in detail about some of the element of challenge, including the state of "flow" that players can reach when the challenge the game offers is perfectly tuned to the participants' skill level. The following list of thoughts and questions addresses several of the most import aspects of challenge to consider when testing your game for fun. Ask yourself and your testers these questions to measure where the challenges in your game are working, and where they can be improved.

Reaching and exceeding goals

The desire to achieve goals is a fundamental part of being human. How can your games tap into this desire? Does you game have one goal at the end, or are there "sub-goals" along the way? Reaching sub-goals can charge your players up emotionally and get them ready for the long haul to the end of the game.

Are your goals too hard to reach? Too easy? Are they clearly defined? Or are they hidden from view? Ask your playtesters to talk out loud about their goals as they play the game; this will help give you a sense if they are engaged in the goals you've planned, or if they are moving off on tangents.

Competing against opponents

Humans are competitive by nature, and competition provides a natural challenge in a game, whether it's directly multiplayer or indirect in the form of rankings or other criteria. We like to see how we compare to others, whether it is in terms of skill, intelligence, strength, or just dumb luck.

Are you missing a chance to create competition in your game? Listen to your players talk to each other, if your test is face to face. Or, if your testers are in different places, make sure they have a way to communicate with each other. Trash-talking, ribbing, and the kind of chest-thumping that happens naturally during playtests may give you a great idea for what is driving the competition in your game.

Stretching personal limits

The goals we set for ourselves often carry a power that the goals which others set for us do not. We know our own limits better than any game designer can. When we set our own goals and surpass those personal limits, there is a sense of accomplishment beyond any in-game payoff system.

Some of the most popular games of all time allow players to set their own goals, challenge themselves so to speak. Of course, not all players enjoy this type of system—they find it too open-ended. Can your game incorporate this phenomenon? You need to know your potential audience and judge whether or not you should strive to offer this type of freedom.

Ask your playtesters to talk out loud about their personal goals in the game as they play—are they setting their own goals, would they like to be able to set goals for themselves? You'll be surprised to find out how often players create their own sub-goals within a system—especially if they know they can't win, but want to feel a sense of accomplishment anyway.

Exercising difficult skills

Learning a skill is hard, but the process has its rewards when you finally master it—even more so when you get to show it off. Presenting your players with the opportunity to learn difficult skills is a

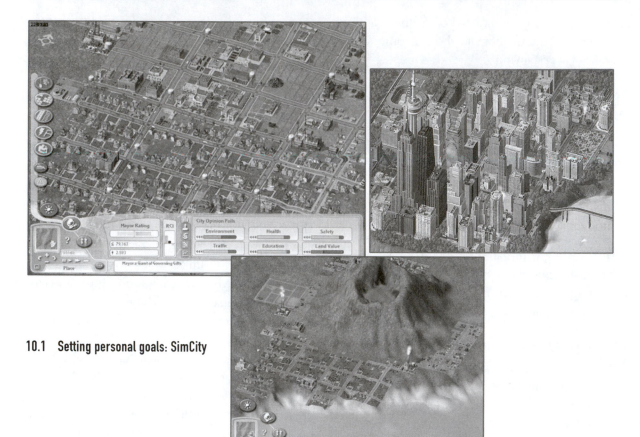

10.1   Setting personal goals: SimCity

challenge, but a hollow one unless you provide ample opportunity for them to master and display that skill. And remember, people don't master skills after five minutes of a tutorial. Learning a new skill often takes time and trials. Rewarding the player for sticking with it will make the process enjoyable.

Making interesting choices

Game designer Sid Meier once said, "Games are a series of interesting choices." These choices can range from where to place your blocks in *Tetris* to how many peons to produce in *WarCraft II*. If the choices have consequences, then they're interesting. If not, they are merely a distraction. Is your game providing choices with consequence? Or are your players simply micromanaging? Are players aware of the consequences as they make those choices? Creating dilemmas, where players must weigh their choices carefully, is a powerful way to challenge your players.

Ask your playtesters to explain what they think the consequences of their choices will be as they play. What factors are weighing into their decisions? Are they correct? Or are they making arbitrary decisions? Arbitrary decisions can kill a player's sense of responsibility for an action. How can you improve the choices, macro and micro, that players are making in your game?

10.2 Making interesting choices: Civilization III

Play

Along with presenting challenges, games are an arena for play. As we discussed in Chapter 4, there are as many different types of play as there are players. What forms of play does your game employ? Are you making the most of that opportunity? Can you offer other areas of play, for different types of players, or do you want to deepen the play for a single type of player? Think about your game in terms of these natural types of play.

Living out fantasies

The desire for pleasure, romance, freedom, adventure, etc. are all powerful forces. Most people dream of being something they're not—an astronaut, snowboarder, general, rap star, etc. Let your players live their fantasies, even for a moment, and you'll have a captive audience. Role-playing games have their basis in this kind of fantasy play, but all games can gain from tapping into people's dreams for themselves. What aspirations does your game put within reach for its players? What fantasies does it fulfill?

This concept can be extended to imaginative play scenarios that are not necessarily "fantasies"

that a player wants to fulfill but rather scenarios that are intriguing to explore even though they go against a player's personal ethics. *Grand Theft Auto III*, for example, fits this description. Players may be compelled by the game even though they don't fantasize about robbing and killing.

Social interaction

People love interacting with one another. Games offer an amazing forum for social interaction, one which is equally about the game and the relationships people bring to the game. Adding this element to your game creates an unpredictable, emergent layer that is often enough for many players to stay hooked on a game long after its release. Some online games with strong social interaction have such loyal players that they have found ways to keep playing even after the official servers and support for the game have ended. Is your game making the most of any potential social interaction? Have you provided time and opportunity for people to get to know one another?

Exploration and discovery

Nothing is so thrilling as venturing into uncharted waters and seeing what you find. If your games make this promise to the player and then fulfills it, you'll create an enchanting experience. Most great adventure, RPG, and FPS games include an element of exploration. The act of discovering something is magical. But creating that sense of trepidation when turning a new corner, anticipation when you think you may have found something, fear of getting lost, and exhilaration of discovery is a difficult task. Are you telegraphing the "right" direction to the secret treasure? You want to help your players, but you don't want the process of exploration to become rote. Try going on adventure yourself—go for a hike on a new trail. Or a walk through a part of town you don't

10.3   Living out fantasies: Star Wars Galaxies

know. Think about the emotions you feel as you make your way—how can you re-create these feelings in your players?

Collection

Some remnant of our hunter-gatherer ancestors must drive this need, but there is nothing like letting players create collections for engaging them in a game. Whether it's a collection that only lasts a single hand of a card game, or a collection of *Magic: The Gathering* trading cards that spans years of play and hundreds, perhaps thousands of dollars of spending, collection is fun for many different types of players.

Stimulation

A game which stimulates the senses and imagination is a treat. Whether it's amazing graphics, music and sound design, or a controller with force feedback, it adds to the fun factor. Never discount eye candy as a major source of entertainment value. Of course, eye candy won't hold up if the stimulation isn't integrated into the gameplay as a whole. Freedom of movement in a 3D space is one of the most successful examples of a sensory experience that has created an entire genre of gameplay.

Self-expression and performance

As human beings, we have a desire to express ourselves, whether it's in the form of artwork, poetry, or building a character in a game world. Giving people the chance to show off who they are and be creative makes for an engaging experience and will add a new dimension to your game.

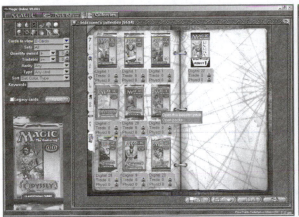 

10.4 Magic: The Gathering Online: card collection screens

Illustrations used with permission of Wizards of the Coast, Inc.

Construction/destruction

Construction is a great tool for making players feel invested in a game. Whether it's constructing cities, armies, space colonies, or characters, building things is fun. If they build it, it's theirs and they won't let go. On the other hand, as much as we humans enjoy construction, we like tearing things down even more. Any ten-year-old boy will tell you how much fun it is to destroy—even precious toys. Let players do this and they'll love your game.

10.5 Destruction: The Hulk

Hulk: TM & © 2003 Marvel Characters, Inc. Used with Permission.
Image courtesy of Universal Interactive, Inc. and is used under license.

Story

A game doesn't have to have a story to be fun, but story can a powerful mechanism for engaging people's emotions. Since we humans could communicate, we've had the urge to tell and listen to tales about one another. By incorporating dramatic elements into your game, you can tap into the human psyche and delight and enthrall your users.

But, as we discussed in Chapter 4, drama in a game has a different source than that in a movie. In movies, it comes from stories where characters struggle to overcome obstacles, both internal and external, while the viewers sit in their seats sweating each turn. In games, drama comes from the player's struggle to overcome those obstacles herself. This puts the human brain in two entirely different states, and presents a very different problem to the game designer.

- How have you used the aspects of drama in your game?
- Do you have a compelling, imaginative premise?
- Unique characters?
- A storyline that drives the gameplay or emerges from it?
- Ask your players if they are playing your game because of its story or in spite of it.
- What is it about the story, the characters, etc. that is working or not working for them?

This list encompasses some of the elements that can, if executed well, improve your game's fun factor. Don't try to cram them all into your game at this late stage, though. The most important thing about fun is its delicate nature. No matter what the marketing slogans say, it's almost impossible to make a game that's "fun for everyone." Pick your audience, find out what they think is fun, and set your goals accordingly.

Let's take a look at a couple very popular games and see how they have incorporated these elements.

EverQuest

- Overarching goal of growing your character, combined with the smaller goals inherent in quests, adventures, and tasks
- Competition among players to become the most powerful, popular, and/or famous
- Fantasy of being in a world of magic and chivalry
- Social interaction with other players online
- Exploration of online world
- Stimulation of 3D graphics and sound
- Self-expression through role-playing
- Stories and legends of the world and characters
- Construction of character, building wealth, accumulating possessions, etc., and destruction of monsters and other players (if you choose)
- Collection of inventory items

Monopoly

- Goal of owning all the property on the board
- Competition among players
- Fantasy of being a real estate tycoon
- Social interaction with other players, trading properties, etc.
- Construction/destruction of houses, hotels, and monopolies
- Collection of property sets

Tetris

- Goal of clearing all your lines of blocks
- Stimulation of catchy music, colorful blocks

- Construction/destruction of rows of blocks
- Collection of all the blocks in a single row

As you can see, *EverQuest* includes ten elements of challenge and play, while *Monopoly* has just six, and *Tetris* has only four. Clearly there's no relationship between the number of elements and the amount of fun a player can derive from the game. *Tetris* may be one of the most universally addictive games ever, and it's quite simple. Making games fun is not about including every possible type of challenge or play, but in finding the right combination. If you can do that, you'll delight your players and keep them interested in your game.

Exercise 10.1: Challenge and Play

As we did with *EverQuest*, *Monopoly*, and *Tetris*, analyze the opportunities for challenge and play that are present in your original game prototype. List the types of challenges players must face, and the ways that they can express themselves through fantasy or play. Describe how these elements interact to make your game fun—or identify how they might be improved.

IMPROVING PLAYER CHOICES

Because it is simply one of the most powerful aspects of fun in gameplay, we need to look more closely at choice as an aspect of fun. What makes a choice interesting versus uninteresting? How can you design choices that are more interesting than not?

One of the most important aspects of choice is consequence. For a game to engage a player's mind, each choice must alter the course of the game. This means the decision has to have both an upside and a downside; the upside being that it advances the player one step closer to victory; and the downside being that it hurts the player's chances of winning. This concept seems simple, but you'd be surprised at how many games force the players to make choices that have no impact upon whether they win or lose.

Remember, the player wants one thing more than anything else, and that is to win. Anything you do that is outside this scope runs the risk of alienating your audience. So when Sid Meier says "interesting choices," what he means is that the game must present a stream of critical decisions

that either directly or indirectly impacts the player's ability to win. No matter what you've been told in the past, drama and suspense in games seldom come from the storyline. It comes from the act of making decisions that have weight, and the more weight each decision carries, the more dramatic the game becomes.

As a designer, this is what you must strive for. But how do you make the choices in your game have significance? To start with, let's step back and analyze your game. What type of decisions are your players making? Are those decisions truly meaningful, or are they tangential to the main objective? To help analyze this, we use a tool we call the decision scale, shown in Figure 10.6.

If there are decisions in your game that seem "inconsequential" or "minor," you have a problem. Go back and rethink the choices you are giving your players. Is there a way to make those choices matter? And if there isn't, those choices need to be eliminated because they aren't adding anything to the game and are probably hurting the experience. Now take a look at the decisions higher up

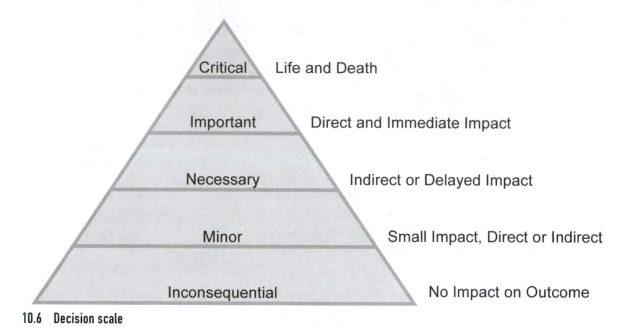

Critical — Life and Death

Important — Direct and Immediate Impact

Necessary — Indirect or Delayed Impact

Minor — Small Impact, Direct or Indirect

Inconsequential — No Impact on Outcome

10.6   Decision scale

on the diagram. Is there a way to make some of your players' decisions fall into these categories? These are the types of decisions your players want to make.

But, unless your game is an arcade-style shooter, the decisions you ask your players to make shouldn't all be life and death. Nonstop action can get boring too—it's in the breather between waves of enemies that we can appreciate our accomplishments, anticipate the next wave, and steel ourselves for the battle ahead.

In order to create a truly engaging game, you want some peaks and valleys. Let the decisions rise and fall, and as the game progresses, ratchet up the tension by making the decisions gradually more important, until by the climax of the game, everything hangs in the balance. This structure mirrors the same dramatic arc that we looked at in Chapter 4 on page 101.

Types of decisions

It's easy to say that games should have interesting choices, but why is one choice more interesting than another? The answer lies in the type of decision you ask to the player to make. If the player has to choose between two weapons, and one weapon is only slightly superior to the other, even though the player may be faced with a life and death encounter, the decision itself does not reflect this. To make this decision interesting, each weapon must have a dramatically different impact on the player's chance of winning.

But if the decision itself is too easy, then it's not a decision at all. If it's obvious that the player should use the golden arrow to slay the dragon, there's no real choice. Why would the player risk using anything else? This decision, although it appears to be life and death, is meaningless. The player will invariably choose the golden arrow, unless he doesn't know about its powers, and in that case, it's an arbitrary choice, not a decision.

The key to making this decision interesting is for the player to know that the golden arrow is the right choice, but also to know that if he uses the golden arrow now, he won't be able to use it later when he has to fight the evil mage. To make this decision truly dramatic, the player must be put in a position where both paths have consequences. If the player doesn't use the arrow now, his faithful companion, who is not immune to dragon fire, may die during the battle. However, if the player uses the arrow, it will be much harder to destroy the evil mage later on. Suddenly the decision has become more complex, with consequences on both sides of the equation.

Decision types

- *Hollow decision:* no real consequences
- *Obvious decision:* no real decision
- *Uninformed decision:* an arbitrary choice
- *Informed decision:* where the player has ample information
- *Dramatic decision:* taps into a player's emotional state
- *Weighted decision:* a balanced decision with consequences on both sides
- *Immediate decision:* has an immediate impact
- *Long-term decision:* whose impact will be felt down the road

In the example of the golden arrow, the decision is a combination of the previous decision types. It's an informed decision because the player knows a lot about situation he is in, it's a dramatic decision because the player has an emotional attachment to his faithful companion, it's a weighted decision because there are consequences balanced on both sides, it's an immediate decision because it impacts the battle which is taking place with the Dragon, and it's a long-term

decision because it impacts the future battle with the evil mage. All these combine to make the decision of whether or not to use the golden arrow a critical choice in the game, and this makes the game interesting.

Exercise 11.2: Decision Types

Take your original game and categorize the types of decisions you ask your players to make. Are there any hollow, obvious, or uninformed decisions? If so, try to redesign these choices.

Not all decisions in a game need to be as complex as the one with the golden arrow. Simple decisions are fine, just so long as they're not hollow, obvious, or uninformed. As a rule, you want to remove all nondecisions from you game, and a player should never be forced to think about anything unless it has some impact, either direct or indirect, on whether they win or lose.

Dilemmas

Dilemmas are the situations where players must weigh the consequences of their choices carefully, and in many cases, where there is no optimal answer. No matter what the player chooses, something will be gained and something will be lost. Dilemmas are often paradoxical or recursive. A well-placed dilemma and trade off can resonate emotionally with a player when encountered during the struggle to win your game.

Game theorist John Von Neumann used dilemmas as a framework for studying how people make choices, and how conflicts are resolved in both game-based and real world dilemmas. Game designers can use the same methodology to study the choices in their own and other designer's games.

Chooser's Strategies:

	Choose Bigger Piece	Choose Smaller Piece
Cut as Evenly as Possible	**Chooser gets a *slightly* bigger piece.**	Chooser gets a *slightly* smaller piece.
Cut One Piece Bigger	Chooser gets a bigger piece.	Chooser gets a smaller piece.

Cutter's Strategies:

10.7 Cake-cutting dilemma payoff matrix

To understand dilemmas, von Neumann broke them down into very simple structures, called moves. Each move was diagrammed on a matrix, showing the potential outcomes of each strategy as they pertain to each player. To understand this concept more clearly, let's next look at a classic dilemma with a simple structure.

Cake-cutting dilemma

A mother wants to divide a piece of cake between her two children. In order to avoid arguments about how large a piece each child should get, she makes one child the "cutter" and one child the "chooser." The cutter gets to cut the cake, and the chooser gets to choose which piece. If we assume that each child wants the bigger piece (i.e., wants to "win" the game), we can diagram this conflict to show the potential strategies for each player, the dilemma they face, and the payoffs for each potential outcome.

As we can see, each child has two possible strategies. We know that it's impossible to cut the cake exactly in half; there will always be one crumb more or less on either side; but the cutter can choose to cut the cake as evenly as possible, or she can choose to cut one piece bigger than the other in an attempt to get the larger slice. Since we've determined that one piece will always be larger than the other, even if just by a crumb, the chooser also has two strategies. He can choose the smaller piece or the larger piece.

By looking at the payoff matrix created by combining these two possible strategies for each player, we can see that in this simple game, there is an optimal strategy for each player. Since we have said that each child will try to get the bigger piece, the chooser's optimal strategy is obvious—he will choose the larger piece. And, since the cutter is also trying to get the largest piece possible, she will try to cut the pieces as evenly as possible. The optimal strategies for each player meet in payoff #1: the chooser gets a slightly bigger piece.

The cake-cutting dilemma is an example of a zero-sum game. By this we mean that the total amount won at the end of the game is exactly equal to the amount lost. In this case, the chooser gains the crumb lost by the cutter. Because of the nature of zero-sum games, the interests of the players are diametrically opposed. What one player loses is gained by the other.

What von Neumann discovered in his study is that there is an optimal strategy for each player in games of this nature that will produce the best possible results in a given situation. He called this concept "minimax theory."

Minimax theory states that there is a rational way for players to make choices in a game, if we are talking about a two-player, zero-sum game. The optimal strategy for all players is to "maximize their minimum potential result." So, in the case of the cake-cutting example, while the cutter cannot "win" the game, her optimal strategy will still maximize the amount of cake she gets to eat.

Games that fall easily into optimal strategies may be interesting for mathematicians, but as game designers, they are often the kiss of death. If you present your players with a game as simple as the cake-cutting dilemma, they will always make the optimal choice and the game will play out the same way every time. How can we create dilemmas that are more complex, where the players must weigh the potential outcomes of each move in terms of risks and rewards?

A game that has a more complex payoff structure was created by two RAND scientists in the 1950s. Called the "prisoner's dilemma," it's a simple, baffling game that shows how games that are not zero-sum can create situations where the optimal strategy for each player can result in sub-optimal results for both.

The prisoner's dilemma

Two criminals commit a crime together and are caught by the police. For the purposes of our example, we'll call the two unlucky criminals Mario and Luigi. Mario and Luigi are held in separate cells with no means of communication. The DA offers each of them a deal and discloses that the same deal was made to his partner in crime. The deal works like this: if you rat on your partner, and he denies it, you can go free and the he gets five years. If neither of you rat on each other, the DA has enough circumstantial evidence to put you both away for one year. If you both rat, you will each get three years. Figure 10.8 shows the payoff matrix for each potential strategy.

Using the same process we used to determine the optimal strategy for the cake-cutting dilemma, we can see that the optimal strategy for Mario is to rat on Luigi. If he rats, he gets either three or zero years. If he doesn't rat, he gets one or five years. The optimal strategy for Luigi is also to rat on Mario for the same reasons. If both players choose the optimal strategy, however, they will both serve three years—more years total will be served in jail than in any other resolution.

The hierarchy of payoffs in the prisoner's dilemma is as follows:

- *Temptation for defection:* zero years
- *Reward for mutual cooperation:* one year each
- *Punishment for mutual defection:* three years each
- *Sucker's payoff for unreciprocated cooperation:* five years

The actual numbers in this hierarchy are not important. What is important is that they ascend in this order: Temptation > Reward > Punishment > Sucker. If this hierarchy exists, the optimal strategy for each player will always result in a payoff that is less than if they had acted cooperatively. Now, we

Designer Perspective: Brian Hersch

Brian Hersch has designed all types of games including CD-ROM games and television game shows. He is best known for his blockbuster boardgames.

Title

General Partner, Hersch and Company

Project list (five to eight top projects)

- *Taboo*
- *Outburst*
- *Oodles*
- *ScrutinEyes*
- *SongBurst*
- *Trivial Pursuit DVD Pop Culture*
- *Hilarium*
- *Out of Context*

How did you get into the game industry?

Trivial Pursuit unlocked my creative curiosity, and my business background led me to conduct a market research study of games in general, and the then-burgeoning adult game category. The interpretation of that research resulted in a recognition that a number of sociological imperatives were all coalescing at that time. A recession was impacting entertainment budgets. The baby boom was strapped with bills, had demonstrated a willingness to entertain at home, and had a predisposition to play boardgames. So the opportunity presented itself, and I jumped in. Happily, our interpretations were correct, and our creative efforts resonated with the public, and our games sold.

What are your five favorite games and why?

- *Taboo:* Because it is one of my babies, and really demonstrated how the simplest concept can be translated into fun.

are talking about a true dilemma—what will Mario and Luigi do?

Exercise 10.3: Dilemmas

Does your original game contain any dilemmas? If so, describe these choices and how they function?

In a recent presentation at the Game Developers Conference, designer Steve Bocska of Radical Entertainment applied the hierarchy of payoffs in the prisoner's dilemma to a hypothetical game design in order to show the usefulness of game theory concepts to designing compelling dilemmas.[1]

---

1. Steve Bocska, "Temptation and Consequences: Dilemmas in Video Games," Game Developers Conference 2003.

- *Carducci:* Though it never licensed this was the game that I am proudest of. It has so many creative and fun elements, and people seem to really enjoy it when we play (even though no company can figure out a marketing strategy for it).
- *Poker:* Because I enjoy taking money from my friends.
- *Trivial Pursuit:* Because it was perfectly suited for my brain-full of garbage, and it was the catalyst for my entry into this business.
- *Snood:* Because it remains the most addictive online game that I have found.

What games have inspired you the most as a designer and why?

I am not sure that my design instincts are inspired as much by games as by outside influences. I happen to design games. And obviously I have an understanding of play-patterns and compelling entertainments. But I think purely from a design standpoint I am often more stimulated and inspired by nongame products: art, photography, architecture, edgy commercial products and innovations. I think I fear being over-influenced by other game designers' works, and worry about the impact on my own desire for originality.

What are you most proud of in your career?

The good fortune to have successfully repeated the creative process of designing new games, and then having those games enjoy retail success. I could probably be satisfied just with the design/creation of new products, but the commercial success has proven to be the validation of my efforts.

What words of advice would you give to an aspiring designer today?

Gamble. Try and do new things. Be original in your thinking. Remember that you are attempting to put entertainment in a box. If you can engage people, make them laugh, spend a compelling hour, then you have succeeded. But it will always feel more satisfying if it is not derivative. Be original—the only thing you have to fear is rejection. And you're going to get plenty of that anyhow.

Bocska imagines an online game in which two players are building and customizing spacecraft with a budget of $10,000. The game requires bartering and trading of raw materials, but at a high transaction cost: $8,000 of "shipping and handling" in a typical game round. A technology can be purchased that allows materials to be "transported" with no transaction cost—but in order for it to work, both players must purchase it. The cost of the technology is $5000.

Bocska asks, "Under these conditions, what is a player likely to do? If both players purchase the transporter equipment, they will reduce their transaction costs for the game from the usual $8,000 to a one-time cost of $5,000 for the transporter—a savings of $3,000. If, on the other hand, neither player purchases a transporter, the transac-

Mario's Strategies:

	Rat on Luigi	Don't Rat
Rat on Mario	Mario = 3 years Luigi = 3 years	Mario = 5 years Luigi = 0 years
Don't Rat	Mario = 0 years Luigi = 5 years	Mario = 1 year Luigi = 1 year

Luigi's Strategies:

10.8   Prisoner's dilemma payoff matrix

tion costs throughout the game for each player will amount to the usual $8,000. What if only one player purchases the machine? With nobody else to connect the transporter to, their machine becomes effectively useless, resulting in them receiving the "sucker's payoff"—the cost of the equipment plus the added cost of continuing to barter using the traditional costly method ($5,000 + $8,000 = $13,000)." The payoff matrix in Figure 10.9 shows the results of the potential strategies.

Unlike the prisoner's dilemma, Bocska envisions a game in which the players can communicate—negotiating with each other when and if to purchase the technology. This complex payoff structure creates a dilemma for the players that can make for compelling strategic moments and potentially deceitful or cooperative decisions play after play.

This is exactly the type of situation you should strive to create in your games. If possible, give the players dilemmas as part of the core gameplay. Make sure to tie the dilemma into the overall objective of the game. If you can accomplish this, it will make the choices much more interesting.

Puzzles

Another format for structuring interesting choices in your games is by incorporating puzzles. Puzzles are solvable systems. They can contextualize the choices that players make by valuing them as moving towards or away from the solution. Suddenly, the act of rifling through a treasure chest takes on new meaning if you are searching for the key to open the door to maze, rather than just looting the castle.

Puzzles are also a key element in creating conflict in almost all single-player games. There's an

Player 1's Strategies:

Player 2's Strategies:		Buy a Transporter	Keep the Status Quo
	Buy a Transporter	Player 1 = $5,000 Player 2 = $5,000	Player 1 = $0 Player 2 = $13,000 (Player 2 goes Bankrupt)
	Keep the Status Quo	Player 1 = $13,000 Player 2 = $0 (Player 1 goes Bankrupt)	Player 1 = $8,000 Player 2 = $8,000

10.9 Transporter game payoff matrix

innate tension in solving a puzzle. If you tie this into a system of rewards for solving the puzzle and punishments for failure, the puzzle transforms into a dramatic element. For example, take *Myst*, the best-selling adventure game of all time. It's essentially comprised of puzzles. It incorporates story and exploration as well, but at its core, it's really a glorified collection of interlocking puzzles.

The popular genre of first-person shooters is also puzzle-based, especially in single-player mode. Take *Medal of Honor*. You have to plant bombs, unlock doors, find medical kits in a labyrinth of rooms, and figure out how to use weapons and explosives in just the right way. The game is one giant action puzzle. The same holds true for many other single-player games.

You'll notice that we keep using the qualification "single-player." This is because in multiplayer mode you don't need puzzles to provide conflict.

The conflict comes from the competition with other players, whether they are human or computer-controlled. But in single-player mode, especially when you are sent on a quest or mission, puzzles play an increasingly important role. That's why every game designer should also consider herself a puzzle designer. The better your puzzle design skills, the better your game will be.

One consideration when designing puzzles in your games is to make sure that the elements of the puzzle are woven into the fabric of the game. By this we mean that it advances the player towards his overall goal. If a puzzle doesn't enable progress, it's a mere distraction and should be redone or removed. A puzzle may also advance the storyline. You can use the puzzle to tell the player something about the unfolding plot.

If you can integrate your puzzles into the gameplay and the story, they won't feel at all like

DESIGNER PERSPECTIVE: BRUCE C. SHELLEY

Title: Senior Designer, Ensemble Studios

Project list (five to eight top projects)

I contributed to the design of these games:

- *Railroad Tycoon* (original edition)
- *Covert Action*
- *Civilization* (original edition)
- *Age of Empires*
- *Age of Empires II: The Age of Kings*

How did you get into the game industry?

I played games of one sort or another all of my life. I began testing board war games by mail for free and eventually landed a job with the company. I was developing boardgames in 1987 when my company asked me to move over to computer games, which I did. In 1988 I landed a job with MicroProse and got a chance to work with Sid Meier. In 1995 an old friend asked me to join Ensemble Studios and have been here since.

What are your five favorite games and why?

I generally dislike this question because tastes change and games that were very important at one time are no longer even available for current operating systems or platforms. Here are five that I particularly enjoyed.

- *Railroad Tycoon:* Working on this game was something I would have done for free if I could have made a living somehow; it was great to see Sid Meier figure out how to make a good game out of something as cool as railroading—not an easy task; the game had a fun economic model, cool trains running, multiple paths to victory, was endlessly replayable.
- *Civilization:* Great fun to work on; we knew we were making something very special. It had a great hidden map, 4X game, multiple paths to victory, endlessly replayable, levels of difficulty,

"puzzles," but rather like integral, interesting choices a player must make to progress in the game as a whole.

Rewards and punishments

The most direct consequences for player choices are rewards and punishments. Obviously, players enjoy being rewarded and dread punishments. Nothing is more natural. So when designing a game, a designer often emphasizes the rewards, while limiting the punishments. This makes sense; players aren't playing games to suffer the hardships of life. And in reality, you don't want to punish players so much that they stop playing your game. But often, the threat of punishment, if not the actual punishment itself, carries a dramatic great topic, deep and rich, and presented a very interesting stream of decisions for the player to make.

- *Age of Empires II: The Age of Kings:* An excellent RTS in a great period, fantastic graphics, tremendous value to customers, lots of different game experiences within the same box, endlessly replayable, and a deep and rich game experience.
- *Empire Deluxe:* A very old game but a classic that is an early and excellent example of many good design principles for strategy games: hidden maps, inverted pyramid of decision-making, a great first fifteen minutes, adjustable levels of difficulty, not beautiful but clean, great opportunities for strategy and tactics, simple but interesting economic system, and a great stream of interesting decisions, but the one negative for me is the end game, which can drag on.
- *Robin Hood: Legend of Sherwood:* I like puzzle and problem solving games that look beautiful and offer a lot of challenge, without being too tough or too easy. I liked the graphics and topic.

What games have inspired you the most as a designer and why?

The single greatest resource for any game developer is all the existing games that can be played and learned from. *Empire Deluxe* and *SimCity* were great inspirations for later games that I helped design. *Populous* offered a lot of ideas about god games and strategy games. At Ensemble Studios we were greatly influenced by *WarCraft I* and *II*, and *Command & Conquer.*

What are you most proud of in your career?

Being a member of the teams that developed *Railroad Tycoon, Civilization,* and the *Age of Empires* series. That's like playing for two different teams that won world championships. Although I did not have a lead role on any of those products, I contributed to them and had a lot of fun doing so.

What words of advice would you give to an aspiring designer today?

Play a lot of games and analyze them. Understand why some games succeed and why others do not. Understand what is actually happening within a player's mind when he or she is being entertained by a game. Think in terms of entertaining a large audience, not a small one. It is okay, even encouraged, to borrow from great games, but be different at the vision level (topic, look, and feel) and innovative at the gameplay level. Don't imitate great games—people have had that experience and probably won't pay to repeat it.

tension that can add layers of meaning to even the most trivial choices a player makes.

Think of a game that forces the player to be stealthy, like *Thief* or *Deus Ex.* The tension, when you are trying to accomplish a task without being caught is tremendous. Getting caught and attacked, and let's face it, killed, is not fun. But that moment when you oh, so quietly pick a lock and sneak past the security bots without incurring any harm is made much more effective by the threat that the anvil of punishment was hanging over your head all the time (see Figure 10.10).

Coming up with a balanced system of rewards and punishments is a way of making the choices in your games much more interesting for players. The type of rewards you offer can vary, but the

10.10 Being stealthy: Thief

best rewards are those that have utility or value in the game. When you develop your rewards system, use the following guidelines:

1. Rewards that are useful in obtaining victory carry greater weight

2. Rewards that have a romantic association, like magic weapons or gold, appear more valuable

3. Rewards that are tied into the storyline of the game have an added impact.

Make each reward count, and if it can both push the player closer to victory and advance the storyline, that's even better.

The timing and quantity of rewards is also critical. If you give a steady stream of small rewards, it can become meaningless. Players know the rewards are coming, no matter what they do and they stop caring.

Psychologist Nick Yee has studied the reward/punishment structure of an extremely addictive game system—*EverQuest*—and believes its addictive power lies in a behavior theory advanced by B.F. Skinner called "operant condi-

tioning." Operant conditioning claims that the frequency of performing a given behavior is directly linked to whether it is rewarded or punished. If a behavior is rewarded, it is more likely to be repeated. If it is punished, it becomes suppressed. It is usually explained by using the example of a "Skinner Box," a glass cage equipped with levers, food pellets, and drinking tubes. Rats are placed in the cage and rewarded with a food pellet for pressing the lever, using reinforcement to shape their behavior.

Yee writes, "There are several schedules of reinforcement that can be used in Operant Conditioning. The most basic is a fixed interval schedule, and the rat in the Skinner Box is rewarded every five minutes regardless of whether it presses the lever. Unsurprisingly, this method is not particularly effective. Another kind of reinforcement schedule is the fixed ratio schedule, and the rat is rewarded every time it presses the lever five times. This schedule is more effective than the fixed interval schedule. The most effective method is a random ratio schedule, and the rat is rewarded after it presses the lever a random number of times. Because the rat cannot predict precisely when it will be rewarded even though it knows it has to press the lever to get food, the rat presses the lever more consistently than in the other schedules. A random ratio is also the one that *EverQuest* uses." [2]

While this might seem surprising, if you relate it to your own actions in games and in the real world it begins to make more sense. Have you ever sat down to play "five minutes" at a slot machine and looked up to realize you'd been there, determinedly pulling that lever for several hours? In many ways, Las Vegas is simply a giant Skinner Box.

---

2. Nick Yee, "EQ: The Virtual Skinner Box," http://www.nickyee.com/hub/home.html.

We may all be just rats in a cage, but there is one type of reward that is very powerful and that can't be delivered like a pellet, and that is peer recognition. Humans crave acknowledgement for their achievements, and there's little that can motivate us more. Especially in multiplayer games, if there's a way for you to make the players, even the ones who aren't winning, feel recognized for their efforts when they do achieve a goal, then you will have a much stronger game.

Many games do this through the Internet, tracking scores or providing tournaments and ladders. There are more immediate ways to provide recognition, in the moment, as well. One is to track and broadcast the players' achievements during the game, highlighting and dramatizing each success for everyone to see. If it's an online strategy game where one team is pitted against another, make it clear when a player pulls off a brilliant maneuver. Let his comrades know exactly what happened and how it impacts the victory conditions. If it's an online RPG, allow the players to show off their conquests to the world, either in the form of legends, artifacts, or admirers who follow them about.

Exercise 10.4: Rewards

Analyze the rewards system in your original game prototype. Look at each reward and determine if it is useful, romantic, and/or tied to the storyline. How are rewards timed? Does the timing reinforce the player's desire to continue playing?

Anticipation

The Skinner Box example works well for game mechanics that are repetitive and apt to become rote. For larger, more complex choices, however, the more clearly you allow players to see, and

anticipate, the consequences of their actions, the more meaningful their choices will be.

In chess, and other games with open information structures, the entire state of the game is visible to both players for evaluation. There's nothing hidden. If players are experienced, they can calculate out moves dozens of turns in advance and see exactly what will and will not happen. The anticipation that players feel in a situation like this is heightened by the knowledge of when they will be able to capture a piece or get in a particular position.

Can games with closed or mixed information structures create anticipation? Definitely. Real-time strategy games often use limited visibility to offer the player a glimpse of the opposition, but only while her units are posted in enemy territory. Since the game state is always changing, the view quickly becomes outdated, and the player winds up making decisions based on only partially accurate information (see Figure 10.11).

In this example, players accept the lack of information as one of the conditions of the game and understand that their job is to maximize their position given the limited information they have available. In fact, the lack of visibility can increase a player's sense of tension. With the knowledge that the game state is in flux, players feel compelled to act swiftly to counter anticipated enemy moves. In many ways, the hiding of knowledge has added a new dramatic twist that is lacking in the completely open strategy games.

Surprise

Surprise is one of the most electrifying tools at a designer's disposal. People love to be surprised, especially when they feel they should have anticipated the event. Too many surprises will alienate players, however, so, how do you know when to use surprise and when to telegraph an event?

10.11 Warcraft III: fog of war turned off (left) and on (right)

A surprise outcome to a player's choice can reinvest them in the game—perhaps they thought they were going to find 20 gold pieces behind door number three, but it turns out to be a trusted friend ready to join their journey instead—a much greater reward.

Surprises may feel random to players, but in a good way. The trick is to find the right balance between the randomness of surprise and the importance of making player choices meaningful. Take the example of a real-time strategy game, where you might send a simple foot soldier up against an ogre because he's all you've got. The foot soldier has strength of one to five, while the ogre has strength of one to 20. Odds are that the ogre will win. But there's always that chance, no matter how small, that the foot soldier will prevail.

Randomness, and surprise, in this case adds a level of drama—the tension of not knowing exactly how a highly probable event will play out. Will this be a David and Goliath story or just another dead foot soldier? In most well-designed games, the element of choice remains dominant. If every choice a player makes results in random

effects, they will feel like their choices have no meaning. But keep surprise in mind; used judiciously, it can create a wealth of fun and excitement.

Exercise 10.5: Surprise

Are there any surprises in your game? Try taking one type of choice and adding an element of surprise to the outcome. How does this affect the gameplay?

Progress

Nothing is quite as satisfying as seeing the choices you make result in progress. It's part of human nature to derive joy from the act of advancing towards a goal. The small payoffs along the way are often sweeter than the final victory. The same is true in a game. Allowing players to feel they are moving forward is the best way to draw someone into a game and keep them engaged.

One approach for structuring progress is to design milestones for the players. These are small

10.12 Mission: Medal of Honor: Mission 2–4 "What Comes Around"

goals along the way to the grand goal of winning. Advertise these milestones to the players so that they know what they're striving for, and reward them after each accomplishment.

Many games do this well. In *Medal of Honor*, the milestones come in the form of missions. They give you a map and let you see where you're headed and what you have to achieve to get there. This helps the player feel like they're making progress throughout a long campaign. The same is true for games that use story to block out their single-player levels, preparing the player at each step and setting out clear and obtainable objectives, and then rewarding the player at the end of each sequence with graphics, praise, and another chapter of the narrative.

No matter what the game, whether it's an arcade shooter or a simulation, providing a path for the player to follow gives a sense of achieve-

ment. Be creative in finding new ways to represent progress for your players. Don't limit yourself to just one system. There's no reason you can't measure progress in several ways at once.

When you consider the pacing of progress that players can make in the game, you might also consider the typical amount of time a player spends with a game. Veteran game designer Rich Hilleman with Electronic Arts says that their designers plan "mini-arcs" of about one hour into the overall game progress. This is because that is what they have found the length of time the average gamer plays for in a single sitting.

At the end of each mini-arc, the designers try to make sure the player encounters a "memorable moment" of gameplay, which makes sure they will return for another play session. These mini-arcs, when aggregated, form the overall dramatic arc of the game.

Exercise 10.6: Progress

Take your original game prototype. Is the ultimate goal clear? Is the player always moving towards this goal? Make sure that you have milestones established along the way. Does your system help motivate the player to reach the final goal? Describe how.

The end

By "the end," we're not talking about when a player dies; we're talking about the moment when the play completely resolves. After investing hours, days, weeks, or even months, this is the instant when your most loyal players deserve a reward for all their effort.

Multiplayer games have their own reward built in: the satisfaction of beating the other players, or, if you have created a cooperative, unilateral, or team interaction structure, the satisfaction of having worked together to beat the game or the other side.

But what of your single-player game? After all the conflict, struggle, and time invested, make sure to give the player a satisfying reward. Too often, the end of all that work is a fluffy animation, where the hero is showered with praise and adulation. If you're going for an ending like this, why not build the reward into the story? Make that animation a moving moment in your hero's quest for whatever he lacks.

Exercise 10.7: Endings

Is the ending or resolution of your original game prototype satisfying? If not, how could you make it even better?

FUN "KILLERS"

For all your efforts, you may have implemented some features that "killed" the fun in your original concept. Here are just a few we've seen come up in first-time games over and over.

Micromanagement

Micromanagement is a classic example of forcing your players to make decisions that don't feel important. Game designers can fall into a trap of believing that the more control they give the players over their universe, the happier they'll be. On some level this is true. Hardcore strategy gamers love control. They want to tweak everything and dissect each element of the game. But there is a fine line between granting your players control and burdening them with chores.

As a designer, how do you know when you've given them enough? Start with the basics. Is the task necessary? Make sure the decision the players are given is not obvious, hollow or uninformed. If it passes these tests, it still may fall into the micromanagement trap. Micromanagement takes place when a task becomes repetitive or tedious. If you're asking the players to make too many small decisions and not enough large ones, then you have a problem. The best way to know this for certain is to bring in fresh playtesters. If they complain that it's too much work or too tiresome, this is a red flag.

The solution in almost every case is to simplify your game. Micromanagement comes from breaking up a task into too many small pieces. The overall impact of the combined decisions may be important on a strategic level, but each individual decision is too burdensome to be worth the effort. The solution is to combine the micro-decisions into one macro-decision. For instance, if deploying an army requires choosing what weapons each unit will use, what supplies they're going to carry, what form of transportation they'll utilize, and what route they'll travel, you're probably asking too much of your players. You can solve this by making some of these choices for them. Set default values that make sense and leave only the most important decisions, like what route to travel, up the players.

In addition to eliminating lesser decisions, you can give the players ways of automating certain tasks, like resource management, troop deployment, and logistics. This provides players with the degree of control they desire. Some players may chose to do everything manually, while others will prefer not to deal with the details. You'll find that different people want different things from your game, and the more flexible a system you can provide, while still keeping the game relatively simple, the better.

Exercise 10.8: Micromanagement

Are there any elements of micromanagement in your game? If so how can you streamline the choices players make so that they are not bogged down by unimportant details?

Stagnation

Some games fall into a pit of stagnation, where nothing new seems to be happening for a long period of time, choices stay at the same level of importance and impact.

A common source of stagnation is repetition, where players are caught doing the same task over and over. For instance, if the players are forced to fight the same type of battle repeatedly, the game can feel like it's at a standstill. The players may actu-

ally be advancing in levels or moving closer to their ultimate goal, but the actions they're performing are so repetitive that they mask any progress being made. In this case the solution is twofold. First, you should vary the type of action being performed. Next, you need to communicate how each action is bringing the player closer to victory.

Another type of stagnation is a balance of power. For instance, you have three players competing to conquer the world, and whenever one player gets ahead, the others gang up and smash the leader down, thus creating an endless cycle where no one is able to achieve victory. The solution here is to create a condition that tips the balance of power so far in favor of the winner that she can defeat the combined strength of the opposition.

A third type of stagnation is the endless loop syndrome. This type of stagnation occurs when a game device traps the players in a cycle. For instance, in a business simulation game, a player may get caught in a trap where all his profits are being eaten up by debt payments. No matter how long he plays, he cannot get over this hump. One solution is to shake things up with an unexpected event, like a windfall or natural disaster that will either push the player over the hump or knock him into bankruptcy. Of course, you could also tweak the game so that players never get stuck in this type of situation. Give the player debt relief or jack up interest rates—whatever it takes to move the game in one direction or the other.

The last type of stagnation is where it feels like nothing is happening, because nothing is actually happening. In other words, no progress is being made, either because the game is poorly designed or because there's no clear goal. An example of this might be an adventure game with a poorly defined objective. The players roam around but have no idea where they're supposed to go or what they're supposed to do. In this case, the solution is to go back and design the game so the objective is clear.

Exercise 10.9: Stagnation

Is there any point in your original prototype at which the game play stagnates? If so, determine what is causing this problem—do you have a repetitive loop? A balance of power? How can you break the cycle and improve the progression of the gameplay?

Insurmountable obstacles

Another problem area to avoid when designing a game is insurmountable obstacles. Despite the name, these may not actually be impossible situations, they just seem that way to a certain percentage of players.

Whether this occurs because of a dearth of information, a missed opportunity, or lack of experience or intuition, the result is always the same: your players wind up banging their heads against the same obstacle over and over and over. Look at your watch—how long now before they shut the game off in frustration, never to return again?

Most of us have been trapped by insurmountable obstacles at one time or another and wound up going in circles looking for that hidden doorway or secret panel. As a designer: make sure that and the game has some way of recognizing when a player is stuck and providing them with just enough assistance to make it past the obstacle without diluting it's challenge completely. Of course, this is easier said than done. Nintendo adventure games, such as those in the *Zelda* series, are typically good at providing info when players are stuck. Game characters are placed in

strategic spots to provide clues and other information that will help you overcome the obstacles. Like with other variables, clues have to be balanced to provide an appropriate level of difficulty for the players.

Building this kind of intelligence into the game is costly and time consuming. Sometimes, it doesn't need to be that sophisticated. In his presentation at the 2003 Game Developers Conference on making games more fun through user-testing, Microsoft User-Testing Manager Bill Fulton used an example from the opening moments of *Halo* to illustrate how a task that seems obvious to the designer may seem like an insurmountable obstacle to the player.

Immediately after the introductory tutorial of this first-person shooter game, your character is asked to follow a guide character to the bridge of the spaceship you are on. Of course, you do, but seconds later, the guide character is killed in an explosion right before your eyes, leaving you trapped behind a partially open doorway with no guide, and no clue how to open the door.

As part of his presentation, Fulton showed a videotape of just one of many user tests in which a playtester stumbled around the corridor, pressing every button on the controller, trying everything he could think of to open the door, all the while talking out loud about how he didn't know what to do. This went on for several minutes until it became clear from his tone of voice that if this player were at home, he would have given up—only five minutes into the game. As Fulton pointed out humorously, "I hope you all recognize this as 'not fun.'"[3]

The goal of the *Halo* designers, in leaving you guideless, trapped behind the door, was to create a sense of confusion and vulnerability that lasted only a few seconds for dramatic purposes. They

---

3.   Bill Fulton, "Making Games More Fun: Tips for Playtesting Games," Game Developers Conference 2003.

10.13 Tape from Halo user test: stuck at a broken doorway—note video insert of player's hands trying different control combinations, lower left

assumed the player would immediately realize the door wasn't going to open, see the alternate exit to the corridor they had planned, and be on their way. User-testing proved that most players needed a little help past this obstacle.

In the final product, a second explosion, timed a few seconds later, drives the player instinctively away from the half-opened door that will, in fact, never open. A text prompt pops up showing the player how to jump over objects, and a carefully designed floor mat points toward another opening in the corridor. The opening is blocked by a set of pipes, but if you know how to jump, that's no problem at all. With just a few modifications, the opening moments of the game were changed from an exercise in frustration to an exciting scene, filled with drama and tension.

Arbitrary events

As much as random events can be used to good effect in certain circumstances, like fortuitous surprises and unforeseen dangers, badly designed randomness can be the downfall of a game. Many games involve some form of randomness—we've seen how randomness can affect combat algo-

rithms in real-time strategy games, and how it can stop movement mechanics from becoming predictable in boardgames. These types of randomness add to gameplay.

But there's a big difference between utilizing randomness to change up gameplay and allowing for totally arbitrary events to disrupt the player experience. For instance, if you've spent weeks building a sophisticated character in a role-playing game, and then suddenly a plague, for which there is no cure, kills your character; you had no chance to defend yourself, and all your hard work has gone down the drain. It's hard not to feel cheated. We all know that life is full of unexpected events, some of which are devastating. So why shouldn't games include them?

The problem is that, as in life, good surprises are welcomed by players, but bad surprises are not. So, how can you include random events that are negative in nature without alienating the player? Whether it's a meteor storm that levels a city, an economic fluctuation which bankrupts a company, or a surprise attack that wipes out an army, you have to make sure it fits into the players' expectations of the game. Prepare your players in advance for the possibility of such an event and give them options to mitigate the damage—just don't tell them when it's coming or how bad it's going to be.

If we take the example with the plague, you should warn the player about the possibility of diseases, and allow them to purchase an antidote in advance. If they choose to ignore the warning signs and take no action, then when the event does come, it's their fault, and they'll know it.

A good rule of thumb is to caution your players at least three times before hitting them with anything catastrophic. Random events that have a lesser impact require smaller warnings, or even no warning at all. It's fine for a player to learn through experience to expect events of smaller consequence. But the bigger the impact, the more of a heads up you should provide. If you follow this rule, the events won't appear arbitrary, and your players will feel like they are in control of their destiny.

Predictable paths

Games with only one path to victory can become predictable. As we discussed in Chapter 5, linear or simple branching structures often lead to this type of predictability. If you want to add a greater sense of possibility to your design, consider treating the structure in a more object-oriented approach. Giving each type of object in the world a simple set of rules for interaction, rather than scripting each encounter separately often leads to creative and unusual results.

An example of this type of thinking is *Grand Theft Auto III*, which has a level structure and story line that the player can follow, or he is free to wander the world, stealing cars, committing crimes, or running a taxi service if that's what he wants to do. While wandering the world doesn't advance the player very far in terms of the overall game objectives, it does give the sense that the world of the game is responsive and unpredictable. At any moment, you might attract the attention of the police and wind up in an unscripted high-speed chase. Simulation games are other examples of this type of design—games like the *SimCity* series can evolve in many directions, all based on the choices of the players.

Another way to keep game paths from becoming predictable is to allow players to choose from several objectives. For instance, in *Civilization III*, the player can choose between six paths to victory: conquest, space travel, cultural advance, diplomacy, domination, and overall score. Each choice takes careful planning and will cause the player to weigh each choice anew, making the game not only interesting the first time around, but extremely replayable. Simply choose another path to victory and the game takes on an entirely new twist.

Not every game has to have the scope of a *Civilization* or a *Grand Theft Auto*, but when finding the balance between too much possibility and too much predictability, it's usually best to err on the side of greater possibility.

Is Your Game Accessible?

The final aspect to refining your game is making sure that it is accessible for the intended players. Can players in Peoria pick up your game and play, without any help from you and, realistically, without much help from the directions?

Accessibility is a strange paradox for the designer, because the better you understand your own game, the less able you are to anticipate problems that players may have in encountering it for the first time. Testing for accessibility is related to testing for usability. The difference is really who is doing the testing. Usability tests are generally done by usability engineers, in usability labs. We highly encourage you to utilize such a group if you or your publisher has access to them.

Usability engineers are generally trained psychologists or researchers whose focus is on testing and evaluating how users interact with various products. The general software industry has incorporated usability testing into its product cycle for years. The game industry lags far behind, although several large publishers, such as Microsoft, now have impressive internal groups dedicated to usability testing for games.

10.14 Microsoft playtesting lab

Multiple participants are playing games, each at their own station. Stations have partitions between them and headphones to minimize distractions. This is done so that one participant's experience doesn't affect another's. Each participant's opinions and preferences are collected via a web-based questionnaire on the monitors at each station. (Photo by Kyle Drexel.)

Professional usability labs are often set up with sophisticated recording equipment, allowing the researchers to insert a close-up view of the participant's hands on the controls—keyboard and mouse, or console controller—within a shot of the main interface. Sometimes another camera shows the participant's facial responses, and her voice talking out loud about what she is thinking is recorded over the sound of the product. The researchers usually sit behind one-way glass with the designers and producers of the product, communicating with the participant via intercom.

The researchers prepare a test script for the session, which asks the participant to walk through a number of areas in the product, or complete a set of tasks. Data on how successful participants are in completing these tasks and an evaluation of how critically any findings will impact the product are compiled in a report.

When we ask you to test for accessibility in your game, we're basically asking you to do a lay-man's usability test. By now, you have probably playtested your game with quite a few different people. Unfortunately, these people are now disqualified for your accessibility testing. The right people to test for accessibility are:

- Part of your target market
- Objective (not friends or relatives)
- Have never played your game

You'll need a fair sized group: Three to five people in each segment of your market (if there is more than one) are sufficient. Eight is preferred.

To make things go smoothly and to get the most out of the session, you need to identify the most critical areas of your game—your list will probably include starting a game, and some of the more critical choices or features. Now, create a script you can use to get the participants to these critical areas and present them with tasks that will give you insight as to how they are working. The

10.15 Microsoft usability lab

A participant (background, on the right) is playing a game. In the foreground, a user-testing specialist is observing the participant play the game in an adjacent room, separated by one-way glass. The one-way glass allows the user-testing specialist and development team members to discuss the game and participant behaviors without being overheard by the participant. (Photo by Kyle Drexel.)

script doesn't have to be elaborate—it is to help you keep the session on track with as little fumbling and forgetting as possible. You want the participants concentrating on your game, not on you.

Unless your game demands a multiplayer environment, it's best to do this type of testing one on one. You want to see where people are stumbling or guessing, and people sometimes try to hide that, or they copy from a neighbor in a group. If you have to have participants in the same room during a test, explain to them that they shouldn't help each other with the tasks.

You may want to have a friend help you out, if you can't record the session, by taking notes while you walk through the script with the participant. Have them sit out of the participant's peripheral view, to lessen distraction. Once you've run several, you will undoubtedly begin to see a pattern—you may be surprised to learn that your game is not as accessible as you believed. The example of the first few minutes of *Halo*, shows how easy it is for game designers to miss potential areas of confusion, simply because they are so familiar with the game. Just remember that participants in a test like this are never "wrong." As tempting as it may be to believe that a feature is "obvious," your opinions don't count in this type

of testing. If your players can't play, there is no game.

Identify the areas that are causing problems, make revisions, and do another series of tests. Continue this until you are satisfied that a majority of your target players can access the most critical areas of your game. In a perfect world, you could test every aspect of your game for accessibility, but you probably won't have the time or resources to do it. What you can do, is make the game easy to get into, easy to understand, and fun to play.

Exercise 10.10: Usability Testing

Conduct a set of usability tests for your original game prototype as described previously:

1. Write a script for a usability test in which you focus on critical tasks like starting a game, understanding objectives, making key choices, etc.;

2. Recruit a group of new testers who have not played your game before.

3. Conduct the tests and analyze the results. Come up with three ideas to improve your game's usability.

Conclusion

You now should have a game that's functional, complete, balanced, fun, and accessible. That's a major accomplishment. Whether you've gone through this process alone, working with a paper prototype, or whether you've managed to get a team together and create a digital prototype of your game, the fact that you've gone through all the phases of design and testing means that you had an idea that was worth the effort. This certainty will be what you need to carry you through the full production and release of this game.

At this point, you probably have a list of things you would have done differently in your design process if you had a chance to do it over. It's a good idea to write these down now, while they are fresh in your mind. Whether these thoughts are simply something you write for yourself, or something you share with a team, they are a road map for making your next design process go even more smoothly.

Chapter 11
Controls and Interfaces

Now that you know how to prototype, playtest, and revise your prototype, it's time to take a look at some of the underlying issues that you'll face when building out your design for a digital platform. If you've begun with a physical prototype, you'll need to translate that core gameplay to a digital format. The main tasks in doing that are envisioning your gameplay using the input and output devices of your digital platform. This means designing for control systems like keyboards, mice, proprietary controllers, etc. It also means visualizing your gameplay in the form of a digital interface.

This doesn't mean starting from scratch—your physical prototype helped you to formalize and test the essence of your game, the essence of what you will be visualizing. The understanding of your game gained from this experience will breathe life into the designs for your controls and interface. It will inform the decisions you make and give you ideas you would otherwise have never thought of.

CONTROLS

What are controls? And as a game designer, how do they impact your job? By controls, we mean whatever input hardware allows the user to affect the game. When videogames were first invented, they were limited in terms of controls. Steve Russell and several other students at MIT programmed *Spacewar* in 1962, often credited as the first digital game,[1] and in doing so, they found the toggle switches built into the front of their DEC PDP-1 to be too cumbersome, so they built their own special controller to go along with the game.

Spacewar had only four controls: rotate left, rotate right, thrust, and fire.

Controls have come along way since the 60s. If we ask you to do a quick impression of a person playing a videogame today, chances are you'll hold your hands out slightly, palms facing each other, and start twiddling your thumbs wildly. Your grandmother may not get the impression, but any teenager will.

Today's controls include the keyboard, mouse, joystick, steering wheels, plastic guns, gloves with

---

1. William Higanbotham is also a contender for this honor. His two-player tennis game, built on a small analog computer and oscilloscope, was created in 1958 at the Brookhaven National Laboratory.

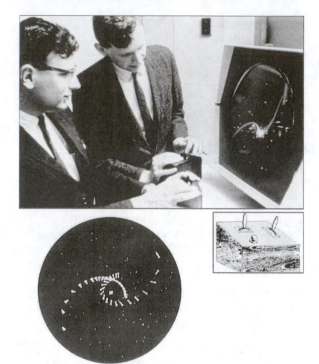

11.1   Spacewar on the DEC PDP-1 and custom controller

11.2   Counterclockwise from top left, controls for: Atari 2600, NES, PlayStation 2 and Xbox

embedded sensors, virtual reality helmets, and more. You name it, someone has thought of it. Not all of these are practical, and most designers only consider a couple of controls when developing their games. The most popular controllers today are simply more elaborate variations on the same directional arrow/selection button design that marked the very first consoles.

There have been a number of interesting forays by arcade companies into the development of radical new types of controllers, including motorcycles you can ride, cars you can drive, the footpad stage of *Dance Dance Revolution*, and the motion sensor frames of *Mocap Boxing*.

But unless you're an arcade game designer, you'll probably forgo the more inventive control systems in favor of the tried and true control pad (for console games) and the mouse/keyboard (for

PC games). This is because every time you design for another controller, it costs the production time and money, and unless the optional controller is deemed a key selling feature of the game, it usually isn't included in the schedule or budget.

The first thing you need to do when conceiving your game is make sure that you understand the standard controller for the platform you are designing to. This means knowing what your audience expects each button to do. These expectations are usually determined by previous games. If you're a rebel and go against the grain, you'll only wind up confusing and frustrating your customers. It's best to stick to normal behavior patterns instead of trying to foist some new scheme upon your users.

That said, this type of decision-making on the part of designers tends to mean that a lot of games will play exactly the same. How many games have you played that use the control button or the spacebar to fire a weapon? Why? Because that is how the designer of the last game did it. We challenge you to be creative and experiment. Don't just fall in line with other games. But when you do venture out and try something different, make certain that the controls work intuitively. Test them on a variety

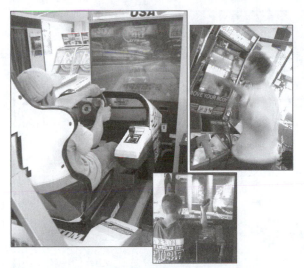

11.3 Race cars, light guns, and motion capture boxing controls

of users, and if your playtesters agree that your design isn't exasperating, maybe you're onto something.

The article by designer Eric Zimmerman of gameLab on page 312 describes how his team's desire to create an interesting new control idea scheme led to the idea for their game *Loop*. In this case, they created a digital prototype of the core mechanic—the "looping" control—and tested that thoroughly to make sure it was intuitive and fun before progressing further with the idea.

Once you understand the input device, you need to think about how your game can best utilize it. You need to decide this in conjunction with your interface design, which we discuss next. Here is a good way to begin: look at the list of procedures for your physical prototype. These procedures need to be translated into a set of digital controls. For example, in our first-person shooter prototype, we had procedures for moving forward, back, turning left, right, etc. We also had procedures for firing weapons, changing weapons, etc. Each of these will need to be mapped to a control. If you have a highly detailed set of controls,

you will probably wind up grouping them under a menu system or other visual device that can be accessed using a single control or set of controls.

Once you've decided how the controls will work, create a control table to make sure you've thought of everything. In one column, list the controls, and in next column, list the game procedure taken when that control is activated. If your game is complex, you may have to make several tables, each representing a specific game state. For the purposes of controls, a new game state exists each time the controls change.

For instance, if it's a game where you can drive a car, fly a plane, or ride a bike, there will be three game states. In this case, the designer should try to keep the controls as similar as possible between the three states to avoid confusing the player.

Exercise 11.1: Original Game Controls

Define a control scheme for your original game. For example, if your game is intended for a game console, such as the PS2, make sure to label every button on the controller. If a button has no function, then label it as "non-functional."

Designing controls, like designing gameplay, is an iterative process. Your first attempt may not be as intuitive as you believed. The only way you'll truly know if the controls work is to test them.

Your goal should be to make the controls as effortless as possible. Gamers don't want to think when they're playing. They want the controls to feel intuitive. In this case, less is more. You'll find that adding too many control options frustrates the average user. For expert players, these detailed controls may come in handy, as will custom control schemes, but it's not worth scaring off novice players.

A wise designer will keep the controls limited to around seven inputs. Most people can't handle

	A	B	C	D	E	F	G	H	I	J	K	
1												
2		**Key**			**Action in each game state:**							
3					**Land**				**Water**			
4		Arrow keys			walk forward, back, left, right							
5		Shift key			run							
6		CTRL or Left Mouse			shoot (hold for continuous shooting)							
7		A Key			look up							
8		Z Key			look down							
9		Spacebar or Enter key			jump				kick to the surface, tread water			
10		C Key			press and hold to duck							
11		C + arrow forward			crawl							
12		A + Arrow Left/Right			side-step							
13		1 Key			Axe							
14		2 Key			Shotgun							
15		3 Key			Double-barrelled shotgun							
16		4 Key			Nailgun							
17		5 Key			Perforator							
18		6 Key			Grenade launcher							
19		7 Key			Rocket launcher							
20		8 key			Thunderbolt							
21												

11.4   Simple control table

more. You can have fifty or more advanced options, but a player should be able to get through the game only having memorized about seven actions. If you can do this, you're designing a game that will appeal to the broadest possible audience.

Exercise 11.2: Control Design

The following exercise is given to prospective employees by game developer Pandemic Studios in Los Angeles. Pandemic requires applicants to complete exercises like this as a way of assessing their capabilities. As William Henry Stahl, the designer of this exercise, pointed out, there are no "correct" answers, and the exercise is just part of the evaluation process for applicants. Complete the exercise yourself.

Control design exercise

As part of a team, you are creating a squad-based, tactical-action game for the PlayStation 2. Entitled *Bravo Leader*, the game places you in the role of a U.S. Army squad leader engaged in contemporary military operations all over the world. It is your responsibility to achieve mission objectives through the skillful deployment and use of four elite U.S. Army riflemen (including yourself).

After an initial series of meetings with the publisher, you have established some basics. The publisher would like to market the game toward an older (18–30), casual-gaming audience. The game should be played primarily from an over-the-shoulder perspective. It will be mostly exterior combat, placing the player in wartime combat situations right away (the publisher would like to steer away from stealth and infiltration objectives).

The core mechanic of the game is the ability to control a team of soldiers and their tactics in combat. The player must be able to issue orders to his team as a group or individually. The most important orders deal with managing the movement of the team so you've been asked to do a first-pass controls mockup that allows the player to do the following in the game:

- Select a single soldier or the entire squad
- Designate a location for that soldier or squad to move to
- Issue a movement order to that soldier or squad

The exact type and number of movement orders the player can issue to his soldiers has yet to be finalized; however, it is safe to assume that there will be more than one. Some suggestions that came out of the design meeting are:

- *Check Position:* Issuing this order causes the soldier or soldiers to approach the designated location cautiously and low to the ground. Should the soldiers encounter the enemy they will stop and engage.

- *Double-Time:* Issuing this order causes the soldier or soldiers to run to the designation. The soldiers will disregard engaging an enemy until it reaches the designated location.

- *Patrol:* Issuing this order causes the soldier or soldiers to casually walk to the designated location. Should the soldiers encounter the enemy they will engage but continue to move to the designated location.

Map out your controls for the "movement orders" feature described earlier using this diagram and control table. You can use as many or as few buttons as you like.

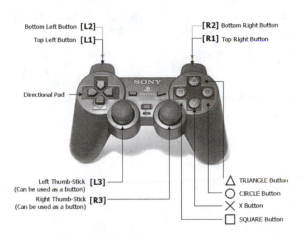

11.5 Sony PlayStation 2 controls

- Main control table
- Left thumb-stick
- Right thumb-stick
- Directional pad
- Triangle button
- Circle button
- X button
- Square button
- L1 button
- L2 button
- R1 button
- R2 button
- Start button
- Select button

Next, write out your design for the "movement orders" feature in detail. Describe how the system functions. Describe how it affects or utilizes other systems—the camera or the HUD (heads-up display) for instance. Include examples of the controls in practice. Feel free to expand or reduce the feature in any way you like. Take as little or as much space as you need but be as thorough as you would be were this an actual design specification.

- Left thumb-stick
- Right thumb-stick
- Directional pad
- Triangle button
- Circle button
- X button
- Square button
- L1 button
- L2 button
- R1 button
- R2 button
- Start button
- Select button

Summary

The preceding example gives you a good idea of the type of thinking game companies are looking for when they hire someone. It also illustrates the importance of understanding controls in today's videogame industry. It's a good idea to play a wide variety of games and take notes on how each system uses the controls. Make sure to remark on schemes that work and ones that don't. This will help you when it comes time to think through your own designs.

When people talk about the art of editing in films and television, they often call it an "invisible" art, commenting that if you noticed the editing while you were watching the film, it wasn't done well. Designing controls for your game is like editing in this way. If players can sit down and start playing, without referring to a manual, your game is well-designed.

VIEWPOINTS

The interface for a digital game is a combination of the viewpoint of the game environment and the visual display of the game status and controls that allow the user to interact with the system. The controls, viewpoint, and interface all work together symbiotically to create the game experience and allow the player to understand and have agency within the system.

As with control systems, the viewpoints for the first videogames were limited, and mainly limited to text descriptions of the environment. This doesn't mean that they were ineffective—just the opposite—anyone who remembers playing an Infocom text adventure probably also remembers the sense of immersion that can come from a well-written storyline.

However, once computer displays were able to move beyond the display of text, several major graphic viewpoints for interfaces were developed fairly early on. These viewpoints have evolved in complexity as technology has advanced, but they remain essentially the same today as they were the first time we looked down on the classic *Pong* tennis court.

Overhead view

Looking directly down at an object is a somewhat unnatural angle, and today, this viewpoint is primarily used for level maps and digital versions of boardgames, but early games used this viewpoint quite a bit, in everything from sports and adventure games, to action puzzles like *Pac-Man*.

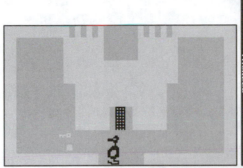

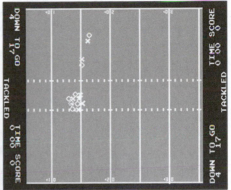

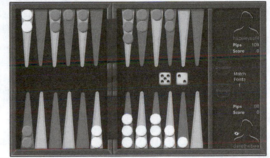

11.6 Overhead views: Atari Adventure and Football, MSN Game Zone Backgammon

MSN Game Zone trademark Microsoft Corporation

Side view

The side view is popular with arcade and puzzle games like *Donkey Kong, Tetris,* and *The Incredible Machine,* but probably has had the most influence in the form of the side-scroller. This type of interface is largely out of favor now, but that doesn't mean that we should ignore the power and simplicity afforded by this viewpoint. The fact that the player only has to control units in two planes leaves a significant amount of brainspace for solving complex puzzles and other forms of play.

Isometric view

Popular in strategy games, construction simulations, and role-playing games, this viewpoint is a 3D space with no linear perspective. It is very good at allowing a "god's eye" view. The distinctive feature of this point of view is the amount of information the player can easily have access to. Recently,

games like *Myth* and *WarCraft III* have used the isometric view in a fully 3D environment, allowing the player to move her perspective closer or further away from the action.

First person view

This is the current favorite among many gamers and designers. It creates immediacy and empathy with the main character, literally putting the player in their shoes. This view also limits the player's overall knowledge—allowing for dramatic moments of tension and surprise as enemies may lurk around any corner, or even approach from the rear.

Third person view

A direct descendant of the side view, this view generally follows a character closely, but doesn't step directly inside their view. Adventure games, sports games, and other games that depend on a more

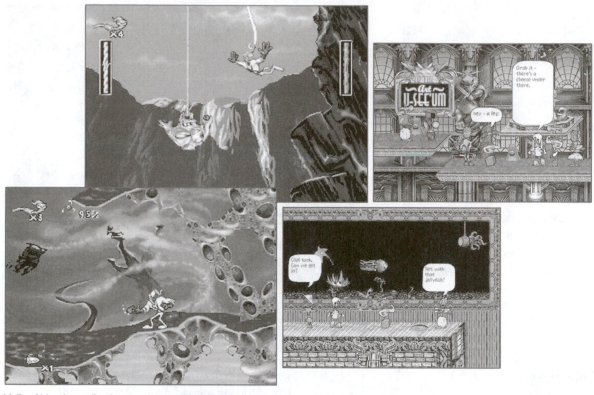

11.7   Side views: Earthworm Jim and Castle Infinity

11.8   Isometric views: Myth and Dungeon Siege

Dungeon Siege trademark Microsoft Corporation

11.9   First-person view: Unreal 2

detailed control of character actions tend to use this viewpoint.

These views have become so ingrained in how we think of games that often a designer will choose without stopping to consider several important questions that lie behind all interface design: what is the purpose of the interface? What is the state of the game, and how much information should the player know about it?

In Chapter 5 we discussed the "information structure" of games—how much and what type of information about the game state was given to each player. The viewpoints we've just discussed provide degrees of access to the state of the world, as well as placing the player in varying relationship to the character or other game objects that they must deal with. This makes the choice of interface view both a formal and a dramatic design element.

Should the player feel extremely close to the game character—sharing its sense of movement, in addition to its lack of knowledge at times? Or, should the player remain close, but somewhat

11.10 Third-person view: Ratchet & Clank

outside of the character, able to see more of the environment, perhaps pick up on clues or tools that might not be in the character's direct vision? Perhaps there is no character in your game, or maybe there's no world—in this case, what is the view of the game state that makes the most sense for your design?

Exercise 11.3: Viewpoint

What viewpoint is the best choice for your original game? Why? Describe how this choice affects both the formal and dramatic elements of your game.

INTERFACE

In addition to the game's viewpoint, there is also the consideration of other information the player will need to know and the actions they will need to take. This might include points or progress in the game, status of other units, communication with other players, choices that are always open to them, or special opportunities to take action. How will you incorporate this information in or around your main view? This "interface" to the game, as mentioned previously, works together with the controls and viewpoint to create the game experience, and needs to be extremely understandable.

Just as with designing controls, the tried and true method usually works better than innovation. Once people become accustomed to a certain type of interface, it's difficult for them to adjust to even small changes. This is a paradox that has plagued designers—and not just game designers—since the beginnings of industrial design. How can we design something new and innovative that is also intuitive and easy to use? The ideal interface would be fresh and new, but feel like something you've used a thousand times before. Is this possible? The answer is yes, but it's not easy. There are no short cuts to good design, but there are some ways of approaching your design process that can help your games reflect both original thinking and sensitivity to user expectations.

Form follows function

You may have heard the phrase "form follows function." Louis Henri Sullivan, the architect who introduced this comment to popular culture, was making the statement that the design of an object must come from its purpose. If you're going to build a building, ask yourself about the purpose of the building before you design the doors. If you are going to build a game, ask yourself what are the formal elements of the game before you design its interface or controls. If you don't, you wind up with a game that looks and acts like every other game.

Today, many designers simply revert to saying things like, "My game is *Halo* but set in a maximum security prison, where you have to escape." In most cases, the designer will borrow the interface and control scheme from *Halo*, and then design the content to fit within these parameters, with perhaps a new feature or two thrown in. That's fine, and it may be a fun game, but it's never going to be very unique. The key to avoiding producing nothing but clones of existing games is to go back to your original concept and ask yourself, "What's special about this idea?"

In the prison example, the concept was to escape from prison. The conflict is clear: the prisoner must outsmart the security. Now how can you do this in a new way? What does a prisoner need to do to break out of prison? What types of tools and weapons and obstacles are there? As designer, you should play with how to represent these onscreen. Don't just copy existing games. Experiment with new ways of visualizing these elements, assign them properties, and allow them to interact with one another. As you can see, the interface is coming from the game, not vice versa.

The best approach is never to design the interface first but let it evolve from the necessities mandated by the function of the game. In other words, form follows function.

Metaphors

Visual interfaces are at root metaphorical. They are graphical symbols that help us to navigate the arcane universe that is the computer. You are probably most familiar with the desktop metaphor that both Microsoft Windows and the Macintosh operating system share. File folders, documents, in-boxes, and trashcans are all clever metaphors for various system features and objects. This metaphor is successful because it helps users contextualize the experience of working with various objects on the computer in a way that is familiar.

When you design your game interface, you need to consider its basic metaphor. What visual metaphor would best communicate all the possible procedures, rules, boundaries, etc., that your game contains? Many games use physical metaphors linked to their overall themes. So, for example, the objects a character can "carry" in a role-playing game are placed in a "backpack." Just like in our discussion of premise in Chapter 4 on page 91, interface metaphors take the dry, statistical facts linked in the computer's memory and display them in a way that fits with the experience of the game.

When creating a metaphor, it's important to keep in mind the "mental model" that players will bring with them to the game. This mental model can either help players to understand your game, or it can cause them to misunderstand it. Mental models include all of the range of ideas and concepts that we associate with a particular context. For example, if I were to make of list of concepts that come to mind when I think about a circus, I might come up with something like this: the ringmaster, the rings, clowns, high wire, barkers, side shows, animals, popcorn, cotton candy, master of ceremonies, etc.

If I were making a game that used the metaphor of a circus for its interface, I might decide to have the ringmaster be the host or help system. The rings might be different game areas or types, popcorn and candy might be power-ups. Using this metaphor helps to visualize this information in an entertaining way.

However, if you are not careful, your metaphor can also obscure navigation. Each of the concepts we listed has its own range of associations as well, and sometimes the mental models we bring to a metaphor can cause more confusion than clarity.

Exercise 11.4: Metaphors

Generate a list of potential metaphors for your original game interface. They can be anything: a farm, a road map, a shopping mall, a railroad—you choose. Now, free associate on each metaphor for five minutes. List any concepts that come to mind.

Visualization

In the midst of a game, players often need to process many types of quantitative information very quickly. A good way to help them do this is to visualize the information, so that a glance will suffice to let them know their general status. We are all

DESIGNER PERSPECTIVE: DAVID PERRY

Title:

President, Shiny Entertainment, Inc.

Project list (five to eight top projects)

- *Enter the Matrix*
- *Sacrifice*
- *MDK*
- *Earthworm Jim*
- *Disney's Aladdin*
- *Global Gladiators*
- *Cool Spot*
- *The Terminator*
- *Teenage Mutant Ninja Turtles*

How did you get into the game industry?

I started getting paid to make games before you could buy games in stores. Back in those days, you bought special magazines or books filled with games written in a programming language called "BASIC." The reader would have to type the entire game that they wanted to play into their computer by hand. Sometimes it would take them hours, then when they tried to actually "play" the game, if they had made one single typo, the game would likely break and they could spend another hour just looking for their mistake. So that's what I did, I wrote tons of games to be printed in magazines and, finally, books. Once games were sold in stores, I was offered a job to start making a "real" game, and that is what hooked me. So I left school at seventeen (without a degree) and never looked back.

familiar with visualization techniques: the gas gauge in your car sweeps in an arc from full to empty, the thermometer bar rises as the temperature goes up. These examples both use cultural expectations to cue us as to what they mean—the arc sweeping left or down means the amount of gas is declining; a rising bar means that something is going up. This is called "natural mapping," and game interfaces can make good use of them.

The *Quake* interface we've looked at before is actually a great example of using natural mapping to visualize an aspect of the game state. The face in the center represents our health—when we start the game, the face is angry and snarling, but healthy. As our character takes hits, the face becomes bruised and bloody, letting us know our status in a glance.

What are your five favorite games and why?

I like *Battlefield: 1942* and *Grand Theft Auto III* because you feel you can do anything. The world is your oyster. You can choose to play the way the game wants you to, or choose to just have fun and entertain yourself. I think that's a great option for gamers, because some of them want to be entertained right now and some of them are very creative and are quite happy to entertain themselves. I like *Halo* and *Max Payne* for their action sequences you feel immersed in their world and can really get into the action. I like *Command & Conquer* for the strategy depth it offers, as you find yourself managing lots of things at once. The more you can handle, the more it can give you to handle. When you think you are good, go ahead and challenge others. Very rewarding.

What games have inspired you the most as a designer and why?

I think the games that kick me up the pants most are games like the ones Peter Molyneux or Warren Spector do. Basically they think big right out of the box. You can take it to the bank that whatever they do next will be interesting and challenging. I like that, and I wish more people did it.

What are you most proud of in your career?

Over the last 21 years, I have taken a lot of risks, and luckily enough of them have paid off. As a result, I've had my share of #1 hits, but I've also had games that even I hate. I think I am most proud of the fact that through very difficult times, I have managed to keep Shiny not only alive but as a really cool place to make games where we are willing to try new ideas. (Shiny turned ten years old in October 2003.)

What words of advice would you give to an aspiring designer today?

I have a free web site called www.dperry.com to help new talent get started in this industry. All I can say is please help me make it better by making sure your questions are answered, or share your experiences with people that you know are going through the same things. Overall? Passion is key. If you feel interested in getting into the industry, that's not enough. You need to be willing to put everything else aside (including sleep) if you plan to compete in this industry. Those with the passion will go far; those without will end up frustrated. Is it worth it? Heck yes!

Exercise 11.5: Natural Mapping

Are there any opportunities to use natural mapping in your original game interface? If so, sketch out these ideas to clarify how the designs might function. You can use these ideas later when you lay out your full interface designs in Exercise 11.8.

Grouping features

When you organize your desk, you probably sort things into similar groups—all the bills go together, all the business cards together, all the pens and pencils together, etc. Designing an interface requires the same kind of thinking. It's often best to group similar features together visually, so that the player always knows where look for them.

11.11 Quake health meter in three states

If you have several types of health meters, for example, don't put them in different corners of the screen—group them together. If you have several combat features, you can make them more convenient to access by putting them on a single control panel. Or, if you have communication features in your game, it will make sense to group these as well.

Exercise 11.6: Grouping

Take a stack of index cards and list one control from your interface on each card. Sort the cards into groups that make sense to you. Try the same exercise with three or four other people. Notice the similarities and differences between each person's decisions. Does this exercise give you any ideas on how best to group your game's controls?

Consistency

Don't move your features from one area to another when changing screens or areas of the game. As Noah Falstein counters in his *Game Developer* column "Better By Design," consistency may be the hobgoblin of small minds, but it is also

important in establishing a usable interface.[2] Have you ever played a game in which the exit button moved from the upper right on one screen, then to the lower right on another? If so, you have experienced the frustration of inconsistency.

Feedback

Letting the player know, through visual or aural feedback, that their action has been accepted is critical. A good designer always provides some sort of feedback for each action the player makes.

Aural feedback is very good for letting the player know that input has been received, or that something new is about to happen. It is not extremely effective for giving precise data like the exact status of a player's resources, or letting the player know where their units are. In this case, you'll need to come up with a method of visual feedback.

Exercise 11.7: Feedback in Your Game

Determine what types of feedback your game needs to communicate effectively to the player. Decide how best to present this feedback: auditorily, visually, tactilely, etc.

Wireframes

One of the best ways to convey your interface design to your production team is to create wireframes. Like an architect's blueprints, wireframes are basic outlines of the structure and functionality of your interface. Wireframes don't have to be artistic. They just need to be well-thought–out and complete. You may find as you work through all the screens that you need to go back and change the ones you did in the beginning. This is precisely

---

2. Noah Falstein, "Better By Design: The Hobgoblin of Small Minds," *Game Developer*, June 2003.

Using Audio as a Game Feedback Device

by Michael Sweet, Creative Director, AudioBrain, Inc.

Sound can have a profound impact on the game. Not only is it important in setting the overall mood for play, it can dictate an emotional responses to the player. Whether you're struggling to make it to the end of a level or waiting for the next monster to appear from around the corner, the music and sound can make the player's heart race or stomach drop.

Several years ago I created sound for a little innovative puzzle game called BLiX. You can still run across it on Shockwave.com if you're interested in playing it. The game brought me several nominations for best audio in a game and the Independent Game Festival Award for Best Audio in 2000.

The object of BLiX is incredibly simple: get the balls into the cup. The game itself was designed to be played by anyone; the interface was iconic, the scoring system didn't use numbers, there was also no real language in the game design itself.

Below is a basic asset list of the sounds that went into the game.

1. Introductory music
2. Interface rollover sounds
3. Play button sound
4. Timer start sound
5. Timer countdown sound
6. Level music (14 versions which cycle among the 300 levels)
7. In-game musical rollovers
8. Bumper place sound
9. Ball bounce sound
10. Ball into cup sound
11. Finish level sound
12. Interstitial music
13. Timer running low sound
14. Special sounds for level power-ups
15. Game over sound

When designing the sound I wanted the player to create the music through gameplay without actually realizing they were participating in it. All the sound effects are musical phrases that get added to an underlying loop of ambient background techno music. In addition the game space is divided into a grid of nine spaces that have rollovers so as the player moves around the screen placing bumpers and playing the game these musical rollovers trigger simple drum hits and synth notes. In essence the score is self-generated by the user.

At the time, with limited toolsets, we introduced some fairly unique concepts to an Internet puzzle game; the creation of music centered around gameplay. Today there are many newer technologies that allow the composer to really shape narrative in real time through seamless branching of the musical score and dynamic created sound effects. At the time BLiX was done we had to be creative about the use of the limited technology, trying to break the rules of the system.

The sounds themselves were created using soft-ware packages Rebirth and Protools. I wanted to inte-grate lots of delays and effects into the individual sounds. I wanted to also recognize a retro arcade feel to the game, taking beeps and blips to a whole new level. The other developers were all old arcade heads and we wanted to recognize our heritage so to speak.

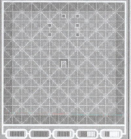

Adding delays on sounds add a lot of file size to the game. The co-designers of the game let me have full reign over file size, which really allowed me to be creative first instead of being led by the technology or inherent difficulties of the limitations of an Internet game. Although we took out assets to maintain file size once Shockwave.com acquired BLiX, it really allowed me to open up creatively and experiment in ways I really hadn't before. I was lucky to be working with designers who let me experiment and try new things.

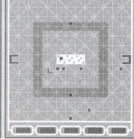

Audio feedback is incredibly important. When I talk to people that play *BLiX* they always mention the game over sound and how they hate hearing it. I was in the process of taking it out during the creation of the game because I felt it was too harsh, when the other designers (Peter Lee and Eric Zimmerman) told me how much they liked it. Players of *BLiX* hate getting to the game over sound, and immediately start a new game as a result.

The one sound in the game I didn't create was the timer running out sound. Peter Lee found this sound and we ended up not changing because it's another sound that jolts you back to reality. After playing the game for a while you get that sort of numb *Tetris*-like feeling where the game is a machine and you're part of it. All of the sudden the timer is running out and it jolts you back to the reality that the game is about to end.

It was really important to me that the audio feedback during the game was a single audio-rich experience. The sound effects in *BLiX* needed to be tightly integrated into the music. Even though we didn't have the ability to sync sounds to the beats the sounds are so well designed (ultimately to my initial disbelief) and synergistic with the background loops that everyone just considers it music instead of two separate elements.

Something frequently overlooked is that audio feedback can also establish the rhythm of interaction for the player. Digital gameplay has a player interaction that has a specific speed of movement, mouse clicks, and keystrokes. These interactions have rhythm all on their own that the music and SFX can support or detract from.

Similar to film, the game sound designer can use motifs and themes to create metaphors for characters, help transitions, and give direct or indirect feedback to the user about how they're doing in the game. The power of sound design can also create emotions that are hard to achieve strictly by the visual representation of the game, things like empathy, hatred, love can all be represented through music and sound.

Each game designer should recognize the power that audio has to increase every aspect of his game. Studies have shown that higher quality audio often gives the game player a perceived increase in the overall visual look of the game and heightened awareness during game play.

Author Bio

Michael Sweet is the creative director for Audiobrain. As a composer and sound designer, he has won numerous awards for his work including the prestigious BDA Promax Award 2000 for Best Sound for a Network Package (HBO Zone) and the Best Audio Award at the GDC Independent Games Festival in 2000. Michael's sound sculptures have traveled around the world, including the Millennium Dome in London, and galleries in New York, Los Angeles, Florence, Berlin, Hong Kong, and Amsterdam.

You can find Michael's sonic imprints on many award winning games and web sites. Award winning work includes: Sesame Workshop's MusicWorks, Shockwave's BLiX & LOOP, RealArcade's WordUp, and many games for the Cartoon Network. In broadcast, Michael's work can be heard in many commercials and network identities, including HBO Zone, Comedy Central, CNN, General Motors, Kodak, AT&T/TCI, and The X-Files.

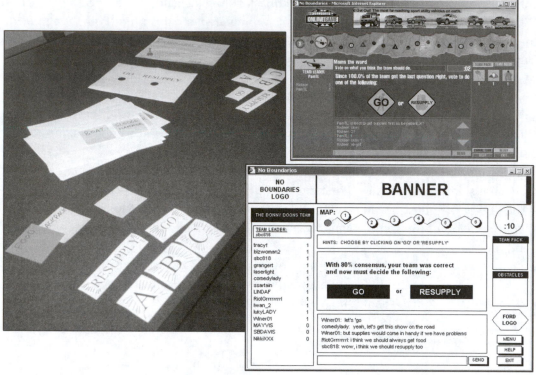

11.12 From a physical prototype (left), to wireframes (lower right), to final interface (upper right)

why we do wireframes, so that we can find and solve issues of metaphor, grouping, and consistency before involving the artists and programmers. Figure 11.12 shows a sample wireframe.

Wireframes also act as a tool to facilitate discussions about the game. Reading a design document is fine, but seeing a wireframe takes it to a whole new level. You'd be surprised at how much it helps to have something visual in front of you when you are explaining how your game functions. Once you are done presenting the wireframes to your team, you should have a very good idea of how your interface will look and function, and this

knowledge will your artists and programmers get off to a smooth start.

Exercise 11.8: Wireframes

Create a full set of wireframes for your original game prototype. Be sure to include every screen. This will force you to think through all elements of the controls, viewpoint, and interface discussed previously. Once you have completed your wireframes, you will be well-prepared for the specification process that we discuss in Chapter 14.

Conclusion

Once you've designed your controls and interfaces, you will work with the artists and programmers to implement them and the rest of the game

logic. This is where the real fun begins. Collaborating with team members can be one of the most rewarding and creative experiences if you approach the process with an open mind and a clear vision. Like the playtesting process, the collaboration process will open your designs up to new ideas and perspectives. The next section deals with this process in depth.

Before moving on though, take a look back at the process you've just been through:

- You not only came up with an idea for an original game, you've learned skills and techniques that will make you a valuable member of any design team. You are an idea generator.

- You've translated your ideas into a prototype of a working game.

- You've playtested your prototype and revised it until its gameplay delighted your testers.

- You've envisioned your game as a digital product, designing controls and interfaces for the target platforms.

At this point, you should feel empowered by your control of the design process. No longer a mystery, the process of game design is one you should feel confident with practicing on your own, with friends, or as a member of a professional design team. You may use your skills to create games in your garage, or you may try to get a job with an established developer or publisher. Whatever you decide to do, you will have the experience and the critical skills to approach the task of game design as both a personal art and a social, collaborative dialogue between the designers and the players of games.

The Core Mechanic: Game Design as Activity Design

by Eric Zimmerman, Co-Founder and CEO, gameLab

The following is adapted from a longer essay entitled "Play as Research" that appears in the book Design Research, edited by Brenda Laurel (MIT Press, 2004). It appears here with permission from the author.

Too often, game designers focus on the content, narrative, or aesthetics of their game design rather than asking more fundamental questions. As participatory, dynamic systems, it is crucial that games be understood not just as content but as action. As you begin working on a game design, ask yourself, what is the actual activity of the game? What is the player actually doing from moment to moment as he or she plays your game?

Virtually all games have a core mechanic, an action or set of actions that players will repeat over and over as they move through the designed system of the game. A game prototype should help you understand what this core mechanic is and how the activity becomes meaningful over time. Asking questions about your game's core mechanic can guide the creation of your first prototype, as well as successive iterations. Ideally, initial prototypes model this core mechanic and begin to test it through play.

Case study: LOOP

LOOP is a single-player game in which the player uses the mouse to catch flittering, colored butterflies. The player draws loops around groups of butterflies of the same color, or of groups in which each butterfly is a different color (the more butterflies in a loop, the more points). To finish a level, the player must capture a certain number of butterflies before the sun sets. The game includes three species of butterflies and a variety of hazardous bugs, all with different behaviors. *LOOP* was created by gameLab and is available for play at www.shockwave.com.

LOOP grew out of a desire at gameLab to invent a new core mechanic. There are ultimately not very many ways to interact with a computer game: the player can express herself through the mouse and keyboard, and the game can express itself through the screen and speakers. Deciding to intervene on the level of player input, we had a notion to cast aside point-and-click or click-and-drag mouse interaction in favor of sweeping, fluid gestures.

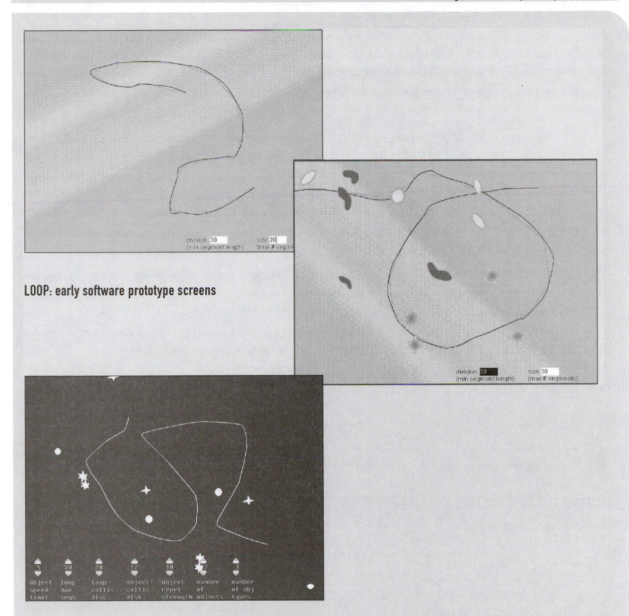

LOOP: early software prototype screens

The first prototype tested only this core interaction, allowing the player to draw lines, but nothing else. Our next step was to have the program detect a closed loop and add objects that would shrink and disappear when caught in a loop.

As you can see in the screenshots, each of these prototypes had parameters that were adjustable as the game was actually running. The length of line and detail on the curve could be tweaked, as well as the number of objects, their speed and behavior, and several other variables. As we played the game, we could try out different parameters and immediately see how they affected the experience, adjusting the rules to arrive at a different sort of play. This programming approach, building accessible game design tools into a game prototype, is a technical strategy that incorporates and facilitates iterative design.

As the butterfly content of the game emerged, so did debate about the game's overall structure and victory and loss conditions. Did the entire screen need to be cleared of butterflies or did the player just have to catch a certain number of them? Did the butterflies gradually fill up the screen or did their number remain constant? Was there some kind of time-pressure element? Were there discreet levels or did the game just go on until the loss conditions were met? These fundamental questions, which grew out of our core mechanic prototyping, were only answered by actually trying out possibilities and coming to conclusions through play.

As the game code solidified, the many adjustable parameters of the game were placed in a text file that was read into the application when it ran. These parameters controlled everything from the behavior of game creatures to points scored for different numbers of butterflies in a loop to the progression of the game's escalating difficulty. Thus the game designers could focus on refining game variables and designing levels, while the rest of the program—screen transitions and help functionality, the high score system and integration with the host site—was under construction. A sample of this game editor code follows:

```
-- LOOP SCORES
score_same=0,5,10,20,40,80,150,250,350,500,700,1000,1400,1900,2500,3100,380
0,4600,5500,7000
score_different=0,0,30,75,200,500
score_badloop=-20



-- # of caught butterflies for each level of loop sound effect
loop_sound_num=1,4,6,8,10



-- BONUSES
-- butterfly-borne bonus (x2):
```

```
bonus_lifetime=60
-- leaf-blown bonus (longer, moretime, freeze, flock):
freebonus_speedlimit=15
bonus_freeze_duration=4
bonus_flock_duration=12


-- HAZARDS
snail_speedlimit=1.2
killerbee_speedlimit=12, killerbee_attackrate=3,killerbee_stingduration=6
beetle_speedlimit=3, beetle_fighttime=4, beetle_aborttime=10,
beetle_effectradius=300
stinkbug_speedlimit=2, stinkbug_tag_radius=40,
stinkbug_effect_duration=10, stinkbug_effect_radius=300
spider_speedlimit=9, spider_climblimit=22,spider_stingduration=6,spider_loop_length=5
```

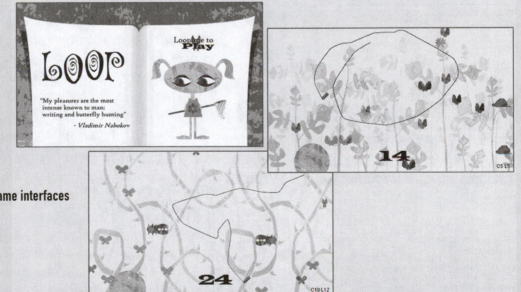

LOOP: game interfaces

LOOP followed an iterative design pattern of testing, analysis, and refinement, moving outward from the game creators to include a larger circle of players. During the development of *LOOP*, gameLab created the gameLab Rats, our official playtesting "club," to facilitate the process of testing and feedback.

The concept for *LOOP* began as the design team questioned the conventions of mouse and keyboard interaction. In the end, *LOOP* managed to achieve the fluid gameplay we had first envisioned, a fresh and original game evolving from a simple idea about a new kind of core mechanic.

LOOP was developed by Ranjit Bhatnagar, Peter Lee, Frank Lantz, Eric Zimmerman, and Michael Sweet and his team at Audiobrain.

SiSSYFiGHT 2000 game interfaces

Author Bio

Eric Zimmerman is a game designer and academic exploring the practice and theory of gaming. Eric has been making games in the game industry for ten years, and presently runs gameLab, a company he co-founded with Peter Lee. GameLab creates experimental online single-player and multiplayer games. Before gameLab, Eric collaborated with Word.com on the underground online hit, SiSSY-FiGHT 2000 (www.sissyfight.com). Other titles include the PC CD-ROM games Gearheads *(Philips Media, 1996) and* The Robot Club *(Southpeak Interactive, 1998). Eric has taught game design at MIT, NYU, Parsons School of Design, and School of Visual Arts. He is the co-author with Katie Salen of* Rules of Play *(MIT Press, 2003) and the co-editor with Amy Schoulder of* RE:PLAY *(Peter Lang Press, 2004). See also his article on iterative design on page 202.*

The first two sections of the book were designed to help you become literate in the structural elements of games and to learn the art of prototyping and playtesting your own game concepts. In this third section we will turn to focus on practical information that will help you to become a working game designer. To succeed as a game designer, you'll need to be able to work effectively on a team, communicate with diverse types of people, and understand how the structure of the game industry can affect your project.

We start out this section with a discussion of how development teams are structured in the industry. We provide insight about the types of people who work on game projects, from the executives at the publishing company, to the QA testers who assure that the game is ready to release. Then, we look the various stages of development that digital games go through—from concept to completion. This includes an explanation of how to plan a production including scheduling and budgeting and how to keep that plan on track during the course of the production.

In addition to having a clear grasp of team structure and the stages of development, you'll need to be able to produce the core deliverable of the game designer: the design document. The design document is the main mechanism through which the designer communicates her game concept to the entire team. We'll show you how to create a document that accurately reflects the gameplay you have designed, prototyped, and playtested.

The final two chapters are about the game industry and how to get a job or sell an original concept. In Chapter 15, we explain the various parties that make up the game business, the platforms and genres that drive the industry, and the nature of publishing deals. The final chapter discusses practical strategies you can follow for getting a job in the industry, or pitching your own original game ideas.

Chapter 12
Team Structures

When digital games were first commercialized in the 1970s, one person, with a decent knowledge of programming, could create the entire product. That person would act as game designer, producer, programmer, and even graphic artist and sound designer. A finished game averaged only eight kilobytes or less in size; onscreen characters were represented by jagged blocks of pixels, and sound effects consisted of generic "beeps" or "bonks" generated from the sound card. To give you a sense of the state of the art, the arcade classic, *Space Invaders* from 1978, was four kilobytes in size, including all art and sound. *Asteroids*, released in 1979, was eight kilobytes in total, and *Pac-Man*, released in 1982, was 28 kilobytes.

As PCs and game console hardware have become more powerful, the size and complexity of the games on these platforms have grown exponentially. The amount of art and audio that can be incorporated into games has surpassed and now dwarfs the computer code. Today's titles take up hundreds of megabytes of storage, with their overall production values fast approaching that of TV and movies. Elaborate visual effects, sound effects, music, voice acting and animation are all standard fare in today's games. Some, such as *CSI: Crime Scene Investigation* or *Enter the Matrix*, rely on the voices and 3D models of well-known television and film actors to give life to game characters, while others like *Medal of Honor*, set their epic cinematic game scenes with music performed by live orchestras.

Along with this rise in production values has come the need for much larger teams composed of people from many different backgrounds. From database programmers to interface designers and 3D graphic artists, game teams are becoming increasingly composed of a wide range of specialized talent. In this chapter, we'll look at the roles of each of these types of individuals, and how the game designer fits into the team structure.

TEAM STRUCTURE

The diagram in Figure 12.1 lists the basic job categories that make up most development and publishing teams in the game industry today. Note that this diagram only shows the types of individuals who are involved in the production at some level. We purposely did not include human resources,

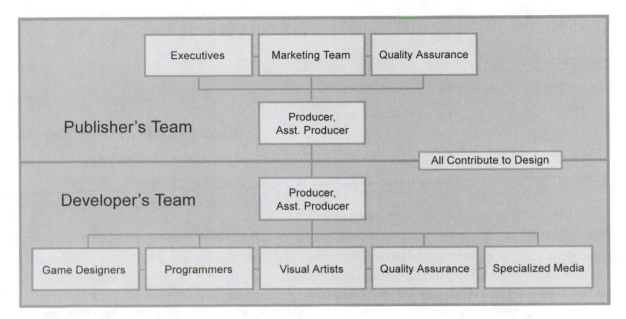

12.1 Team Structure

accounting, public relations, sales, and support, as they don't typically become involved in the actual production and are outside the scope of this discussion.

Publisher versus developer

To understand team structure, we must first examine the relationship between the publisher and the developer. As any game developer can tell you, this relationship is critical. It determines how everything else will be structured. The types of relationships vary. Sometimes the developer will do almost everything but sell and market the game. Other times, the publishers will pick up much of the development and internalize it, utilizing the developer only for specific tasks. But in most cases, the arrangement will break down according to the chart in Figure 12.2.

Typically, the publisher gives the developer an advance against royalties, and the developer uses this money to pay the team members, cover over-

head, and subcontract certain portions of the work. The developer's main task is to deliver the product, while the publisher's is to finance and distribute it.

Figure 12.3 shows examples of some typical publishers and developers in the industry today. One confusing aspect of this relationship is that many game publishers also develop games internally. Electronic Arts is one example of a publisher that develops a number of its titles in-house. Additionally, some game developers are owned by publishers. For instance, Blizzard Entertainment is wholly owned by Vivendi Universal Games.

Even in these cases, however, there's a basic publisher/developer relationship between the internal development group and the rest of the company. In many respects, in-house development teams, as they're called, are forced to act like small companies, responsible for their own cash flow, profit and loss, schedules, and staffing. This

DESIGNER PERSPECTIVE: STARR LONG

Title: Producer, NCSoft

Project list (five to eight top projects)

- *Tabula Rasa* (in production): Producer
- *Ultima Online:* Project Director
- *Bioforge:* QA Lead
- *Ultima VIII* (French): QA Lead
- *Wing Commander: Privateer:* QA
- *Wing Commander: Armada:* QA
- *Ultima Underworld 2:* QA
- *Ultima VII: Part 2: Serpent Isle:* QA

How did you get into the game industry?

I was working in theatre in Austin (I have a degree in set/lighting/sound design) and not making very much money. I needed a steadier income so I answered an ad in the local paper that said Origin was looking for playtesters. I have always loved games of all kinds and I had no idea that people actually got paid to play games. I got the job and went on to project direct *Ultima Online*, the first large-scale success in online gaming.

What are your five favorite games and why?

- *Diablo II:* I have spent more time playing *Diablo II* than any other game. The game is very simple but incredibly deep. The item and monster generation in this game are some of the best ever. Each time I play I find some new combination of weapon attributes or boss monster abilities. When combined with the multiplayer aspect there are few games that can match this one. They also have provided stellar support over many years on Battle.net. I still play to this day.
- *Grand Theft Auto: Vice City:* The immersive quality of this game has no equal. The possibilities the designers built into the game for emergent behavior are almost limitless. Being able to solve almost every single mission in a myriad of ways (drive-by shooting versus sniper, moped versus semi, etc.) was thrilling. Just driving or flying around the game was fun. To top it all off the radio station soundtrack of 1980s tunes was a stroke of genius.
- *Tony Hawk Pro Skater:* I attempted to be a skater when I was young but alas I am neither coordinated nor athletic so I was terrible. This game let me do all the tricks I could never do in real life. It also introduced me to the idea of multiple objectives within a given game context (skate parks in this game), which I have used as a model in the game I am currently working on.
- *Command & Conquer:* The first real time strategy game to truly leverage multiplayer. While the game only had a few units compared to recent titles each of those units was very differentiated so strategies from session to session could vary immensely. They also nailed the luck factor

through their "crates" so it was possible to come back and win even if you fell really far behind. To this day I have yet to see another RTS that you can come back from behind like this.

- *Ultima IV: Quest of the Avatar:* The first role-playing game where what you did in the game actually mattered. You could not just go around killing and stealing to win the game. You really had to be a good guy by following the virtues or else the game would become un-winnable. A game with a conscience if you will.

What games have inspired you the most as a designer and why?

- *DOOM:* This game was the first to really open my eyes to the possibilities of multiplayer games. For the first time I truly understood how human beings were infinitely more entertaining and unpredictable than any artificial intelligence. This game more than any other was my inspiration for *Ultima Online.*

- *Diablo: Diablo* showed me how an incredibly simple game mechanic in an RPG could be so captivating. The mechanics of starting up games with small groups and having that play space to yourself is what has inspired the focus on instantiated spaces in my current project.

- *Tony Hawk Pro Skater:* Placing multiple objectives in a single game context was brilliant. This inspired how we are building missions in my current project to encourage replay.

What are you most proud of in your career?

1.	Starting in QA

I am most proud of the fact that I worked my way up from the very bottom of the organization to leading multi-million dollar projects. The perspective I gained from having to test broken games informed every aspect of how I make games today. My QA experience inspired my mantra: "Stable, fast, and fun. In that order."

2.	Ultima Online

UO started out as the bastard child of EA/Origin. At one point they had us sitting in a hallway while they were remodeling an entire floor of the building around us. Despite the hardships I supported my team and kept us going. The result was the first large-scale success in online subscription based gaming. However what made me most proud was a letter we received from a physically challenged individual who thanked us for giving him an alternate world that he could live in where he could run.

What words of advice would you give to an aspiring designer today?

Play every game you possibly can. Then analyze them carefully. Ask yourself what you would change if you could. Figure out what feature was best executed and which one was the worst executed. Finding inspiration from outside of games is extremely important. Read books, watch movies, see plays, look at art, listen to music, watch people interact with each other—there is inspiration everywhere. We take books and mark passages for directing level design. We show each other clips from films for art direction ideas. Finally always make sure you are having fun. If you are not having fun making your game, then your customers will not have fun playing it.

Publisher	Developer
- Chooses which titles to produce - Finances titles - Provides QA testing - Markets titles - Distributes titles	- Pitches creative ideas and demos to publishers - Uses money from publishers to produce titles, including game design, programming, art, audio, etc.

12.2 Publisher/developer responsibilities

12.3 Example publishers and developers

Publishers	Developers
- Electronic Arts - Activision - Nintendo - Sony Computer Entertainment - Microsoft Games - Take Two Entertainment - Disney Interactive - Vivendi Universal Interactive - Atari - Eidos	- Blizzard Entertainment (*Warcraft, Starcraft* and *Diablo* series) - Rockstar Games (*Grand Theft Auto* series) - Ensemble Studios (*Age of Empires* series) - Westwood Studios (*Command & Conquer* series) - Naughty Dog Entertainment (*Jak and Daxter*) - Ion Storm (*Deus Ex*) - Shiny Entertainment (*Enter the Matrix, Sacrifice, Earthworm Jim*) - Bioware (*Baldur's Gate*) - Big Huge Games (*Rise of Nations*) - Firaxis Games (*Alpha Centauri*) - Gas Powered Games (*Dungeon Siege*) - Maxis (*The Sims, SimCity* series) - Epic Games (*Unreal* series) - Lionhead Studios (*Black & White*) - Digital Illusions (*Battlefield 1942*)

helps the publisher to gauge the success of each developer and analyze whether it's more cost effective to work with internal or external groups.

We'll look at the typical individuals involved in a game production from the publisher's side on page 334, but first, let's focus on the production team from the developer's perspective.

DEVELOPER'S TEAM

Game development companies often begin life as small groups of people, usually friends, who enjoy working together. Many times, especially in the beginning of a company's existence, the exact job descriptions may not be clear. "Everybody does everything" is a common comment at small, start-up game companies. But as the team grows larger, budgets grow bigger, and projects grow more and more complex, even the best of friends have to determine who is responsible for what—and when.

Most established game developers clearly delineate job descriptions for every member of their team. This doesn't mean that individuals don't work together closely—they just sometimes ignore the exact lines of their formal job descriptions. It does mean that each individual has a specific focus, however, and a set of skills that makes him the best person to be ultimately responsible for certain aspects of the project.

Let's look at each of these types of individuals closely, beginning with the game designer, since our primary goal is to understand how the game designer fits into the structure of the team, and interacts with all of these other individuals.

Game designer

As we've already discussed, the game designer is responsible for the play experience. From conception through to completion, it's the designer's job to ensure that the gameplay works at all levels. Because gameplay is so intricately linked with how that play is programmed, visualized, and supported by music, voice-over, etc., the game designer must collaborate closely with just about every other team member.

Since you've had experience designing your own games by now, you know the designer's primary responsibilities. To review, they are:

- Brainstorms concepts
- Creates prototypes
- Playtests and revises prototypes
- Writes concept and design documents and updates throughout production
- Communicates vision for the game to the team
- Creates levels for the game (or works with level designers; see page 333)
- Acts as advocate for the player

Not all companies have dedicated game designers. This role is sometimes undertaken by programmers, artists, executives, or producers. Depending on the scope of the project and the skill of the individual taking on multiple roles, this practice can sometimes have a detrimental effect on the design process.

For example, a game designer who is also the programmer of a game may not be objective about the success of a crucial feature of gameplay, simply because the feature took them several weeks, or even months, to code. If the roles are divided, the game designer can approach playtests and feedback with a more objective mindset.

This conflict of interest is true of game designers who also play the part of producers, artists, or executives. It is seen most clearly when the role of game designer is combined with that of the producer. Because the producer is ultimately responsible for the schedule and budget of the project, there is a natural conflict with their role as designer. How can a single person advocate expenditures of time and money to ensure the best gameplay possible, while on the other hand forcing himself and the team to stick to a strict bottom line?

As a solution to this problem, at some companies, like Electronic Arts Canada, the producer does act as the game designer, but many of the producer's traditional responsibilities are handled by another individual, called the development director.

In the end, exact titles aren't as important as job descriptions. What matters most is that on every game there is someone who is able to focus specifically on the workings of the game play, without the distraction of too many other responsibilities. We call this person the game designer.

To take on this responsibility, especially on games as complex as those being made today, is a full-time job, and the industry has begun to move towards a system where dedicated game designers can concentrate on the gameplay and the player experience without being burdened by budgeting, scheduling, resource allocation, and other production duties.

DESIGNER PERSPECTIVE: RICHARD HILLEMAN

Title

Father to Rachel and Christopher

Project list (five to eight top projects)

Too many to list, but…

- John Madden Football (the original)
- NHL Hockey (the original)
- *Chuck Yeager's Flight Trainer*
- *Jurassic Park II: The Lost World*
- *American McGee's Alice*
- *Racing Destruction Set*
- *Ferrari Formula One*
- *Kasparov's Gambit*
- *Tiger Woods Golf*
- *Indianapolis 500*

How did you get into the game industry?

I had a friend, David Gardner, who used to work at the computer store I haunted. He told me about going to EA and the fact that Tim Mott worked there. I knew about Tim from his Xerox Parc/Bravo days and knew it beat business applications in Fortran, which is what I was learning in school. I started out copying discs, making cables, and making Apple IIs and IBM PCs work. Then EA figured out I could do some other things.

Producer

The simplest definition of a producer for the developer's team is that she is the project leader. The producer is the person who is responsible for the delivery of the game to the publisher as promised. In order to make this delivery, the producer must create a plan for that delivery, including a schedule, budget, and resource allocation.

In most productions, there's a producer on the publisher's team as well as one on the developer team. These two, in a good working structure, serve collectively as the "single point of contact" for important decisions regarding the production that have to pass between the publisher and developer. By making this single point of contact the main conduit of information between the two

What are your five favorite games and why?

- *Chess:* Just the most perfect game ever invented, true mental warfare.
- *Hold 'em poker:* The best game of chance ever invented.
- *Quake III:* For what it became after the public got a hold of it.
- *Quake:* For the work that American and John did to redefine what a shooter could be.
- *M.U.L.E.:* The best multiplayer game for computers. As close as computers have to a classic like *Monopoly*.
- *Indianapolis 500:* The first real driving simulation that was also fun.

What games have inspired you the most as a designer and why?

- *F15 Strike Fighter:* Sid Meier shaped more of my views as a designer than anyone else.
- *TV Sports Football:* Got half of the idea right. Madden, the game series, put the rest of the game with the presentation.
- *Nintendo Golf:* This might actually be Miyamoto's greatest game. Look at how much fun it still is today on 8-bit hardware. Then, you try and make a game that is still fun after almost 20 years.
- *Pole Position:* The first great racing game.

What are you most proud of in your career?

That sports and simulations are no longer the backwaters of interactive entertainment. When I started producing and designing, *D&D* games where about half the market.

What words of advice would you give to an aspiring designer today?

Get as broad a background in the liberal arts as you can. The technology will change enormously in your lifetime, but people won't.

teams, the producers can work together to make sure both teams are acting on the same assumptions and that important decisions are communicated to the right people on each team as they are made.

In brief, the responsibilities of the producer for the developer are:

- Team leader for developer's team

- Main communication link between developer and publisher
- Responsible for schedule and budget for the production from the developer side
- Responsible for tracking and allocating resources, as well as forecasting
- Manage developer team to make sure deliverables are completed on time

- Motivate team and solve production related problems

Meeting the delivery schedule usually involves making some tough decisions during the course of the production; some of the producer's many responsibilities may include hiring or firing employees, as well as saying no to excessive resource or spending requests. But ultimately, being a producer can be an extremely rewarding role. Producers interact with the contacts on the publisher's team more than the other team members. They may also be asked to represent the team in public, at conferences or in the press. The office of the producer often serves as a "United Nations" for the production team—the place where everyone comes to air their grievances and concerns and, hopefully, to resolve them.

There may also be an executive producer on each team whose job it is to oversee multiple productions or sometimes an entire development group. Additionally, there may be assistant producers and associate producers on each team whose job it is to support the producers. Most producers start out as assistant producers and associate producers, then work their way up the ladder to producer, senior producer, and eventually executive producer.

As a game designer, you must work hand-in-hand with the producer. This means sitting down together at the start of any production and going over the design document in detail. It's your job to make certain that the producer crafts a realistic schedule and budget and the producer can't do this without a clear understanding of the game you plan to make. If you don't clearly explain the entire scope and vision of the project, the producer will wind up using canned numbers or rough estimates, and both the schedule and budget for your game will be inaccurate, potentially insufficient, and the cause of a lot of unnecessary anxiety.

This means that to be a really efficient game designer, you need to understand the ins and outs of scheduling and budgeting almost as well as the producer. You don't have to create these documents, or be responsible for tracking them, but you should review them carefully and understand each line item. Make sure they match your vision of the project and articulate any issues you see as early as possible in the process.

The producer and the game designer must work in concert; otherwise the production team will receive mixed messages. Nothing is more destructive to a team than an atmosphere in which these two critical individuals are working against each other. An understanding of the importance of each role, and a respect for the pressures and constraints placed on each individual can make for a productive and successful team environment, and provide the foundation for the production of the best game possible.

Programmers

We use the term "programmers" as a catchall to refer to everyone involved in technically implementing the game. This includes high- and low-level coders, network and systems engineers, database programmers, computer hardware support, etc. Programmers are also referred to as engineers and software developers at some companies. Advanced positions in this track are senior programmer, lead programmer, and technical director, all the way up to CTO. Some companies break down the titles according to specific areas of specialization, such as tools programmer, engine programmer, graphics programmer, database programmer, etc.

The most common way to become a game programmer is to study computer science or engineering at a four-year university. However, there are also some game programmers who come from other fields of expertise and have learned programming skills on their own. These individuals, depending on their level of skill as programmers, can make valuable additions to a team because of their knowledge in their other areas of interest.

In general the programming team's responsibilities include:

- Drafting technical specifications
- Technical implementation of the game including:
  ◊ Software prototypes
  ◊ Software tools
  ◊ Game modules and engines
  ◊ Structuring data
  ◊ Managing communications
- Documenting code
- Coordinating with QA engineers to fix or resolve bugs

As a game designer, if you don't have a technical background, you may find it difficult to communicate your ideas to the programming team. While you don't need to become a programmer, if you're going to design digital games, you do have to learn the basic concepts of programming in order to have a common language with which to speak to the engineers. There is no right way to do this. If you learn best by reading, then buy a book on programming for beginners. If you need a structured environment in which to learn, then take a class. If you have a good relationship with a programmer, then ask him questions about his work. Everyone likes to talk about things they are good at. If you express genuine interest, most programmers will talk your ear off about how games are programmed.

Once you have a strong understanding of how games are implemented technically, you can use this knowledge to write better design specifications, and to describe your game concepts more clearly to the technical team. This, in turn, will make programmers more open and accessible to talk to about tweaks and changes to the gameplay as they are required.

Throughout the production cycle, you'll find that almost every change you need to make to the gameplay requires alterations in the code. If you've designed your game modularly, as we discussed in Chapter 9 on page 253, this won't mean drastic repercussions to the entire system, but it will still mean additional work for the programming team. To achieve the kind of relationship with the programming team that will allow you to suggest these changes without uproar, you'll need to use all your communication skills and your knowledge of programming.

Whether your team is large or small, there is likely a hierarchy you'll need to respect to get things done. No matter how much you'd like to circumvent the technical director, for example, and go straight to the database engineer to ask for a quick change, try to avoid such an action. This undercuts the technical director's authority, and there's no better way to create an adversary out of this person.

You need to partner with the technical director, lead programmer, or whoever is in charge of your programming team. It is this person's job to communicate your ideas to the other team members, and you want to establish a relationship where they will respect your ideas in the same way that you respect their expertise and contribution.

In general, you should try to avoid making huge changes to the gameplay once the production begins in earnest—and if you've done prototyping and playtesting work up front, you won't need to. Most people, programmers included, don't like to see weeks of work changed on a whim or because you didn't do your homework. Try to avoid situations where it seems like you're making the programmers' work harder. If they view every change you make to the game as "extra" work, then you've got a problem.

One way to do this is to make sure that time for "playtesting tweaks" are built into the initial schedule. In addition to this, you should try to invest the programmers in the playtesting process so that they understand why each change is necessary. Bring them into the playtesting sessions. Or if that isn't feasible, share with them the results of sessions via video or detailed reports and playtester quotes. Let them draw their own conclusions. If they realize that players are not responding as anticipated to a game feature they've been working on for weeks, they'll be the first ones to try and salvage it, rather than see it cut later on.

The goal is to have your programming team become active participants in the iterative improvement of the game. Soon, they'll be asking you when the next playtest session is—looking for validation of the work they've been doing. And you'll have a solid partnership with one of the most important groups who will work on your game.

Visual artists

As with the term "programmers," we use the term "visual artist" as a catchall to refer to those team members who are tasked with designing all of the visual aspects of the game. This includes the char-

acter designers, illustrators, animators, interface designers, and 3D artists. Advanced positions in this track include art director, senior art director, and lead animator. In some companies there are even positions like creative director and chief creative officer, whose responsibilities include making sure there's a consistent look and feel across a company's entire product line.

Visual artists come from many different backgrounds. The best artists may or may not have a degree in the field. Some artists have always worked on computers, others may have come to computers after gaining a background in traditional tools. Before hiring your artists, you need to think about what skills your team will need. Will the game require predominantly 3D art? Will you need someone who can animate? Does your interface need to appeal to a specific market segment?

As you look at various portfolios, you'll find that some artists are brilliant at creating intricate cityscapes and imagining 3D worlds, but when it comes to animating a character, they simply can't do it. For this reason, teams tend to be structured around the key tasks required in the production, and artists will be hired for specialized tasks like 3D modeling, animation, texture mapping, interface design, etc.

Overall, the responsibilities of the visual artists are to design and produce all visuals for the game including:

- Characters
- Worlds and world objects
- Interfaces
- Animations
- Cut-scenes

Game designers and artists can also have trouble communicating even if there is no technical barrier of understanding, as with the programming team. It is the job of the artists to make the game as visually appealing as possible. Sometimes, the needs of the game design can get in the way of a beautiful screen. You may find yourself in a situation where the wireframes you created, showing each important feature and detail of the design, have been only loosely followed. Artists may take it upon themselves to "condense" features in order to make the layout look better.

In a situation like this, your first reaction might be to insist that your designs be followed to the letter. This is one way to get things done. Another way might be to evaluate the work of the artists more objectively—after all, if they thought your design was convoluted, perhaps players will as well. You may be able to compromise and find that your designs become better and more intuitive as they are re-thought by someone with a skilled artistic eye. Of course, you need to make sure that features are not hidden or lost for the sake of beautiful artwork. Remember, it's your job to think about how a player will respond to these screens. They won't care about the beauty if they can't find the feature they need to continue on in the game.

Another issue that may come up between artists and game designers is in the overall style of the game. As you work with different artists, you'll find that each one has their own unique style and techniques. While most artists are trained to work outside their personal style, they will always respond more enthusiastically to a project that mirrors their own interests more closely. To use an analogy, if you were starting a rock-and-roll band, you might think twice about hiring a percussionist from a philharmonic orchestra to play drums for you. In the same way, try to assemble an art team that is passionate about the look and feel you are striving for.

It may not be possible to choose the specific artists who will work on your project. If you are at a larger company, you may be simply assigned a team of artists. In this case, you'll have to make a decision: either change your vision to utilize the skills of the people you have, or find a way to communicate your ideas clearly enough so that the team can implement them.

Artists are visual people and a great way to communicate with them is through visual reference material. Most art departments have a great deal of reference material—other games, magazines, art books, etc. For example, game artist Steve Theodore uses video to capture reference, as well as textbooks on human and animal motion to create visuals.[1] If need be, bring in your own reference material to get the conversation going. When Tracy and Chris, two of the authors of this book, were working on a game for Microsoft that had a retro space age style, the art team collected samples of brightly designed 1950s fabrics from flea markets, and scanned their patterns and colors in order to create the visual palette for the game.

As with the programming team, you'll get the best results if you partner with the lead artist or art director in the process of design. Explain your vision, but listen to their responses. Chances are, your artists have seen and studied far more visual references than you have and they may have some fantastic ideas that take your initial concepts much further than you could have yourself. Look at these references together, and be specific about what you like and don't like about them.

Once you've decided on an approach, the artists will begin creating concept art and you will

---

1. Steve Theodore, "Artist's View: And a Partridge in a Poly Tree," *Game Developer*, November 2003.

need to start giving criticism. Keep in mind that the purpose of criticism is to move the project forward. Even if a sketch or design is not exactly what you want, there may still be some elements in it that are useful. Search for those elements before you start speaking. Try to see what the artist was going for. And when you do start speaking, it's always nice to begin on a positive note: "This is beautiful. Really nice. I like this area right here. In fact, if we could expand on what you're doing there…"

Giving and taking feedback is probably one of the hardest things to do in life. As you saw when players were critiquing your gameplay, it is often a complete surprise to find that people don't respond to a part of the design that is very close to your heart. Your most important ally in the process of giving feedback to the artists is the art director. You must work together with this individual to set the tone of the project. Listen carefully to your art director and try to come up with solutions that appeal to both of you. Remember, there's more than one answer to each design problem, and by creating an open dialogue, you may find another approach that neither of you has considered.

Ultimately, unless you have the skills to create the art yourself, you need to allow the artists some freedom to move beyond your initial concepts and bring their own ideas and passion to the project. If you've created a good working relationship with the art director, chances are you will feel a strong sense of authorship in the final artwork, even if it's not what you initially imagined, just as the rest of the team will feel that they have contributed to the overall game design.

QA engineers

QA (quality assurance) engineers are also referred to as testers or bug testers. Many game professionals start their careers as QA engineers, and then move to other tracks such as producer, programmer, or designer. Advanced positions on this track are QA lead and QA manager. As is noted on the team structure diagram, there are QA engineers on both the publisher side and the developer side. Publishers typically QA projects themselves before they accept delivery of the code.

The responsibilities of the QA team are:

- Create a test plan for the project based on the design and technical specifications
- Execute the test plan
- Record all unexpected or undesirable behavior
- Categorize, prioritize, and report all issues found during testing
- Re-test and resolve issues once they have been fixed

As the designer, you should take it upon yourself to make sure the QA staff has everything they need to create a comprehensive test plan. Don't assume that they have a complete understanding of the game just because you've distributed a design document. Offer any assistance they may need to create the best test plan possible. But don't be surprised if they want to experience the game first without your input—as with playtesters, it's often best if QA testers have some objectivity about the game when they begin the testing process.

QA testers can be the designer's best friends. Other than your playtesters, they are the last line of defense you have before your game ships out to the masses. Don't be upset if some of your design features come back listed as "bugs." This isn't a criticism of your design—this is QA's way of helping you make sure your design is working properly. Their job is to make sure your game is functioning both technically and aesthetically. If you get a bug back that says the font you've chosen for the character screen is illegible under certain circumstances, don't bristle defensively. Be grateful that you have the chance to fix it before the game goes to the players.

It may help for you to sit down with the QA team and observe their process. You can learn a lot by consulting with your QA engineers and going through the game element by element. Because they are seasoned testers, they may be able to provide you with insights no one else can.

Another consideration is to let your QA manager review your wireframes early in the process. They may find problems with your design before you even start to implement it. Starting the QA process early and making the QA team part of the design process will mean they are more invested in your game. This means that in crunch time, they will make your game a priority and put in the extra hours it takes to find every last glitch.

Specialized media

As we've seen, games have grown to include many specialized types of media—too many to address each possible role on all game productions. Your game may require the skills of writers, sound designers, musicians, or even motion capture operators, karate instructors, and dialogue coaches. We include these in a group as "specialized media" because they are too many to list. These types of individuals are usually hired for a short period of time on a contract basis, rather than coming on as full-time employees.

One of the most important things that you can do as a designer is to define what you need from these professionals as clearly as possible before they start working. When people are hired as contractors, they are often charged by the hour. If you bring in contractors and waste time trying to figure out what to do with them, you can wind up wasting a lot of money that would be better spent elsewhere in the production.

Some of the most typical contractors that you will work with include writers and sound designers. In the case of a writer, the responsibilities can range from creating bits of dialogue where needed to scripting the entire story. How much writing you will need depends on what skills you have as a designer. If your strength is writing, you may not need a writer at all. If you are not a strong writer, you may bring a writer in very early and work with them throughout production.

In the case of a sound designer, the task might be limited to creating special effects and music for the game once it is almost completed. Or, if you are striving for a more integrated sound design, it may encompass laying out a plan for the entire audio design for the project up front and working with you to make sure the audio supports the gameplay effectively. Sound and music affect players at a very emotional level; if you involve a sound designer more deeply in the project, you may be surprised at the improvement it can make to the player experience.

As productions continue to grow more complex, they'll invariably require more media professionals in a diverse range of fields. There's a lot of talk about bringing in Hollywood talent to make games more like movies. This means that everyone from gaffers to makeup artists may soon be involved in creating games.

As the designer, you'll have to interact with many of these media professionals and give them direction and support. As you deal with people who may not work exclusively on games, it's

DESIGNER PERSPECTIVE: MATT FIROR

Dark Age of Camelot

Title

Executive Producer, Mythic Entertainment

Project list (five to eight top projects)

- *Dark Age of Camelot* (and expansions)
- *Silent Death Online*
- *Rolemaster: Magestorm*
- *Starship Troopers: Battlespace*
- *Aliens Online*
- *Godzilla Online*
- *Spellbinder: The Nexus Conflict*

How did you get into the game industry?

I was a big fan of dial-up BBS multiplayer role-playing games in the 1980s, and a few friends and I decided to make our own game. We worked nights and weekends over the course of about four years on the project. The game, *Tempest*, came out in 1992 and was a fantasy role-playing game that allowed up to sixteen players to play simultaneously on dial-up modems in the Washington, D.C. area. This was strictly a hobby, though—it was for fun, and we all had day jobs. Eventually our lawyer hooked us up with another company, we merged, got some contracts, and I started full time in the industry in January 1996.

important to communicate with them in terms they are familiar with. Many of these media professionals will not be hardcore gamers, and they may get lost if you use shorthand or game jargon. To bring out the best of their talents, you'll have to learn as much as you can about their specialty, and act as their guide when it comes to game production.

Because the games industry is still relatively young, there's a lot to be learned from other media. For instance, you may find that many of the processes employed in filmmaking can help you in your game production. In the same way, when you're choosing media professionals to collaborate with, you should pick ones that are open minded and who want to learn about the games

What are your five favorite games and why?

In no special order:

- *Fallout:* It had the best story and immersion of any game I've played.
- *Half-Life:* The best shooter of all time, with a great story.
- *Wizardry:* My favorite fantasy single-player RPG, the one that got me hooked.
- *EverQuest:* Proved that online role-playing games were just as good (if not more so) than single-player games.
- *Dark Age of Camelot:* Of course! Seriously, it was the first online RPG that successfully let players fight one another in an organized fashion.

What games have inspired you the most as a designer and why?

I think it's safe to say that every game I play, to a certain extent, gives me design ideas. *Half-Life* and *Fallout*, though, really inspired me, because they showed that a game can be deceptively simple to play, yet enormously fun and compelling.

What are you most proud of in your career?

Being the producer/designer of one of the most successful online games to date.

What words of advice would you give to an aspiring designer today?

Don't be afraid to do whatever it takes to get into the industry. If you have to start as an artist, QA tester, programmer, whatever—just do it. Once you're in the door, it's a lot easier to get your voice heard. And be patient. People won't respect your ideas until they know that you are competent and level. This takes time.

business. These individuals can grow with you and become lifelong resources.

Level designer

Games that are organized into levels will need someone to actually design and implement each level. If your project is very small, you may design all the levels yourself. On a larger project, however, the game designer often leads a team of level designers who implement their concepts for the various game levels and sometimes come up with ideas for levels themselves.

Level designers use a toolkit or "level editor" to develop new missions, scenarios, or quests for the player. They lay out the components that appear on the level or map and work closely with the game designer to make these fit into the overall theme of the game.

Responsibilities of level designers include:

- Implementing level designs
- Coming up with level concepts
- Testing levels and working with designer to improve overall gameplay

Level design is an art, and it's a great way to enter the industry. Good level designers often go on to become game designers—an example is American McGee, who won notoriety for several of the levels he designed while working at id Software. Other level designers may move on to become producers.

As a game designer, you'll want to develop a close working relationship with your level designers. Levels are the structure within which the players will experience the gameplay you've designed. They may include story or character elements that are crucial to the development of the game. Because levels are so critical, sometimes game designers can become somewhat controlling of how they are implemented.

As with artists however, you can usually achieve better results by fostering creativity in your level designers rather than making them tow a strict line. If you've created an amazing system of gameplay, it will inspire your designers to come up with combinations and situations that you may not have even thought of in your initial pass at the game levels. Try not to micromanage your level design team, and you will find that they will work harder and come up with better results than if they had implemented your designs to the letter.

The fact is that you're the designer of the game, and their hard work and innovations will only make you look better. So tuck any insecurity away and treat your level designers as partners with which to experiment and take the game to places that even you did not think possible.

Exercise 12.1: Recruit a Team

Now that you know a little bit about the roles of team members in a game production, think about enlisting some friends or recruiting some talent to work on the original game idea you have prototyped in Part II. Decide which of these positions you can't fill yourself and go out and try and fill them. Post notices on local bulletin boards or web sites—you are sure to get a response, because many people out there are eager to work on game projects.

PUBLISHER'S TEAM

Publishing companies are often huge corporations, with offices in many cities and sometimes countries. They employ thousands of people who you may never meet, but who may work indirectly or directly on your game in the process of getting it to the shelves. Here, we have focused on those you are most likely to interact with while working on your game.

Producer

As with the producer on the developer's team, the producer for the publisher is also a project leader. Unlike the producer on the development team, however, the producer for the publisher will spend less time interacting with the production team, and more time marshalling the forces of the marketing team, and making sure that the executives at the company continue to stay behind the game concept throughout development.

The responsibilities of the producer for publisher are:

- Team leader for publisher's team
- Main communication link between publisher and developer
- Responsible for schedule and budget for the production from the publisher's side
- Responsible for tracking and allocating resources, as well as forecasting
- Approve work accomplished by developer so milestone payments can be made
- Coordinate with internal executive management, marketing, and QA personnel

The producer for the publisher is one step removed from the actual production, although they are usually more involved than any other person from the publisher's team. This position means that they have a vested interest in the success of the game when it goes to market, but they are also somewhat removed from the day to day struggle of production and sometimes able to see the game and its potential more objectively than the game designer and the rest of the production team.

There is a sense in many creative industries—the game industry is no exception—that executives and producers who are removed from the process don't understand the plight of creative teams. The suggestions and direction of these people are often met with resistance and scorn. While it is true that no one understands your game design the way that you do, it is also true that these individuals are skilled at publishing and marketing successful games and they may have some good points to make if you remain open to their feedback.

No one gets into the game industry because they want to make bad games. The producer and executives on the publisher's team are no exception. They want to make great games, games that they feel a sense of authorship in just like everyone else on the team. And if you can find ways to incorporate their suggestions into your game in ways that improve the gameplay, rather than dragging your heels, you will find when it comes time to sell the game that the publisher is behind it all the way.

Marketing team

The goal of the marketing team is to find ways to sell your game to the buyers. In some cases, they may have direct involvement during the production process—giving feedback on game concepts, and holding focus groups for various character designs. In other cases, you may never meet them until the game is almost ready to ship. The marketing team can be an asset to the open-minded game designer. This is because they are the strongest link to the demands and desires of buyers. It's their job to know the market, and if you can interpret the data they have creatively, you can address the trends and features that people are interested in without sacrificing your core gameplay.

One important factor that the marketing team has a strong influence on is the target hardware platform for PC titles. Marketing professionals study things like the projected penetration of different processors, available RAM on consumer PCs, average screen sizes, etc. In other words, a marketer in 2004 can estimate how many potential buyers will have a 3GHz computer in 2006, and they set the target hardware specs for games scheduled to be released in 2006 accordingly.

If it is important to you as a designer to have a best-selling product, it's smart to bring the marketing team in early. Tap them for information, invest them in the project, and give them credit for their insight. Sometimes having a clear concept of what those key bullet-point features will be on your box can help you stay on track with your designs when ideas are flying in from all directions. The marketing team can help you with this, and you'll have a powerful ally when it comes to publicizing your game or getting a new project off the ground. Nothing speaks louder than sales, and the marketers often represent the voice of the buyers.

Exercise 12.2: Marketing

Design the box for your original game idea. Come up with a slogan or tag line that will capture buyer interest. Write "call outs" for the top three or four features in your game. Really try to "sell" your game through your box design. Think about what aspects of the game will illustrate these points. Will your box show screenshots, character designs, or original artwork?

Show your box design to some of your playtesters and do an informal focus group on your design. This process will help you develop a good sales pitch for your idea—which we address in Chapter 16.

Executives

Executive management can include the CEO, President, CFO, COO, assorted VPs, and directors of the publishing company. It's beyond the scope of this discussion to detail all the responsibilities of all these individuals. Suffice to say that it's the job of the executive management to run the publishing company. This means providing leadership and direction, overseeing every department, and ultimately publishing great games.

Of course, there may be upper management on the game developer's team as well, if the company is large enough. In many cases, executives at game development companies are the founders of the company, or have risen up from the core design team to take on more responsibility.

At publishing companies, people in upper management can come from all types of backgrounds. Some may have business or marketing degrees, or experience in other industries. Others may have extensive experience in game production, but otherwise no business background. The nature of the game industry is that it grew out of a hobbyist culture, so there are many people who are very skilled in the development and publishing of games, though their academic credentials wouldn't tell you so.

The best-case scenario for a game designer is when an executive has considerable experience with game development, a deep understanding of the market, and are willing to take a hands-on approach. Unfortunately, most game designers don't see it this way. As a rule, designers tend to resent upper management's involvement in the production process. They want management to put out the money for the game, and then leave them alone to create their masterpiece.

As we said before, no one wants to make bad games, executives included. You might want to take the time to find out what games or products the executive you're dealing with has worked on, and what their expertise was before they moved up the ladder, before disregarding their input or pushing back on their suggestions.

If you do this, and still find that you just can't get along with an executive, try to learn from their mistakes. What are they doing that you don't like? Is it the way they present their ideas, or the ideas themselves? Is it their attitude, or the content of their suggestions? Use this interaction as an opportunity to improve your own management skills. Write down what it is that they're doing that's ineffective, annoying or counterproductive, then make sure that you're not doing the same thing when it comes to your own team.

If all else fails, at a certain point, you may find that the decisions coming down to you from the executives are "ruining" the game. You may be fed up and ready to walk. But before you blow a gasket, consider this: its part of your job to communicate the vision for the game to the upper management, and you may be partly to blame if they're on the wrong track. Design specs are long and tedious documents, and they may not have read yours. Development code is clunky and unstable, and they may not have had time to install and play with your latest build. All in all, they may not have a clear idea of the finished product from either of these sources.

Take a step back from the situation and try to educate them. Perhaps you can have a brainstorm on the area under question with the entire team, and invite the executives to participate. This will allow them to give advice in an open forum, and to see some of the issues you are up against in implementing their suggestions.

In most cases, everyone will walk away from such a discussion feeling that their ideas have been taken seriously, and they will be invested in the decisions that were made. No one wants to be told what to do—not you, and not the executive team. Everyone wants his or her opinion to be heard and respected. An open discussion for the purpose of solving design issues accomplishes both of these objectives. In the end, you may wind up having to make the changes anyway, but perhaps you will have formed a new channel of communication for the next project.

QA

The QA team for the publisher's team functions in much the same manner as that of the developers' team. The two exceptions are that they probably aren't as familiar with the game, since they don't work side by side with the production team, and that their overall goal is to determine whether or not to "accept" the build as a deliverable. This acceptance generally triggers a payment to the developer, so it's important that the build passes muster with the publisher's QA team.

Usability specialists

Some game companies use the services of usability specialists as part of the development process. As we discussed in Chapter 10, usability specialists can be an important part of making sure your game is intuitive and accessible to your target market. They evaluate a user's abilities to perform important tasks in the game, and understand key concepts. Usability testing generally focuses on the interface and controls, rather than the core gameplay, which distinguishes it from playtesting.

Usability specialists are almost always third-party companies that are hired by the publisher or the developer for a specific series of tests at a point fairly late in the development cycle. Some larger publishers, however, such as Microsoft Game Studios, have recently established in-house usability labs, and are beginning to integrate usability into the development process from start to finish.

This is the ideal situation if it is available to you. Usability testing can make an incredible difference in the player experience of your game. Like playtesting, it brings the player to the forefront of your design process and allows you to respond to their input before your game ships and it's too late to make changes.

Responsibilities of the usability specialists are:

- Heuristic evaluation of interfaces (this is an application of general interface principles and reporting of potential issues)
- Creation of user scenarios
- Identify and recruit test subjects from target market
- Conduct usability sessions
- Record and analyze data from sessions (this may be visual, in the form of video and audio, or quantitative, in the form of task success/failure reporting or questionnaire data.)
- Report findings and recommendations

A common mistake game designers make is to push off usability testing until the end of development. Some designers associate it with focus testing and marketing. In general, usability testing has not been as widely accepted in the game industry as it has been in the rest of the software industry. For many game designers, there is a resistance to "outside" input on the game that makes them fear and dislike the testing process.

Unfortunately, these designers are missing out on a great opportunity to improve their game and learn more about how players interact with games. Every usability session can teach a designer something new about the craft of game design. And interacting with usability engineers can also teach designers how to break down issues with play, navigation, control, etc., to test these issues and solve them.

It seems obvious that learning how to solve issues with gameplay will make you a better designer. A smart and successful game designer will not only bring usability engineers into the process as early as possible, but try to learn as much as possible from them during their work on the project.

Exercise 12.3: Usability Experience

Contact a third-party usability lab and find out if you can either watch one of their test sessions or participate as a user. What types of tasks were you or the subjects asked to complete? Were you able to use the software being tested successfully? Why or why not? How do you think the input from the usability tests helped the designer of the software that was tested?

TEAM PROFILE

As we touched on at the top of this chapter, the number of people involved in a typical game production has grown steadily since the beginnings of the industry. Additionally, both budgets and timelines for production have increased. Because of this, the expectations for sales of each game have grown higher as well.

For a major publisher like Electronic Arts to justify producing a game title today, they have to project that it will sell at least one million units. This means that they are only interested in producing games that have the potential to be blockbusters.

Figures 12.4 and 12.5 show the evolution of team size and development time for an A-list title on each of the major console systems. A-list PC games have experienced a similar growth in team size and development time. These estimates were provided by Steve Ackrich, Vice President of Product Development at Atari, based on his eighteen years in the game industry. Ackrich has extensive experience producing console games,

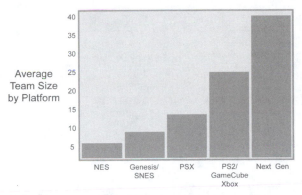

12.4   Average console development team size

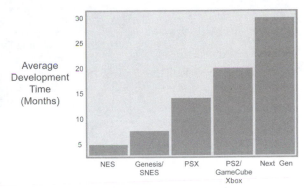

12.5   Average console development time

managing internal and external developers, and overseeing product acquisitions among other responsibilities. He's worked for many publishers and developers including Sega of America, Activision, and Accolade.

You may be wondering how many people from each job category work on a typical title. Ackrich shared the estimates in Figure 12.6 with us. As you can see, not only have team sizes grown over time, but specialization in areas like

programming and art have created new categories of employment.

As teams have grown and production schedules have lengthened, the stress on the team, professionally and personally, has grown as well. The following sections are designed to help you understand what factors can make a team come together, how to build a team, and how to keep that team communicating during the entire production.

ALL CONTRIBUTE TO THE DESIGN

Notice the phrase "all contribute to design" on the team structure diagram in Figure 12.1 on page 319. This does not mean that everyone will literally participate in the design process, but it does mean that in a well-run project, each and every member of the team is able to contribute their special talents to the articulation and execution of the design at whatever level they may be involved.

In some cases, this may just mean that every suggestion is always received with respect and consideration. In other cases, it may mean that the designer actively solicits input from the team when making decisions about the design. Every

designer and every team will have their own process. But the end result should be that everyone who works on the game should have a sense of authorship the final product, and be able to say with pride about some aspect of the experience, "I worked on that."

As the designer, and also as a producer, fostering this sense of authorship is a vital part of the job. You should take the time to establish good channels of communication with each of the team members we've discussed in this chapter and to structure your interaction with the team so that everyone's input is heard. There's no single way to

12.6 Team profile by platform

NES	Playstation

- 1 Producer/Game Designer
- 2 Programmers
- 3 Artists
	- 1 Lead Game Designer
	   - 2 Level Designers
	- 1 Producer
	   - 1 Associate Producer
	- 1 Lead Programmer
	   - 3 Programmers
	- 1 Lead Artist
	   - 4 Artists

Genesis/SNES	
- 1 Game Designer - 1 Producer - 3 Programmers - 4 Artists	
PS2/GameCube/Xbox	**Next Generation**

- 1 Lead Game Designer
   - 4 Level Designers
- 1 Producer
   - 1 Associate Producer
- 1 Lead Programmer
   - 2 Engine Programmers
   - 4 Game Programmers
- 1 Lead Artist
   - 10 Artists
	- 1 Director of Game Design
	   - 2 Game Designers
	   - 4 Level Designers
	- 1 Executive Producer
	   - 2 Producers
	   - 1 Associate Producer
	- 1 Lead Programmer (Engine)
	   - 3 Programmers
	- 1 Lead Programmer (Game)
	   - 6 Programmers
	- 1 Art Director
	   - 3 Lead Artists
	   - 14 Artists

orchestrate something like this, but there are some tips we can give you that will help.

- Set up weekly "leads meetings," where the heads of each group gather to discuss the current status of project.

- Start a suggestion box—old fashioned but it works.

- Take time for one-on-one creative talks with key members of the team.

- Have open brainstorming sessions during the design phase for anyone who wants to attend—this includes everyone from the production assistants to the QA team. Shutting people out of the design process fosters cliquishness and might deprive you of hearing some great ideas.

- If you get stuck on a design issue, ask your coworkers to help solve it. Make the process fun, like a puzzle or a challenge.

- Ask members of your group if they have hobbies, talents or knowledge that may aid in the production.

- Share authorship. When you speak, make sure to use "we" not "I." This is a subtle but effective way to let everyone share in the ownership of the ideas.

TEAM BUILDING

In addition to having a great idea, the next most critical thing you can do to make sure your produce a great game is to build a team that can bring that idea to life. This doesn't just mean that hiring a group of talented people, throwing them together, and expecting miracles. The structure you define for your team and the working environment you create will determine their ability to succeed.

Talent is always a key ingredient to team building, and of course, you want the most talented individuals you can find. Microsoft is an example of a company with a corporate philosophy of hiring the smartest, most talented individuals available. But talent only goes so far. Finding the right mix of talent and personality is even more crucial. Some people are brilliant at what they do individually, but, when put on a team, they are unable to interact productively with their teammates and cause more trouble than their contribution is worth.

When assembling your team, you have to look at each person as an individual, and as a potential team member. Examine their track record and make sure to talk with people who have worked with them before. Ask about both their individual performance and how they interact in a team.

Here are some qualities you might look for when bringing on new team members:

- *Attitude:* Positive people with an optimistic outlook are by far the best teammates.
- *Experience:* Unless you are hiring for a low-level position, make sure the person has the right experience for the job. Game production is a pressure cooker environment, and the worst thing you can do is put someone who's unprepared on your team. It will be bad for you and worse for them.

- *Friends:* Though conventional wisdom tells us not to mix business with pleasure, there's no substitute for bringing onboard people that you know and trust. If your friend is the best person for the job, then by all means get them on the team. Conversely, don't hire a friend if they are not the best person for the job—this can cause incredible stress on the team and in your relationship.
- *References:* You can't always hire someone you know, so when checking references make certain to talk to former employers. Friends, coworkers, and relatives will always say nice things, but employers will often be more honest. Insist on these reference checks, and try to make it a phone call, rather than taking a written recommendation.
- *Diversity:* Seek out diversity. Combining people with different backgrounds and skills on your team can create a rich and creative environment.
- *Track Record:* Look for people with a history of success. Small personal successes can count as much as large corporate ones. Try to bring on people who have set goals for themselves and achieved those goals.
- *Maturity:* There's no substitute for someone who is mature and well-balanced. You want stable people who are in control of their emotions.
- *Excellence:* People who strive for excellence are worth their weight in gold. Look at their history. Did they do well in school? Have they proven that they can deliver under pressure? What is their approach to problem solving?

- *Creativity:* Bring onboard people who think creatively. Do they ask good questions? Are they curious about the business? What ideas do they have?

Team Communication

Notice on the team structure diagram that in addition to the vertical lines of hierarchy, there are also horizontal lines of communication connecting the different groups. This is to illustrate that all of the groups interact with each other laterally, as well as reporting to the producer. This doesn't mean that the production has no hierarchy; it is the job of the producer and the leads from each department to make decisions about the big picture vision for the project and the day-to-day tasks each group should be working on.

There is also one communication line on the diagram between the producer's lines for the developer and the publisher. This line is important because it signifies that one person from each team is responsible for communications between these two groups. Veteran developers know that it's important to have a single person on the publisher side that's empowered to approve their work and authorize payments. It would be problematic if team members from each side were making decisions without having the producers involved to maintain consistency.

Imagine if someone from marketing on the publisher's team requested creative changes directly from the art director without involving the producer. An art change may cause a ripple effect in the animation production or programming, or it might mean that the QA engineers will have to re-test an area of the code. The schedule might have to shift because of this request, which could wind up costing the developer not only time, but money. If this happens enough times, the developer may find themselves out of business—simply because the team was trying to be responsive to the publisher's requests. What happened? There was a breakdown in communication that could have been avoided if proper channels were respected.

The same goes for communication within the development team. As we mentioned, if you need to work with the database programmer, or make changes to part of the interface, go to the technical director or the art director to make your request, not to the person directly responsible for that change.

The following simple courtesies can help maintain respect and communication within your team and avoid numerous misunderstandings:

- Respect the chain of command.
- Understand the resource needs, time requirements, and cost implications for requests that you make.
- Be open to the requests of others.
- Communicate decisions and changes to the design both up and down the ladder.
- Don't engage in turf warfare or cliquishness.

Conducting meetings

Meetings are the best way of getting your team members to communicate. But conducting effective meetings is not as simple as gathering your coworkers together in a conference room and beginning a conversation. You need to structure the meeting so that it produces the desired results.

If you are calling the meeting, you will need to set the agenda. The best meetings are ones for which there is a definite goal, everyone knows the goal ahead of time so that they can come prepared, and by the resolution of the meeting the goal has been accomplished. If you don't have a clear agenda in mind, you are likely to waste everyone's time and accomplish very little in your meeting.

If you are asked to participate in a meeting, you will need to come prepared. Find out the agenda and goal and make sure you have all the material you will need in order to contribute. This may mean doing some research for a brainstorming meeting, or evaluating your workload for a status meeting. If you don't come prepared to a meeting, you will also be wasting other team members' time and have very little to contribute.

At the meeting, the person who called it will most likely function as the discussion leader. This person may designate other individuals to run certain parts of the meeting, but it's still up to the discussion leader to keep the meeting on track and moving toward the goal.

As in our rules for brainstorming, many of the rules of meetings involve personal and social skills. No one should be left out of the conversation intentionally, and those who speak should be able to do so without being criticized. No personal attacks should be permitted. If anyone makes a personal remark, they should be warned, and if it continues, they should be asked to leave the meeting. Make it clear that differences of opinion are helpful in sorting out the problem, and allow people to approach the same topic from multiple angles.

As the meeting draws to a close, you should make sure to review the decisions that have been made and any action items that have been assigned to the team. If the discussion requires a follow-up meeting, determine when it will be and make sure that everyone will have time to prepare for that follow-up. And last, if you have called the meeting, you should always send out notes and reminders of the decisions and assignments to the participants and to any key team members who were unable to attend.

Games and teamplay

Another great way to get your team to communicate is by playing games together. Everyone on your team probably loves games if they are in this business, so why not use that common interest as a way to forge stronger relationships between the various groups.

When choosing a game, try to pick one where players have the opportunity to work cooperatively or to express themselves. Multiplayer online games, boardgames, or sports work great for this. Games you make yourselves or games that are personalized for your team can also be a great way to get people talking. Whether it is a company softball league or weekly poker game, playing together can work wonders in building morale, enhancing communication, and fostering a feeling of connectedness.

Don't limit yourself to one type of game; try new games each week. Having a designated game night is a great way of bonding. Each week a different team member can bring in a favorite game, or a new game they are dying to try. In this way, your team will learn more about each other and have the chance to play games they otherwise might have missed.

THE RIGHT ENVIRONMENT

A great team doesn't materialize in the first week of a project. It takes time and the right environment to grow. The following reminders can help you to establish a great working environment from the beginning and make sure that your team has the potential to come together as the project moves forward.

Everyone belongs

Make sure that everyone feels as if they're part of the team. Many times cliques form and no one realizes it. This is especially apparent to new employees, who often feel left out. Do your best to avoid excluding anyone.

Fairness

Just like parents, managers shouldn't have favorites. Showing favoritism demoralizes and excludes those who are on the outside. When dealing with employees, try to treat them all according to the same set of rules. This builds trust and respect in the workplace.

Cooperation

Emphasize hard work and cooperation. Try to build a culture where everyone is committed to working together to produce the best game possible.

Goals

Achieving a goal gives us a sense of completion that can re-invigorate us for the next leg of the race. But often the big goals—the major milestones of a production are months apart and filled with stressful moments. Don't hang the morale of the team on these major milestones, instead, set mini, internal deliverables along the way. Publicize the completion of these mini-deliverables within the team to boost confidence and re-energize the team.

Results

Define success. Point out what success and failure mean in terms of the business and its customers. Provide a mechanism for monitoring results, and make sure each employee knows exactly how they fit into the overall success of the company.

Eliminate fiefdoms

Try to break down the walls between groups. Make each group see itself as part of greater whole. Structure rewards and recognition around company-wide objectives, not group politics. Emphasize the big picture and the vision, so that everyone feels like part of the larger organization.

Tracking

Make sure that everyone is on the same schedule and adheres to a single plan. Many times one group's deliverables are contingent upon another's. Bring the groups together at the start, even if they are in totally different departments, and open up channels of communication whereby everyone in the company can track the progress of everyone else. This way each group can adjust their schedules accordingly.

Responsibility

Make sure each group knows what its tasks are and accepts responsibility for deliverables and deadlines.

Roles

Make sure every individual knows his or her role. All team members should have a clear idea about what is expected of them. Also, everyone in the company should know who to turn to for various functions. Clarify any confusion in roles or overlapping duties. Allow people to take ownership and fulfill on their obligations to the other team members.

People

You must know exactly who you need on your team. A great team is made up of people with different kinds of expertise. Make sure you have the right combination of people with the right skills to get the job done. Good planning in advance is crucial if you are going to bring together the right people.

Evaluation

Set up a mechanism by which individuals and groups are evaluated. Both managers and peers should be involved in the evaluation process, and it should be based on clear criteria so that everyone feels it is as fair and accurate as possible. The evaluation should then be delivered in an open and constructive environment so that it helps the employee to improve and become better integrated with the team.

Delegate

Decisions shouldn't be made from the top down. Good managers delegate decisions and monitor results. Hire people you trust and give them the freedom to make mistakes. Teams run from the top down can become bottlenecked and inefficient.

Diversity

Accept that different people have different cultural backgrounds, personalities, outlooks, skills, strengths, and weakness. Encourage everyone to be themselves. Don't look for one type of person, but look for the best in each person. Try to find jobs that suit each individual and allow them to contribute the most they can to the team effort.

Communication

Make sure there's lateral as well as vertical communication. Problems should be addressed between groups. Structure your teams so that they are constantly talking to each other. Schedule weekly or even daily meetings between and within groups. Every group should know exactly what every other group is doing and who to talk to if there's a problem. Make these details public and distribute them to every member of your team.

Support

Ensure that each group has the support it needs to get the job done, whether this is technical support, computer equipment, training, etc. Monitor this and have a way for groups to obtain the support they're lacking.

Honesty

Encourage an environment of where people accept blame for their mistakes. Make it an issue of pride to stand up and admit that you make an error. Discourage blame shifting and political games. Foster a culture of honesty by holding up examples of people who take responsibility for their actions.

Rewards

Make sure your team is rewarded for their actions. Small gifts or simply recognition of a job well done can be a huge morale booster.

CONCLUSION

Understanding your role in a team and having the interpersonal skills to work within a team structure are as important as any of the design skills we've discussed to this point. Game development is a collaborative art, and game teams are getting larger and more complex every day. We urge you to take the time to practice your team-building skills before you are thrown into the maelstrom of production.

Take the time to understand the roles of the other team members and to learn to communicate with them. Make sure they know who you are and what your role is on the production. Participate at the highest level possible in team discussions—always come prepared, and focus your input toward achieving the goals of the meeting. Whether you're starting at the bottom, or you're leading the team, be the best team member you possibly can, and your contribution will act as an inspiration to others.

Just as there is no one way to design a game, there's no one way to go about structuring and building the best team. The concepts we've introduced here are just a starting point. You'll need to find the right way to set up your specific project and the individuals who work on it. Feel free to experiment; take the rules we've given you as a starting point and expand from there. But remember, your objective is to create an environment where every individual is able to contribute to the very best of their abilities. Succeed at this, and your game will reflect excellence in every aspect of its development.

Chapter 13
Stages of Development

Producing electronic games is a complex and expensive process. A developer's goal is to produce the highest quality game within the limits of their resources and budget. The publisher's goal is to produce the best-selling game while limiting their risk by keeping costs low. There is a common interest in producing a successful product between these two parties, and also a conflict of interest in how much money and time that product should require.

Estimating the schedule and budget for a game is a difficult task. There are many variables and uncertainties that make it hard to pin down what the exact timeframe for delivery will be—especially if you are inventing new technologies or tools to get the job done. It's easy for a production to spin out of control or for unexpected costs to crop up, and many developers do not always have the financial expertise to foresee these problems. Conflicts can arise between developers and publishers when productions go over budget or fall behind schedule. If a project is delayed, how much more money will it cost to complete? And if

a production goes over budget, who will pay for the overages? The publisher may have added features or delayed the process by requesting changes. Or, the developer may have overpromised, only to find out they now need more time to complete the game.

To combat these issues, the industry has evolved some best practices for producing games efficiently. A core aspect of the process is that a project is developed and approved in stages. Each stage is defined by milestones. Contracts between publishers and developers are typically based on these milestones, and the developer is paid a predetermined amount for each milestone it reaches. Even if you do not plan to be a game producer, as a game designer, you will need to work with a producer and understand these stages of development clearly. In this chapter, we will walk through each of the stages of development and talk about how to create a project plan that takes into account the unpredictable nature of developing games.

STAGES DEFINED

Figure 13.1 is a graphical representation of the stages of development. Notice that the five stages are drawn in a "V" shape. This is to represent that in the beginning of a project, the creative possibilities are broad, open and changeable. Early on, changes can be made with little financial consequence. If you want to alter your idea from an ant simulator to a submarine combat game, for example, the concept stage is the time to do it. As the process moves along, ideas must become more focused, smaller and smaller changes can be made to the design without disrupting the production.

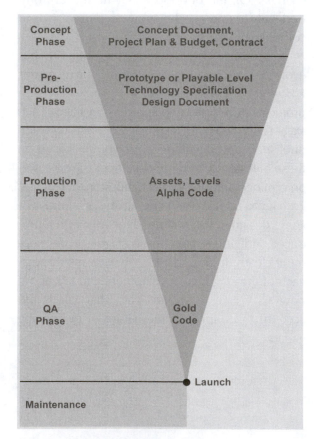

13.1   Stages of development

By the time you reach the middle of a production, it's virtually impossible to alter the broad vision of a game, but you can tinker with some features or concepts within it. For instance, during the production stage, you might find yourself discussing whether or not to create nine submarine models instead of five. This is will change the gameplay but won't require significant restructuring of the application, or starting over in terms of the existing art and animation. During later stages of production, it becomes increasingly difficult and more expensive to make any modifications to the game design beyond tweaking variables that have been set up to be flexible.

As you approach the testing stage, only the completion of details is an open area of discussion. Any major or even moderate changes are usually out of the question. At this point, you might discuss things like whether the controls for a German U-577 submarine have been implemented to spec, but you'd never suggest adding another model of submarine.

But what about the playtesting process, you are wondering? How can we implement changes to the gameplay based on our playtesting if our decisions are dictated by the needs of the production process? The answer to this is why we insist that you prototype and playtest your gameplay early. If you do so, the major issues will be found in the concept and pre-production stages—before you've even begun to create the art or program the actual code for the game. The playtesting you do during the production and QA stages will reveal smaller problems, requiring the type of focused changes we are talking about.

The time estimates given in the headings for each stage are based on typical schedules for today's big console titles. Naturally, estimates will be different for PC, cell phone, and online titles. Time is also a function of the experience of your team and tools they have at hand. If a team begins a project with a ready-made engine from the last project they worked on, they may be able to cut out significant development time. If they must start from scratch, this equation is reversed. You need to be aware of the limitations and resources of your team, and how these may affect your development schedule.

Concept/contract (Month 1)

Selling a game is one of the hardest tasks for a developer. Unless you're an "A+" developer with at least one hit under your belt, getting a publisher to even consider funding your idea can be a challenge. The goal at this stage is for the developer is to get a publisher to commit to funding at least the first milestone. Unfortunately, publishers don't like to work with unproven talent because the risks are too high, so they put up a number of barriers to entry. Even getting in the door to make a pitch can be difficult.

We'll talk about how you can get in the door in Chapter 16, but for now, let's assume that you found the right contacts and you've made your pitch. In this case, the publisher will base their decision on three things: the team, the project plan (which includes schedule and budget), and the idea.

The team

Above all, a publisher wants to see an experienced development team. This is because game production is expensive, complex, and risky, and the publisher can reduce their risk considerably by going with a proven group of individuals.

When listening to a game pitch, the publisher is going to weigh it considerably in regards to the team. Remember, you're not the only one out there with great ideas. In the publisher's mind, ideas are a dime a dozen. It's implementation that counts. Can you deliver a ground-breaking game on budget and on time? The best gauge of this is a proven track record, and publishers tend to fund the teams who have already published games, dismissing even brilliant ideas from lesser-known developers.

What makes up a winning team? First, it's important that the group has worked together in the past. As we discussed in the last chapter, teamwork is critical. If you have talent from all across the industry, but they've never worked together, the risk is higher than a less talented team that has demonstrated they can deliver a product. The publisher will look closely at your team's history and try to determine how long you've been together and how you operate. Are there clear leaders in each area of production? Who performs what functions within the company? What obstacles have you overcome and how have you dealt with them? Is there a good history with previous publishers?

Second, the publisher will want to know if your team can deliver the type of product that you're proposing. If your team is known for producing simulation games, but what you're proposing is a first-person shooter, there's obviously more risk involved. The publisher will wonder if your group can really deliver a compelling game in a different genre. Do you have a handle on the technology, which is quite different from that of a simulation? What about the gameplay elements? A good first-person shooter and a good simulation game are two entirely different play patterns. Because of this, publishers often pigeonhole developers,

DESIGNER PERSPECTIVE: TROY DUNNIWAY

Title

Lead Game Designer, Electronic Arts, Los Angeles

Project list (five to eight top projects)

- *Command & Conquer: Generals Zero Hour*
- *Oddworld: Munch's Oddysee*
- *Bruce Lee: Quest for the Dragon*
- *Legend of the Blademasters*
- *Armor Command*

How did you get into the game industry?

I started off working in the film industry doing effects work on movies. I eventually began doing art for games and eventually joined a small game developer in Northern California full time around nine years ago. I was hired as the lead animator, but quickly began doing design work on games. Every year I did more and more design work and less art. I eventually moved over to Microsoft as a lead designer and first party action and strategy design director. After a few years I moved to EA, where I am now.

What are your five favorite games and why?

This is a tough question, which always changes. We used to think that *Pac-Man* and *Joust* were awesome, then *Doom*, *Ultima*, and *Command & Conquer* were killer. Every year games keep getting better and better. I still go back and play the classic games that used to be my favorite, but they're getting very hard to compare directly anymore. I now tend to spend most of my game-playing time playing competitive games to what I'm currently working on. However, my most favorite games probably include: *Ultima 7*, since it was the first time I got fully immersed in a world to that degree, *Star Wars Knights of the Old Republic*, since it immersed me in a huge world better than any game since *Ultima 7*, *X-Wing* allowed me to fulfill my *Star Wars* fantasy like I never thought was possible at the time, and *Age of*

expecting them to produce the same type of games that they are known for.

Lastly, the publisher will want to know if you can deliver on the platform of choice. This varies, depending on the publisher's internal objectives. Some publishers only focus on console games, while others cover PC and handheld games as well. If it's a console game, then a developer who

has produced hundreds of PC games may be deemed less worthy than another developer who has produced one hit console game—the point being that platform matters. Publishers want a team experienced in exactly what has to be delivered. This is because both the schedules and budgets are so tight that there's little room for error.

Empires: The Age of Kings was an incredibly fun RTS that allowed me to play in more ways than I ever thought was possible in a strategy game.

What games have inspired you the most as a designer and why?

Every game I work on has a different set of games that inspire me. I grew up owning and playing practically every game that came out, so it's hard to say which of those had the most influence on me. Early on professionally, games like *WarCraft, Ultima, Command & Conquer*, and *System Shock* had a lot of influence on me. I liked games that showed me that it was possible to play a game, have a story, and be able to think through them instead of just fight or jump your way through them. I've always been more into role-playing and strategy games than anything else, even though I play most action games on the PC and consoles. I like games that pushed the limits, allowed players to find their own paths and have fun doing it. I get tired of games with little to no innovation or originality.

What are you most proud of in your career?

The design work that Lorne Lanning and I did on *Munch's Oddysee* was pretty incredible. I had to completely redesign the game and rebuild it in a very short time period. While the final design may have had a few flaws, if you look at the time spent on actually building the final levels of the game and how they turned out, they were pretty darn good. *Munch* went on to win a lot of critical acclaim from many different sources, which also shows that a lot of people really had fun playing the game. In the end, what makes me the most proud about my work on *Munch* is knowing that I made millions of people's lives a little more enjoyable, even for a brief moment in time. But, I'm even more proud knowing that I did it facing impossible odds.

What words of advice would you give to an aspiring designer today?

To be a great designer, you have to be a great student. Never stop learning, studying, thinking, or rethinking what you are doing. You have to be motivated and willing to work hard to succeed. Learn from the good and bad lessons that other designers make. Look outside of games for inspiration, learning, and help. Always ask, "Why?" Don't design games for yourself, and leave your ego at home.

So if your team meets all those qualifications, then at least you're in the running. We're not saying this to discourage you. What we want is for you to focus your efforts on the areas that maximize your chances of success. The bottom line is that if you're starting out, you'll have to work your way up, by joining an established developer or publisher and establishing a track record before you can take on projects of your own.

The project plan

Next in importance is the project plan, which includes a budget and schedule. The project plan shows the publisher that you've thought through every element of the production and understand what it will take to implement. The more detailed a plan you can provide the publisher, and the further along you are in the process, the greater your chances of getting funding. The logic behind this is simple: each step you take in advance of funding reduces the publisher's risk, and that means the publisher is more inclined to step forward with the money.

The project plan is arguably the most important document in the whole production because the signed contract typically includes the project plan as an addendum. This means that once it's approved by the publisher, the developer is legally obligated to adhere to it. If the developer misses any of the milestones laid out in the project plan, it can spell disaster. The publisher may view a missed milestone as a red flag, and because the project plan is now part of the contract, they can cancel the project, leaving the developer in a dire position. Our advice is to take your time thinking through the project plan, evaluating it with each group lead, and making sure that everyone is on board to execute the plan. We will go through the process of developing a project plan in detail later in this chapter.

The idea

In many ways, the idea is the least important thing to the publisher. This is not to say that publishers are not interested in great ideas. But the criteria by which a publisher judges an idea is very different than that of a developer. Throughout this book, we have taken the perspective of a designer and developer—we have encouraged you to seek the essence of great gameplay and to pursue it, no matter the genre or precedent. This is the way to develop great game ideas, but unfortunately, it is not necessarily the way to sell great game ideas.

And publishers want to find and fund games that they can sell.

Publishers rely on market data to determine what types of games the audience wants buy. Because of this, if your game doesn't fit into a top-selling genre, a publisher will be hesitant to fund it. While publishers do like to see innovation, they like to see it implemented on top of a proven genre of game. For example, *Deus Ex* is a truly innovative game. But its gameplay has a solid basis in two proven genres—the first-person shooter and the role-playing game. While *Deus Ex* actually has more innovation than most publishers would feel comfortable supporting, it also had an amazing team behind it, including the game designer and project director, Warren Spector, whose years of experience in the industry balanced the risk involved in such an innovative project (see Warren's profile on page 39).

One way for you to support your game idea is by doing your own market research prior to presenting it to publishers. Search out sales data on games that include elements of the type of play you are planning. Look at market trend analyses from reputable research companies. Hire a third-party marketing team to focus test your concept. Include a summary of the research you've done in the presentation of your idea. Don't rely on your high-end concept graphics or exaggerated feature points to sell your idea. The best way to reach a publisher is to have a great idea and to prove that it is a saleable one.

When you present your idea to the publisher, it is called a "pitch." Pitching is an art, and we'll go into more detail on this art in Chapter 16 on page 430. But briefly, your pitch materials need to communicate the strength of all three things we've talked about: the team, the plan, and the idea. You may only get a few minutes in a crowded hallway to pitch your idea, so preparation and practice are essential.

An excellent resource for understanding what materials will be most effective for selling to a publisher is the IGDA's Game Submission Guide. This document is based on a survey of publishers and developers across the industry and details some best practices for selling concepts. The document can be found at http://www.igda.org/biz/submission_guide.php.

It may take a long time to get there, but at the end of the concept/contract stage, the developer should have a signed agreement with a publisher. This agreement will spell out the terms of the association, including rights, deliverables, and the payment milestones. The first milestone is signing the contract and approving the project plan. Subsequent milestones occur during each stage of development, as described next.

Pre-production (Months 2–6)

During pre-production, a small team will be put on the project to verify the feasibility of the idea. This team will work to create one playable level or environment of the game, focusing on proving out differentiating features and risky technology. As Steve Ackrich of Atari pointed out to us, this is the most critical period in development. If a game looks like a dog after six months of pre-production, he'll kill it.

The team at this point will be small because a small team is inexpensive. Until the publisher is certain that the game concept and technology are going to work, they won't fund a full team. The job of the small team is to further refine the plan for the design, technology, and implementation of the entire production, from staffing and resource allocation through to schedules and deliverables.

If a software prototype was not created in the concept stage, now is the time to make it and playtest it. This is also the time to write up a detailed design document and technical specification. When the full team is hired for the production stage, they will use these documents as a guide. The more clearly these documents describe the elements of the gameplay, visual design, and technology, the more efficient the production can be.

The design document and technical specification impact the project plan and vice versa. The project plan cannot be fully fleshed out until the design is complete, and the limitations of schedule and budget will impact decisions that are made regarding the design. Typically, these documents are refined in parallel, each one influencing the other.

In addition to refining the game design, pre-production is the time to build much of the risky technology and prove its feasibility. This helps to reduce the potential risk for both developer and publisher. It would be foolhardy to begin a technically ambitious project without a clear sense of the viability of the ideas or the time to complete implementation. At this point, the technology does not need to be 100% complete, but the publisher needs to see that the game is technically achievable before funding the next stage of development.

At the end of pre-production, the publisher will evaluate the prototype or completed level, the progress on the technology, the design and technical documents, and the fully developed project plan, in order to make a decision to finance the production or kill the project. Smart publishers will not hesitate to kill projects that they think are too risky or do not seem marketable. At this point, their overall investment is fairly low and the loss is negligible, compared to the cost of releasing a product that doesn't sell.

DESIGNER PERSPECTIVE: STAN CHOW

Title

Executive Producer, EA Canada

Project list (five to eight top projects)

- *Def Jam Vendetta*
- *NBA Street*
- *NBA Live '95*
- *NBA Live 2001*
- *PGA Tour Golf '98*
- *Skitchin'*
- *World Tour Tennis*
- *4D Boxing*

How did you get into the game industry?

I spent most of my teenage years either playing videogames at the arcade or on my Apple II computer. In 1989 my best friend, Don Mattrick, who started his own videogame company in 1982, asked me if I wanted to join his company and help design games. I was in university studying computer science at the time; it was a no-brainer.

What are your five favorite games and why?

- *Robotron:* Mowing down hundreds of robots with my blaster and escaping against all odds gives me a sweaty, heart-pounding, white-knuckled adrenaline rush.
- *Metal Gear Solid:* It's the first game to let me play out my fantasy of sneaking around and taking people out. The game triggered feelings of fear and anticipation as I ran and hid from the enemy or snuck around a corner. It also has a good story.

If the publisher does kill the project at this point, they will pay the developer the milestone payment for the pre-production and cancel the rest of the development. Then, depending on the rights negotiated in the contract, the developer may either go to another publisher with their work or start over on a new idea. Problems can crop up if the developer has spent more money than planned during the concept and pre-production stage, counting on the next milestone payment to make up the difference. More than one developer has gone out of business at this stage.

Production (Months 7–22)

Production is the longest and most expensive stage of development. The goal in this stage is to

- *Pikmin:* I love this game for its fresh concept and great execution of gameplay.
- *WarCraft:* As a player, real-time strategy is my favorite genre of games. The most important thing in a RTS game is balance. Once you find an imbalance in a RTS game that you can exploit it is no longer fun to play. In terms of balance, *WarCraft* is the best execution of a RTS game.

What games have inspired you the most as a designer and why?

I can't really name one game that inspired me the most. What inspires me the most are games that feel fresh and original in concept or design. Games that have fallen into that category in their time are: *Test Drive, SimCity, Goldeneye, Metal Gear Solid, The Sims,* and *Pikmin.*

What are you most proud of in your career?

I am the most proud of my involvement in building the *NBA Live* franchise from *Live '95* to *Live 2001.* It was and still is the number one selling basketball simulation on the market.

What words of advice would you give to an aspiring designer today?

Understand the structure of games and what makes them fun. Ideas and concepts are cheap. Structure and execution are what make a game great.

Two Stan Chow faves: Metal Gear Solid and WarCraft

execute on the vision and plan established in the previous stage. In the process of improving and executing the design, some changes will inevitably be necessary that must be reflected in the design document. However, in most cases, larger creative changes will not be possible in order to meet deadlines and stay within budget.

During this stage the programmers write the code that makes the game function. The artists build all the art files and animation. The sound designers create sound effects and music. Writers write dialogue and other in-game text. QA engineers familiarize themselves with all aspects of the project and do some light testing of early builds. The producer works to make sure everyone on the team is communicating and is aware of the overall progress, while tweaking the schedule and monitoring resources to ensure that everything remains on track.

As the production gains momentum, the levels and environments are fleshed out, art and sound files are integrated into the working builds of the code, and the game begins to take shape. One recommendation that Steve Ackrich makes to his teams is to build the first levels last. This is because the team will have worked out kinks in their production process and tools, they will know the limitations of the game system, and because of this the levels built last will likely be the best designed ones in the game. You want users to have an amazing experience with the first levels because that is what will get them hooked on the game.

The goal in this stage of development is to get to "alpha" code. This means that all features are complete and no more features will be added. Sometimes the team has to cut ambitious features in order to meet the alpha milestone and stay on schedule. For instance, let's say the design document called for a feature that allows users to import names from their e-mail address book into the game. Then, during gameplay, those names would appear on units as they came into the game. That would be fun—and it's actually a feature in the game *Black & White*. However, if the team's running out of time and this feature isn't complete, the producer may classify it as "low priority" and cut it.

As the programmers work on the code, they will periodically assemble versions of the project, which are called "builds." Each build is given an incremental number, so that any issues or bugs can be referenced as to what build they were found in. When the developer achieves alpha code they send a build to the publisher's QA team. If approved, the publisher pays the developer for

reaching the milestone, and the team moves on the QA and polishing stage.

QA/polish (Months 23–24)

In the last few months of production, the focus shifts from producing new code and features, to making certain that what has already been built functions as expected and that the levels and artwork are complete and polished. The team shrinks down in size because the majority of production artists and outside talent such as sound designers and writers are no longer needed.

During this stage, the developer takes the Alpha build and transforms it into the final product that we see on the store shelves. The user experience grows tighter and more complete. Levels are fine-tuned. Game designers, programmers, and QA engineers work together to iron out timing issues, bugs, and annoying interface and control problems. As Steve Ackrich points out, 70% of the quality of a game comes during this last 10% of development. He cautions developers to leave enough time in their production schedule to truly refine the game.

It is in this last stage that the developer has a chance to truly see their game for what it is and to make sure it offers the best possible experience for the player. The difference between a game rushed off to market and one which has had the luxury of a good polishing can be enormous. It's the subtle tuning of gameplay and tweaks to timing and controls that can create an unforgettable player experience, and this is the level of quality that makes blockbuster games.

As we've mentioned before, QA testing is an art, and it's something that shouldn't be taken for granted. There are numerous books dedicated to the implementation of good testing procedures, and it would behoove you to read as much as you can about this detailed and vital process. In brief, the QA team creates a test plan, a document that describes all the areas and features of the product, and the various conditions under which each will be tested. This test plan is based on the design document and technical specifications, so it is important that these be up to date. The QA engineers run the tests against the current build and note when the game doesn't behave according to spec. This is called a "bug."

Bugs are entered into a database with a description of the exact steps to be taken to re-create the problem, the severity of the issue, and the name of the tester who discovered it. Severity is a judgment of the technical level of a bug. While exact nomenclature may differ from team to team, the four major levels of severity are:

- *Critical:* the software will not run
- *1 or High:* unexpected fatal errors (includes crashes and data corruption)
- *2 or Medium:* a feature is malfunctioning
- *3 or Low:* a cosmetic issue

In order to keep track of what has been fixed, by whom, and in what build, bugs are assigned to specific individuals. For example, a bug related to a game's database, will be assigned to the database programmer. When the programmer has fixed the bug, they send it back to the QA team for re-testing. Once the QA team is satisfied that the bus is fixed, they mark that issue "resolved" in the database.

The order in which bugs are fixed is dictated by their priority. While severity is a technical judgment, priority is often a business judgment. For example, a bug that is low severity because it is essentially cosmetic may have a high priority for business reasons. As with severity, the nomencla-ture for priority may also differ from team to team, but the basic priority levels are:

- *Now:* Drop everything and take care of it as soon as you see this (usually for blocking bugs).
- *1:* Fix before next build to test.
- *2:* Fix before final release.
- *3:* We probably won't get to these, but we want to track them anyway

When the development team gets together to assess the current state of the code, prioritize and resolve bugs, it is called a "triage" meeting. A typical console title will have several thousand bugs in the database. The programmers work through the database systematically, eliminating the highest priority bugs first. Bugs may be found in all areas of the game—there may be bugs that require the attention of the visual designers, the programmers, and even the legal staff, if there are outstanding questions on things like disclaimers or registration. When all of the features are complete and there are no more "priority 1" bugs in the database, the project is considered at beta.

The final goal of this stage is to reach what's called "gold code." This means that all bugs have been resolved. Interestingly, nearly every game ships with some minor bugs in the code. At the very end of the project, the producer resolves remaining minor bugs as "deferred." This means that time has run out and the producer has determined that the remaining bugs are so unobtrusive that they can ship with the game. An example would be something like a slightly wrong font size on an alert message. It may be annoying to the art director, but it doesn't impact gameplay, so it's left in.

Maintenance (ongoing)

Now that the Internet is so accessible to most game players, games are often updated via "patches" distributed online. This means the team monitors user feedback once the game is shipped and continues to fix bugs even though the product has shipped. These "patches" are reasonably small downloads that correct pervasive problems.

Patches are usually not released for cosmetic or low-severity issues. Generally, they address feature problems, incompatibility issues, or other medium- and high-level bugs that managed to make it past the testing team. For example, here's a list of fixes from the first patch of many released for the game *StarCraft*. The list is taken from the developer Blizzard's web site.

StarCraft patch information

Changes in version v1.01

- Fixed cheat that allowed one player in a multi-player game to see the map.

- Fixed bug that allowed players to receive extra resources when canceling building construction multiple times by exploiting lag in a multiplayer game.
- Fixed pathing problem related crash bug that was most commonly exhibited in Terran 10.
- Fixed "C Runtime Library" crash bug exhibited during saved games when year was greater than 2098.
- Fixed sprite allocation errors that prevent normal combat and creation of units.
- Fixed occasional hang when joining and leaving Battle.net.
- Enemy science vessels no longer continually unmask after irradiating units.
- Missile turrets controlled by the AI properly acquire targets.
- Fixed blank game names in Battle.net game list.
- Game names with high ASCII characters now show up properly.

HOW TO MAKE A PROJECT PLAN

As we've mentioned, the project plan is the most important document that the developer creates. This set of documents is a road map for producing the game. It includes the schedule and the budget, which are generally attached to the contract for the production. The diagram in Figure 13.2 provides an overview of the process for creating a realistic project plan and budget. Notice how each step directly affects its successor. Here is a description of each step of the process.

Goals

First articulate all the goals of the project. Include gameplay goals, such as features and levels, and technical goals, like enabling multiple players over the Internet. Also include the target platform and proposed launch date. An example might be to launch on the Xbox and PlayStation 2 for Christmas 2006.

Exercise 13.1: Goals

Working with the team you've recruited, write down the goals for turning your original game idea into a finished product. Make sure to include both gameplay goals and technical goals.

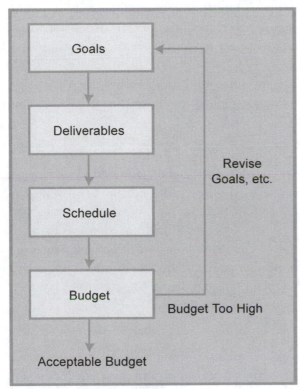

13.2 How to make a project plan

Deliverables

The goals have a direct impact on the deliverables, which are the materials that you produce as part of the project. List out everything you envision making, and organize them under the stages of development. For instance, you would list a design document under the design stage. If your game has levels, you should list the number of levels or environments under the production stage. Likewise, you would detail out exactly how much artwork, animation, and other media you will need to produce and during the production as well, defining things like the number of 3D models, characters, sound effects, minutes of music, seconds of linear animation, seconds of voice

recordings, etc. Each one of these is a deliverable, and it has to be both budgeted for and placed on the schedule.

Exercise 13.2: Deliverables

List out the deliverables for your production based on the goals you just stated. Think of every single element that goes into making up your game, from code modules to sound effects. Work with your team members to make your deliverables as accurate as possible.

Schedule

A schedule is an estimate of how long it will take your team to complete each deliverable. The deliverables are made up of tasks, and these tasks are assigned to specific team members. The best way to begin creating your schedule is to break down each deliverable into a list of tasks. If you are experienced, you will know the tasks already. If you are not experienced, you may need to confer with your team members to get an idea of what tasks will need to be done and how long each task will take. Next go through the tasks and define what resources (i.e., team members) you will assign to each one and how long, in terms of days, it will take to complete.

Finally, assign start dates to each task on the list. Some tasks can be done in parallel, while others won't be able to begin until certain other tasks are completed. These are called dependencies, and they must be accounted for in the schedule. It can become quite complex when one aspect of the game requires fifteen tasks to be completed by three different groups in a very specific order. You will also need to make sure you are balancing the workload for each team member. If you schedule a programmer to be coding three features at once, you will undoubtedly be disappointed when only one task actually gets accomplished.

Many game producers use a software program like Microsoft Project to create schedules. Microsoft Project and other scheduling programs allow you to drag tasks around the schedule visually and create links and dependencies between tasks. If you don't have a scheduling program, you can use a spreadsheet like Excel or even a paper calendar. The key is to organize all the tasks that will need to get done during each stage of development and to estimate how long each one will take and how many people will need to work on it. When you are done, you will have an overview of your production time line, and a list of resources you will need and for how long. This list is what you need to produce the budget.

As you'll see, the schedule forms the foundation of your project plan and will become an indispensable tool for managing the production. The sample schedule in Figure 13.3 is shown in Gantt chart format—a typical view for looking at schedules.

Exercise 13.3: Schedule

Using either scheduling software or a paper calendar, create a detailed schedule for the production of your original game. Don't leave any tasks unspecified. Also, make certain to identify any dependencies. You may need to estimate the length of time it will take to complete many of these tasks. Don't worry, the important thing is not how accurate your schedule is right now, but that you think through the process and see how the pieces all fit together.

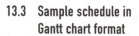

13.3 Sample schedule in Gantt chart format

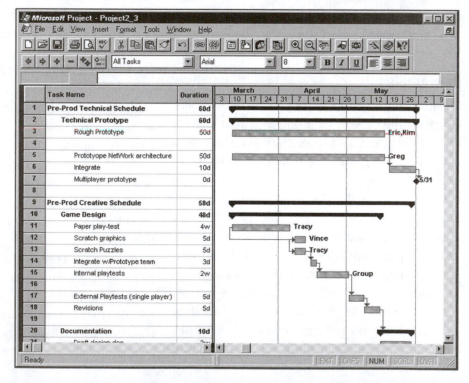

Microsoft Excel - BudgetForm.xls

Vendor	Generic Games	Date Prepared:	
Address	555 Main Street		
	Los Angeles, CA	Client:	
Telephone #	(310) 555-1212	Client Contact:	
FAX #		Address:	
Producer		Telephone:	
Interactive Designer		FAX:	
Technical Director			
Art Director		Revision 1 Date:	
PROJECT TITLE		Revision 2 Date:	
Multiplayer Shockwave Game		Revision 3 Date:	
		Revision 4 Date:	
		Revision 5 Date:	
PRODUCTION LABOR			
Project Management			57,500
Game Design			46,000
Graphic Design			34,500
Digital Video			-
2D Animation			-
3D Animation			-
Software Development			128,800
DIRECT COSTS			
Testing			20,000
Production Supplies			5,000
Media & Replication			-
Licensing			15,000
General & Administrative			7,000
Subtotal			313,800
Production Insurance	(0.0%)		-
Production Markup	(25%)		78,450
Contingency	(0%) of Subtotal)		-
		Grand Total:	$392,250
COMMENTS			

Microsoft Excel - BudgetForm.xls

		NO.	WEEKS	RATE	BENEFITS 0%	EQUIP/FACILITY 15%	TOTAL
	Project Management						
100	Executive Producer	0.5	20	2000		300	23000
105	Producer	1	20	1500		225	34500
107	Associate Producer			1000			
110	Production Coordinator			1000			
115	Production Assistant			650			
120	Other						
	Project Management Total:						57500
	Interactive Design						
125	Creative Director			3000			
130	Senior Game Designer	1	20	2000		300	46000
135	Game Designer			1600			
140	Writer			1200			
145	Editorial Coordinator			1000			
150	Other						
	Interactive Design Total:						46000
	Graphic Design						
160	Art Director	1	10	2500		375	28750
165	Senior Designer			1600			
170	Designer			1000			
175	Art Assistant			800			
180	Illustrator			800			
185	Sound Design	1	1	5000		750	5750
	Graphic Design Total:						34500
	Digital Video						
190	Digital Video Editor			2000			
195	Video Digitizing			1800			
200	Avid Edit			1800			
205	On-Line Edit			1300			
208	Duplication			1000			
210	Other			1000			
	Graphic Design Total:						
	2D Animation						
215	Animation Director						
220	Sound Designer						
225	Assistant Animator						
230	Layout Artist						
235	Ink & Paint						
240	Other						
	2D Animation Total:						

13.4 Sample budget

Budget

The budget is a direct function of the schedule. This is because the schedule tells you exactly how many people you'll need and for how long, and salaries comprise the majority of a game budget. Other "direct" costs include things like software licensing and specialized services.

The sample budget in Figure 13.4 was created using Microsoft Excel and shows several important elements of a budget. The cover page on the left shows total costs for various types of production labor: project management, game design, graphic design, digital video, 2D/3D animation, and software development. It also shows the direct costs

for testing, production supplies, media, licensing, and administrative costs. In this instance, the testing costs are probably being paid to a third-party testing facility. If they were internal resources, the producer would have included them under production labor. Every production will have its own way of handling specific things like this.

The right hand page is an example of how each of the labor totals on the front page is calculated from a breakdown of line items. In this case, on a small web game, one game designer is going to work 20 weeks at $2000 per week. It looks like this is a very small company, because they aren't paying any benefits to this employee and they are only calculating an overhead cost (the cost for equipment and facility) of 15%.

Overhead expenses refer to all nonlabor expenses required to operate the business. For game developers it generally includes rent, utilities, supplies, insurance, and other such costs. A true overhead percentage can be calculated by an accountant as a function of the developer's real labor and nonlabor costs. This percentage is extremely important because many developers do not calculate it correctly and wind up shortchanging themselves. A typical overhead amount for developers is 100%. That means a typical developer should charge at least double their labor costs in order to cover their actual costs. This developer has probably underestimated their overhead, which may cause difficulty for them down the line.

After the benefits and overhead are calculated for a specific line item, it is included in the total for the group of resources and carried over to the front page. All the various costs are added in a subtotal. And then, several important percentages are calculated. The first is "production insurance." If you have taken any insurance out to back-up your company's ability to complete the job, you'll need to add that cost here. In this case, the developer has not done so.

The second percentage to be calculated is "markup." This is a percentage that the developer charges above their costs. Thus it may be possible for a developer to actually make some money on a production if they manage it closely and meet their expectations. A standard markup amount for developers on a work-for-hire agreement is about 25%. The percentage varies depending on the developer's total compensation. A lot of developers spend everything they're given and rely upon the royalties to yield their profits.

If you're starting out as a developer, we recommend that you get your hands on budgets from similar game titles or ask a more experienced producer to review your work. Short of hiring an experienced producer, this is the best way to make sure you have considered everything. In the end, you will probably forget something, so keep in mind that it's always better to estimate just a tiny bit high—the fat you build in will get worked out during the next part of the process.

Exercise 13.4: Budget

Now it's time to create the budget for your original game. Use the sample schedule form in Appendix A on page 444 to build out a budget for your original game idea. It's okay to put down your best guess for the various costs, because you will be revising your estimates later.

Revise

After you've gone through the first four steps, don't be surprised if you wind up with a gigantic budget number that far exceeds what you know the publisher will advance you. Let's say a typical budget for a console title is $4 million, but yours comes out to be more like $6 million—what do you do? First, don't panic. This is normal. Second, don't give in to the urge to just cut the budget number down to match the publisher's expectations.

Your next step is to go back to the beginning: look at your goals and revise them. Once your revised your goals, you'll need to revise the deliverables, which should now require a shorter schedule. Once you've revised your schedule, you'll need to reflect those changes in your budget. If, for example, you cut down your goals down from "recreate the submarine battles of WWII" to "recreate three major submarine battles of WWII," this would cause a ripple effect in your deliverables, your schedule, and, of course, your budget. This is because the change in goals in this case would drastically cut the amount of media and levels you needed to produce, reducing resource requirements and effectively lowering the budget.

The biggest mistake that beginning developers make during the budgeting process is to not change their goals and deliverables but instead fiddle with the numbers until they come out looking "reasonable." Always start with your goals and work down through the deliverables and schedule, item by item. If you over-promise and under-budget you will run the risk of losing money, overworking your team, and being unable to complete the project as promised.

Exercise 13.5: Revise

Now assume the publisher has asked you to cut 20% out of your budget. Starting with your goals, and working your way through the deliverables, schedule, and finally the budget, revise your plan to reduce costs.

Milestones and approvals

Each time a stage of development has been completed and approved by the publisher, the developer receives a milestone payment. It's important that the developer keep a written record of all approvals and decisions from the publisher. This is a time-consuming but necessary process handled by the producer that helps manage the production.

Quite often the publisher will ask for changes to the design in the middle of production. For instance, let's say a developer was producing the submarine game we've been talking about. The developer has received written approval for the concept/contract stage and the pre-production stage.

Then during production, the publisher decides that the submarine game should be set in modern times instead of WWII. This kind of radical change in direction is not uncommon. This means that the developer would have to re-think the project, starting with the early concept deliverables and the schedule and budget would have to be extended accordingly. A proper response from the developer would be, "We will be happy to make the change if you extend the schedule and pay us an overage that covers the additional expense."

Naturally, the publisher won't want to pay more money or extend any deadlines, and they may even threaten to withhold approval and payments if the developer doesn't acquiesce. Despite how it may seem, in this scenario, the developer is in the position of strength. The record of signed approvals should show that the developer has followed the contract unequivocally, and it is the publisher who is pushing to alter the scope and direction of the game. If the producer for the developer has been thorough about getting signed approvals, the developer should be in a defensible position. Without a signed record of approvals, the publisher could say that they had not agreed on the concept for the game and demand that the developer fulfill the original schedule and budget terms with the requested changes.

Unfortunately, many times the developer will want to please the publisher, and so they'll make the change without defining the overage costs at that point—believing they can make up the time later in production. This is a strategy that is sure to fail. Eventually, the team will fall behind, and the developer will have to ask for an extension on the schedule. If the developer asks for overages at this point, without any record of how the requested changes have affected the costs of production, the publisher is sure to deny the request.

The bottom line is that nothing should be left up to good faith. The developer can and should manage the publisher to the schedule and contract in the same way they manage their own team. Approvals should be handled in writing, as should change requests and overage estimates. These

details that seem so formal and unnatural in the rather casual environment of game production can mean the difference between completing your game on time and on budget, or having the project terminated. Again, it comes to down to maintaining a clear line of communication and letting the publisher know the consequences of every request that they make.

PREPARING FOR THE INEVITABLE

The process we've described here is designed to create an environment where everyone on the team has the opportunity to do the best work they are capable of. The schedule is sound, the budget is fair, and the deliverables are achievable. If the world were a perfect place, all game designers who followed this process would go home at a decent hour every night and have happy, stress-free lives. Inevitably, though, no matter how well you prepare, something will either go wrong, or turn out to take longer than you thought.

How you deal with a slipping schedule is as important as setting up a good process in the first place. First, understand that most software schedules slip. Usually, this comes from a combination of aggressive estimations up front and additions and changes to features during development. The question isn't how can you keep your schedule from slipping—it will—the question is, what should you do about it when it happens?

Jim McCarthy, Microsoft team leader for Visual C++ among other products, has written a book on this problem called the *Dynamics of Software Development*. McCarthy describes many of the critical moments that a development team will face, including the inevitable slipping schedule. "When you slip, don't fall," he says, recognizing

that slipping is a natural part of the process, but that good management of the situation can keep the team from falling, and from failing.

Some of the points that McCarthy makes include:

- Try to anticipate slips as soon as possible and communicate them to the team and the publisher. Re-define milestones *before* you slip.
- Keep the team psyche up—slipping is not failure; don't let it infect the rest of the process.
- If necessary, prioritize outstanding features and cut those that are not critical to its operation.

Recognizing that you are slipping and being honest about it with the publisher is a tough problem. On the one hand, you don't want them to lose confidence in you, so you want to put up a good front. On the other hand, if you completely blow a milestone, you really will lose their confidence. McCarthy's policy advocates honesty—only you can know the limits of your relationship with your publisher and whether this policy will work for you. If possible however, an open and honest relationship with the publisher will save you the heartache of driving your team into the ground to meet a deadline, missing it anyway, and having both a pissed-off publisher and a burned-out team.

Keeping the team psyche up is one of the benefits to re-defining milestones with the publisher before they are missed. It's true that working hard and achieving the impossible together will bring a team together like nothing else. But by going this route you risk not achieving the impossible together. Defeat and exhaustion are a killer combination. If you can find a way to redefine milestones before they are missed, so that your team is able to achieve the possible, it will keep the morale up and keep everyone focused on the next milestone, instead of reliving the last one.

Having to cut features in order to make a milestone can be a hard, emotional process. One way to avoid cutting core features is to prioritize them early on—before you start slipping—and make

sure the most important ones are implemented early. Another way is to design the program modularly, in groups of features. So, for instance, if you just don't get to the multiplayer components, your entire single-player game is still playable. If it does come down to cutting, make sure you involve the entire team, including the publisher and the marketing team. Features are the basis of how games are sold—you may wind up cutting a feature that could be responsible for a big percentage of projected sales.

The take-away from all of this is: be sure to put a good process in place, but when the project slips, be prepared to react quickly and efficiently to solve the problems and keep the project moving forward.

TEAM STRUCTURE PLUS STAGES OF DEVELOPMENT

As a project moves through the stages of development, different members of the team will work on it for varying amounts of time. For instance, the pre-production stage may require 100% of a game designer's time but none of a QA tester's time. On the other hand, the QA/polish stage may require 10% of a game designer's time and 100% of a QA engineer's time. Figure 13.5 shows a visual estimate of the amount of time required by various team members during different stages of production. More lines on the diagram imply more time spent.

This diagram provides a glimpse at how a development studio could run multiple projects at one time. For example, a game designer would have enough time to work on two projects at once if she was in pre-production on one and QA/polish on another. This concept applies to every member of the company across all of the company's projects.

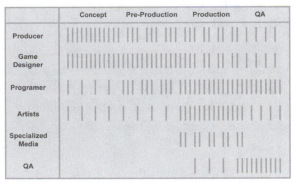

13.5   Team structure plus stages of development

This brings us back to our original concern about what happens when a project is terminated and a developer is left fully staffed but without any revenue. The fact is that this happens all the time—not just with terminated projects but with gaps between projects. Smart (and lucky) developers find a way to overlap their projects, allocating resources and scheduling stages so that they can maximize their employee's time and cover any naturally occurring breaks between projects.

As you can imagine, running multiple projects at once can be quite complex, and some developers simply aren't capable of managing such a situation, but in today's world, if a developer is going to thrive, it's wise to put these processes into place. Development jobs are inherently uneven, with lengthy gaps in between. The more you can plan ahead to smooth out cash flow, the better off you and your employees will be.

Conclusion

A great plan is the first step to a great game. Smart planning can give a talented team the environment in which to take an average idea and execute it excellently. Conversely, bad planning can mean that an excellent idea never reaches its full potential. Understanding the stages of development and how to prepare for each stage is a critical part of successful game development. Although designers are not typically responsible for creating the project plan or managing it, the more you know about the process of development, the better a designer and the better a team member you'll become.

Games tend to be some of the most technically advanced software in the world, and the challenge in creating them keeps growing as the teams get larger and the player expectations increase. Knowing how to put a good process in place, taking time to learn what certain types of features cost, how long it takes to develop art and animation, are all ways that you can ensure the success of your ideas. Additionally, knowing what to do when the schedule slips, how and when to respond are skills that you'll need to have, no matter what role you play on a team.

The outline we've given you here is just the bare bones of the real experience. You will find that shipping a project you have worked on from concept to delivery and living to tell the tale is, in spite of all the challenges, long hours and hard work, one of the most satisfying experiences you will have as a game designer.

Designer Perspective: Josh Holmes

Title

Producer, EA Canada

Project list (five to eight top projects)

- *Def Jam Vendetta:* Producer/Designer
- *NBA Street:* Lead Designer
- *NBA Live '98, '99, 2000:* Assistant/Associate Producer

How did you get into the game industry?

I was a struggling film actor with a series of dead-end jobs on the side to help pay my bills. I started looking for something I could do that might interest me as much as acting. I had always been a gamer and dreamed of creating my own games, so I applied with EA. In the interview I told them my goal was to be a game designer within five years. I started as a game tester, and after a year and a half in the QA department, I moved into production and started making games.

What are your five favorite games and why?

- *Sid Meier's Pirates!:* This is my all-time favorite. It was (and still is) the most successful example of a hybrid game, combining several different game styles to create a cohesive overall experience. While the game experience was predominantly nonlinear, it gave the impression of creating a rich narrative each time you played, based on the actions of the user. It also featured multi-layered goals and rewards, so the replay value was extremely high.
- *SimCity:* This was the ultimate sandbox game. By providing a simple, yet rich simulation, it gave the user the tools with which to create his own fun. There are just so many ways you can play *SimCity.* That's what makes Will Wright's games so amazing; he helps you unlock your inner creativity while playing his games.
- *Tetris:* If there was only one game I could play for the rest of my life, I would choose *Tetris.* Simple, abstract, and devilishly addictive, I never seem to grow bored of playing. There is a lesson on the value of simplicity here.
- *Grand Theft Auto III:* It successfully combined a compelling action experience with the sandbox concept of building your own fun, and then threw in a dark humorous fiction "borrowed" from many of my favorite films. It came the closest to realizing my vision of what games will one day be: a complementary part of mainstream entertainment and culture.

- *Virtua Fighter 2:* This is my favorite fighting game. I love the characters, the variety of fighting styles, and most of all the immersive control system. Once you learned the controls, it had a feeling of connection with your fighter that all other fighting games seemed to lack. It wasn't just a matter of memorizing long strings of button presses to initiate scripted combos; fights were back-and-forth dances of action and reaction. It really captured the essence of what fighting is all about.

What games have inspired you the most as a designer and why?

- *Diablo:* For demonstrating the impact and importance of simplified RPG aspects like item collecting and character-leveling.
- *Pirates!:* For being such a genre-busting title.
- *Grand Theft Auto III:* For leading the way toward truly mature gaming entertainment.
- So many games for so many reasons.

What are you most proud of in your career?

Creating *NBA Street*. Everyone's expectations for the game were basically just that we deliver an arcade-like basketball experience. We took the game much further, introducing bold new gameplay concepts and representing streetball culture. The gameplay engine was created from scratch, and became a step forward for basketball games in a lot of ways.

What words of advice would you give to an aspiring designer today?

1. *Think of the consumer*

You aren't designing for yourself. It doesn't matter what game you personally want to play, you have a responsibility to create the experience that the audience wants. That doesn't mean you should be predictable. Give them what they want, just not how they expect it.

2. *Fun first*

Whenever you have a choice between realism and fun, go with fun. Anybody who chooses realism at the expense of fun needs a smack upside the head.

3. *Always strive for balance*

As a designer, game balance should be foremost in your mind whenever you introduce a new feature or concept. For every reward, there must be risk. For every attack, there must be a defense. Balance is the key to a great game experience.

4. Think big

Any time you have an idea, take it as far as you possibly can. Subtleties rarely play.

5. Remember pacing

Design your game experience to be a series of emotional peaks and valleys. If the experience remains at one level, it becomes flat and boring, even if it's "action packed" (see *State of Emergency* for a one-note action-packed experience). Always remember: you can't have highs without lows.

6. Play bad games

Learn from the mistakes of others. Compare successful games against their hurting counterparts and analyze what went wrong. Then make sure you don't fall into the same traps.

7. Look outside of games

The best and most innovative designers create new experiences that seem different from anything we've played before, though the core mechanics are often familiar. Look outside of games for new ideas and then marry them to proven gameplay mechanics. A perfect example of this is *The Sims*. Life is filled with new experiences just waiting to be expressed as games. Don't be content to "photocopy" existing games. The world does not need another sassy female adventurer with big boobs.

Holmes favorites and inspiration: **Sim City, Tetris, Diablo**

Chapter 14
The Design Document

We've said throughout this book that digital game development is an inherently collaborative medium. In the last two chapters we've looked at all the various types of people that make up that collaborative environment, as well as best practices for structuring the production process to ensure that these people can achieve success. One of the most important parts of managing this process is communicating the overall vision of the game to each and every team member. If your team is very small, or if you're working alone, this might not be a problem. But most games are complex enough, and most teams large enough that the most effective way to ensure communication is to write down that vision as well as a detailed plan for executing it.

This plan is called the design document, or sometimes the design bible, and the game designer is its primary author. The design document describes the overall concept of the game, the target audience, the gameplay, interfaces, controls, characters, levels, media assets, etc. In short, everything the team needs to know about the design of the game. The artists use it to lay out interfaces that reflect the features you've designed, the programmers use it to define the software modules for those features, the level designers use it to understand how their level fits into the overall story arc, the producer uses it to generate an accurate budget and schedule, and the QA department uses it to develop a comprehensive test plan.

The reliance on a design document is a relatively new trend in game development and there are many ways to go about creating such a document. Until the 1990s, games were made by individuals or very small teams who worked together so closely they were able to communicate their designs to each other with little or no documentation. As team sizes, schedules, budgets, and the overall complexity of game designs have grown exponentially in the last 10 years, the need for clear, comprehensive documentation has become clear. Most game developers and publishers today would never think of going into production without a detailed design document. Writing and maintaining this document throughout production is a critical responsibility of the game designer.

COMMUNICATION AND THE DESIGN DOCUMENT

A good design document is like a sound blueprint for a building. Everyone can refer to it while they do their separate tasks and understand how their work fits into the game as a whole. Without a design document to direct their efforts, the individuals on a team may interpret what they know about the game in their own unique ways, working hard, but not necessarily towards the same ends. When it comes time to integrate that work, art may have been made to unusable specs, technology may reflect out-of-date features, or the essence of the gameplay may have been lost in the level designs.

In order to create an effective design document, the game designer needs to work with every other member of the team to make sure that the areas of the document affecting their work are accurate and achievable. In this way, the writing of the document itself becomes a process for communication. By conferring on the details of the document, team members have to think through the entire game, from the highest-level vision concepts, to the lowest-level art specifications, the file types, and the font sizes.

Because the design document is so important, and because games are so complex, there is a trend in writing these documents to make them very, very long. It's not unusual to see design documents that are 400 or 600 pages. We certainly can't criticize the zeal that has gone into documents of this size; however, it's important to remember the audience and objective of the document when you write something of this size. You are writing for very busy people, and you want them to read it, not use it for a doorstop. If you can get your point across in fewer pages, you will probably have more success in actually communicating to your team.

A good design document can be created in 50 to 100 succinctly written pages, well-organized and labeled, so that a busy executive or programmer can find the areas that affect them quickly and easily. If there are areas that need to be expanded on as production moves forward, one strategy is to create sub-documents that delve into these areas more deeply. These can be referenced in the main document, but only distributed to the team members they actually affect.

Always keep in mind that you're not writing the design document for the sake of writing it—your objective is communication, do whatever it takes to accomplish that goal. Documents are also not a substitute for talking to your team—just because you've written it down, don't assume that everyone has read and understood your vision. Writing the document provides a process for establishing communication and serves as a touchstone for the entire team in terms of creative and technical designs, but it is not a substitute for team meetings and in-person communication.

CONTENTS OF A DESIGN DOCUMENT

There are as many different ways to write a design document as there are designers. The game industry has no standard way of documenting designs. It would be nice if there were a set formula or style to follow, like the standards for screenplays or architectural blueprints, but this simply doesn't exist. Everyone does agree that a good design document needs to contain all the details required to create a game, however, what those details are will be affected by the specifics of the game itself.

In general, the contents of a design document can be broken up into the following areas:

- Overview and vision statement
- Marketing and legal information
- Gameplay
- Characters (if applicable)
- Story (if applicable)
- World (if applicable)
- Media list

The design document may also include technical details, or these may be articulated in a separate document called a technical specification. The technical specification or the technical sections of the design document are generally prepared by the technical lead or director.

Exercise 14.1: Researching Design Documents

To get a feeling for the various ways that designers approach the writing of design documents, go on the web and do a search using Google or Yahoo! for game design documents. You'll find dozens posted on the Internet. Pick two and read through them. What are their strengths and weaknesses? If you were a member of the design team, would you be able to execute the design as described? What questions do you have for the designers after reading the documents?

When you approach the writing of a design document, it's easy to get distracted by the scope of the document and forget the ultimate goal—to communicate your game design to the production team, the publisher, the marketing team, and anyone else with a vested interest in the game. This is one reason why we advise you not to write your

14.1   **Character sketches from Jak & Daxter and Ghost**

design document until you've built and playtested a working prototype of your idea. Having this type of concrete experience with your proposed gameplay can make all the difference in your ability to articulate that gameplay in the design document.

You should also think of your design document as a "living document." You'll likely have to make a dozen passes before it's complete, and then you'll need to constantly update it to reflect changes that are made during the development process. Because of this, it's important to organize your document modularly. If you organize your document carefully from the beginning, it will be easier to update and manage as it grows in size and complexity. Also, as we mentioned earlier, it will be easier for each group to find and read the sections that affect their work.

The following outline is an example of how you might organize your design document. We've noted under each section the types of information it should contain. Keep in mind that our goal here is not to give you a standard format which will work for every game, but rather, to provide you with ideas for the types of sections you may want to include. Your game and its design should dictate the format you use for your own document, not this outline.

1. **Design history**

   A design document is a continuously changing reference tool. Most of your teammates won't have time to read the whole document over and over again every time that a new version is released, so it's good to alert them to any significant modifications or updates that you've made. As you can see, each version will have its own section where you list the major changes made in that iteration.

   1.1 Version 1.0

   1.2 Version 2.0

       1.2.1 Version 2.1

       1.2.2 Version 2.2

   1.3 Version 3.0

2. **Vision statement**

   This is where you state your vision for the game. It's typically one or two pages. Try to capture the essence of your game and convey this to the reader in as compelling and accurate a way as possible.

   2.1 Game logline

   In one sentence, describe your game.

   2.2 Gameplay Synopsis

   Describe how your game plays and what the user experiences. Try to keep it concise—no more than a couple of pages. You may want to reference some or all of the following topics:

   - Uniqueness:
     What makes your game unique?
   - Mechanics:
     How does the game function? What is the core play mechanic?
   - Setting:
     What is the setting for your game: the Wild West, the moon, medieval times?
   - Look and feel:
     Give a summary of the look and feel of the game.

3. **Marketing information**

   3.1 Target audience

   Who will buy your game? Describe the demographic you're targeting, including age, gender, and geographic locations.

   3.2 Platform

   What platform or platforms will your game run on? And why did you choose these platforms?

   3.3 System requirements

   System requirements may limit your audience, especially on the PC where the hardware varies widely. Describe what is required to play the game and why those choices were made.

   3.4 Top performers

   List other top-selling games in the same market. Provide sales figures, release dates, information on sequels and platforms, as well as brief descriptions of each title.

   3.5 Feature comparison

   Compare your game to the competition. Why would a consumer purchase your game over the others?

   3.6 Sales expectations

   Provide an estimate of sales over the first year broken down by quarter. How many units will be sold globally, as well as within key markets, like the United States, England, Japan, etc.?

4. **Legal analysis**

   Describe all legal and financial obligations regarding copyrights, trademarks, contracts, and licensing agreements.

5. **Gameplay**

   5.1 Overview

   This is where you describe the core gameplay. This should tie directly into your physical or software prototype. Use your prototype as the model and give an overview of how it functions.

   5.2 Gameplay description

   Provide a detailed description of how the game functions.

   5.3 Controls

   Map out the game procedures and controls. Use visual aids if possible like control tables and flowcharts, along with detailed descriptions.

5.3.1 Interfaces

Create wireframes for every interface the artists will need to create. Along with each wireframe should be a description of how it functions. Make sure your detail out the various states for each interface.

5.3.2 Rules

If you've created a prototype, describing the rules of your game will be much easier. You'll need to define all the game objects, concepts, their behaviors, and how they relate to one another in this section.

5.3.3 Scoring/winning conditions

Describe the scoring system and win conditions—these may be different for single-player versus multiplayer, or if you have several modes of competition.

5.4 Modes and other features

If your game has different modes of play, such as single and multiplayer modes, or other features that will affect the implementation of the gameplay, you'll need to describe them here.

5.5 Levels

The designs for each level should be laid out here. The more detailed the better.

5.6 Flowchart

Create a flowchart showing all the areas and screens that will need to be created.

5.7 Editor

If your game will require the creation of a proprietary level editor, describe the necessary features of editor and any details on its functionality.

5.7.1 Features

5.7.2 Details

6. Game characters

6.1 Character design

This is where you describe any game characters and their attributes.

6.2 Types

6.2.1 PCs (player characters)

6.2.2 NPCs (nonplayer characters)

If your game involves character types, you'll need to treat each one as an object, defining its properties and functionality.

6.2.2.1 Monsters and enemies

6.2.2.2 Friends and allies

6.2.2.3 Neutral

6.2.2.4 Other types

6.2.2.5 Guidelines

6.2.2.6 Traits

6.2.2.7 Behavior

6.2.2.8 AI

7. Story

7.1 Synopsis

If your game includes a story, summarize it here. Keep it down to one or two paragraphs.

7.2 Complete story

This is your chance to outline the entire story. Do so in a way that mirrors the gameplay. Don't just tell your story but structure it so that it unfolds as the game progresses.

7.3 Backstory

Describe any important elements of your story that don't tie directly into the gameplay. Much of this might not actually make it into the game, but it may be good to have it for reference.

7.4 Narrative devices

Describe the various ways in which you plan to reveal the story. What are the devices you plan to use to tell the story?

7.5 Subplots

Because games are not linear like books and movies, there may be numerous smaller stories interwoven into the main story.

Describe each of these subplots and explain how they tie into the gameplay and the master plot.

7.5.1 Subplot #1

7.5.2 Subplot #2

8. **The game world**

If your game involves the creation of a world, you need to go into detail on all aspects of that world.

8.1 Overview

8.2 Key locations

8.3 Travel

8.4 Mapping

8.5 Scale

8.6 Physical objects

8.7 Weather conditions

8.8 Day and night

8.9 Time

8.10 Physics

8.11 Society/culture

9. **Media list**

9.1 Interface assets

9.2 Environments

9.3 Characters

9.4 Animation

9.5 Music and sound effects

List all of the media that will need to be produced. The specifics of your game will dictate what categories you need to include. Be detailed with this list, and create a file naming convention up front. This can avoid a lot of confusion later on.

10. **Technical spec**

As mentioned, the technical spec is not always included in the design document. Often, it is a separate document prepared in conjunction with the design document. This spec is prepared by the technical lead on the project.

10.1 Technical analysis

10.1.1 New technology

Is there any new technology that you plan on developing for this game? If so, describe it in detail.

10.1.2 Major software development tasks

Do you need to do a lot of software development for the game to work? Or are you simply going to license someone else's engine or use a preexisting engine that you've created?

10.1.3 Risks

What are the risks inherent in your strategy?

10.1.4 Alternatives

Are there any alternatives that may lower the risks and the cost?

10.1.5 Estimated resources required

Describe the resources you would need to develop the new technology and software needed for the game.

10.2 Development platform and tools

Describe the development platform, as well as any software tools and hardware that are required to produce the game.

10.2.1 Software

10.2.2 Hardware

10.3 Delivery

How do you plan to deliver this game? On CD-ROM, over the Internet, on wireless devices? What's required to accomplish this?

10.3.1 Required hardware and software

10.3.2 Required materials

10.4 Game engine

10.4.1 Technical Specs

What are the specs of your game engine?

10.4.2 Design

Describe the design of your game engine.

10.4.2.1 Features

10.4.2.2 Details

10.4.3 Collision Detection

If your game involves collision detection, how does it work?

10.4.3.1 Features

10.4.3.2 Details

10.5 Interface technical specs

This is where you describe how your interface is designed from a technical perspective. What tools do you plan to use and how will it function?

10.5.1 Features

10.5.2 Details

10.6 Controls' technical specs

This is where you describe how your controls work from a technical perspective. Are you planning on supporting any usual input devices that would require specialized programming?

10.6.1 Features

10.6.2 Details

10.7 Lighting models

Lighting can be a substantial part of a game. Describe how it works and the features that you require.

10.7.1 Modes

10.7.1.1 Features

10.7.1.2 Details

10.7.2 Models

10.7.3 Light sources

10.8 Rendering system

Rendering is a big part of games these days, and the more details you can provide the better.

10.8.1 Technical specs

10.8.2 2D/3D rendering

10.8.3 Camera

10.8.3.1 Operation

10.8.3.2 Features

10.8.3.3 Details

10.9 Internet/network spec

If you game requires the use of the Internet, LANs, or wireless networks, you should make the specs clear.

10.10 System parameters

We won't go into detail on all the possible system parameters, but suffice to say that the design document should list them all and describe their functionality.

10.10.1 Max players

10.10.2 Servers

10.10.3 Customization

10.10.4 Connectivity

10.10.5 Web sites

10.10.6 Persistence

10.10.7 Saving games

10.10.8 Loading games

10.11 Other

This section is for any other technical specifications that should be included, such as "help menus," "manuals," "setup and installation routines," etc.

10.11.1 Help

10.11.2 Manual

10.11.3 Setup

11. Appendices

The appendix is the perfect place for reference documents, such as agreements with third party developers, subcontractors, or talent. Also details on hardware or software can be included in the appendices so that they don't clutter up the main design document. In general, if there are lengthy pieces of information and data that your team may need but that don't belong in the body of the design document, you can place them in the appendices.

11.1 Appendix A

11.2 Appendix B

11.3 Appendix C

We want to emphasize that the previous outline is merely a list of suggested topics that may need to be addressed in order to communicate your design. Every game will have its own specific needs and the organization of your design document should reflect these needs.

The following table of contents from a game design document is an example of how one game has dealt with these topics. The game is *Godzilla: Destroy All Monsters Melee*, published by Atari and developed by Pipeworks Software. The game

DESIGNER PERSPECTIVE: CHRIS TAYLOR

Title: President, Gas Powered Games

Project list (five to eight top projects)

- *Hardball II*
- *4D Boxing*
- *Test Drive II*
- *Triple Play Baseball*
- *Total Annihilation*
- *Total Annihilation: The Core Contingency*
- *Dungeon Siege*

How did you get into the game industry?

I started in the business by answering a small classified ad in the newspaper. I started as a programmer at a game developer in Burnaby, B.C., Canada called Distinctive Software. My first assignment was to do *Hardball II*. It was a sequel to the hugely successful *Hardball* by Bob Whitehead, and was a great learning experience. I worked almost every single day for the eighteen months it took to develop the game.

What are your five favorite games and why?

This list changes over time, but some of them include *Populous* (PC), *Duke Nukem 3D* (PC), the original *Command & Conquer* (PC), *Ratchet & Clank* (PS2) and now *Battlefield: 1942* (PC).

What games have inspired you the most as a designer and why?

The most inspirational games are the early Sid Meier and Peter Molyneux games, and then without a doubt *Dune II* and *Command & Conquer* from Westwood Studios. Without *Command & Conquer* I would never have left EA to create *Total Annihilation*.

What are you most proud of in your career?

Total Annihilation because of the very short timeline we created it in—20 months from beginning to end, and that it had such a huge mod community, and then *Dungeon Siege* for the sheer engineering complexity.

What words of advice would you give to an aspiring designer today?

My advice would be to get a job in the business at any level to get your foot in the door. Once you see how games are really made you will change your strategy and get your game made much sooner, even though it could take you ten years to learn the business. Read every book you can find and play every game you can get your hands on. Pick your role models and look carefully at how they find success.

designer and producer, Kirby Fong, has provided an excellent overview of the design in the manner in which the sections and subsections are organized. In just a brief glimpse, you can get a good idea of whether or not the topic your interested in is covered in the design document and where to find it.

Godzilla: Destroy All Monsters Melee Design Document, Version 2.1

Copyright 2000 Pipeworks Software

1. **Legal notifications**

2. **Essence of Godzilla**
   2.1   Gameplay emphasis

3. **The story**

4. **Features**

5. **The look**
   5.1   Game views

6. **Gameplay**
   6.1   The battles
        6.1.1   Weapons play
        6.1.2   Hand-to-hand combat
        6.1.3   Fight again?
        6.1.4   Health and energy
        6.1.5   Rage
        6.1.6   Power-ups
        6.1.7   City destruction
        6.1.8   Human armies
        6.1.9   Fight boundary

7. **Play modes**
   7.1   Adventure mode (1 player)
        7.1.1   Scoring
        7.1.2   Rounds
        7.1.3   Fight again (reset)
        7.1.4   Elapsed time counter
        7.1.5   Unlocking the "hidden" monster
        7.1.6   MemCard data
        7.1.7   Adventure options

   7.1.8   Adventure mode game flow
   7.2   VS mode (1 or 2 players)
        7.2.1   Scoring
        7.2.2   End game options
        7.2.3   MemCard data
   7.3   Melee mode (2 to 4 players)
        7.3.1   Melee rules settings
        7.3.2   MemCard data
   7.4   Team battle (3 to 4 players)
        7.4.1   Rules settings
   7.5   Destruction Mode (2 to 4 players)
        7.5.1   Scoring
        7.5.2   Destruction game flow
   7.6   Survival mode (1 player)

8. **Game flow chart**

9. **Art components**
   9.1   Front end screens
        9.1.1   Intro
        9.1.2   Title screen/main menu
        9.1.3   Adventure screen
        9.1.4   VS: monster select screen
        9.1.5   Melee: monster select screen
        9.1.6   Team battle: monster select screen
        9.1.7   Destruction: monster select screen
        9.1.8   Survival: monster select screen
        9.1.9   City selection screen
        9.1.10 Main options screen
        9.1.11 Adventure "Top 10" screen
        9.1.12 Survival "Top 10" screen
   9.2   Fight Screen
        9.2.1   3D elements
        9.2.2   Overlays
   9.3   Environments
        9.3.1   Tokyo
        9.3.2   San Francisco
        9.3.3   Los Angeles
        9.3.4   London
        9.3.5   Monster Island
        9.3.6   Osaka

Under each of the sections in your design document, you need to answer all the questions that a team member may have. For instance, the "character designs" section would include drawings and a description of each character in the game, while the "levels" section would include not only the intended gameplay for each the level but explanations of any story elements that would be found in each level.

Writing Your Design Document

Before you sit down to write your design document, you should have spent a considerable amount of time thinking through the gameplay. The best way to do this, as we already discussed, is to build a physical or software prototype of your game and playtest it, improving and expanding your design until you have a solid foundation for your full game. Only after you have gone through several iterations of prototype can you really be ready to write your design document.

Many designers will move to an outline, and start pounding out the text of the design document at this point. We recommend flowcharting your entire game and building a set of wireframe interfaces for every screen in the game first. As we briefly discussed in Chapter 11 on page 306, a wireframe is a rough sketch that shows all the features that will need to be included on an interface screen. By sketching out both the flow of the game and every required screen, you will be forced to think through the entire player experience for the game—finding inconsistencies and issues before any artwork or programming has been done.

Figure 14.2 is an example of a game flowchart created using typical software, like Microsoft Visio. This is for an online multiplayer version of the *Wheel of Fortune* game. As you can see, it illustrates how players move through the game and interact with it. Notice how the flowchart shows all possible paths through the game and all possible results, including how the player wins and loses, as well as what happens if the player disconnects.

You can use flowcharts to map out all sorts of processes within your game. The more detailed you are, the easier it will be to communicate your ideas to your teammates.

After you create your flowcharts, you'll need to sketch out the main interfaces for the game in wireframe format. Figure 14.3 shows an interface wireframe from *Wheel of Fortune*, an early concept sketch for the interface, and the final interface as released. If you look closely, you'll see that several changes were made during production—notably in the way that chat is handled in the game. Wireframes are not the end of the design process, but the beginning. They give the game designer, the artists, programmers, and producers a visual reference point to discuss the game in its early stages. They can also be usability tested at this point. Changes can be made to the design at this point, when they cost nothing to make, rather than months down the road when they would have much higher repercussions.

Exercise 14.2: Flowchart and Wireframes

Either on paper or using a software tool like MS Visio or Flow Charting PDQ, create a full flowchart for your original game design. Complete the set of wireframes you created in Exercise 11.8 if you have not yet done so. Now, annotate your wireframes with callouts describing every feature as described in the next paragraph.

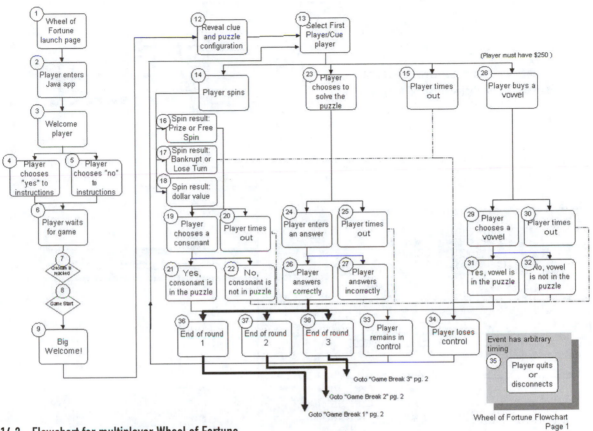

14.2   Flowchart for multiplayer Wheel of Fortune

Now that you've created a prototype, a flow chart, and a full set of wireframes, you will have a very good idea of what you need to communicate in your design document. You'll also have a set of visual aids for explaining the features of you game. Most people can absorb information more clearly from visual displays like your wireframes than from long paragraphs of text explaining the features of your game. Because of this, your wireframes are not only a good tool to help you think through your game, but they are an excellent reference point for your readers. As you outline your document, use the flowchart and wireframes to explain the areas and features of the game. You may want to create callouts on your wireframes explaining how various features will work. These callouts can be supported by bullet points that expand on the visual diagrams.

Ideally, by working through your concept from prototype to flowchart and wireframes to documentation, you will find that the document is actually quite simple to write. Instead of being faced with the mammoth task of thinking through the game while you write the document, you will have broken the task down into smaller stages that

14.3 Interface wireframes, sketches, and final interface for multiplayer Wheel of Fortune

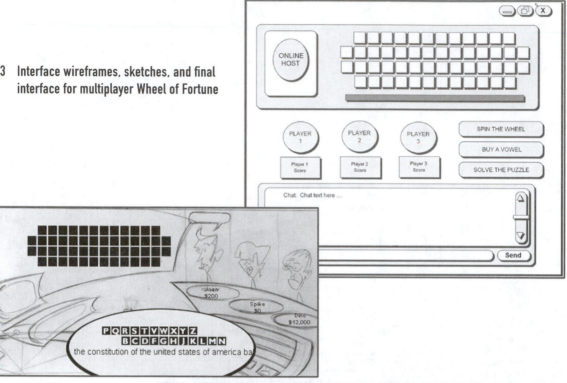

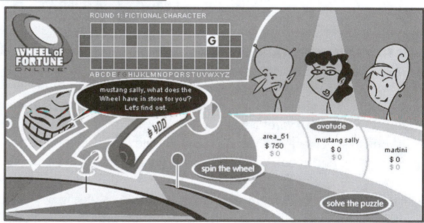

allow the game itself to dictate how the design document should be written.

As with the rest of your design experience, the document should be an interactive process. Don't try to complete it in a single pass. Let it grow over time. Fill out sections as they become clear, then go back to other sections and refine them.

Exercise 14.3: Table of Contents

Outline the table of contents for your original design document. Consider every aspect of your prototype, flowchart, and wireframes when you are deciding how to describe your game. Draw from the example documents you downloaded from the web and the ones shown in this chapter.

You may realize while writing a later section that your thoughts from an earlier section need to be revised. Since everything in the design document is linked, you'll be continually going back and forth between the sections, modifying and updating them. Here's an example as to how the process might go for the "level design" section:

- *First pass:* Make outline of all levels and give them names
- *Second pass:* Write one paragraph descriptions of what takes place on each level
- *Third pass:* Design maps for each level
- *Fourth pass:* Populate maps with content

Exercise 14.4: Fleshing Out Your Design Document

Flesh out your design document using your table of contents, your flowchart, wireframes, and the documentation you created while designing your prototype, such as your concept document, rules, etc. Work with your team members to complete each section as described earlier.

USING THE DESIGN DOCUMENT

Writing the design document will help you clarify the details of your design. Once the document is written, it is used to manage team members from both the publisher and the developer. The core concept as detailed by the design document will be approved by the publisher before the team moves into production. Then, the document will evolve as the project progresses. It is part of the game designers's job to keep the design document current with the changes that occur during production and to make sure the team knows that these changes have been made.

In most cases, it's best to use a standard word processor like Microsoft Word to create your design document, unless your company has a particular piece of software that they require. The advantage of using a common file format like a word processing document is that it can be easily distributed, and other team members can modify it or make suggestions.

Some designers like to create their design document as an internal web site rather than a text document. This has both advantages and disadvantages. If well done, it's easy for everyone to access and update. You can easily post links to new sketches, builds, levels, and other works-in-progress for everyone to see. One problem with this method is that it's not as portable as a standard document, or as easy to print out. Also, a web site can be more difficult to code and maintain.

A better strategy is to have a weekly update schedule, and to remind all the team members via an e-mail that lists the revised areas. This way, if your teammates are affected by the revision, they can download the new document. If you send updates more often than once a week, you'll find that you begin to lose your audience—remember

Design Documents—An Interview with Chris Taylor

Chris Taylor is a prolific game designer and CEO of Gas Powered Games. He created an excellent template for writing design documents for digital games. The template is available for free on the Internet.

Game Design Workshop: Why did you write a design document template? And why did you decide to make it freely available?

Chris Taylor: I can't remember the exact reason, but I think it was after a talk I gave where someone asked me if I had a sample design doc they could look at. I took the design for *Dungeon Siege* and basically used that by removing all the specific *Dungeon Siege* design. I took what was left and used that as a framework that I could share with others. As for sharing it, that wasn't even something I thought about... I am happy to share stuff like this, that's a no-brainer.

GDW: What is your personal approach to writing a design document?

CT: Each time I have sat down to write a game design the approach is usually evolved from the last one. When creating a new design I describe the high level stuff at the start of the document, and then cover the details later. One of the key things I do right up front is to answer the 10 most difficult and jaded questions that someone may ask that challenges my design. Like I have always said, if I can't answer these questions, it's a good time to reconsider why making the game is a good idea in the first place.

GDW: What is the role of a design document in a Gas Powered Games production? How often does one typically change during a production?

CT: A design doc is very important, but to the individual members of the team it's the specification docs that are really key. These docs are what people actually use to create the game with. It's very important to have the design docs, but they are only a starting place. In general it is possible that the design process be a fluid one but we try not to do that... anymore. It's too expensive and confusing to constantly change design. It's better to have a long pre-production phase where

that these are very busy people. All they want to know is the vital information that they need to get their jobs done. If that is clearly presented in the document, easy to find, and updated regularly, your design document will be an effective tool for the production.

Conclusion

In this chapter, you've learned how to take your original game concept from the prototype to a full design document. You've created detailed flowcharts and wireframes for every area of your game.

the design gets locked down, and then go into full production where the game is created. Sometimes an intermediate step is needed to prove-out the fun factor and playability of a game, but that's a decision you make on a case-by-case basis.

About Chris Taylor

Chris Taylor began his career in the videogames business at Distinctive Software in Canada. His first title, Hardball II was a sequel to the popular Hardball, and won the SPA (Software Publishers Association) award for best sports game of the year. Next, Chris created 4D Boxing, which won many accolades for its innovation as a 3D title. Chris later served as designer and project lead for the original Triple Play Baseball at Electronic Arts. Chris went on to create the highly acclaimed RTS, Total Annihilation, at Cavedog Entertainment. After completing the expansion pack, "The Core Contingency," he decided to start his own company. Chris founded Gas Powered Games in May of 1998. GPG released its first title, Dungeon Siege for the PC in April of 2002. Gas Powered Games has established itself as an innovator in both technology and gameplay, and is now working on its next round of games to be released in the near future.

Dungeon Siege

Dungeon Siege trademark Microsoft Corporation

You've worked with your team, if you have one, to flesh out both the technical and creative tasks that will need to be accomplished to make your game a reality.

Writing and updating your design document is a monumental and sometimes tedious responsibility. The design document can be a useful tool, or a millstone around the designer's neck. Always remember that the purpose of your design document is communication and articulation. A designer huddled in a cubicle writing in isolation for weeks on end will produce a document that is far less valuable than a designer who engages the team, includes them in the process, and works with them to build out each section.

By working with the team, a designer will not only wind up with a better design document but will also help focus the team on the project at hand. This is how living design documents are cre-ated, and when you have a living document, in which everyone is an acting co-author, it becomes a force in and of itself, which serves to unite the team and give them a common platform from which to understand the game as it evolves.

PERSPECTIVE FROM THE TRENCHES: CHRISTOPHER RUBYOR

Chris Rubyor is a seasoned game professional who recently earned the title "Game Designer" at Electronic Arts.

Title: Game Designer, Electronic Arts, Los Angeles

Project list

- *Command & Conquer: Generals Zero Hour* (2003): Game Designer
- *Command & Conquer: Generals* (2003): Community Manager
- *Command & Conquer: Renegade* (2002): Community Manager
- *Command & Conquer: Yuri's Revenge* (2001): Community Manager
- *Emperor: Battle for Dune* (2001): Community Manager
- *Command & Conquer: Red Alert 2* (2000): Community Manager
- *Command & Conquer: Tiberian Sun: Firestorm* (2000): Public Relations
- *Nox* (2000): Public Relations
- *Command & Conquer: Tiberian Sun* (1999): Public Relations
- *Lands of Lore III* (1999): Public Relations
- *Recoil* (1999): Public Relations
- *Dune 2000: Long Live the Fighters!* (1998): Public Relations
- *Blade Runner* (1997): Public Relations
- *Games People Play: Hearts, Spades, and Euchre* (1997): Public Relations
- *Lands of Lore: Guardians of Destiny* (1997): Public Relations
- *Command & Conquer: Red Alert* (1996): QA Analyst
- *Command & Conquer: The Covert Operations* (1996): QA Analyst
- *Command & Conquer* (1995): QA Analyst
- *Monopoly* (1995): QA Analyst
- *Lion King* (1994) (Nintendo, Sega): QA Analyst
- *The Legend of Kyrandia: Malcolm's Revenge* (1994): QA Analyst

How did you get into the game industry?

Well, I was fortunate enough to know someone who worked in the industry. At the time (1994), I was working at a computer store selling games and hardware. One day my old boss called the store and asked if I was interested in working as a QA analyst for the company that created *Dune II* (Westwood Studios). Being a big fan of *Dune II* and *The Legend of Kyrandia*, I couldn't refuse.

What's the most interesting thing that's happened on the job?

During the project it was very inspiring when the team would put in long hours to get features into the game, that otherwise, might not have made it into the final version. We would often find ourselves at the studio until 1:30 a.m. fine tuning and polishing missions to make them that much better for our fans. It's a great feeling when you have a team that dedicated to making great games.

What experiences have taught you the most about game design?

For every designer it's different. I knew from the day I started working at Westwood Studios that I wanted to be a game designer. Unlike most, I made a conscious decision to learn more about the industry, thus my foray into marketing and community support.

From 1997 through 2000 I worked as a PR manager for Westwood Studios under Laura Miele (VP of Marketing) at the time. This position gave me the opportunity to learn about marketing products to our consumers and the importance of PR and how it related to gaming. I traveled to various trade shows, worked with some of the top gaming magazines from around the world, and helped set up events to promote Westwood's games. It was great experience that I look back on with fond memories.

Starting June 2000, I made the decision to take on a new community manager (*Command & Conquer*) position at Westwood Studios. It was something new to the company and dealt exclusively with the fans. For the next year I worked very closely with Brett Sperry, the company's co-founder and visionary behind the *Command & Conquer* series, and Ted Morris, the web development director, to carve out the role. Working with these two individuals gave me the chance to learn a great deal about web design and the importance of an online community for a multiplayer product.

Over the next three years I did everything from helping design web sites and managing message boards to creating six-month community plans layered with events for both pre- and post–launch of a product. I also put on the PR hat at times and set up online chat events, contests, and fan site events at the main studio to help excite and promote growth of our community. From this I walked away with a wealth of knowledge about online gaming, community integration, and a realization that multiplayer gaming is my passion.

In July of 2003 I made the decision to begin working my way into a design position. Westwood Studios was just beginning work on a new project and the team was limited to only a few developers. So, after hours I began working with the creative director on concepts and big ideas. We also talked a lot about multiplayer gaming and what we should try for our next game. After about six months an assistant design position became available and I gladly took on the role.

Now I'm working as a full-time game designer at Electronic Arts in the RTS division. I credit the choices I made and people I met for my smooth transition into my dream job.

Where do you hope to be in five years?

I plan on to continuing my pursuit of creating great games, wherever that my take me.

What words of advice would you give to a person trying to get into the industry today?

Don't be afraid to take chances; it would be a shame for gamers to miss out on the next killer game experience.

Chapter 15
Understanding the Game Industry

Unless you are a producer or an executive, you may never even see the contract or terms under which your game is produced. You may not feel the need to understand the royalty structure of the agreement, or the rights assignments for the characters you create. You may want to ignore all the lengthy contract language and business mumbo jumbo and stay focused on what you love—designing games. But if you are going to be a smart, effective, and successful game designer, you might want to think again before dismissing the business side of things so quickly.

Understanding the basic structure of the game industry—the players, the market, and how business deals are structured between publishers and developers—is knowledge that can make you a better designer, especially in a commercial sense. This chapter provides a basic overview of how the game industry works and how deals are structured to produce and publish games. It is not a comprehensive explanation, but it will give you enough understanding to participate intelligently in the deal-making process for your game if you are invited to do so. Even if you are not part of that process, this information will help you to understand the concerns of, and communicate more clearly with, the executives and marketing people working on your game.

Our advice to all game designers is to embrace business knowledge in the same way you would embrace technical knowledge. You may not specialize in either, but understanding how the business aspects of the industry work, and how they affect your designs, will help you be a more effective creative person and a more valuable resource on the team.

THE SIZE OF THE GAME INDUSTRY

The game industry currently brings in around $36 billion dollars annually worldwide. In the United States alone annual revenues are about $10 billion, which is slightly bigger that the U.S. domestic box office revenues from the film industry. Because of this, many people refer to games as "bigger than movies" these days. This isn't precisely true—movies make most of their money today on DVD sales, as well as rights for broadcast, cable, and foreign distribution. The $10 billion number for games revenue also includes hardware sales. If we only look at software sales alone, which are a

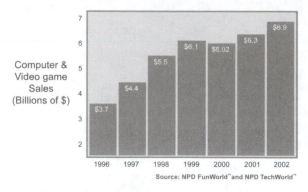

Computer & Video game Sales (Billions of $)

Source: NPD FunWorld™ and NPD TechWorld™

15.1 Videogame sales growth

more equivalent comparison to box office revenues, the U.S. game industry makes about $6.9 billion annually. So while games are large and growing, they still have a ways to go before they truly surpass the film industry in terms of domestic revenue.

It may not take long before the games industry bridges this gap, however, because the industry has remained strong, even in the face of recession, and has grown steadily over the past decade. Figure 15.1 shows the growth of videogame sales (PC and console) in the U.S. since 1995.

Digital games have become a significant form of entertainment since their introduction in the 1970s. Today, more than 60% of all Americans, or about 145 million people, play games on a regular basis.[1] The split between men and women players is closing as well, with women comprising 38% of PC gamers and 28% of console players. As several generations of players have grown up with digital games, most have continued to play as they grew older: 40% of PC gamers are over the age of 36, and 26% are between 18 and 35. The majority of game players have been playing for more than six

years. Figure 15.2 shows that gaming is a phenomenon that people tend to continue once they've begun.

According to Entertainment Software Association President Doug Lowenstein, "Video games have become a leading form of mass market entertainment as the core user has aged from the teens into adulthood, and millions more casual gamers join the hard core gamers to drive market growth and expansion."[2] All of these statements point to the fact that digital games are no longer a niche market. They are making the transition from being a pastime to becoming an integral part of the entertainment industry. In many ways, they are redefining our culture and our expectations about media and entertainment. Journalist Bob Schwabach said in a New York Times article, "The video game industry has been on the threshold of seizing dominance in entertainment for several years. Ultimately, it will. It's inevitable."

This phenomenon is not limited to the United States. The game industry is growing worldwide. The U.S. may be the single largest market, but countries like Japan, the U.K., Canada, and France are also known for their game industries and high-

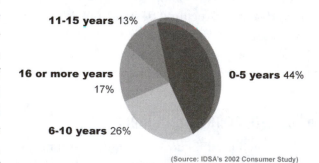

(Source: IDSA's 2002 Consumer Study)

15.2 How long have most gamers been playing games?

---

1. Peter D. Hart Research, as quoted in "Essential Facts about the Computer and Game Industry," Entertainment Software Association.

2. Entertainment Software Association, "Essential Facts about the Computer and Game Industry."

quality products. The worldwide sales of video-games are nearly $18 billion annually, with another $18 billion in hardware and peripheral sales mak- ing the total worldwide game market approxi-mately $36 billion per year.[3]

PLATFORMS FOR DISTRIBUTION

One way to define the basic segments of the game industry is by the platforms for which games are distributed. Consoles dominate the sales of the industry by far. Of the $6.3 billion in sales in 2001, $4.6 billion of that were sales of console games, with computer game sales bringing in $1.42 billion, and edutainment titles the remaining $322.6 mil-lion (see Figure 15.3).

Console

Within the console market, there are various com-petitors. Historically, the console market has always been dominated by one or two players, with cutthroat competition and technological advances meaning new platform releases every three to five years. The console machines of today have astounding processing power and graphics capabilities. This enables designers to create dra-matic experiences with production values rivaling television and film. Here's a breakdown of today's top console platforms.

Sony PlayStation 2

The PS2 dominates the current console market. As early as 2000, Sony had already shipped 51 million PS1 boxes, giving them a healthy head start, and with the release of the PS2, Sony now has the number one platform. As of early 2003, they had shipped 52.5 million units worldwide and seemed only to be gaining momentum. Sony added broad-band connectivity to the PS2, is developing the upcoming PlayStation 3, is recruiting software developers, and is preparing to take console wars to a whole new level.

Microsoft Xbox

The Xbox is in second place and doing well in the U.S., but not so well in Japan and Europe. As of July, 2003, Microsoft had sold just over 9.4 million Xbox consoles worldwide, according to its quarterly financial statement. Microsoft projects the Xbox installed base will grow to between 14.5 and 16 million consoles by June 2004. Microsoft has also launched Xbox Live, with more than 500,000 sub-scribers worldwide to date. Despite heavy compe-tition, Microsoft looks like it's in the game for the long run, and with a mighty war chest and strong developers, it should continue to draw a healthy audience.

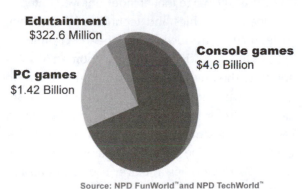

Edutainment
$322.6 Million

PC games
$1.42 Billion

Console games
$4.6 Billion

Source: NPD FunWorld™ and NPD TechWorld™

15.3   Console game sales versus computer game sales

3.   Global Information, Inc., "Video Games: The Dominant Form of Electronic Entertainment."

Nintendo GameCube

The GameCube looks like it may slip into third place, which historically is not a good place to be in the hyper-competitive platform wars. The GameCube is roughly even with the Xbox, having sold 9.4 million units as of April 2003. While Sony and Microsoft seem to be targeting the same market, Nintendo has aimed at a younger demographic and has produced some outstanding and original games. Time will tell if Nintendo's strategy pays off. If anyone can survive as a third player, it's Nintendo, which has a devoted following based on its years of domination in the marketplace and its history of releasing innovative games with memorable original characters.

Computer

The computer game market is much smaller than the console game market, and is divided by games created for the two dominant operating systems. Computer game players tend to be older than console game players, and more evenly divided between male and female.

Microsoft Windows OS

Games made for Windows dominate the computer game market. With high-end graphic cards, DirectX, and broadband connectivity, PCs are a powerful platform for gaming—especially online gaming. PC gamers tend to prefer strategy and simulation games to the action and sports games that dominate the console market.

Apple Macintosh OS

The Mac operating system is a distant second. Despite what many true believers feel to be a much more elegant OS, Windows dominates both the home and office, while Apple's share continues to hover between 3% and 5% of the desktop market. As a result, most PC games today are made for Windows, and only ported to the Mac OS if there is strong market reason to do so.

Other platforms

In addition to consoles and PCs, digital games are distributed in several other ways. Handheld devices, arcade games, and emerging platforms such as cell phones, PDAs, and interactive television systems are other aspects of the industry that game designers need to pay attention to.

Nintendo Game Boy Advance

The GBA dominates the handheld gaming market. Others have tried to break the hold that Nintendo has had on this market since their release of the original Game Boy system, but have met with very limited success. Possible competition in the future may come from Sony's PSP. Touted by Sony as a "21st century Walkman," this multi-use device is scheduled to be released in 2004.

Coin-op arcade

Arcade games are dwindling as a market these days. The advantage that arcades enjoyed in terms of superior graphics and technology when they were first introduced has been completely eclipsed by the advancements in home consoles and PCs. The only lingering advantage that arcade games have is in their ability to deliver sophisticated control systems—such as footpads, motion capture frames, mock race cars, and immersive VR environments. The success of games like *Dance Dance Revolution* lies in clever use of this advantage.

Emerging platforms

Emerging platforms are a next frontier for games. Many companies are working to develop the next great gaming platform, whether it's interactive television systems, mobile phones with color screens, or DVD players that double as game machines. Most of these fall by the wayside as quickly as they crop up, but every now and then, one surprises us. Mobile phone games seem to be big as a new gaming platform in Japan right now, but in the U.S. they haven't gained much traction. Similarly, pay-per-play games have made a big impact on the interactive television systems in the U.K. and Europe, but in the U.S. these systems have been slow to deploy.

GENRES OF GAMEPLAY

In addition to platforms, another important way of looking at the game industry is in terms of game genres. You've probably noticed by now that we did not emphasize the concept of genre in any of our discussions about design. This is because we believe genres are a mixed blessing to a game designer.

On one hand, genres give designers and publishers a common language for describing styles of play: They form a shorthand for understanding what market a game is intended for, what platforms the game will be best suited to, who should be developing a particular title, etc. On the other hand, genres also tend to restrict the creative process and lead designers toward tried and true gameplay solutions. We encourage you to consider genre when thinking about your projects from a business perspective, but not to allow it to stifle your imagination during the design process.

That said, genre is a big part of the today's game industry, and as a designer, it's important for you to understand the role it plays. The top-selling genres differ between platforms, and between market segments. When publishers look at your game, they want to know where it falls in current buying trends of the gaming audience. Without the benefit of genre, this would be a difficult task.

Although we don't want you to inhibit your design process by too great an emphasis on genre, designers can learn something from the publishers' emphasis on creating product for players who enjoy specific types of gameplay. In order to better understand today's top-selling genres, we've briefly listed their key differentiators.

Action games

Action games emphasize reaction time and hand-eye coordination. While store shelves are packed

2001 Computer Game Sales by Genre

15.4 Top-selling genres in 2002

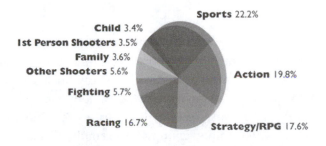

2001 Video Game Sales by Genre
(Sources: NPD TechWorld™ and NPD FunWorld™)

Beginner Perspective: Jim Vessella

Title: Production Intern, Vivendi Universal Games / Student, University of Southern California

Project list: Six unannounced titles with Vivendi Universal Games

How did you get into the game industry?

I always wanted to get into the industry, but like most people had trouble finding an open door. I thus spent all my time learning about the industry so I would be prepared when an interview came up. I would read about the industry on a daily basis, analyze reviews, and play as many different games as possible. I would also take every opportunity to talk to people in the industry, you'd be surprised how eager some people are to simply share their experiences or give some inspirational words of wisdom.

During our Spring 2003 career fair at USC, I met the recruiter from Vivendi Universal Games who was looking for applicants to their summer internship program. I jumped at the opportunity, and kept in touch with her for several months after sending in my application. I was also fortunate enough to meet their VP of Product Development during my game design class at USC and again at E3. Through continuous networking I finally scored an interview and was lucky enough to be selected for the position.

What's the most interesting thing that's happened on the job

I was responsible for directing and creating game trailers for internal demonstration and promotion. I would constantly look at competitive titles, reviews, previews, and videos to compare and thus improve our current projects, along with perform market research to evaluate risk in new concepts.

Since I was with a publisher, we often had up and coming developers pitch us projects in the hope of gaining a publishing contract. On one specific occasion, a developer came in with a great looking game almost 3/4 complete. I was amazed at how innovative and polished the game looked without prior publishing overhead. It was a great opportunity to see how beautiful a game can be made without having a ridiculous amount of time or money.

with titles that utilize 3D graphics and the first-person perspective, this is more of a trend than a genre requirement. Action games can include titles as disparate as *Unreal Tournament*, *Grand Theft Auto III*, and *Tetris*. Action as a genre often overlaps with other genres, for example, *Grand Theft Auto III* is an action game, but it is also a driving/racing game and an adventure game. *Tetris* is an action game and a puzzle game. *The Legend of Zelda: The Wind Waker* is an action adventure game, and *Diablo* is considered a role-playing action game. Action games are without exception real-time experiences, with an emphasis on time constraints for performing physical tasks.

What experiences have taught you the most about game design?

In the School of Cinema at USC, I took a class in game design taught by the authors of this book. The class took an in-depth look at how games operate as interactive systems, and analyzed game history in an attempt to unfold why certain design traits are successful and why others fail.

During my internship one producer instructed me to map out the levels of certain games on paper, and write walkthroughs as though I were explaining the level to programmers, artists, and sound designers. The exercise made me realize how every room in a level should have a purpose, and how on every level the player should be learning new tactics or introduced to new challenges.

Where do you hope to be in five years?

I hope to be working with a major publisher or developer, with an opportunity to give input on design and the creative process. I am fascinated by the current trend in hybrid genres, and hopefully I will have a chance to someday work with these innovative projects.

Jim Vessella, left, testing one of his game prototypes with other student designers.

What words of advice would you give to a person trying to get into the industry today?

Be passionate and be persistent. Play games from all genres and platforms, read about the industry on a daily basis, and constantly search for internships or entry-level positions. Use these positions as a chance to network with employees and prove that you can handle greater responsibility.

Strategy games

Strategy games focus on tactics and planning, as well as the management of units and resources. The themes tend to revolve around conquest, exploration, and trade. Included in this genre are *Masters of Orion, Civilization, Settlers,* and *Risk.* Originally, most strategy games drew upon classic strategy boardgames and adopted turn-based systems, giving players ample time to make decisions; however, the popularity of *WarCraft II* and *Command & Conquer* changed everything, ushering in the subgenre of real-time strategy games. Today there are even action/strategy games, which combine physical dexterity with strategic decision-making. *Uprising* and *Shogun: Total War* are examples that fit into this hybrid genre. Pure strategy games like chess and checkers are increasingly rare in the world of digital entertainment, as the market has moved toward incorporating some elements of chance with the strategic decision making, as well as plenty of action.

Role-playing games

Role-playing games revolve around creating and growing characters. They tend to include rich storylines tied into quests. The paper-based system of *Dungeons & Dragons* is the great-grandfather of this genre, which has inspired such digital games as *Baldur's Gate*, *Dungeon Siege*, *EverQuest*, and the pioneering *NetHack*. All role-playing games begin and end with the character. Players typically seek to develop their characters, while managing inventory, exploring worlds, and accumulating wealth, status, and experience. Many role-playing games take weeks, if not months, to complete, and the play can be quite slow when compared to action games. However, a new breed of role-playing/action games, made popular by *Diablo*, has sprung up and combines traditional elements with fast-paced twitch play.

Sports games

Sports games are, quite simply, simulations of sports like tennis, football, baseball, soccer, etc. Since the success of *Pong*, simulations of sports have always made up a strong segment of the digital game market. Some of the most popular sports games today are *Madden NFL*, *FIFA Soccer*, *NBA Jam*, as well as *Sega Bass Fishing* and *Tony Hawk Pro Skater*. Most sports titles rely on real-world games for their rules and aesthetics, but increasingly, there's a new breed of sports titles that take more creative liberty, like *Def Jam Vendetta*, which combines hip-hop celebrities, wrestling, and fighting. Many sports games involve team play, season play, tournament modes, and other modes which mimic sporting conventions.

Racing/driving games

Racing/driving games come in two flavors, the real-world simulations, like *NASCAR Thunder*, *F1 Career Challenge*, and *Monaco Grand Prix Racing Simulation,* and the popular fantasy racing games, like *Carmageddon*, *Test Drive*, and *Diddy Kong Racing*. One thing that all of these games have in common is that you're racing and you're in control. This includes the horse racing games, like *G1 Jockey* and *Gallop Racer,* and the spaceship racing games, like *Star Wars Episode I: Racer*. Arguably, you could even include luge and ski races, although they are really sports games. But then again, there's a big overlap between racing and sports. To differentiate the two, another iconic part of racing games tends to be the point of view (POV): the cockpit with instruments POV, the cockpit-removed POV, the chase POV, and the overhead POV. How these games use viewpoints, instrumentation, objects whizzing past, and sound effects plays a large part of creating the illusion of speed and control which makes racing games so addictive.

Simulation/building games

Simulation/building games tend to focus on resource management combined with building something, whether it's a company or a city. Unlike strategy games, which generally focus on conquest, these games are all about growth. Many simulation/building games mimic real-world systems and give the player the chance to manage her own virtual business, country, or city. Examples include: *The Sims*, *SimCity*, *RollerCoaster Tycoon*, *SimAnt*, *Gazillionaire*, and *Capitalism*. One of the key aspects of simulation games is the focus on economy and systems of trade and commerce. Players tend to be given limited resources to build and manage the simulation. Choices must then be made carefully because an overemphasis on developing one part of the simulation results in the failure of the entire system. Another important factor in these games is the balance between direct and indirect control. Players are often given direct control over construction, and placing or purchasing items, but only have an indirect influence over other aspects of management. This tension provides a nice dynamic as the player struggles to maintain control over the growth of the simulation.

Flight and other simulations

Simulations are action games that tend to be based on real-life activities, like flying an airplane, driving a tank, or operating a spacecraft. Flight simulators are the best example. These are complex simulators that try to approximate the real-life experience of flying an aircraft. These cannot be put squarely in the action camp because they aren't focused on twitch play and hand-eye coordination, but instead require the player to master realistic and often complex controls and instrumentation. Good examples include *Microsoft Flight Simulator*, *Spearhead*, and *Jane's USAF*. These types of simulations usually appeal to airplane and military buffs, who want as realistic an experience as possible.

Adventure games

Adventure games emphasize exploration, collection, and puzzle-solving. The player generally plays the part of a character on a quest or mission of some kind. Early adventure games were designed using only text, their rich descriptions taking the place of today's graphics. Examples include the text-driven *Adventure* and *Zork*, as well as graphic adventures like *Myst*. Today's adventure games are often combined with elements of action, such as *Jak and Daxter* or *Ratchet & Clank*. Shigeru Miyamoto, the creator of the *Zelda* series of adventure games, summed up the nature of the adventure game in his comment that "the state of mind of a kid when he enters a cave alone must be realized in the game. Going in, he must feel the cold air around him. He must discover a branch off to one side and decide whether to explore it or not. Sometimes he loses his way."[4] Although characters are central in adventure games, unlike role-playing games, they are not a customizable element and do not usually grow in terms of wealth, status, and experience. Some action-adventure games, like *Ratchet & Clank*, do have the concept of an inventory of items for their characters, but most rely on physical or mental puzzle-solving, not improvement and accumulation, for their central gameplay.

Edutainment

Edutainment combines learning with fun. The goal is to entertain while educating the user. Topics range from reading, writing, and arithmetic to problem-solving and "how to" games. Most edutainment titles are targeted at kids, but there are some which focus on adults, especially in the areas of acquiring skills and self improvement. Good examples of kids edutainment software include *Putt-Putt Saves the Zoo*, *Reader Rabbit's Kindergarten*, and *Curious George Learns Phonics*, and for adults, Sierra's *Driver's Education*, a simulation that teaches you how to drive safely, and

---

4. David Sheff, *Game Over: How Nintendo Conquered the World*" (New York: Vintage Books, 1994), p. 52.

BEGINNER PERSPECTIVE: JESSE VIGIL

Title

QA Tester, Vivendi Universal Games

Project list

- *Battlestar Galactica*: QA
- Several unannounced titles: QA

How did you get into the game industry?

I always dug videogames, being a member of the Nintendo generation, and all, but it was always just recreation. It was in college that I really began to appreciate the design aspects. So I threw myself into it, and after being encouraged to pursue it, I went looking for a career in games. Fortunately, I had a good friend in a QA department who was awesome enough to make sure my resume got to the right people. I am told by nearly everybody that QA is the best way to get your foot in the door, so here I am, climbing the ladder.

What's the most interesting thing that's happened on the job?

Many of my best stories right now are unfortunately inside jokes, though I often don't realize they're inside jokes until I try to tell my girlfriend about this hilarious bug we found or this bizarre e-mail from a developer and can't help but notice that she isn't laughing. I used to work for an architecture firm and the resident engineer often laughed out loud about some engineering-related flub on a plan. The rest of us in the office came to the conclusion that it was the kind of joke that was only funny if you had a masters in mechanical engineering; I'm getting the feeling that the same is true of those of us in the gaming industry. We have our own subculture and our own unique brand of humor.

As far as war stories go, I have pulled a couple of eighteen-hour days while the game was in final candidate. It's a bit of a bonding experience when you're working with the rest of your crew and you watch the sun both set and rise again before your work is done. Plus, if you're lucky, you will get to watch the associate lead spontaneously burst into a funny little jig somewhere around 4:00 in the morning when the build that took three hours to upload from England turns out to be corrupted or incomplete. That's always a good time.

What experiences have taught you the most about game design?

QA is a great way to see the game slowly evolve over time. I just finished two months of core testing on a game. Every few days you get a new build and you see the changes that were implemented and then you, as a tester, have as one of your jobs the task of seeing if the changes were beneficial to the game. It's like being able to peek over the designer's shoulder and watch the designer work.

Depending on your situation, you may even be allowed to offer suggestions. It's a real rush when you make a suggestion and then, a few days later, you're playing the newest version and you say, "Oh wow, they actually did it."

Where do you hope to be in five years?

I'm doing all this because I want to write games, and I make sure that I tell everyone constantly that what I really want to do is write. I'll write the cut scenes, I'll write manual, I'll write the surveys on those little postcards that fall out of the box when you open the game, it doesn't matter.

Eventually, of course I want to write the actual game. I'm not really a designer, but I look forward to collaborating with designers. Five years from now, it would be awesome to overhear even one seventeen year-old saying, "The game is great and the story is superb." In general, it would be a kick to hear some seventeen year-old say "superb," now that I think about it.

If I had one wish, though, I would also like to overhear said seventeen-year-old tell his buddy, "This is the first game I've played in a long time where the ending doesn't suck." A lot of the games I've played lately just stink when you get to the end. The game was great and the story was good and you've put a ton of hours into beating the sucker, only to get to the end and see a two-minute (if you're lucky) cut scene that is "blah" at best and then the credits. Where's the payoff? Where's the drama? Where's your reward? I'd like to make my mark as the writer whose games have an ending that's worth the trouble of unlocking.

What words of advice would you give to a person trying to get into the industry today?

Make friends. Don't schmooze. But do make friends and make sure they know what you can do and what you want to be doing. You never know when they might come across an opportunity, and you want as many people as possible to think of you when that happens.

I've been noticing that it's easy to *get* a job in QA. It's keeping the job that's tough. Really throw yourself into it. Make yourself invaluable. A mentor of mine in college always said, "Be excellent at whatever you do and you won't do it for long," and I think that's great advice for people starting out at the bottom. QA is a rough job and lacks glamour, but if you're a hard worker and your work is quality, you'll get noticed.

My last piece of advice is related to that. Keep doing a good job once you've started. I know of someone who started doing very well but then slacked off once he knew the lead thought he was doing a good job. The lead also noticed he was slacking off, and that sort of thing can really harm you, especially when you're just starting out.

Chutes and Lifts, a simple online game that helps foreign speakers to learn and read English.

Children's games

Children's games are designed specifically for kids between the ages of two and twelve. These games may have an educational component, but the primary focus is on entertaining. Nintendo is a master at creating these games, though its franchises such as *Mario* and *Donkey Kong* are also loved by adults. Other examples include Disney's *Aladdin Activity Center,* Kidsoft's *Ozzie's Funtime Garden,* and Humongous Entertainment's *Freddi Fish* series.

Family and mass-market games

Mass-market games are typified by the fact that they are meant to be enjoyed by everyone: male and female, old and young. This means they eschew twitch play, violence, and complex gameplay in favor of attracting the broadest possible audience. Most of the time these are simple games, like those found on Yahoo!'s game site, where you'll see everything from *Canasta* to *Gem Drop* to *Literati.* Other examples include games like *Trivial Pursuit, Scrabble, Yahtzee,* and *Monop-*

oly. One of the most popular types of family game is the game show. The *You Don't Know Jack* series, as well as the versions of *Jeopardy!* and *Wheel of Fortune* made for almost every platform available are perennial family favorites.

Puzzle

Puzzle games incorporate the solvable systems (i.e., puzzles) into the overall competitive system of a game. *Tetris* is probably the most famous digital puzzle game ever made, but as you'll find if you look closely, many games include puzzles, including most role-playing games and practically all adventure games. *Myst* is a good example of an adventure game that is clearly a series of puzzles. Puzzle games may emphasize story, as in *Myst,* or action, as in *Tetris.* They may also include elements of strategy, as in *Scrabble* or solitaire, or construction, as in *The Incredible Machine.*

Exercise 15.1: Your Game's Genre

What genre does your original game fit into? And why does it fit this genre? Given this information, what platform should your game be released on and who is your target audience?

PUBLISHERS

The publishing landscape has changed dramatically over the past decade with a myriad of mergers, closures, re-branding, and re-structuring. Finding a publisher for your game in the best of times is a difficult task. In today's ever-shifting industry, just knowing who to call is a challenge in itself. In a recent report by *Game Developer* magazine, the top 20 publishers were featured and analyzed as to their overall revenue, the number of

titles released in 2002, the types of games released, and their relationship with developers. Much of the data included in the following list of publishers was gleaned from this survey.[5]

Electronic Arts

EA, as it's commonly called, is the world's largest independent publisher. By independent, we mean

---

5.   Tristan Donovan, "*Game Developer* Reports: Top 20 Publishers," *Game Developer*, September 2003.

that it's not part of a platform company, like Sony, Microsoft, or Nintendo. EA published just over 100 titles in the 2002 fiscal year. About 60% of these were developed by the company's internal development studios. EA focuses heavily on licenses and sequels, with original titles making up only about 16% of their games. Key titles include *Madden NFL, FIFA Soccer, SSX Tricky, Def Jam Vendetta, The Sims, Medal of Honor,* and *Command & Conquer.*

Sony Computer Entertainment

Sony focuses on titles for its PlayStation 2 console, for obvious reasons. In the 2002 fiscal year, they released 44 titles, 45% of which were produced by external developers. Sony releases titles in all genres, but action, sports and racing game together make up about 54% of their output. As opposed to EA, Sony invests heavily in original ideas—about 45% of its games in the year surveyed were new intellectual properties. Titles from Sony include *SOCOM: U.S. Navy Seals, The Getaway, ICO, Gran Turismo 3 A-Spec,* and *Twisted Metal: Black.*

Nintendo

Nintendo is the oldest game publishing company in the business; the company was founded in 1889 as a publisher of "Hanafuda" playing cards in Japan. From the mid-1980s through the 90s, Nintendo dominated the console business. Now, it is still a major player and one of the most innovative publishers in the business. While the company is reliant on sequels and spin-offs of its key properties, licenses made up only 3.5% of its titles in the 2002 fiscal year. About 46% of Nintendo's titles in that year were produced by third-party developers, but these mainly consisted of Japanese teams. Key Nintendo titles include the *Mario* and *Donkey Kong* series and spin-offs, the *Zelda* series, *Pokémon, Pikmin, Animal Crossing,* and many more.

Activision

Activision has been one of the top publishers in the business since its formation in 1979. The company tends to rely on licensed properties and sequels, with original ideas making up only about 14% of its titles. Like EA, Sony, and Nintendo, Activision focuses mainly on console titles—69% of its releases in the 2002 fiscal year were in that area. Handheld games made up 22% of its titles in that time period, and computer games just 9%. Activision titles include *Return to Castle Wolfenstein,* the *Tony Hawk* series, *Spider-Man,* as well as *Quake III: Arena* and *X-Men.*

Vivendi Universal Games

Vivendi Universal Games continued as one of the biggest publishers in the industry during the 2002 fiscal year despite the financial troubles of its parent company. The company has a strong presence in the edutainment area—43% of its titles in the year surveyed were for children. Because of this, it also tends to release a higher percentage of computer titles—61% of all their releases are for the PC and Macintosh—than any other top publisher. About half of Vivendi's titles are produced by external developers, and original ideas only make up 11% of their releases. Titles from Vivendi include the *WarCraft* series, *The Incredible Hulk, Crash Bandicoot: the Wrath of Cortex, Jurassic Park: Operation Genesis,* the *Barbie* titles, and the *Fisher-Price: Rescue Heroes* titles.

Take-Two

Take-Two is considered one of the top publishers mainly because of the amazing success of its internally produced *Grand Theft Auto* series. But in the 2002 fiscal year over 80% of its 25 titles were produced out of house. Take-Two titles tend to be in the action and sports genres. Aggressive and original, 41% of the company's titles are new concepts—with 50% being sequels and only 10% licensed properties. In addition to the *Grand Theft Auto* titles, Take-Two has released *Max Payne*, *Myth III: the Wolf Age*, *Oni*, *Railroad Tycoon II*, and *Big Bass Fishing*.

Atari

Atari started as a console maker in the 1970s. It became a publisher and was sold several times over the years. The most recent owner, Infogrames, recently changed the company name to "Atari" to capitalize on the tremendous brand recognition. Infogrames had built itself up into one of the biggest publishers by buying a number of other companies, including Hasbro Interactive, which held the rights to the Atari name. About 74% of the new Atari's games in fiscal year 2002 were produced by external developers, with 22% based on original ideas rather than sequels or licenses. The company leans somewhat heavily toward developing for the PC—about 53% of its releases in the year surveyed were computer titles. They're known for such titles as *Neverwinter Nights*, *Unreal Tournament*, as well as the highly publicized *Enter the Matrix* game.

Konami

Konami is an extremely prolific publisher with an emphasis on producing titles internally. Of the 64 titles they published in the year surveyed; only 7% were produced by external developers. Konami also focuses heavily on sequels—78% of the titles released in the 2002 fiscal year were sequels. Konami focuses heavily on consoles and hand-

helds, but they also make arcade games, toys, and card games. Konami titles include the *Silent Hill* series, *Metal Gear Solid*, the *Dance Dance Revolution* arcade games, and the *Yu-Gi-Oh!* card and digital games.

Microsoft Game Studios

Microsoft publishes titles for both its Xbox platform and the PC, with the console titles making up about 55% of their releases. Like Sony, Microsoft titles tend to focus on original concepts, rather than sequels or licenses, with 58% of the titles released in the 2002 fiscal year based on original ideas. About 64% of Microsoft's titles are produced by external developers. Microsoft scored several important hits in its early releases for the Xbox, including the highly successful *Halo*. But they are also well-known for their PC titles like the *Age of Empires* series and the ever-popular *Microsoft Flight Simulator*.

Sega

Sega is an ex-console maker turned publisher. With the demise of its Dreamcast platform, it has turned exclusively to publishing, but is highly reliant on sequels and licenses. Sega also continues to make amazing arcade games, but as we mentioned, that market is suffering. Recently, some of Sega's internal development teams have started creating games for other publishers, including Nintendo. Titles from Sega include *Virtua Fighter 4*, *Phantasy Star Online*, *Shinobi*, *NFL 2K3*, and *House of the Dead III*.

Summary

Rounding out the list of top 20 publishers are:

- Square Enix
- Ubi Soft

- THQ
- Capcom
- Bandai
- Namco
- Acclaim
- Koei
- Eidos Interactive
- Midway Games

As Tristan Donovan, author of the *Game Developer* report points out, "awareness of a publisher's general attitude toward external development, its treatment of other developers, and what genres it concentrates on can be highly valuable when dealing with a publisher." We encourage you to research publishers before approaching them. Knowledge of their products, their business focus, and trends they seem to be a part of can help you present you own game in the context of their goals and plans.

Exercise 15.2: The Right Publisher

Do some research of your own and find a publisher you think would be right for your original game idea. Don't just choose the biggest or the most well-known publisher—find a company that is a match for your game in terms of focus, market, and other games they've published.

DEVELOPERS

There are so many game developers, large and small, that it would be unhelpful to list them all. In general, there are three types of developers: independent studios, wholly owned studios, and partially owned studios. Most developers start out small. Many times, it is a group of friends who have either worked together in the past, or perhaps gone to school together. Like starting a band, starting a development studio is a usually a labor of love.

Many start-up developers never make it past the concept stage. Perhaps they build a demo and shop it around. Only a few very lucky teams actually sign a deal to produce a game. And even fewer wind up producing a hit. Being a game developer is a very risky business. Many small developers produce one or two games, but don't have the financial cushion to deal with a dry spell or a spate of unexpected costs. These companies go out of business, but the talent always seems to reemerge at another company under a new name.

Some developers may make a series of successful games for a publisher who decides to invest in them, or to buy them outright and make them an internal development group. The following list describes several very different developers, some of whom have been bought by publishers and some who have remained independent or taken on investment. The list is by no means comprehensive; we've just tried to give you a sense of the companies out there, their history, titles, and some of the people behind them.

2015

2015 is a fairly small independent developer founded in 1997 with a focus on 3D action games. Scoring a hit with its *Medal of Honor: Allied Assault*, the Tulsa, Oklahoma company has a strong relationship with Vivendi Universal Games and a deal for a military action game on multiple consoles.

BioWare

BioWare is a Canadian company of about 135 people formed in 1995 by two doctors who met at medical school—hence the name. Dr. Ray Muzyka and Dr. Greg Zeschuk are joint CEOs and Co-Executive Producers of BioWare's games. They're known for their top-notch RPGs including the *Baldur's Gate* series, *Neverwinter Nights*, and *Star Wars: Knights of the Old Republic*. Publishers they've produced titles for include LucasArts, Atari, and Microsoft.

Blizzard Entertainment

Blizzard was established in 1994 and quickly became one of the most respected producers of PC strategy games. Its blockbuster hits include the *WarCraft*, *Diablo*, and *StarCraft* series. The company has changed hands several times, being passed from Davidson & Associates, to CUC, to Cendant, to Havas, and finally to Vivendi Universal Games, of which it is now a wholly owned subsidiary. These ownership gyrations have not seemed to impact the quality of Blizzard's games, and the company continues to produce high-quality, exquisitely designed and tested work.

Firaxis Games

Legendary game designer Sid Meier and his partner Jeff Briggs founded Firaxis in 1996. The company has released a series of successful strategy games including *Gettysburg!*, *Alpha Centauri*, and *Civilization III*. Firaxis is an independent company, but has strong ties to both EA and Atari, which acquired the rights to the *Civilization* franchise with its purchase of the Hasbro Interactive and its MicroProse division in 2001. Meier was one of the original founders of MicroProse, and developed the first two *Civilization* titles for that company. Firaxis produced the third *Civilization* title for Atari and is developing a new version of *Sid Meier's Pirates!* for that publisher.

id Software

id Software has been responsible for some of the best-selling computer games of all time. Founded in 1991 by John Carmack, Adrian Carmack, John Romero, and Tom Hall, the company went on to transform the game industry with the release of *Wolfenstein 3-D*, followed by *DOOM*, *Quake*, and its sequels. Not only renowned for the development of the 3D graphics technology that changed the industry, the company also pioneered a unique model of software distribution wherein the first levels of a game can be downloaded from the Internet for free, but subsequent levels have to be purchased once the player was hooked.

Lionhead Studios

Peter Molyneux, the pioneering game designer behind *Populous* and *Dungeon Keeper*, formed Lionhead in 1997. Lionhead's first game, *Black & White*, was published by EA in 2001. Molyneux has a history of focusing on innovation in his game designs. His first company, Bullfrog, was founded in 1987 with a goal to create games that were more "cerebral" than the average title. Their first game, *Populous*, created an entirely new genre of play, the "god game." The game, turned down by every publisher except EA, was a commercial and critical success and the company continued to push the boundaries with each new product. EA purchased Bullfrog in 1995, but Molyneux broke off on his own again in 1997 to start Lionhead.

Naughty Dog

Sixteen-year-old entrepreneurs Andy Gavin and Jason Rubin founded Naughty Dog in 1986. Formerly called JAM software, the company developed a couple titles for the Apple II and early PCs, but really got going once they signed first with EA, then later with Universal Interactive Studios, and changed their name to Naughty Dog. In 1996, they released the first *Crash Bandicoot* title on the PlayStation to critical and commercial success. Their current titles include *Jak and Daxter* and *Jak II* for the PlayStation 2.

Oddworld Inhabitants

Computer and animation special effects wizards Sherry McKenna and Lorne Lanning started Oddworld in 1994. Their *Oddworld* series of games has received an enormous amount of critical acclaim for both its inventiveness and humor. The first two titles in their *Oddworld* series were published by GT Interactive, which was subsequently bought by Infogrames (now Atari). Oddworld's current publisher is Microsoft, and the third title in the *Oddworld* series was developed for the Xbox.

Pandemic Studios

Activision veterans Josh Resnick and Andrew Goldman formed Pandemic in 1998. When the two approached Activision about their plans to leave the publisher and start their own company, Activision reacted by investing in that new company and giving them the rights to produce sequels to two Activision properties: *Battlezone* and *Dark Reign*. The company has also produced titles for EA, LucasArts, and the U.S. Army.

Rockstar North

Rockstar North, formerly DMA Design, was acquired in 1999 by publisher Take-Two Interactive. Best known today for its *Grand Theft Auto* franchise, the company was also responsible for the classic *Lemmings* series. Founded in 1989 by David Jones when he was still a college student, the company was self-financed, and their first *Lemmings* game was produced entirely by Jones and two employees over the course of a year. Professional management, a hit franchise, and acquisition by Take-Two made the company a huge success story.

Shiny Entertainment

Shiny was founded in 1993 by David Perry and soon thereafter released *Earthworm Jim*, a hit game which spawned several sequels and licensing deals, including action figures, comic books, and a syndicated television series. Since then, Shiny has produced a number of hit games such as *Messiah*, *Sacrifice*, and *Enter the Matrix*. In 2002, Shiny was purchased by Atari, who published the *Enter the Matrix* game, in a $47 million deal.

Summary

This list could go on and on, with hundreds of stories of developers who have started out with nothing, taken risks, stood by their ideas, had both amazing successes, and heartbreaking failures. It's impossible to list even a fraction of the developers out there. The one clear link between them all is that they all love games and no matter what their level of success, are trying to find a way to balance managing a business and staying true to their artistic vision while staying alive and in the game.

THE BUSINESS OF GAME PUBLISHING

From a business perspective, designing a game is just one small part of the elaborate process of producing the game. And producing is also a smaller part of the lengthy process for publishing a title. Game publishing involves all the steps needed to get a game from the glimmer of a concept to a polished product that is distributed to the store shelves. This section explains the four key elements of publishing: development, licensing, marketing, and distribution. Game publishers are the primary source of funding in the game industry; so understanding these elements of how they work will help you interact with them more effectively.

Element 1: Development

The basic task of development involves financing a team to create a title and then managing that process so that a high-quality game is delivered on time and within the budget.

Industry trends

The average cost of game development has risen steadily since the 1980s. Today, it typically costs $3.5 million to produce a console title, and that number continues to rise. The reason for the increase is simple: customers expect games to have more media of better quality to utilize the features of newer, better hardware systems. Back in the days of the Sega Genesis, for example, a game cartridge could hold 4 MB of data. Today, an Xbox DVD can hold 4.7 GB. That's a 100,000% increase in capacity, and more capacity equates to greater customer expectations, and to more costly production of graphics, sound, music, gameplay, etc.

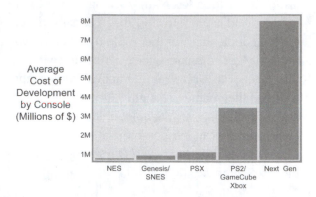

15.5 Average cost of console development

Steve Ackrich of Atari shared with us the diagram in Figure 15.5, showing the cost of console development over his time in the industry. Ackrich points out that the launch price for console titles over the same time period has remained steady at about $50. So with the cost of development for each title going up and the price of each title remaining static, game publishers have been forced to adopt a "fewer, bigger, better" strategy.

This means that publishers must produce fewer titles, because the costs are so high, and each title must sell more units. To do this, the production values must be better and the audience appeal broader. This dynamic leads to an extreme hits-driven business, where the top 20 game titles generate 80% of the industry's revenues, while the other hundreds of titles make up the remaining 20%.

This is why, if you're a designer, you may find it difficult to find a publisher for a truly amazing, original design that appeals to only a niche market. While everyone, publishers included, would like to see more diversity in the industry, the economics make this difficult to accomplish. Additionally, publishers don't hesitate to cancel weaker products during the development cycle, saving their money and resources for games that promise to be stronger sellers.

A number of truly innovative independent game designers can be found working on the Internet today for this reason. Web games, often produced in Shockwave or Java, can be produced for far less money, and so present less of a risk in terms of innovative gameplay. Shockwave.com is a good place to see the work of some of these smaller developers and niche games.

Developer royalties

Typically, publishers pay development costs to a developer as an advance against the royalties generated by the title. A royalty is a percentage of the overall revenue earned by a publisher that is paid to a project participant. Here's a basic explanation how a standard publisher developer deal works:

Base deal

In most basic development deals a publisher advances all development costs to the developer in the form of milestone payments. This means that if the budget is $3.5 million, the publisher pays the developer a percentage of the total after each stage of development: concept, pre-production, production, and testing.

These milestone payments are treated as an advance against future royalties. Typical royalty rates for a developer range from 10% to 18% of a publisher's net sales revenue after deductions. The publisher starts paying royalties after the development costs have been recouped via sales. In our example, this means that the publisher keeps 100% of the revenues generated by a title until the royalties reach $3.5 million.

After the royalties reach the amount advanced, the publisher shares the revenues with the developer according to the royalty schedule. So, if the agreed-upon royalty rate were 15%, from this point onward, the publisher would give the developer 15% of the net sales revenues earned and keep 85% for itself. Developers can ask for royalty rates to "step up" when certain sales goals are met. For instance, the royalty rate may be 10% until 60,000 units are sold, then 15% until 120,000 units are sold, then 20% until 240,000 units are sold, etc.

First-time developers are a risk for the publisher, so their royalty rates are low. Established developers, who have proven that they can deliver hits, can negotiate for a higher rate because they represent less risk.

Royalty calculation

Royalties are calculated on "net sales revenue" or "adjusted gross income," meaning the developer gets paid after the publisher makes deductions, such as: sales tax, duties, shipping, insurance, and returns. This can open the door for creative accounting. A developer is wise to ask that these deductions be narrowly defined and that the publisher not include its overhead costs.

Affiliate label deal

In an affiliate label deal, the developer shares in development and marketing costs. This reduces the publisher's risk, and thus the royalty percentages tend to be much higher—typically 65% to 75%.

Element 2: Licensing

There are two basic kinds of licensing in which publishers engage: content licensing and console licensing.

Content licensing

As you saw in our list of the top publishers, many rely heavily on licensed properties for game title. Of the 103 titles EA released in fiscal year 2002, 51% were based on licensed properties. By licensing recognizable characters, personalities, music, or other entertainment properties and integrating them into a game, publishers can increase its exposure and sales, thereby decreasing their risk of investment. The following top-selling games are examples of games based on licenses: *Tony Hawk Pro Skater 4, Harry Potter and the Chamber of Secrets, Enter the Matrix, Madden NFL 2004, The Lord of the Rings: The Two Towers, NBA Jam, Dark Angel, The Simpsons: Road Rage,* and *WWE Raw 2.*

When a game uses a licensed property, the publisher pays the rights holder a fee for use of the property. So, in the case of the *Madden NFL* series, EA pays a license fee to John Madden and the NFL. With videogames pulling in record profits, licensors of content are holding out for higher and higher prices. Because of this, some publishers, like Sony Computer Entertainment and Microsoft Game Studios are actually quite aggressive about developing original game concepts, or intellectual property, as it's called.

Nevertheless, it's not uncommon for large titles to spend hundreds of thousands of dollars on a license, in addition to giving away anywhere from 1% to 10% of net revenues to the rights holder. The bottom line in terms of licensing is that it helps reduce publisher risk. Branded products have proven strong sellers time and time again, whether they have good gameplay elements or not.

Console licensing agreements

When you produce a game on the PC, you don't have to pay Microsoft, Apple, or the hardware manufacturer a royalty for distributing on their system. However, when a publisher distributes a game on a console system, they must enter into a strict licensing agreement with the console maker, in which they agree to pay a licensing royalty for every unit sold. Typically this ranges from $3 to $10 per unit—that's on top of the retail markup, advertising, shipping, overhead, and development costs for the unit.

Here's how the responsibilities for a typical third party console licensing deal breaks down.

Publisher's Responsibilities:

- Come up with game concept
- Develop the game
- Test the game
- Market the game
- Distribute the game

Console Maker's Responsibilities:

- Approve the game concept
- Test the game
- Review and approve the final game
- Manufacture the game

Console licensing agreements generally give the console maker the right of final approval, which means that if they don't approve of the game or its content they can prevent it from being released. The testing and approval process can be quite rigorous. The console maker wants to ensure that the game works under all conditions and that it meets their quality standards. If they find flaws that they deem significant, they can send the game back to the publisher and demand that it be fixed before release.

Changes at this stage of development, as we discussed in Chapter 13 can be very costly, and can also impact the release date, potentially missing important market schedules. If and when the publisher finally gains approval to release the game, they must pay the console maker the royalty fee for every unit manufactured up front. Only after this payment are the games delivered to the publisher and then redistributed to retailers.

Element 3: Marketing

A big part of the publishing task is marketing the game. A marketer's job is to make decisions that will result in maximum sales. The marketing department is typically involved in a game's entire life cycle, from conception through to the bargain bins. Only once the game is no longer saleable does the marketing team stop working. The marketing department handles everything from idea approvals and setting system specs through to buying up advertising on local radio stations, as well as coordinating in-store promotions and publicity. Marketing budgets are typically double the development budgets. So, for our example of a $3.5 million game, the marketing budget would come in at around $7 million.

Element 4: Distribution

Publishers have very important relationships with the wholesalers and retailers who comprise the distribution chain. Without these relationships, a publisher would not be able to sell enough products to pay back all the costs they incurred in the production of the game. Getting the game onto the shelves of large chains like Wal-Mart, Target, and Babbages is a must, and that process costs more money. Here is a breakdown of the costs involved in distributing a typical console game:

- Retail price of $50.
- Wholesale price (the amount retailers pay publishers for the title) = approximately 64% of the retail price or $32.00 per unit.
- Cost of goods incurred by publisher = approximately $5.00 per unit.
- Co-op advertising costs incurred by publisher = approximately 15% of wholesale price or $4.80 per unit.
- Marketing costs incurred by publisher = approximately 8% of wholesale price or $2.56 per unit.
- Return of goods contingency estimated by publisher = approximately 12% of wholesale price or $3.84 per unit.

If you subtract the cost of goods ($5.00), the co-op advertising costs ($4.80), the marketing costs ($2.56) and the return of goods contingency ($3.84) from the wholesale price ($32.00), you'll find that the publisher reaps about $15.80 per unit sold or approximately 32% of the retail sale price. This is less than most people imagine.

Even if a title is fortunate enough to be sold on the shelves of Wal-Mart, there's no guarantee it will stay there for long. If the product doesn't sell right away, or in sufficient quantity, retailers reserve the right to return product, which means that the publisher can wind up with a warehouse full of unsold games.

Even for larger publishers, who have a rich pipeline of games that the retailers desire, there are risks involved in producing games. The shelf life for most games is three to six months—not very long. And if you look at the publisher's other expenses, including production budget overruns, high return rates, approvals being withheld, schedules slipping, etc., you'll understand why so many of the smaller publishers go out of business or are bought by larger companies. It's not easy to make a profit in the games industry unless you can control costs, produce the best products, and have the right relationships to make sure that your products get placed on the shelves and stay there.

CONCLUSION

To the game designer entirely focused on gameplay and production, the business aspects of publishing games may seem a confusing cutthroat environment, best left to producers and executives. But as in all things, knowledge is power, and the more you know and understand about the industry you work in, the better-equipped you will be to deal with the ups and downs of getting your original game ideas produced and published.

Creative people should not shy away from understanding the issues presented in this chapter. Understanding the needs and goals of all the parties involved in the publishing process, from the executives at the publishing company, to the representatives of the console makers, to the salespeople at the retail outlet will help you make better decisions and will pay off over and over again in your career.

Think of yourself as a creative businessperson, as well as a game designer, and educate yourself at every opportunity about the industry. Read marketing research, ask questions about contracts, understand the deal structure for your game, and treat each opportunity to deal with the business aspects of the industry as a chance to learn and expand your skills. The respect you show for this process will improve your relationships with the businesspeople involved in your game, and make you a better designer in turn.

UNDERSTANDING THE BOARD AND CARD GAME INDUSTRY: A GUIDE FOR INVENTORS

by Brian Tinsman, Wizards of the Coast

In the board and card game industry—a.k.a. the tabletop game industry—game designers are called "inventors." Brian Tinsman is a professional game inventor with over 25 published tabletop game products. As lead concept acquisitions representative for Wizards of the Coast, Brian has reviewed hundreds of games submitted for publication and helped many beginning inventors get their first games published.

The following is excerpted from his excellent book: The Game Inventor's Guidebook. *It is used here with permission.*

How New Games Happen

Design

Most tabletop game companies don't have a staff of full-time inventors creating new games. It's usually more cost-efficient for them to buy or license at least some amount of games from independent inventors. Inventors drive the whole creative process. They take the germ of an idea and play around with it until it's a working game. They create a prototype and test it out with lots of players, collect feedback, and make numerous revisions until it's ready to sell.

Pitching

The designer's next step is to convince a publisher to risk his money getting the game manufactured. Just like movies, books, and music, the game industry is overflowing with people who think they're more talented than they really are. For that reason, the most desirable publishers have to screen out the hacks. In many cases you need to demonstrate you're a legitimate prospect and have some talent before your game reaches the reviewer's desk.

Manufacturing

When a publisher gives the go-ahead to publish a new game, he hands it off to his art department. Once the art and graphic design are finished, the rules are edited, the game goes to production. The production people select what kind of paper and plastic are going to be used for each component and convert the artwork from computer files or photographs to films, which are fed into the printing machines at the factory. The presses churn out boxes, boards and cards, the molds spit out the pieces, and a worker puts them all together and shrink-wraps it. Once the entire print run is complete, it goes on a truck.

Distribution

Once the game is on a truck it needs to get to stores. The very largest publishers can call up the largest chain retailers like Toys R Us and ask how many copies to ship, but what about all the small publishers and retailers? There are about 5,000 game and hobby stores in North America that aren't part of any chain. It doesn't make sense for a small publisher to call each store up and ask if they want to carry a few games. Likewise, a retailer that carries 50 different games doesn't want to call 50 publishers every time he places an order. This is where the distributors come in. Distributors buy games from publishers, store them in a warehouse, mark them up about 50%, and send retailers a catalog from which to order.

Retailing

Retailers fall into two major categories: mass-market retailers and specialty/hobby shops. Mass-market retailers are mostly composed of big department stores like Target, Wal-Mart, and the 800-pound gorilla of the industry, Toys R Us. Toys R Us alone accounts for 19% of all tabletop game sales in the U.S. Hobby shops, on the other hand are usually small stores privately owned and run by dedicated people who love games (and/or comic books).

Markets For Games

From an inventor's perspective, there are basically four markets (categories) in which to sell games to publishers. They're defined by the type of consumer who buys the games in that market, methods of distribution, and product expectations of the publishers. The categories are mass market, hobby games, American specialty games, and European games.

Mass market

Mass-market games are most recognizable of all games to most Americans. They're the ones you see on the shelves of Wal-Mart and Toys R Us. They mostly come in two types. The first is adult party games like *Pictionary*, *Taboo*, and *Cranium*. Alongside these newcomers are the venerable classics and family games that many of us grew up with, such as *Monopoly*, *Clue*, *Life*, *Boggle*, and *Scrabble*. Most young children's games fall into this category too.

Hobby games

Hobby games are mostly the domain of males in their teens and twenties who play religiously every week or more. In general these games are extremely complex and it's not unusual for fans to spend hundreds of dollars a year buying supplements, cards, figurines, or new rulebooks for a single game.

Hobby games fall into three major categories: roleplaying games, miniatures games, and trading card games.

American specialty

This is sort of a catchall category for American games that aren't mass market or hobby games. It includes products targeted at a certain segment, such as strategy games, drinking games, "how to host a mystery" games, and so forth. Generally you should expect small print runs from small publishers, but it's definitely the easiest category to get started in. There are also a number of games in this category that would be appropriate for the mass market, but for one reason or another haven't gone through that distribution channel.

European

When someone talks about the European game market, they're mostly talking about games published by German companies. The German game market is a big one. In Germany, games are quite a bit more popular as a mainstream entertainment choice when compared to North American tastes. German companies put out dozens and dozens of new games each year, only a small fraction of which ever get translated and make it over to the United States. German games in general tend to be much more complex, abstract, and strategic than most Americans are used to.

Others

These four markets are by no means the only places you can sell games. If you have a football game and you can get sporting goods stores to carry it, or if you can find some other way to skip traditional game retail outlets, that can work in your favor. Some companies sell directly to the consumer by mail order. Others sell on eBay or via a web site. There's also a modest amount of sales to educational distributors and schools. There are innumerable other options for getting your game into consumers' hands. However, as of yet, none of them have been able to generate sales figures that come close to those of the four traditional markets.

Idea to Store Shelf in Seven Steps

1. *Invent your game.* Start with a certain type of consumer in mind. Refine it by getting people who don't know you to play it. They'll discover more problems than you expected. Solve them.
2. *Research publishers.* You want a company that publishes games that are different from yours, but are aimed at the same target market. These publishers already have good distribution in places where those consumers shop and will be most receptive to a game like yours. Try to find out what's missing from their product line by visiting their web site.

3. *Contact your targeted publishers one at a time.* Ask if they're interested in seeing your game. If not, find out why not and what they'd rather see instead. There are four recommended methods of contact:

- *Cold call:* Call up and ask the best way to submit a game. Be professional. (Works best with smaller companies.)

- *E-mail inquiry:* E-mail their customer service department with a professional-sounding query letter asking if they would be interested in seeing your game.

- *Approach in person:* If you have the chance to attend a game convention or trade show, companies will often have booths with development staff in attendance. Ask how you can submit a game concept.

- *Broker/agent:* You will only need an agent to reach the large mass-market companies. But good agents can often give you valuable objective feedback on your product. Stay away from the shady ones that advertise on TV.

4. If they are interested in your game, send them a prototype or meet with the R&D representative to give a demonstration.

5. Wait to hear the company's decision. (Usually six weeks maximum.)

6. Get feedback and continue development until you make a sale.

7. Negotiate a contract and let the publisher take it to market.

Top Ten Reasons Games Get Rejected

1. *Poor gameplay:* Lots of submissions just aren't fun to play.

2. *Unoriginal mechanics:* Poor inventors use play elements stolen from a traditional game or a competitor's game, whether intentionally or unintentionally. While no game is 100% original, it shouldn't feel like something they've played before.

3. *Game is not appropriate for that company:* Reviewers see games all the time for categories they just don't publish. Either people don't do their research or are hoping a war game company will change their minds and publish a preschool game.

4. *Too focused on theme, not gameplay:* Many inventors like the idea of using a certain intellectual property or theme, but don't have the time or talent to put together a compelling game. Instead, they take a traditional game like Go Fish, introduce a board, and slap some pretty pictures of Barbie on it. If a publisher wanted to do a product like that, they wouldn't need an inventor to show them how.

5. *Game is submitted without required legal forms or with inventor's own legal forms:* If the company asks you to sign a disclosure form and you don't, your submission goes right in the trash.

Asking a publisher to sign a confidentiality agreement usually has the same effect. This is like stamping "I don't understand the procedure" on the front of your submission.

6. *Poor marketing potential:* Some games are aimed at a consumer segment that's too narrow. *How many people are going to be interested in your subject?*

7. *Not feasible to produce:* New inventors tend to over-design games with too many rules and too many extraneous components. If your game has lots of pieces or anything that would be complicated to manufacture, ask yourself if it's absolutely necessary.

8. *Game depends on an unobtainable license:* Sure it would be nice to do a *Star Wars*-themed boardgame, but Hasbro has the license locked up for the foreseeable future. Even if it were available, very few publishers could afford the licensing fees. If your game depends on a license you need to make sure the license is available and affordable before you pitch.

9. *Unclear rules:* It's a little-known truth that rules are unbelievably tricky to write. If you want a demonstration, watch someone try to play your game for the first time from your rules while you say absolutely nothing. If a publisher has that much trouble, he's just going to quit.

10. *Competes directly with another product in the company:* Some people assume that if a company has a hit product they'll want another one just like it. In fact, the opposite is true if it's aimed at the same consumer segment. A new product is just as likely to pull customers away from the old game as it is to bring in new players. This is called cannibalization risk.

Chapter 16
Selling Yourself and Your Ideas to the Game Industry

There is no one way to get into the game industry. If you have been reading along with the designer perspectives throughout this book, you've probably noticed that each individual designer has a unique story to tell about how he or she got a start designing games. No two took the same path, and you too will have to find your own way. But in this final chapter, we provide you with a number of strategies for selling yourself and your vision to the game industry. The three basic strategies we discuss are:

1. Getting a job at a publisher or developer
2. Pitching and selling an original idea to a publisher
3. Producing your ideas independently.

Most game designers don't start out by selling original concepts; they get a job at an established company and work their way up the ladder. Once they have some experience, they may break off to start their own company, or pitch ideas internally to the company they work for. But how do you find your first job in the game industry? What are the qualifications? What should you bring to an interview? These are questions that don't have easy answers. Unlike many career paths, game design doesn't have an established route to success. The ideas we suggest are ways to maximize your chances in very competitive arena.

If you can get a job at an established company within the industry, even if that job does not involve game design directly, you will still be exposed to the process of game production and be able to gain a real understanding of how games are developed, the technologies involved, the roles and responsibilities of the team, and current trends in the industry. Once you have a significant amount of production experience, you will have a better chance of getting your own ideas heard and know how to present them when you do.

As we said in Chapter 12, it's very hard to sell original ideas to a publisher. If you have some production experience with an established developer or publisher, you will be in a much better position to get your ideas heard. But what exactly is involved in pitching original game ideas? What materials will you need to prepare? How do you follow up afterwards? Again, we've laid out some solid strategies for this process, based on information gathered from companies across the industry.

The last part of this chapter takes a look at developers who have decided to just go out and "do it." Independent game developers face huge challenges in today's high-profile industry, but they are driven by their passion for their ideas and are free to explore those ideas to the extent their resources allow. More and more, small development teams are turning to the web as a way to distribute their independent games to niche audiences. If you have the resilience and the resources, independent development may be the answer to getting your original game made.

No matter which route you take, the exercises you've done throughout this book will help you develop an excellent beginner's portfolio. Whether you are trying to get a job, or trying to convince your friends to work on an independent game, having a working set of prototypes and several well-written concept documents will lend credibility and focus to your efforts, and differentiate you from other candidates.

GETTING A JOB AT A PUBLISHER OR DEVELOPER

Getting a job at an established company is the most practical way to start off in the game industry. You will gain knowledge and experience, meet and work with other talented people, and see the inner workings of game production first hand. But even at the entry level, the game industry is very competitive. Aside from the obvious routes of responding to job postings and contacting the HR departments of game companies, we have several strategic recommendations that may help you get your first job.

Educate yourself

When contacting companies and going on interviews, the most important thing you bring with you as a beginning game designer is a solid knowledge of games and the game industry. Being able to articulate concepts in gameplay and mechanics, knowing the history of games, and understanding how the companies you are speaking to fit into the business of games are all important ways to show your skills. There are many ways to educate yourself about games and the industry—everything from academic programs to a do-it-yourself regime of games and research.

Academic programs

Many colleges around the country are beginning to offer degrees in multimedia studies and game design. This includes some top-tier universities, like NYU, USC, and Carnegie Mellon, which are just beginning to develop their programs. There are also well-established trade schools, like DigiPen and Full Sail, which specialize in placing people in the game industry.

Although the game industry to date has not had a strong emphasis on higher-level education as preparation for careers, according to Rusty Rueff, EVP of Human Resources at Electronic Arts, larger game companies, like EA, are looking forward to a time when the majority of their new hires will come from university programs.

If you choose to attend one of these schools, keep in mind that a well-rounded program may better prepare you for a career in game design than a curriculum focused only on tools and techniques. Additionally, studying subjects outside the field, such as history, psychology, economics, literature, film, or other topics you are passionate about, will stimulate your mind and imagination and give you interesting perspectives from which to design games.

That said, there's one bias that game companies do have: they are more likely to hire people with technical skills. So if you take some courses in engineering or computer science, it will give you an edge over the competition. And while you shouldn't make tools your learning focus, you should become familiar with the applications used to make games. Programs like Adobe Photoshop and Illustrator, 3D Studio Max, Maya, Macromedia's Shockwave and Flash, Microsoft Project, Word, and Excel are all important tools that you may want to become familiar with and most game programs will offer some training in these tools.

Play games

Even if you are not at a university or trade school that offers a program in game development, you can teach yourself about design by playing as many games as you can, reading about their history and development, and analyzing their systems.

We assume you love games, so playing them a lot is probably something you do already. But just playing is not enough. Get in the habit of analyzing the games you play. Challenge yourself to learn something new from each game you play. With the concepts you've learned from this book, you should now be seeing the structure of games in a different light. Try branching out to new genres and platforms—web games, card games, boardgames, classic games, cutting edge games, and independent games can all teach you about the craft and make you a better candidate for a job in the industry.

Design games and levels

If you are following along with the exercises in this book, you should have designed at least one original game prototype by now. This experience is one of the most valuable tools you have in your search for a game design job.

Good solid paper game prototypes and well-written concept documents can form the basis for a great beginning portfolio. If you have the skills to turn your designs into software prototypes as well, you should do so. Even if you don't plan on pitching your ideas to a publisher at this point, polish your prototype and concept document anyway. During that crucial moment in a job interview when they ask you what experience you have, you'll be able to show your work and discuss the process of design, playtesting, and revision in detail. This will differentiate you from other applicants, because even though you are a beginner, you'll be able to display actual experience of the development process, even though your games have not yet been published.

In addition to making physical and digital prototypes of original games, you can demonstrate your game design skills by building levels for existing games. As we discussed in Chapter 7, many games ship with level editing and mod building tools that are both powerful and flexible. Several quite famous game designers have gotten their start by designing mods that become so popular a publisher took notice. There are also mod and level-making competitions that you can enter, which may help give you the visibility and recognition you need to secure that first job. One strategy for getting in the door at a game company is to make levels or mods of that company's games, then submit these examples of your work along with your resume.

APPLYING FOR A JOB IN GAME DESIGN

by Tom Sloper, President, Sloperama Productions

Get this, and get it straight. The job of "game designer" is a much sought-after position with a prerequisite of a lot of game industry experience. So even if you have just graduated from college, don't hold out for the vaunted title of "game designer." Just apply for any game industry job you can get.

The key is getting in in the first place. Your first goal must be simply to get inside the industry. We're talking about a career—a way of life—not a sinecure.

Once you are inside, you have to work hard, volunteer to help out in any way you can, learn everything you can, and prove yourself, before you can gain the title of "game designer."

After proving yourself as a game designer once, you will have to prove yourself time and time again. Know that ahead of time, steel yourself, and be willing. And you'll be fine. Okay, the necessary basic info is out of the way now. Here's how to apply for that game industry job.

First, you must be prepared for the job.

Presumably you have completed the exercises in this book. Presumably, you are a high school graduate and have a college degree. Presumably, you are an avid game player. Presumably, you have already been participating in the game newsgroups, to wit:

- news:comp.games.development.design
- news:comp.games.development.industry
- news:rec.games.design

Next, you need to have a well-written resume.

I'm not going to tell you how to write a resume. There are lots of books and web sites about that. One way to sweeten your resume, though, is to mention your personal design projects. You will differentiate yourself a lot if you list prototypes you've made, treatments you've written, mods you've created, game groups you've organized, newsgroups you participate in, etc.

Next, prepare your portfolio.

What's a portfolio, you ask? According to Merriam-Webster, a portfolio is:

1. A hinged cover or flexible case for carrying loose papers, pictures, or pamphlets
2. A set of pictures (as drawings or photographs) either bound in book form or loose in a folder

If you're an aspiring game designer, you can create a portfolio with samples of your writings and drawings, photographs of your paper prototypes, flyers, newspaper clippings, or photos from game events you organized—anything that shows off your creativity and desirability as a job candidate. Just the best stuff, though. A portfolio should fit into a 1/2" flexible three-ring binder (it shouldn't be too thick; you'll only have a few minutes to show it off). Protect the paper by encasing it in "sheet protectors" (available at office supply stores). And make copies of your portfolio, so you have the option of leaving one with a hiring manager.

Organize your portfolio with your most striking stuff in the front. In an interview, the interviewer may open the binder, look at the first few things, then close it. So you need to make the best possible impression with the first things, right up front.

Don't put complete designs into your design portfolio—game companies almost always have prohibitions against receiving game concept "submissions" without signed agreements in place, and they might perceive your portfolio as a stealth submission. There shouldn't be more than about 20 sheets in a portfolio.

If you've created animations, audio pieces, or programs, collect those on a CD. Don't bring demos on Zip disks, 8-tracks, Syquests, or reel-to-reel tapes! But, as with the paper portfolio, make a copy.

So that's what a portfolio is, and how it's used. If you can't make a spectacular portfolio, don't make a portfolio at all. It's okay to show up for an interview without a portfolio. However, having one is important if you want to set yourself apart from the competition.

Next, you have to have a target list of game companies.

I can't give you a target list; each aspirant has to make this for himself. Any game company worth working for has a web site. And there are lots of game industry job web sites. Assuming you're active in the newsgroups you will find them. Ideally, your list contains companies in your local area, or in an area you are willing to move to.

Next, you need to educate yourself about your target companies.

Read their web sites. Learn their product lines. Find out about their stock, if they're publicly owned. It looks bad if an applicant comes in and says, "Well, I don't know anything about your company, but I'd like to work here."

Now you're ready to contact the target companies.

Don't pin all your hopes on one specific company. Have multiple companies to contact. You never know what's going to happen. Find out the name of a person to contact at each company. If you know someone who knows someone at a company, get in touch with that person and find out whom you should send your resume to. You need a name to put at the top of each cover letter. If you don't know anybody who knows somebody, call the company and ask for the name of the studio head (the VP in charge of the game production department) or for the name of the Human Resources head.

Write a good cover letter.

As with resumes, you can find information about how to craft a good cover letter on the Internet. Being a game designer means being a creative writer. Your cover letter should showcase your creativity and your communication skills. Mention the games you've created on your own. The cover letter (especially if there's basically nothing on your resume) is arguably even more important than the resume.

It's unrealistic to say "I'm seeking a job as a game designer," and it's not helpful to say "I'll take any job you have open." Find out what job openings are available. Figure out which opening is suited to your skills and interests. That's the job you should be applying for.

Mail the resume and cover letter, or deliver them in person.

If you do not live in the local area of the target company, mail your package to the person identified above. But if you do live in the local area of the target company, call the person and request an interview. If you mailed your package, follow up with a phone call a week or so later. Ask the person if she's received your package. Your goal is to come in and meet with the person. A game company will not pay your airfare to fly out for an interview for an entry-level position so don't ask.

When speaking with the person on the phone, be your normal personable self. Don't say you want to come in for a job interview, just ask if you could come in to introduce yourself. You're interested in learning about the game industry, you're a college graduate, you've done some stuff on your own, and you'd appreciate a short chat.

Eight times out of ten, that straightforward approach will get you in the door. And that's exactly where you want to get—in the door.

The interview

Don't put on a three-piece suit. Nobody in a game studio (aside from some top executives) wears a suit. Wear clean presentable clothes. Long pants. Shoes and socks. Bring two or three copies of your resume and cover letter and bring your portfolio along with extra copies of that as well.

The main goody, the best thing you bring to the interview, is you. Be eager, attentive, charming. Your goal is to get a job, any job, so that you can eventually be a game designer. Find out what job openings are available. Figure out which opening is suited to your skills and interests. That's the job you should be angling for.

What the company is looking for is hard working, smart, capable communicators first and foremost. That's the impression you want to convey, through your appearance, your eye contact, and what you say during the interview.

Show your portfolio, if possible.

In an in-person interview, you could, at a logical point in the conversation, show samples of your work. If you're a game designer, sample game concepts might be construed as an unsolicited submission, making the game company liable to a lawsuit from you if they ever did anything similar. It would be wise to put your designs on your own web site (like a free Geocities web page for instance), which would make them public knowledge (taking your portfolio out of the realm of "submission" and into the realm of "portfolio"). Letting the interviewer know this in advance could prevent what might otherwise turn into an awkward moment if someone perceives your portfolio as an unsolicited submission. And it shows that you are both savvy and sensitive to the company's needs.

Be prepared with your portfolio, in paper form, CD form, and/or web form but realize that the interviewer may not have the time to look at it. Do not expect the interviewer to navigate through whatever labyrinthine path you have on the web or on a CD during the interview. It doesn't work like that. If you have the opportunity to show it, that's great. If not, don't be upset.

An important point about game concepts you developed on your own (oft stated on the game design newsgroups): It's unlikely that anybody is going to steal your idea and make your game idea without you. It's also unlikely that they'll take your idea and make the game with you. Game companies are teeming with more ideas than they can ever make. What game companies need is people, not game ideas. Your purpose in showing them your portfolio is purely to show them that you're a creative individual that they should hire.

After the interview

It's unlikely that the interview will end with you walking out the door with a job offer in hand. That's possible, and that's desirable, but it's more likely that the interviewer will discuss you and your resume with others before any decision is made about offering you a job. When you leave the interview, you will probably have a sense of how well the interview went. If it didn't go very well, then just spend a few minutes thinking of what you could have done to make it go better. Then use that thinking on the next interview. When a stumbling block is in your way, use it as a stepping-stone.

Send thank-you notes to the people who interviewed you. I know it sounds old-fashioned, but we're not talking about robots, we're talking about human beings with whom you want to build human relationships. Some folks send thank-yous electronically, some will tell you a paper letter is best. Here are some tips on thank-you letters from the *Los Angeles Times* CareerBuilder (latimes.com/careerbuilder):

- Send the thank-you letter within 24 hours of the interview. The idea is to show them that you have follow-up skills.
- One page max.

- Each one you send must be written specifically for the individual. If you met multiple individuals, get their business cards so you have proper spellings and job titles, and take notes immediately after the interview so you recall details for personalizing the letters.

- An important purpose of the letter is to restate why you are a good candidate, and also to answer any potential objections, especially those you may have heard the individual mention during your interview.

- Just like with a cover letter or resume, the smallest writing error can spoil any good impression they may have gotten of you.

Again, don't pin all your hopes on one company. Go for other interviews. The worst thing that can happen is that you don't get any offers. The second-worst thing that can happen is that you get one offer. The third-worst thing (the same thing as the best thing that can happen) is: you get more than one job offer to choose from.

Author Bio

Tom Sloper's game biz career began at Western Technologies, where he designed LCD watch and calculator games, and the Vectrex games Spike and Bedlam. Subsequently, he worked in designer, producer, and director roles at Sega Enterprises, Rudell Design, Atari Corporation, and Activision. Sloper participated in the completion of 121 game products—78 in the role of project leader, 27 in the role of designer—winning six awards along the way. Sloper has produced games with developers in the U.S., Japan, the UK, Australia, Russia, Europe, and Southeast Asia, and lived for several months in Tokyo, working for Activision's Japan operation. Doing business as Sloperama Productions, Sloper is currently consulting, writing, speaking, teaching, and developing original games.

Know the industry

As we discussed in the previous chapter, it's important to stay informed about the industry you want to be a part of. Read books, magazines, and web sites that can help you find out the latest news and trends. Having a grasp on the latest industry news when you go into an interview or meeting is a good way to show your knowledge of the space and it will allow you to take advantage of opportunities that may arise with the latest announcements.

Networking

Networking is a powerful tool for people at all levels of the game industry. By networking, we simply mean getting out and meeting people within the industry. You can do this by going to industry-related events, attending conferences and conventions, reaching out to people in the industry via the Internet, and getting introductions via friends and relatives who know people in the industry. Networking may not come easily for you, but the payoffs are great. You can learn a lot by interacting with industry professionals, and when a job becomes available, you may be the person they think of first.

Organizations

Joining organizations related to the industry is one way of meeting people. One of the best to consider joining is the International Game Developers Association, or the IGDA. The IGDA is an international organization of programmers, designers, artists, producers, and many other types of industry professionals, which fosters community and action for the furthering of games as a medium. The organization has local chapters in many geographic locations—you can find out if there is one near you by going to www.igda.org/chapters.

Chapters often hold networking events, lectures and other opportunities to meet people working in the industry. There are membership fees for this organization, but if you are a student, you can get a reduced rate.

Conferences

Another great opportunity for networking is at conferences. Two of the top conferences in the U.S. are the Game Developers Conference and E3. Developers and publishing executives attend these events *en masse*, and you will have the opportunity to meet people from all levels and areas of the industry. There are lectures and seminars on any number of topics, and you may be surprised at how accessible some of the top talent in the industry is at these events.

Exercise 16.1: Networking

Make it your goal to attend at least one networking event per month. This can be a conference, a party, a meeting, a lecture, or any other opportunity in which you can meet people in the game industry. Start a database of the contacts you make at these events.

Internet and e-mail

Another networking resource is the Internet. You can meet many people in the industry in online communities, such as the forums on IGDA.org. Or you can find internships or positions in the jobs and projects sections of Gamasutra.com. E-mail is a very efficient tool for reaching out to people, but not necessarily the most powerful or persuasive way to introduce yourself. You can find lists of developers and publishers in the companies area of Gamasutra.com, and you can go to their web sites and contact them via a "cold" (i.e., unsolicited) e-mail, but don't be surprised if you don't get a response. Game companies are flooded with e-mail from people who want to work in the game industry, and the chance of your e-mail getting to the right person without an introduction is slim. That doesn't mean you shouldn't try, but don't be dismayed if the response to your carefully written e-mail is silence.

One problem is that HR departments are often not the best way to reach the decision-makers for project hiring. We recommend searching for the individual addresses of people inside the company. Find out who is the producer or line producer on a particular game title, and then try to get an introduction to this person. Do you know someone in the industry, or otherwise, who knows him? If so, get a personal introduction. If not, try to find his e-mail address from press releases or postings on the web and contact them directly.

Before sitting down to write your e-mail, research this person's background and the games he's worked on. Personalize your e-mail to him, based on your research. A little knowledge and a well-written introduction to yourself and why you are contacting him can go a long way. If you're lucky, your e-mail will get a response—even if there is no job at the moment, you'll have made a contact and you can introduce yourself in person at the next industry event or conference.

Good research and writing notwithstanding, don't expect too much from each message that you send. Professionals working in the game industry receive a lot of unsolicited inquiries. If they don't write back, don't be surprised or upset. They are probably in the midst of production and too busy to answer their mail. But if you continue to persevere, your odds will increase with every message you send.

Exercise 16.2: Follow-Up Letter

Write a follow-up letter to a person you've met via your networking efforts to talk about job opportunities in her company or to show her your original game idea. Try to make your letter both persuasive and courteous. Be sure you are prepared for the meeting should they respond—the next few exercises will help you to do that.

An important note about networking is to not expect too much from each activity you do. If you go to an event and don't meet anyone who can help you, don't consider it a failure. Networking is a cumulative endeavor. It's seldom that a single meeting will result in a job opportunity. Usually, you'll have to meet people several times at events and follow up with them each time before opportunities open up. Even if a networking event opens up no opportunities, you'll still learn a lot by simply mingling and interacting with the people there.

Starting at the bottom

What jobs should you be trying to get in your quest to enter the industry? If you are an artist or a programmer, there are entry-levels positions in these tracks at most companies. You'll need to have a good resume/portfolio. These positions are competitive, but demand is high for this type of talent. As the size of game teams has grown, the largest percentage of new jobs has been created in the art and programming groups.

If you want to produce games, there may be production assistant or coordinator jobs (or internships) you can apply for. But if you want to design games, the outlook is a bit more complicated. The best job you could get would be as an assistant designer or level designer. Truthfully, however, these positions are difficult to come by unless you're experienced or already working within a game company. Many people who become game designers do so by starting in another track and jumping over into design once they have gained experience in the industry. For example, many game designers first work as programmers or producers.

Exercise 16.3: Resume

Create a resume focusing on your game design experience. Even if you don't have much professional experience, make sure to include references to all the design work you've done in the exercises throughout this book, courses you've taken, or organizations you belong to, such as the IGDA.

Interning

A good way to get into the industry in any career track is by interning. Game companies, especially publishers, bring on summer interns from colleges regularly. These are generally not paid positions, and are not as hard as getting a paying job. But before you take an intern position, make sure the company is serious about letting you become involved in actual projects. You don't want to spend three to six months making photocopies or acting as a receptionist. This won't advance your career much, or teach you about the industry. A good internship will allow you to learn about some aspect of the business. Interns often do research, testing, or assist producers or executives. It's a great way to get to network and to increase your knowledge.

Exercise 16.4: Internship

If you are a student, an internship is a good place to start. Go to the career center on campus or visit the web site and look for postings. Another option is to approach game companies directly and ask them if there are any internship openings.

QA

The most common paid entry-level job is as a QA tester. The pay is usually low and hours can be long, but it's a good way to start your career because QA testers are exposed to the whole development team. You'll be writing bug reports that go directly to the programmers, artists, and producers. Managers may take note of talented QA testers because many of them started in QA themselves. When production teams are being built for new projects, some companies will give a good QA tester, who has paid his dues, consideration over an outsider. More importantly, QA testing gives you front row seats to the development process. You'll get to see games evolve and come together from early builds to the final release.

Once you've proven yourself as a QA tester, it's easier to transition into other roles, including assistant producer, programmer, assistant designer, or level designer. Be dedicated to your work in QA, but take the opportunity to communicate to your managers and co-workers the path you hope to take. Don't be pushy, but if the occasion arises, invite your colleagues to see the work you've done on your own as a game designer, and be open to opportunities to advance, even it means extra work or volunteering some time to another department.

An Interview with a Game Agent

Richard Leibowitz is the president of Union Entertainment.

Game Design Workshop: How did you become a game agent and why?

Richard Leibowitz: After considering careers in law, finance, and politics, I decided to combine the three in entertainment and took a position at Paramount Pictures as an attorney in the Domestic Television department. From there, I went on to head Rysher Entertainment's International Business and Legal Affairs department, and later returned to Paramount when Paramount acquired Rysher. During that period, I became enamored with the videogame industry and left Paramount to apply my entertainment deal-making and legal experience towards the production of games. Eventually, I established my own agency and partnered with Sean O'Keefe, a feature film producer, in 2003 to form Union, a feature film and videogame production and management company.

GDW: What's the role of an agent in the game industry today?

RL: In my opinion, there are three types of agents in the game industry today: recruiting agents, packaging agents, and Hollywood agents.

Recruiting agents simply make phone calls to publishers on behalf of developers, whether clients or not, to solicit and secure work-for-hire deals. For example, a recruiting agent calls a publisher and learns that the publisher is requesting proposals from developers to make a game based on a recently acquired license. The recruiting agent then calls random developers, tells them of the opportunity, finds or settles on one interested developer, and pitches that developer to the publisher. If the publisher hires the developer, then the recruiting agent successfully used his contacts and networking abilities to secure a project for the developer. Typically, the developer will pay the recruiting agent a percentage of the development budget.

Packaging agents identify and secure content, whether original or licensed, attach the best available developer, and pitch and sell the package (i.e., content and developer) to a publisher. For example, the packaging agent is offered or identifies a property that has been successful as a television series, but has yet to be made into a game. The packaging agent secures an agreement from the licensor to represent the property in the videogame industry, attaches an interested developer to the property, and pitches the package to publishers. If a publisher buys the package, then the recruiting agent has successfully secured a license agreement for the licensor, secured a development project for the developer, and provided the publisher with an opportunity to start and develop a game franchise. Typically, the licensor will pay the packaging agent a percentage of the license fee and the developer will pay the packaging agent a percentage of its development budget.

Hollywood agents include those at Endeavor, CAA, ICM, William Morris, and a host of other agencies. Each of the agencies has at least one person dedicated to games, although the services they provide vary greatly. For the most part, Hollywood agents represent their film clients' interests in the game world. For example, if a publisher wants to secure an actor's name and likeness rights and/or hire the actor for voice recordings, the publisher will have to deal with the Hollywood agent to secure such rights and/or services. Several Hollywood agents are more proactive, though. Such agents, for example, package developers with film projects at the agency and sell those packages to publishers. Typically, the publisher will pay the Hollywood agent a percentage of the package (i.e., license, actor's rights and services fees, and development budget).

GDW: How is a typical deal structured between a developer, publisher, and your company?

RL: Union provides a wide array of specialized services and has a successful track record. As a result, there are many developers that utilize Union's services. The most common deal structures between Union and its clients include: (1) straight retainer (i.e., an amount per month for services), (2) fees (i.e., a percentage of development budget), and (3) retainer plus fees (i.e., compared to straight retainer and fees, a lesser amount per month plus a lesser percentage of development budget).

GDW: What do you look for in a client?

RL: Talent. Publishers hire two types of developers: (1) established developers with robust and proven technology, or (2) brand new developers with superstar talent and capable management.

GDW: What do you think the role of a game agent will become?

RL: There will always be a place for game agents—even the biggest and best developers can take advantage of an agent's contacts and deal-making abilities. That being said, I believe the role of a game agent in the future will be more of the packaging variety than recruiting for at least two reasons:

Internal business development personnel: Developers have business development personnel on staff to secure and sell projects. Typically, the associated costs to employ such personnel are equal to or less than what the developer would pay a recruiting agent to secure a work-for-hire deal.

Publisher demand for projects: Publishers are extremely risk averse. One way publishers reduce risk is by hiring the best development companies, and another is to green light projects based on pre-existing and identifiable underlying content (i.e., *Harry Potter*).

Packaging agents add value to developers and pique publishers' interest when they attach developers to desirable content. By so doing, the packaging agent will most likely either (1) secure a deal for a developer that the developer wouldn't have otherwise secured, or (2) make it possible for the developer to charge a premium for its game development services (i.e., higher development budget or a larger share of royalties).

GDW: *Will agents be as established in the game industry in the future as they are in the film and television industry today?*

RL: Eventually. The Hollywood agencies are big and powerful because they were established many years ago and are unequivocally accepted by both talent and movie studios as standard operating procedure. At this time, developers demand agents less than Hollywood talent does and publishers haven't fully embraced the role of the game agent. However, the game industry is slowly but surely modeling itself after the Hollywood industry and, after some time, game agents will surely act similarly and be as influential as their Hollywood brethren.

Just as in Hollywood, content is king in the game industry (followed closely by technology). The packaging and Hollywood agents are best suited to assist and add value to developers since they often control the underlying content demanded by publishers. In the not so distant future, publishers will follow the movie studios' lead and rely upon the game agents to package and present compelling projects.

Other ways in

There are countless other ways to establish yourself in the industry. You may find work in public relations or human resources, and then transition by networking and interacting with other departments. You may start in the sound department as a production assistant, or as we said earlier, as a programmer or a producer. There have been lawyers, accountants, and office managers who've managed to transition into game design. What really counts is that you start working within the game industry in some fashion, and while you're in that position, network with the rest of the team and show them your skills. If your ideas are good, people will notice, and they'll think of you when openings come up.

PITCHING YOUR ORIGINAL IDEAS

Once you have built up some experience by working in the industry, you may want to develop and pitch your own original ideas to publishers. As we discussed in Chapter 13, publishers are more likely to fund ideas that come to them with an experienced team, a stellar idea, and a good, solid project plan. But how do you get a meeting with a publisher to give them your pitch?

If you've been following our advice and networking with your peers and with other individuals in the industry, perhaps you know someone who can get you a meeting. If not, start researching various publishers and find a way to meet or contact them at the next industry event. Conferences like E3 and the Game Developers Conference are times when publishers set aside time to meet with new developers and hear pitches. If an event like this is coming up, try contacting them and suggesting a meeting then. You're much more likely to get a positive response.

Another way to get your idea heard is to work through an agent. Game agents work like most talent agents, in that they sign a contract with you to represent you to their contacts in the industry. If you sell an idea via these contacts, they will negotiate the deal for you, in conjunction with your lawyer, and for this service, you pay them a percentage of your fee. Agents are not as established in the game industry as they are in other areas of media. However, as the sidebar in this chapter with Richard Leibowitz discusses, agents may be used for recruitment, business development, or deal packaging. When you are first starting out, it will be difficult to get agents interested in representing you, however, so this route is an unlikely one for a beginner.

Let's assume that you've been able to get a meeting with a potential publisher. What do they expect to see? How will the process unfold? The following section explains some industry practices for established developers seeking to sell their ideas to publishers. Even if you are not yet at that stage of your career, it is worth understanding the process so that you can anticipate what you will have to do when you do get to that point.

The information and recommendations in this section are based on the IGDA Business Committee's *Game Submission Guide*. In preparing this document, the IGDA surveyed and interviewed professionals throughout the industry to get a picture of trends and common practices for game submissions. The full report is available for download from http://www.igda.org/biz/submission_-guide.php. With the IGDA's permission, we've used the report to create the following recommendations.

Pitch process

Game publishers receive thousands of submissions a year from developers. Many of these are immediately rejected for a variety of reasons, including inadequate submission materials. Less than 4% of submitted ideas are actually published. Of the ones that become products, only one or two become hits. Don't be discouraged by these statistics, though, because the odds of rejection are similar in all creative industries.

As a developer, you can increase your chances of getting past the first step with a publisher by making acceptable pitch materials. Good pitch materials will identify your team as experienced professionals and they will convey your ideas in an exciting way. When you are pitching to a publisher they are asking themselves: "Can these people be trusted with millions of my dollars?"

The first step in pitching is to get to some one who reviews third party submissions. You can sometimes find a contact address on the publisher's web site or by calling the main switchboard and asking for someone in "third party product acquisitions." Again, don't be surprised if your phone calls don't get returned. Always be courteous, but also be persistent.

When you eventually get a pitch opportunity, you should be prepared to sign a submission agreement or confidentiality agreement. This document will basically say that whatever idea you are going to present may already be in development at the company or presented to them by another developer. In any case, you will have no recourse if they end up producing a similar idea without you. Despite the one-sidedness of this document you should sign it. Refusing to sign will show that you are not familiar with the process. Submission agreements are standard practice in every creative industry including books, film, and television.

It's best to pitch in person. However sometimes publishers will request to review the materials on their own first. Either way, present yourself and your materials in as professional a manner as possible. You don't need to wear a suit, but ripped jeans and an old T-shirt are not appropriate.

Depending on how aggressive you are, getting through the pitch process can take anywhere from four to sixteen weeks. Make a checklist or spreadsheet of every publisher you contact. It's okay to present the same pitch to multiple companies, but dealing with publishers that have multiple individuals evaluating your project can get confusing and you don't want to lose track of your progress.

Pitch materials

The package you present has to instill confidence in different types of people within the publishing company. They will be evaluating your team first, your creative materials second, and your schedule and budget third. Make your materials easy to understand in a very short time frame because not everyone at the publisher is going to read them in their entirety. Here are some materials that the IGDA guidelines recommend preparing:

1. Sell sheet
2. Game demo
3. Game AVI
4. Game design overview
5. Company prospectus
6. Gameplay storyboards
7. PowerPoint presentation
8. Technical design overview
9. Competitive analysis

1. Sell sheet

This is a "short attention span" document that explains your idea as well as the target market. It's good for the sales and marketing folks that may

Selling Ideas to the Game Industry

by Kenn Hoekstra, Raven Software

To be brutally honest, it's *very* difficult for someone outside the games industry to get their ideas past a company's front door. For that matter, it's not all that easy to get a game company to look at your ideas if you work for them. There are a number of reasons for this.

First of all, there are legal reasons that revolve around the legal possession of an idea. Let's say a company had a similar idea a year ago and they've spent a million dollars or more developing that idea up until this point. The company says, "Sure, I'd love to hear your new, innovative game idea" and it turns out the idea is the same as the one the company has been working on. When the game comes out, you have a "he said/she said" lawsuit on your hands over whose idea the game was in the first place. That is a hassle that no company wants. To combat this situation, most companies delete ideas and suggestions unread or send them back "return to sender" through postal mail.

Another reason game ideas are hard to sell is that most people outside the industry don't understand the fundamentals of game development. They don't understand technology limitations, development times, financial concerns, scheduling or any of the multitudes of other headaches involved in developing a new product. Their idea proposals say things like, "You would recreate New York City to scale and have four million unique-looking and -sounding individuals that you can interact with and you can have 500,000 of them on the screen at the same time when you join them in Times Square for the New Year's Eve ball drop. That's when the aliens attack and severely damage the city, so all of the buildings have to be half-destroyed as the city is plunged into chaos and eternal night. Then you and your band of 10,000 resistance fighters lead the charge with 50 different weapons and squad-based tactics and the game would toggle between first-person, third-person, top down, and map views and on and on and on and on and on. You see what I mean? A vast majority of game idea submissions suffer from this problem. I call it "newbie ambition." Game development is mostly about figuring out "what cool stuff you can do in a limited time period with limited cash."

Yet another reason for not accepting game ideas is a question of "who takes the risk?" The game company is spending three to six million dollars (or more) on the development cycle for the game and, in turn, they are taking all of the risk. Why, then, should they pay someone from outside the company for their game idea when they aren't taking any of the risk? Generally speaking, every game company has more ideas of their own on the back burner than they will ever have time to produce and thus, there's no reason to accept outside ideas.

Think of it this way. Everyone at one time or another has tried to write a novel or has had a great idea for a novel. How many book publishers will take an idea for a novel if they have to pay someone else to do the writing? None. Therefore, the people with the ideas have to write their own books. How many of them start writing? How many of them actually *finish* the novel? When they're finished, how many get published at all? And of those that are published, how many are published without changes made by the publisher? See what I mean?

Think of game companies as established entities in the entertainment business. Generally speaking, game companies think they know everything there is to know about gaming because they've paid their dues and worked their way to the top. Just as you won't sell a *Star Wars* sequel to George Lucas or a Spec Ops book to Tom Clancy, odds are you won't sell your big idea to a game developer. Sadly, it's just the nature of the business.

The only possible exception to the "outside game ideas" rule is if you are a world-famous person in the entertainment industry. If Stephen King, for example, came to a game company with an idea for a horror game, who wouldn't listen? The potential to have a famous name on the box can sometimes outweigh the "we have our own ideas" rule.

Now, if you do want to get your idea made into a game, there are a few things you can do:

- *Inquire with the company first.* Ask them if they want to hear your idea and offer to sign an NDA agreement. If you're not interested in money or lawsuits, tell them in writing they can have your idea "no strings attached" if they want to use it. Don't just send the idea in unsolicited. It will be deleted unread, ignored, or mailed back to you.

- *Get a job at a game company.* If you're on the inside, your chances of getting your ideas noticed or accepted are much greater because most of the legalities disappear.

- *Get a team together and make the game yourself.* If not the whole game, make a solid, working demo. This will show publishers that you're serious and it will give them something concrete to look at. Game development is a very visual business and it's a lot easier to judge a game idea from a demo than from a piece of paper or a wordy verbal description.

It's a great misnomer that game companies (or any companies for that matter) employ "idea people" or think tanks to push the company in bold new directions. Hard work and contribution to a greater goal or the greater good of a company is the only way to get anything done in the business world. That goes for your own company or any company you're working for. Unless, of course, your family owns the company. Then all bets are off on the hard work and contribution part.

Author Bio

Kenn Hoekstra has a Bachelor of Science degree in English from the University of Wisconsin—Whitewater. He has designed 3D game levels for Raven Software's Take No Prisoners, Hexen II: Portal of Praevus, HexenWorld, *and* Soldier of Fortune: Gold Edition. *He also served as Project Administrator for* Heretic II, Soldier of Fortune, Star Trek: Voyager—Elite Force, *the Elite Force Expansion Pack,* Jedi Knight II: Jedi Outcast, *and* Soldier of Fortune II: Double Helix. *Kenn has written several game manuals, the official* Soldier of Fortune Strategy Guide *the screenplay for* Soldier of Fortune II: Double Helix *and has published several articles on the games industry. He is currently working on* Jedi Academy, Quake IV, *and* X-Men: Legends. *Kenn lives in Madison, Wisconsin with his wife, Michele and his Jack Russell Terrier, Toby.*

look at your pitch. The sell sheet should include: game title, genre, number of players, platform, ship date, two paragraph description, bullet point list of features, and some game art.

2. **Game demo**

A playable demo is one of the most important submission materials you can produce. 77% of the respondents to the IGDA's publisher survey say that a playable demo is essential to a pitch package. Demos can be built in differing degrees of completeness. The important thing is that the publisher can get to evaluate the final gameplay. Ideally, contents will include: a game level, quality artwork and sound, and an easy interface.

3. **Game AVI**

If you can't produce a playable demo then a game AVI is the next best thing. It's a video file that shows the characters and gameplay. The most credible AVI will be one created using your game code. However some established developers make them using just storyboards and narration.

4. **Game design overview**

This is a game design explanation written without excessive details. If a publisher is interested they'll want to see that you've thought through the whole project but they will not want to read every last detail. Ideal contents include: game story, game mechanics, level design outline, controls, interfaces, art style, music style, feature list, preliminary milestone schedule, and a list of team members with short bios.

5. **Company prospectus**

This is a short document that talks about the managers in your company and the team members. It's like a resume for your company. Ideal contents include: company info (including location and project history, and proven abilities),

company details (including technologies used, number of employees in each department, other differentiating information), titles in development, titles shipped (including platform info), and full team bios.

6. **Storyboards**

These are still images from your game. They can be in sketch form or final art or both. They are nice to include in a paper package because an executive might want to review your documents when they are away from a computer and can't run your demo or game AVI. Ideal contents: visual walkthrough of gameplay with text explanations, play control diagrams, and character profiles.

7. **PowerPoint presentation**

This is a compilation of key visuals and points from your other pitch materials. It's easy to make and it may be useful if the publisher wants to get the top points when you are not in the room. For instance, one person inside the publisher may want to present the idea to another when you are not around.

8. **Technical design overview**

This is a technical design document without excessive details. It describes how your technology works, as well as the intended development path. It should include complete explanations while being accessible for nonengineers. Ideal contents: general overview; engine description, tools description, hardware used—development and target, history of code base, and middleware used, if any.

9. **Competitive analysis**

This identifies titles you are competing against. It shows that you understand the market and your relative position within it. Ideal contents: summary of your concept's market position and reason for success, and pro and con descriptions of competitive titles—with sales figures if you can get them.

Exercise 16.5: Preparing Your Submission Materials

Go over the previous list, and with your team members prepare as many of the submission materials as you can. Make sure to include all of the work you have done on your original game prototype, your design document, and your project plan.

The psychology of the pitch

Publishers only engage their time and resources with what they consider attractive opportunities. So if you represent yourself and your company as anything other than a competent, creative, and attractive opportunity from which both parties will benefit, then you will have very little chance with them. Remember that publishers literally have hundreds of properties to choose from—and they might only pick two or three for the whole year. Your submission needs to be complete and professional; your in-person presentation should be no more than 30 minutes to an hour in length.

Make sure you get enough sleep the day before your pitch, be at your best energy level, your most articulate, and if you receive criticism, be sure to take it gracefully. Keep everything in the perspective of business, and remember not to take rejections personally. The odds are against you, but they are not zero. Also, bear in mind that the rejection or criticism you get from a publisher is not failure if you learn from it. Any input you receive and act on can improve your pitch for the next publisher.

Exercise 16.6: Pitching

From your networking database and the research you've done, target a list of companies to whom you can pitch your original game. Use all the methods described previously to find a contact within the company and set up a pitch. Even if this exercise doesn't result in the sale or funding of your idea, this is a great way to network and will help you to meet more people in the industry and possibly get a job.

What happens after the pitch

Before leaving your pitch meeting, you should ask when you should expect a preliminary response to your pitch. This will set both your own expectations for a response as well as the publisher's expectations that you intend to follow up.

Prompt follow-up on the developer's part is important, but over-eagerness can quickly wear on a publisher. A good guideline is to follow up with a short "thank you" e-mail immediately after your pitch, and provide any supplemental materials or copies of documents that were requested during the meeting.

If a publisher is interested they will likely get back to you quickly, but if you don't hear from them immediately, it may just mean that your contact is traveling, or busy in other meetings. If you do not receive a response after seven to ten days, you should contact the individual who set up your meeting with no more than one e-mail and one phone call per week to check on the status of your pitch. Contacting the person more than this will be seen as bothersome and is unlikely to help your cause.

What will likely be happening at the publisher during this time is an internal review process among multiple people. It is unlikely that one person will be empowered to make a decision. Most publishers are organized around three groups:

- Sales and marketing
- Production
- Business/legal

Within each group are decision makers who have input on external submissions. The people you pitch to will likely be from the business/legal group. If they like it they will take it to the other internal groups and try to build consensus. These groups often have competitive relationships because of their differing roles in the company. Ideally someone will feel strongly about your idea and fight to convince the other groups that it will be successful. If these groups like it, the publisher may ask a technical executive to dig deeper into your project. It's a great sign if the publisher starts asking for technical details.

In essence the final decision will be based on a combination of many possible risks. These risk factors may include: time to market risk, design risk, technology risk, team risk, platform risk, marketing risk, cost risk, etc. If the publisher goes through

their process and decides your project is worth the risk they will prepare a detailed return on investment (ROI) analysis that will determine profit potential for the title.

If the publisher deems all risks and the projected ROI acceptable then the publisher may send you a letter of intent for the project. This is a great day, but your submission process is still not over. As a final step, the publisher will probably want to execute a full contract. Or, they may unexpectedly kill the project at this point for internal reasons. As a rule of thumb, don't believe you have a deal until you see a signature from the publisher on the final contract. And don't spend any of the money you expect to see from the publisher until it is actually in your company bank account.

If your pitch doesn't make it to this stage, know that you are not alone: you are in the company of 96% of all other submissions that the publisher has reviewed and passed on that year. Each time you go through this process you will learn more about how to pitch your ideas and you will have more and better contacts to pitch them to.

INDEPENDENT PRODUCTION

Like other large media industries, the game industry has its share of independents, who choose to self-produce and distribute games. This is a hard route to take, and scraping together the money to support a team through months of production can be an arduous process. Some independent developers have other jobs, some do work for hire to support their original game development, some use credit cards and loans from friends and family. Like independent films and underground music, independent games are a long shot for their creators—more often than not they are never finished, or never find a distribution channel. But independence has its privileges as well—the ability to experiment with truly original concepts, the freedom to change ideas mid-stream, and the knowledge that you own your ideas and their implementation.

One independent studio, gameLab, eloquently sums up its philosophy on their homepage at www.gmlb.com: "gameLab is a new kind of game developer. Cinema has its independent filmmakers. The music industry has alternative and underground bands and DJs. And the gaming industry needs its independent voices. Our games break new ground by finding new audiences, inventing original forms of gameplay, and by exploring narrative content and visual and audio styles that aren't normally found in games. What drives us? We're doing our part to expand the boundaries of the gaming world and reshape the culture of games. If we don't, who will?"

For most independent developers, the goal is to produce a game that will be picked up and distributed by a major publisher. If this happens, the developer will be able to negotiate a fairly good deal in terms of ownership and royalties, and the publisher will be taking much less risk in terms of advances. Unfortunately, most independently produced games do not get picked up and their developers must resort to trying to sell them directly via the Internet, or using them as a demo to get a publishing deal for a different game. But that's no reason not to go the independent route if you have a truly original idea and the passion to produce it. The edges of industries are where innovation often thrives, and your game may turn out to be exactly what the game-playing public didn't know it was looking for.

Conclusion

As you can see, there are many ways to become a game designer and to get your ideas produced. Whether you get a job in the industry and you work your way up the ladder, or try to get a deal to develop an original game for a publisher, or strike out on your own and produce your ideas independently, what really matters is not the path you choose, but that you find a way to realize your dreams and make the type of games you truly believe in.

To do this means that you should take the time to think deeply about what it is you want to do with your life, and what types of games you want to develop. Don't just follow in the footsteps of others. Great thinkers and creators have always made their own way. We hope you'll challenge yourself to create your own games your own way, even if everyone else believes it is impossible or unwise.

Whether you find yourself working at a large company, wind up producing games on a shoestring, or just wind up designing games as a hobby, never lose sight of your own personal vision, and keep in mind that the only way to fail is by not making games at all.

Indie Game Jam—
An Outlet for Innovation and Experimental Game Design

by Justin Hall

Austin Grossman is fleeing through a city, fervently searching through tens of thousands of shuffling, pixellated citizens for the wide sombrero of the man who wants to kill him. Austin's movements with the mouse are jerky, and he's holding his breath. Suddenly he hears a loud reverberating ping, off to his left. Austin whirls to face the sound. The crowd parts, and before Austin can react, the man in the Sombrero shoots him down.

Thatcher Ulrich watches over Austin's shoulder, gently nibbling his finger. Austin and his colleague Doug Church are playing Thatcher's game, Dueling Machine. In Dueling Machine, one player hunts another, using sonar pings to find or avoid their enemy amidst tens of thousands of innocent bystanders. Few games use sound in such an integral way; this idea came from Marc LeBlanc. Thatcher works at Oddworld Inhabitants, a videogame development studio owned in part by Microsoft. At the time, Marc worked for Visual Concepts, a videogame development studio owned by Sega. Given the competitive nature of the modern game industry, it doesn't make much sense that these two would be coding a videogame together.

Thatcher and Marc are both working on Dueling Machine as part of the Indie Game Jam. Tired of calcification in commercial videogames, a small group of game designers decided to jump-start some experimental game design. In March of 2002, they built a system for simultaneously displaying up to 100,000 moving characters on the screen at one time. Then they invited a dozen designer-programmer friends from a half-a-dozen game companies to join them for collective quick and dirty garage-style programming in a barn on a marina in Oakland, California.

The roots of electronic entertainment lie in these sorts of collaborations, in garages and basements and dank laboratories—places where people gathered over rudimentary machines to make virtual worlds. Twenty years ago, the people responsible for electronic entertainment were not yet game professionals, they were simply dedicated hobbyists. They tinkered with computers and code to make small simulations, establishing rules and parameters that their friends would break.

These tinkerers gave birth to a $20 billion industry. Electronic gaming has expanded rapidly; now twenty years later most games are made by massive teams of specialized developers working for years with a marketable product in mind. Still there are some folks who hope to encourage a generative creative spirit, to inject some creativity and vitality into a medium that's increasingly conservative.

This "Indie Game Jam" was organized in part by programmer Chris Hecker, who sees a games industry that is "too risk adverse." He believes videogaming needs a more independent subculture, a Sundance Film Festival or garage band ethos feeding new ideas to commercial publishers. His office is

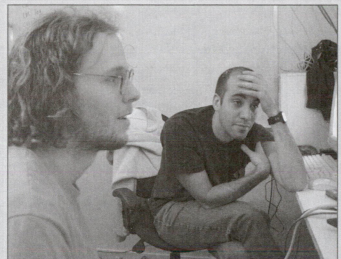

Indie Game Jam participants in action

Top left: Chris Hecker and Doug Church working on their game FireFighter, top right: Chris Corollo and Brian Sharp of Ion Storm working on their game Wrath, bottom: 2002 Indie Game Jammers, left to right: Austin Grossman, Robin Walker, Art Min, Brian Jacobson, Chris Hecker, Sean Barrett, Zack Simpson, Ken Demarest, Jonathan Blow, Doug Church, Brian Sharp, and Chris Corollo. Photos by Justin Hall.

a center for this kind of activity; he works out of the top floor of a red barn in a cluster of antique buildings surrounded by office parks and industrial sites. This space is shared by a revolving cast of independent game programmers—sitting on a futon couch propped up with old CPU cases, these game industry refugees brainstorm on whiteboards.

Hecker opened up his Oakland office to serve as the site of the Indie Game Jam. Over a bowl of dry noodles at a nearby Vietnamese restaurant, Hecker speaks passionately about the evolution of gameplay: "Games of the future will be interactive not only at the second-to-second level, which we focus on now, but also at the minute-to-minute and hour-to-hour levels. This means that not only can you walk left or right interactively, but your decisions impact the overall flow of the game." Deeper interactions require richer simulations; Hecker works primarily on physics, the system of game rules determining how objects in games interact. Do you want to stack those crates over there against the door to keep the bad guy from following you into this room to eat you alive? As Hecker points out, most games today won't allow that kind of strategy—crates are for climbing on or smashing up only.

But if physics can develop to allow more creative solutions to game problems, then, as Hecker hopes, the medium of games might develop further: "Physics has the potential to increase the richness and subtlety of the interaction with the world, but at the same time stay airtight and consistent so that we maintain a suspension of disbelief." For Hecker, that consistency involves simulating the proper way to hang off of rocks. For the last two years, he's been translating rock climbing into a shareware game that "evokes the rhythm" of that sport.

Trained initially as an artist, Hecker brings an understanding of the humanities to an aspect of game development typically characterized by attention to mathematical programming details. Independent game design gives him a chance to work as the sole writer, artist, designer, and programmer.

The second Indie Game Jam replaced 100,000 sprites with one main actor—the human body. Borrowing from Zack Simpson's Shadow Garden work, fourteen programmers had one weekend to build games that used the shadow of a human body cast on a wall as the interface for electronic entertainment. Casey Muratori and Michael Sweet created Owl Simulator where a player's outstretched arms control their flight path. In Atman Binstock's Squisy Marshmallow Maze, two players struggle to move their colored block through a maze, while using their shadow to block the progress of the other player. Squisy Marshmallow Maze games typically devolve into wrestling matches; a kind of physicality rarely encouraged by videogames.

Saleable product may seem a long way off from experiments like these, but these ideas feed the mainstream. Programmer Doug Church explains in an e-mail interview, "The game industry has always been about smoke and mirrors, and making the correct tradeoffs. So even little baby steps and experiments which seem silly now may lead to some real and unexpected successes later." Now that game development schedules have extended out beyond eighteen months, it can be difficult to work through a few different game design concepts. The format of the Indie Game Jam weekend codefest is a good uninhibitor; as Doug explains, "Given a lack of research money and time, Game Jam-like no-time-to-think-just-type-and-see-what-happens sort of events may help provide some of the ideas which eventually help us make progress."

IGJ co-organizer Sean Barrett is a refugee from the game industry, working independently in Hecker's office to move beyond "people doing simple games and high-end graphics." He's been working on a few different games and game engines, free to follow his research interests. Some projects are echoes of older titles, within which he develops what might be best described as "interpersonal physics." Experienced gamers can tell you that even if a game has good writing, it's unusual to have the feeling that players can truly affect the other characters or the plot of the game.

In e-mail correspondence, Barrett writes of developing "some sort of character 'simulator' which actually has some meaningful state and attitude and reacts to the conversation, rather than just being a menu maze that you navigate no differently than a voice mail system." Touching on Hecker's idea that a player's style of playing should affect a game over time, Barrett has been integrating personality and conflicting priorities in a hovercraft fighting game he's programming: "Your squadmates have personal agendas (derived from their allegiances to various political and religious groups) and become satisfied or unsatisfied with you based on whether you cooperate with those agendas in game." Choosing which objects to blow up may not seem like much of a step towards richer interaction, but any in-game motivation other than scoring and linear progress is remarkable. As Barrett points out about game making, "We do violent conflict great, but we don't do any other kind of conflict, especially interpersonal relationship sorts of conflict, at all."

The weekend-long Indie Game Jam may not be enough time to develop character-driven, plot-oriented games. Most of the programmers participating have day jobs with studios like Valve, Ion Storm, gameLab, or Oddworld Inhabitants. For them, the Indie Game Jam gives them a compressed version of Sean's freedom, a weekend where personal inclination and a sense of playful experimentation direct game design more than market concerns.

On the last day of the first Indie Game Jam, most of the games had been finished and many of the programmers had headed home. Sean Barrett stood over Chris Hecker's shoulder as Hecker's dirty glasses reflected tens of thousands of tiny figures being mowed down by a single warrior onscreen. As he killed with mouse and keyboard, the camera panned out slowly until his character was shown to be surrounded by an impossible sea of enemies. There was clearly no way he could survive. The artful futility of Barrett's Very Serious RoboDOOM put a wide grin on Hecker's face.

The next week at the Game Developer's Conference in San Jose, Hecker would join numerous upstart game designers rallying for more independent game development culture. Hecker proposes the creation of the videogame equivalent of film festivals and film schools, the systems that have given rise to independent film in America, alongside giant Hollywood productions. He hopes these programmers at the Indie Game Jam, infected by the spirit of loose creative game programming, might start making games that earn the respect commanded by other art forms.

More about Indie Game Jam can be found online at www.indiegamejam.com.

Author Bio

Justin Hall participates in digital culture and electronic entertainment. Present at the birth of the popular web, Hall invested his mortal soul in the exchange of personal information online. Later consumed by machine stimulation, Hall set out to study videogames to better understand his life-long computer babysitters. Justin lived in Japan for the early part of the 21st century. His writing can be found online on Game Girl Advance (www.gamegirladvance.com), and on his personal web site at www.links.net.

Conclusion

If you have been following along with the exercises in this book as you read the text, you have not only broadened your understanding of games and game structures, but you have learned to conceive, prototype, playtest and articulate your own game ideas.

You have thought through what it will take to produce at least one of your original game ideas, by creating a production plan with goals, deliverables, a schedule, and a budget. You have a draft of your game's design document and presentation materials such as art boards, a PowerPoint show, and perhaps a working demo of your game. You may even have a list of contacts in the industry to whom you can pitch your idea. In other words, you are well on your way to working as a game designer.

It has been our goal throughout this book to empower you with the knowledge and skills to go out and work as a game designer, either by getting a job at an established company, by selling your game ideas to a publisher, or by producing your ideas independently. If you feel confident in your ability to do this, then we've accomplished our goal.

Alongside this confidence, however, should exist the knowledge that "becoming" a game designer is a lifelong process that is never finished. Hopefully, you will continue growing and learning as a designer for the rest of your career, and the ideas we have presented in this book will just be the first step in a very interesting journey—the first level of your life as a game designer, so to speak.

Now, you are ready to move on to tackle more challenging concepts in design, more professional responsibility, or perhaps to refine your focus to a particular field—such as visual design, programming, producing, or marketing. Wherever your future path in game design directs you, we hope you take with you a sense of the infinite possibility that exists for game design today, the potential for developing an entertainment form with the ability to move people to involvement and action far beyond traditional media.

The future of game design rests not only in the ever more immersive qualities of technological devices we read so much about today, but more importantly in the ability of those technological wonders to serve some deeper sense of play and interaction. The potential is wide open to bring richer emotional qualities to the experience of games we know, and to create new and unique mechanics for games we've yet to play. The game designers of the next few decades will show whether this medium will live up to that promise or not. We believe that you are up to the challenge.

Thanks for playing!

Appendix A
Sample Budget Spreadsheet

Producer	Date Prepared:	
Address		
	Client:	
	Client Contact:	
Telephone #	Address:	
FAX #		
	Telephone:	
Exec. Producer	FAX:	
Line Producer		
Designer	Revision 1 Date:	
	Revision 2 Date:	
PROJECT TITLE	Revision 3 Date:	
	Revision 4 Date:	
	Revision 5 Date:	

PRODUCTION LABOR	
Project Management	0
Game Design	0
Graphic Design	0
2D Animation	0
3D Animation	0
Software Development	0
DIRECT COSTS	
Production Subcontractors	0
Digital Video	0
Production Supplies	0
Media & Replication	0
Licensing	0
General & Administrative	0
Subtotal	0

Production Insurance (2.5%)		0
Production Markup (()% of Subtotal)		0
Contingency (()% of Subtotal)		0

Grand Total:	$0

COMMENTS

	NO.	WEEKS	RATE	BENEFITS 21%	EQUIP/FACILITY 87%	TOTAL
Project Management						
Executive Producer				0	0	0
Producer				0	0	0
Asst. Producer				0	0	0
Project Management Total:						0

	NO.	WEEKS	RATE	BENEFITS	EQUIP/FACILITY	TOTAL
Game Design						
Game Designer				0	0	0
Level Designer				0	0	0
				0	0	0
Interactive Design Total:						0
Visual Design						
Art Director				0	0	0
Interface Designer				0	0	0
Production Artist				0	0	0
				0	0	0
Graphic Design Total:						0

	NO.	WEEKS	RATE	BENEFITS	EQUIP/FACILITY	TOTAL
2D Animation						
Animation Director				0	0	0
Character Animator				0	0	0
Assistant Animator				0	0	0
Layout Artist				0	0	0
Ink & Paint				0	0	0
				0	0	0
2D Animation Total:						0

	NO.	WEEKS	RATE	BENEFITS	EQUIP/FACILITY	TOTAL
3D Animation						
CG Animation Director				0	0	0
CG Animator				0	0	0
CG Animation Assistant				0	0	0
				0	0	0
3D Animation Total:						0

	NO.	WEEKS	RATE	BENEFITS	EQUIP/FACILITY	TOTAL
Software Development						
Technical Director				0	0	0
Lead Programmer				0	0	0
Programmer				0	0	0
Assistant Programmer				0	0	0
Software Tester				0	0	0
				0	0	0
Software Dev't Total:						0

	WEEKS	COST	TOTAL
Production Subcontractors			
Sound Design			0
Illustration			0
Voice Over Talent			0
			0
Subcontractors Total:			0

	WEEKS	COST	TOTAL
Digital Video			
Video Digitizing			0
Avid Editing			0
On-line Video Session			0
			0
Digital Video Total:			0

	WEEKS	COST	TOTAL
Production Supplies			
Software Purchase			0
Art Supplies			0
Reference Media			0
Film & Processing			0
			0
Production Supplies Total:			0

	UNITS	COST	TOTAL
Media & Replication			
CD-ROM One-offs			0
CD-ROM Replication			0
Exabyte Tapes			0
Syquest Cartridges			0
Magneto-optical Discs			0
Zip Cartridges			0
1/2" Dubs			0
3/4" Dubs			0
D-1 Tapes			0
			0
Media & Replication Total:			0

			TOTAL
Licensing			
Stock Footage Licensing			0
Stock Image Licensing			0
Stock Audio Licensing			0
Software Licensing			0
Licensing Total:			0

	WEEKS	COST	TOTAL
General & Administrative			0
Phones			0
Shipping			0
Travel			0
Working Meals			0
			0
G & A Total:			0

Appendix B
Industry Magazines and Web Sites

Gaming News, Reviews, and Features

The Adrenaline Vault (www.avault.com)

Blue's News (www.bluesnews.com)

Classic Gamer (www.classicgamer.com)

Computer Games (www.cgonline.com)

Computer Gaming World (www.computergaming.com)

Digital Games (www.digitalgames.com)

Edge (www.edge-online.com)

Electronic Gaming Monthly (www.egmmag.com)

Expert Gamer

Game Informer (www.gameinformer.com)

GameNOW (gamenow.gamers.com)

Game Pro (www.gamepro.com)

Game Revolution (www.game-revolution.com)

GameSpot (www.gamespot.com)

GameSpy (www.gamespy.com)

Gamers.com (www.gamers.com)

Happy Puppy (www.happypuppy.com)

IGN (www.ign.com)

The Next Level (www.the-nextlevel.com)

MobyGames (www.mobygames.com)

Official XBox Magazine (www.officialxboxmagazine.com)

PC Gamer (www.pcgamer.com)

PlayStation Magazine (www.playstationmagazine.com)

PSM (www.psmonline.com)

TotalGames.net (totalgames.net)

Video Game News (www.videogamenews.com)

Game Design and Production

Gamasutra: The Art and Science of Making Games (www.gamasutra.com)

Game Developer (www.gdmag.com)

GameDev.net (www.gamedev.net)

Journal of Game Development (www.jogd.com)

Game Studies

Center for Computer Games Research Copenhagen (game.itu.dk)

Digiplay Initiative (www.digiplay.org.uk)

Game Culture: Thinking About Computer Games (www.game-culture.com)

Game Studies: The International Journal of Game Research (www.gamestudies.org)

Ludogoly.org: Video Game Theory (ludology.org)

Re:play: Game Design + Game Culture (www.eyebeam.org/replay)

Data and Research

DFC Intelligence: Game Industry Research
(www.dfcint.com)

Gartner (www4.gartner.com)

International Data Group (www.idg.com)

Jupiter Research (www.jup.com)

NPD Group (www.npd.com)

The Yankee Group (www.yankeegroup.com)

ORGANIZATIONS

Academy of Interactive Arts & Sciences (www.interactive.org)

Academy of Television Arts & Sciences: Interactive Peer Group (www.emmys.org)

Digital Games Research Association
(www.digra.com)

DGA New Technology Committee (www.dga.org)

Entertainment Software Association
(www.theesa.com)

Interactive Advertising Bureau (www.iab.net)

IGDA: International Game Developers Association
(www.igda.org)

Producer's Guild of America: New Media Council
(www.pganewmedia.org)

Screen Actors Guild (www.sag.org)

SIGCHI (www.acm.org/sigchi)

SIGGRAPH (www.siggraph.org)

Usability Professional's Association (http://www.upassoc.org/)

Visual Effects Society (www.visualeffectssociety.com)

WGA New Media Committee (www.wga.org)

CONFERENCES

Austin Game Developer Conference (www.gameconference.com)

International Consumer Electronics Show
(www.cesweb.org)

CTIA Wireless I.T. & Entertainment (www.wirelessit.com)

COMDEX (www.comdex.com)

DICE: Design, Innovate, Communicate, Entertain
(www.interactive.org/dice)

Digital Games Research Conference
(www.gamesconference.org)

Digital Hollywood (www.digitalhollywood.com)

Digital Media Summit (www.digitalmediasummit.com)

ECTS (www.ects.com)

Electronic Entertainment Exposition
(www.e3expo.com)

Game Connection (www.game-connection.com)

Game Developers Conference (www.gdconf.com)

Game Developers Conference Europe (www.gdc-europe.com)

GENCON (www.gencon.com)

iHollywood Forum: The Business of Digital Entertainment (www.ihollywoodforum.com)

Independent Games Festival (www.indiegames.com)

Indie Games Con (www.indiegamescon.com)

iWireless world (www.iwirelessworld.com)

London Games Week (www.london-gamesweek.com)

MILIA (www.milia.com)

Mobile Games (www.ef-telecoms.co.uk/mgames/pr)

Nielsen Norman Group events
(www.nngroup.com/events/)

SCoRE (www.score-event.co.uk)

SIGCHI Conference (sigchi.org/conferences)

SIGGRAPH (www.siggraph.org)

Xtreme Game Developers XPO (www.xgdx.com)

Index

Postmortems from Game Developer

Insights from the Developers of Age of Empires, Unreal Tournament, Black and White, and other Top-selling Games

Austin Grossman, editor

"Wow! What a fantastic book! Postmortems provides simply a wonderful survey of the pains and joys of game development." — Grady Booch, chief scientist, Rational Software Corporation (IBM)

Improve your development processes by learning how the superstars of the game industry have succeeded—and how they would improve upon their successes. This collection of the most popular columns from Game Developer magazine has been edited to reveal best practices for development challenges that include managing complexity, software and game design issues, schedule difficulties, and changing staff needs.

$29.95, Softcover, 328pp, ISBN 1-57820-214-0

The Complete Guide to Game Audio

For Composers, Musicians, Sound Designers, and Game Developers

Aaron Marks

"An exhaustive and indispensable resource for game audio, from initial concept to cashing the royalty checks." —Jennifer Olsen, editor-in-chief, Game Developer magazine

Turn your musical passion into a profitable career with this essential guide to the business and technical skills you need to succeed in the multibillion-dollar games industry. Step-by-step instructions lead you through the entire music and sound effects process—from developing the critical skills and purchasing the right equipment to keeping your clients happy.

$34.95, Softcover with CD-ROM, 318pp, ISBN 1-57820-083-0